ADVANCE PRAISE

"The CEDAW Convention is one of the great milestones in the history of human rights. Through the eyes of those who have shaped the Convention over the past 25 years this book brings the challenge and the struggle to life. It sheds invaluable light on the difficult questions of how and why the treaty's impact has been so great."

—**Philip Alston**, NYU Law School

"This book is essential reading for those interested in moving the agenda forward on women's equality. Written by an extraordinary group of CEDAW experts, it provides invaluable insights into the global challenges of eliminating all forms of discrimination against women."

—**Rebecca J. Cook**, professor of law, Faculty Chair in International Human Rights, Faculty of Law, University of Toronto

"A significant contribution to the history of women's human rights internationally, this book will become a classic, required reading for lawyers, students, and those interested in international affairs or international jurisprudence. Once into it, one can't stop reading, for despite differences among women, their common humanity transcends world politics and provides hope for the future."

—**Arvonne S. Fraser**, cofounder and former director of International Women's Rights Action Watch (IWRAW); former U.S. ambassador to the UN Commission on the Status of Women

"The title of this book does not do justice to its importance as both a history and a guide to the establishment of women's human rights as a serious global issue. This collective account by former and current CEDAW experts underscores the key accomplishment of the CEDAW Committee: moving the focus of the gender discussion from development and empowerment to rights and equality. This has made all the difference for millions of women in the last twenty-five years and will continue to do so for decades to come."

—**Marsha A. Freeman**, current director of International Women's Rights Action Watch (IWRAW)

"This insightful collection brings together the wide-ranging expertise of the CEDAW Committee in taking on long-standing and deep-seated obstacles to women's equal rights—economic, political, social, and cultural—as well as critical new challenges to those rights brought by globalization. Now celebrating its 25th year, the Convention has been ratified by nearly every nation in the world. UNIFEM has supported CEDAW and its Committee since its inception, and will be there to help it reach new heights over the next 25."

—**Noeleen Heyzer**, executive director, UNIFEM

"This book is essential reading for anyone concerned with women's equality and a sobering reminder to U.S. women of how their country's failure to ratify the Women's Convention has resulted in their exclusion from a vital international conversation."

—**Ann Elizabeth Mayer**, Department of Legal Studies and Business Ethics, The Wharton School, The University of Pennsylvania

THE CIRCLE OF EMPOWERMENT

Mariam K. Chamberlain Series on Social and Economic Justice

Taking on the Big Boys: Or Why Feminism Is Good for Families, Business, and the Nation
Ellen Bravo

Taxes Are a Woman's Issue: Reframing the Debate
Mimi Abramovitz and Sandra Morgen with the National Council for Research on Women

THE CIRCLE OF EMPOWERMENT

TWENTY-FIVE YEARS OF THE UN COMMITTEE ON THE ELIMINATION OF DISCRIMINATION AGAINST WOMEN

Hanna Beate Schöpp-Schilling, Editor
Cees Flinterman, Associate Editor

The Feminist Press
at the City University of New York
New York

Published by The Feminist Press at the City University of New York
The Graduate Center, 365 Fifth Avenue, Suite 5406, New York, NY 10016
www.feministpress.org

Library of Congress Cataloging-in-Publication Data

The circle of empowerment: twenty-five years of the UN Committee on the Elimina-
tion of Discrimination against Women / Hanna Beate Schöpp-Schilling, editor / Cees
Flinterman, associate editor.
  p. cm.
Includes bibliographical references.
ISBN-13: 978-1-55861-563-2 (pbk.)
ISBN-10: 1-55861-563-6 (pbk.)
ISBN-13: 978-1-55861-564-9 (library binding)
ISBN-10: 1-55861-564-4 (library binding)
1. Sex discrimination against women—Prevention. 2. United Nations. Committee on
the Elimination of Discrimination against Women. I. Schöpp-Schilling, Hanna Beate. II.
Flinterman, C., 1944-
HQ1237.C57 2007
305.4209'045—dc22
2007021442

This publication was made possible, in part, by the Federal Republic of Germany through
the German Ministry of Foreign Affairs, the Foreign Offices of The Netherlands, and by
Mariam K. Chamberlain.

Text and cover design by Lisa Force
Printed in Canada by Transcontinental

11 10 09 08 07   5 4 3 2 1

CONTENTS

HUMAN RIGHTS I: OVERARCHING CHALLENGES

HUMAN RIGHTS II: SPECIFIC CHALLENGES

REMAINING CHALLENGES AND THE WAY FORWARD

MESSAGE ON CEDAW'S TWENTY-FIFTH ANNIVERSARY

KOFI A. ANNAN, SECRETARY-GENERAL OF THE
UNITED NATIONS,1997–2006

From the birth of the United Nations, women have made judicious and skillful use of our organization as a platform to voice their demands for equality and nondiscrimination. From the signing of the Charter—which proclaims the equal rights of men and women—and the adoption of the Universal Declaration of Human Rights, through subsequent instruments that codify human rights and fundamental freedoms, the United Nations has been a constant partner and ally of women in the work for full equality.

Among those instruments, the Convention on the Elimination of All Forms of Discrimination against Women stands out as a landmark, because it aims to secure these rights for women in practice. The General Assembly adopted the Convention in 1979 after many years of heroic efforts by women's rights advocates, both with governments and outside. To this day, the Convention remains the foremost global tool in the work for true gender equality in the home, the community, and society; and for freedom from discrimination, whether perpetrated by the State or by any person, organization, or enterprise.

That achievement is mirrored by the outstanding efforts of the UN Committee on the Elimination of Discrimination against Women, the 23-member expert body that oversees implementation of the Convention. Since it began work in 1982, the Committee has had a unique and professionally diverse profile: With very few exceptions, all its members have been women, and it has established itself as a source of expertise on issues of concern to women in all parts of the world. The Committee has contributed to our understanding of human rights, including the duty of States Parties to promote gender equality and the advancement of women, while taking action against private as well as public acts of discrimination. It has made us aware of the need to examine laws that appear to be gender-neutral but that, in fact, have adverse effects on women. And it has played a pioneering role in the area of violence against women, in particular by establishing that violence against women is a human rights

1

violation—a form of discrimination that prevents women from enjoying rights and freedoms on a basis of equality with men.

The monitoring role of the Committee has assisted States Parties in putting in place the policy and program measures needed to translate the provisions of the Convention into reality. And thanks to information and education campaigns conducted by the Committee together with civil society, women are increasingly aware of the rights the Convention exists to defend.

In 1999, a new milestone was achieved with the adoption of the Optional Protocol to the Convention. In States that have ratified the Protocol, women whose rights have been violated are now able, once they have exhausted national remedies, to seek redress from the Committee. And the Committee will be in a stronger position to ensure, through the Optional Protocol procedure, that the Convention is effectively implemented, by addressing specific violations of a woman's rights and recommending an appropriate remedy.

Clearly, much has been achieved under the watchful eye of the Committee. But we all have a long way to go in achieving compliance with all the Convention's terms. Women remain significantly underrepresented in public life. The scourge of violence afflicts uncounted numbers of women in their daily lives. Atrocious acts of violence continue to be committed against women in conflict situations. In many societies, the effects of migration flows and economic upheaval threaten to unravel the gains made by women. Sexual harassment remains all too common in the workplace. Even discriminatory laws remain on the books and are applied in many countries, in all parts of the world.

I hope this anniversary will provide an incentive for greater public debate at the national level about all these issues, and act as a catalyst for new policy initiatives to increase compliance with the Convention. I hope it will inspire parliamentarians to accelerate legislative action. I hope it will encourage civil society to support women from all walks of life in claiming their rights, and give new impetus to the work for the Convention's universal ratification. It is the duty of all of us—individuals, governments, and the international community, men and women alike—to be vigilant and articulate custodians of this precious instrument.

INTRODUCTION AND ACKNOWLEDGMENTS

HANNA BEATE SCHÖPP-SCHILLING, *GERMANY*
CEES FLINTERMAN, *THE NETHERLANDS*

This book tells a story of success. It celebrates twenty-five years of the work and achievements of the UN Committee on the Elimination of Discrimination against Women (the Committee) in monitoring the implementation of the Convention on the Elimination of All Forms of Discrimination against Women (the Convention), the most important international human rights treaty for women. As of December 2006, 185 member States of the United Nations were States Parties to the CEDAW Convention. Their efforts to implement the Convention are scrutinized by the Committee on a regular basis through various procedures.

The CEDAW Committee—then consisting of twenty-two women and one man—met for the first time in Vienna in October 1982. At that time, those few who knew about the Convention and its Committee had low expectations for it. The many reasons for this are fully illustrated in this book's essays and personal reflections by current and former members of the Committee and UN staff connected with it, which describe various obstacles of a conceptual, political, organizational, and technical nature to its work. These obstacles had been—knowingly or unknowingly—put in place by member States of the United Nations, by States Parties to the Convention, by the organizational culture of the United Nations, and by Committee members themselves, and they have impeded the Committee's work in allowing women to exercise and enjoy their human rights on an equal basis with men. The contributors to this book also describe the story of how many of these obstacles have been overcome since 1982 and of the patient contributions of many, including international and national women's human rights organizations, to this goal.

Today, the CEDAW Committee is considered a vital and essential part of the UN human rights treaty bodies system. A celebration of such success has not blinded the Committee to existing and newly emerging challenges. A number of contributions identify such issues and formulate recommendations for overcoming them, which hopefully will guide the Committee in its future work.

One aspect of the twenty-five-year-long history ends in 2007, since the Committee will no longer be serviced by the UN Division for the

Advancement of Women (DAW) in New York. Starting in 2008, the Committee—like all other human rights treaty bodies—will be serviced by the Office of the UN High Commissioner for Human Rights (OHCHR) in Geneva. Thus, this book is also a grateful tribute to the support of DAW and its staff, which grew in intensity and excellence over the years. At the same time the book is also a gift to the OHCHR for taking over this responsibility.

The book introduces readers to examples of various forms of discrimination against women, as experienced in all regions of the world and which the Committee—in its constructive dialogue with States Parties—tries to make them understand and eliminate. Beyond the Committee's own work, the book also recounts the efforts of women and men who have worked in a context of multicausal influences, e.g. in a variety of international, regional and national institutions, human rights and women's movements, forums and conferences, to make the legal provisions of the Convention a reality for women worldwide. Like Committee members these activists and officials are also committed to the achievement of substantive equality for women with men and are convinced that only through the achievement of this goal can peace and sustainable development be achieved around the globe.

The original concept of the book included *all* relevant articles and aspects of the CEDAW Convention as well as all facets of the work of its Committee. The personal interests of current and former members in certain topics as well as the very nature of each expert's unique perception of the Convention and its Committee moved the book slightly off that course. Moreover, some views expressed in this volume do not necessarily reflect those of its editors. Still, the book treats most of the important topics arising from the Convention, its Committee, and global and specific realities of women's lives, while other aspects have been covered as much as possible in introductory essays. For ease of referencing, the text of the Convention and its Optional Protocol have been included, while in the interest of providing a book of a modest size, the general recommendations of the Committee are only listed. They are easily accessible at the UN websites (http://www.un.org/womenwatch/daw/cedaw).

The editors and contributors of this volume have written for a wide audience not only in the United States, but potentially also in other countries around the globe. They want the general public, college students, and members of nongovernmental organizations—really, all those who are interested in women's human rights, general law, social movements, development, women's and gender studies—to read this book. The writers also expect a scholarly audience to find new facts and ideas about the Convention and its Committee.

The United States is still the only industrialized country that has not ratified the Convention, though it signed it in 1980, thus expressing its will for ratification at some later point and for accepting a so-called "obligation of good faith" not to contravene the purpose of the treaty in the interim period. Efforts by Presidents, Senators, Congressmen and women and nongovernmental organizations so far have unfortunately not succeeded in achieving ratification, though the goal was in reach in the fall of 1994. It is our hope that the book will contribute to a speedy ratification of the Convention by the United States of America and that it will dispel the fears and misconceptions of those who are currently opposed to such an act.

While working on the final editing of all contributions in February 2007, we learned the sad news that Angela King had passed away. In 1997, the UN Secretary-General Kofi A. Annan appointed her as the first Special Adviser on Gender Issues and Advancement of Women with the rank of an Assistant Secretary-General. In this position she supported the work of the Committee with all her strength. On her many missions she exerted strong efforts to increase the number of ratifications of the Convention, including efforts addressed to the United States Senate. In recognition of her struggles and important achievements for women's equality within the United Nations as well as around the world throughout her career of thirty-eight years at the United Nations, we dedicate this book to her as well as to deceased Committee members who are not able to celebrate the twenty-fifth anniversary of the Committee's work with us.

ACKNOWLEDGMENTS

We are most grateful to Florence Howe who immediately embraced the idea of publishing a book on the occasion of the twenty-fifth anniversary of the work of the CEDAW Committee, having encouraged the idea for a book on the CEDAW Convention almost ten years ago. Her long-term publishing experience was decisively helpful, guiding us from the early drafts until the final effort of cutting repetitions and making this book more than a mere collection of interesting texts. Naturally, we also are more than grateful to the contributors who took the time to write for this book, often in the context of pressing professional obligations. Aurora Javate de Dios kindly let us use the title of her personal reflection on the Committee's work as the book's title.

Since most contributors are nonnative English speakers, we are grateful to the editorial work of Tina Johnson, who also checked facts, styled sources in a consistent manner, and advised constructively regarding the improvement of texts and the table of contents. This process was followed up by Anjoli Roy, Assistant Editor of The Feminist Press, who also contributed a number of valuable ideas. Hadassah Gold proofread the final manuscript. Marsha Freeman confirmed facts regarding the early years of the support of the Committee by international women's rights organizations and enlightened us about the problems surrounding ratification of the Convention by the United States. Many people assisted us in checking facts, quotations, and sources, and gave us technical and organizational support, including Malte Bahrenfuß, Ramona Biholar, Katharine Fortin, Philomena Kintu, Ginney Liu, Anne Sieberns, and Anna Rita Tarant. Carolyn Hannan and Christine Brautigam of DAW answered many questions concerning the UN context of the Committee's work and kindly let DAW staff assist us.

The book would not have been possible without the financial contributions of the Foreign Offices of the Federal Republic of Germany and The Netherlands, and we are grateful to Peter Rothen and Birgitta Tazelaar and their colleagues for procuring these grants to The Feminist Press. Finally, we thank our spouses, Ulrich Redmann and Miekje Flinterman, for their patience over a period of more than two years, for their intellectual and emotional support, and for taking up all the tasks in home and garden, which we neglected due to our involvement with this book.

NOTE

1. The editors and contributors of this volume have referenced electronic versions of UN documents whenever they are available. Such sources refer to relevant paragraphs only, while printed UN documents also refer to page numbers. All references are to the English version of documents.

PERSONAL REFLECTION:

IN CELEBRATION

RACHEL N. MAYANJA, ASSISTANT SECRETARY-GENERAL OF THE
UNITED NATIONS AND SPECIAL ADVISER ON GENDER ISSUES AND
ADVANCEMENT OF WOMEN

*Since the coming into force of the Convention on the Elimination of All
Forms of Discrimination against Women (CEDAW) on September 3,
1981, there has been significant progress in the promotion of the human
rights of women. In many countries, constitutions now include provisions
guaranteeing equality between women and men. Laws that prohibit
discrimination in general—as well as in regard to specific rights such as
education, employment, marriage, and divorce—have become standard
components of the regulatory framework. Many countries have repealed
discriminatory provisions in civil, penal, and personal status codes to bring
them into conformity with the Convention. Equal opportunity laws have
been aimed at improving women's legal and de facto status. New legislation
has been adopted on gender-based violence, especially domestic violence,
to provide protection and remedies for women. Some countries have
introduced temporary special measures for the advancement of women to
improve women's political participation and to ensure their representation
in decision-making and executive positions at all levels of government.*

*However, obstacles still remain in many countries, and women's
representation in parliament and in public life remains low. Deep-rooted
stereotypes, including negative customary and traditional practices, persist.
Many women have no access to or control over land, while social security
protection, especially for women in the informal sector, is nonexistent.
Violence against women—including rape, trafficking in women and
girls, and sexual harassment at work—continues to undermine women's
enjoyment of their rights.*

*The persistence of a wide range of discriminatory and criminal
practices, including gender-based violence, causes tremendous suffering for
individual women and girls, as well as exacting incalculable social costs. In
fact, there are fewer women living on earth today than we would expect:
Roughly 90 million women who should be alive today are "missing" due
to gender-based violence, including battery and sexual assault within the
family setting. Sexual violence is being used as a weapon in the context
of war and State militarism and in a range of other political, social,*

7

and cultural upheavals. Women are more likely to become the victims of trafficking and involuntary prostitution in times of war and upheaval.

CEDAW provides all States Parties with comprehensive guidelines for the adoption of antidiscrimination policies. More important, it outlines women's fundamental rights in the form of a legally binding international treaty. Undoubtedly, ratification of or accession to the Convention by all States would be an important commitment to the goal of full equality between women and men. With the implementation of the Convention usually comes a realization that women who are burdened by discriminatory practices, intended or unintended, will contribute less to the economy, to the community, and to good governance.

As a result of the work of the Committee on the Elimination of Discrimination against Women, States Parties are beginning to recognize the breadth of human rights violations women experience in their respective countries. While no State Party denies women's right to equality in principle, States Parties differ about the specific contents of rights, in particular about practices that constitute violations of rights. In this regard, the Committee's focus on the content of the Convention and its enforcement is welcomed.

THE CONVENTION AS A LIVING INSTRUMENT

THE NATURE AND SCOPE OF THE CONVENTION

HANNA BEATE SCHÖPP-SCHILLING, *GERMANY*

A historical perspective on women as individual holders of human rights clearly identifies them as latecomers. The adoption of the Convention on the Elimination of All Forms of Discrimination against Women (CEDAW, 1979; the Convention) and later of its Optional Protocol (1999) was a milestone in the long and arduous process toward this goal. Human rights is one of the three pillars of the United Nations, the other two being the safeguarding and promotion of economic and social development and the maintenance of international security and peace. As UN members, all nations have committed themselves to work together toward these goals. Human rights are inalienable; every human being is born with them. States and their governments do not "grant" rights to their citizens, nor can they take them away with impunity. Rather, it is their duty to respect, protect, and fulfill them.[1] Human rights underpin all areas of life and include civil, political, economic, social, and cultural rights.

It was a victory for the international women's movement and individual diplomats that, due to their untiring efforts, the basic human rights architecture—the Charter of the United Nations (1945), the Universal Declaration of Human Rights (UDHR, 1948), and the International Covenants on Civil and Political Rights (ICCPR, 1966) and on Economic, Social and Cultural Rights (ICESCR, 1966)—all stipulated women's equality with men in the exercise and enjoyment of their human rights. All prohibit discrimination on the ground of sex. Why formulate then a separate Convention on the very same norms? As a "specialized" Convention, CEDAW spells out the meaning of the norms of nondiscrimination against *women* and their formal and substantive equality with men as to all human rights in all areas of their lives. To monitor its implementation, the Convention set up the UN Committee on the Elimination of Discrimination against Women (the Committee).

THE UN COMMISSION ON THE STATUS OF WOMEN AND ITS ROLE FOR CEDAW

Although always in the shadow of the erstwhile UN Commission on Human Rights (CHR), now the UN Council on Human Rights, and never having its work sufficiently recognized within the UN system or by the general public, the UN Commission on the Status of Women (CSW) has been of extreme importance to women since its creation in 1946. Within the context of its mandate to "'prepare recommendations and reports to the Economic and Social Council [ECOSOC] on promoting women's rights in political, economic, civil, social and educational fields,' and to make recommendations 'on urgent problems requiring immediate attention in the field of women's rights'" (United Nations 1995d, 13, para. 46), the CSW initiated and conducted numerous studies and programs over the years. It also drafted important conventions on women's rights, which were later adopted by the UN General Assembly: the Convention on the Political Rights of Women (1952), the Convention on the Nationality of Married Women (1957), and the Convention on Consent to Marriage, Minimum Age for Marriage and Registration of Marriages (1962). Based on additional work of the CSW, the General Assembly also adopted the Declaration on the Elimination of Discrimination against Women (DEDAW) in 1967, which prepared the way for CEDAW.

In addition, the UN General Assembly and various UN specialized agencies have addressed aspects of women's human rights in other important conventions.[2] Despite such efforts it became clear by 1972 that persistent discrimination against women could not be eliminated with the existing treaties alone. Thus in 1972, using the opportunity of its twenty-fifth anniversary, the CSW recommended to both ECOSOC and the General Assembly that 1975 should become "International Women's Year" to remind UN member States that new and increased efforts were needed to deal with the legal and practical manifestations of this phenomenon. Once this recommendation was approved, the CSW set out to formulate its program for the year, which included an international conference to be convened in Mexico City. This First UN World Conference on Women (1975) was a watershed for women worldwide. Its World Plan of Action, endorsed by the majority of the government delegations, called for high priority to be given "to the preparation and adoption of the convention on the elimination of discrimination against women, with effective procedures for its implementation" (United Nations 1976, para. 198), thus reaffirming the 1972 CSW view that a new, legally-binding instrument on women's human rights was necessary, and supporting its drafting efforts, which had begun in 1974 (United Nations 1995d, 40, para. 158).

After lengthy and difficult negotiations in the CSW and within UN working groups of the Third Committee of the UN General Assembly, the assembly adopted CEDAW on December 18, 1979 (Rehof 1993). The Convention was opened for signature, ratification, or accession by UN member States on March 1, 1980 in New York. A special ceremony was conducted on July 17, 1980, during the Second UN World Conference on Women in Copenhagen, to accelerate this process.[3] The Convention entered into force on September 3, 1981, after the twentieth State had become a party to it.

RATIFICATION AND RESERVATIONS

Nobody had expected the rapid ratification of the Convention only later surpassed by the Convention on the Rights of the Child (CRC) adopted in 1990. At the same time, the Convention is also the UN human rights treaty to which the highest number of reservations has been entered (Schöpp-Schilling 2004). According to Article 28, countries ratifying or acceding to the Convention can enter reservations. These, however, must be compatible with its "object and purpose." Reservations can be objected to by other States Parties when they consider them incompatible. In the eyes of scholars, objecting States Parties, and the CEDAW Committee, most of the general reservations as well as those entered to Articles 2 and 16 are, in fact, considered as incompatible with the Convention's object and purpose. Article 29 (1) allows for a dispute regulation between two or more States Parties concerning the interpretation or application of the Convention. But in addition to the fact that this regulation has never been used, it also can be made inactive by a reservation. Both the UN International Law Commission and a working group consisting of members from all UN human rights monitoring treaty bodies are currently trying to formulate a common and consistent point of view on the issue of reservations to UN human rights conventions and the function of their monitoring bodies in dealing with them.

Reservations to the CEDAW Convention have been entered by States for legal, religious, and often, political reasons (Mayer 2001, 109–10). Reservations can and sometimes also have been withdrawn when legal and political obstacles have been removed. Entering reservations allows a State to proceed with accepting the nonreserved parts of the Convention and thus makes scrutiny of its implementation by the Committee possible. However, the high number of reservations and their lack of specificity often affect the universal validity and integrity of the Convention as well as the status of women's right to nondiscrimination on the basis of their sex as international customary law: e.g. as a norm that is binding regardless of whether a State has become party to the CEDAW Convention or to the two Covenants (ICCPR and ICESCR). In contrast to the prohibition of discrimination on racial grounds, discrimination against women on the basis of their sex has not yet reached the status of international customary law.

Various patterns among States Parties to the Convention as to the timing of their ratification or accession and to their use of reservations can be identified. One group of States quickly became party to the Convention and without reservations, since they believed that equality for women had already been fully achieved in their countries. Another group waited until it had changed some or all existing domestic discriminatory legislation so that its legal system complied with the Convention. A third group became party with either very specific or rather general reservations, because parts of their legal systems did not conform with the Convention. Some of these States Parties later lifted specific reservations, due to positive changes in their political climate or jurisprudence, or to interaction with the Committee and to pressure by their civil society groups. Others consider it to be unlikely that they will be able to remove their specific or general reservations, due to religious factors reflected in their legal systems and their political realities. Some countries became States Parties without reservations, despite existing widespread discrimination against women in law and practice.

Countries participating in the Fourth UN World Conference on Women in 1995 in Beijing agreed on the goal of universal ratification of the Convention by the year 2000 (United Nations 1995a, para. 230 [b]). Despite individual and concerted efforts by members of the Committee; by the staff of the Division for the Advancement of Women, which has been servicing the CSW and the Committee since their inception; by the two Special Advisers to the UN Secretary-General on Gender Issues and Advancement of Women;[4] by UN specialized agencies; and, last but not least, by national and international nongovernmental organizations (NGOs), this goal has not yet been achieved. As of December 2006, 185 States have ratified or acceded to the Convention, while eight UN member States and one UN observer State are still missing.[5] Of those 185, 85 are also States Parties to its Optional Protocol. Thus, the second highest number of States (after the CRC) have accepted the CEDAW Convention as a source of legally binding obligations.

THE CEDAW CONVENTION AND THE UNITED STATES

The United States, which signed the Convention at the Second UN World Conference on Women in Copenhagen, remains the only industrialized country not to have ratified it. Signing the Convention indicates only that a State agrees not to contravene its provisions, but it carries no legal obligation to be bound by the treaty. Reasons for the failure of the United States to ratify the Convention, to date, are both constitutional and political.[6]

The U.S. Constitution provides that the President may sign a treaty on his or her own but may ratify a treaty only with the "advice and consent" of two thirds of the Senate, e.g. the agreement of sixty-seven of the one hundred senators. The ratification process thus involves intensive negotiation between two equal branches of government. This negotiation is particularly difficult because it involves significant constitutional issues. First, the U.S. Constitution does not include, either on its face or as a result of judicial interpretation, a sex discrimination norm that would meet the requirements of Article 2 of the Convention. The failure to adopt an Equal Rights Amendment in the 1970s, when the political climate was more propitious than it is now, suggests that this gap is likely to remain and would have to be clearly dealt with. Second, because of its federal system, with fifty state constitutions and fifty separate state governments, U.S. treaty ratifications must account for the relationship between the obligations and rights of the states and those of the federal government. While UN treaty monitoring bodies indicate that treaty obligations run to the states as well as to the federal government, the U.S. takes the position that the federal government has limited authority to impose international norms on states. Such issues are generally dealt with by adopting reservations, declarations and "understandings" (RDUs) that render the ratification politically acceptable within the U.S. and that are usually criticized by scholars and external observers (Mayer 1996, 754–819).

Additional political considerations also have slowed ratification. Each senator must consider the political repercussions of a "yes" vote in his or her own state. A high valuation of individualism and self-empowerment—which Alexis de Tocqueville identified as a problematic strength within early nineteenth-century Euro-American culture, and which in many respects still prevails—consistently renders American voters suspicious of political and economic involvement with even their closest neighbors. Moreover, in recent decades the right wing has become both more vocal and more influential in American politics than ever before—and right-wing ideology is opposed to involvement in multilateral agreements, particularly human rights treaties, and to any domestic policy that could conceivably threaten traditional concepts of family and morality.

Thus, building political will for any treaty ratification is a long, hard process, if not a battle. Ratifying a treaty on discrimination against women, with all its implications of challenging traditional beliefs that subordinate women and providing accountability for equality policy, is beyond difficult. Even when ratification has not been on the agenda of the U.S. Senate, conservative think tanks and their associated social movements have attacked the Convention and its monitoring body by deliberately misconstruing provisions of the Convention and quoting parts of the Committee's concluding comments to specific States Parties out of context.[7] Still, U.S. Presidents, individual senators and representatives, and the Senate Foreign Relations Committee have made various efforts to move ratification forward. From the history of the ratification effort, however, it is clear that ratification would be accompanied by a collection of reservations, declarations and "understandings" (Halberstam 1997, 54–62).[8]

While ratification has been stalled, U.S. advocates of the Convention have been hard at work at the local level. Today, over 190 U.S. organizations—including professional organizations, trade unions, civil rights groups, and religious groups—support its ratification. A number of publications and websites on CEDAW have emerged (CEDAW: Treaty n.d.). Arguments currently offered to support U.S. ratification primarily point to the need for the Government's international credibility as it monitors other countries' human rights in general and women's human rights in particular. Another argument focuses on the domestic impact of ratification, e.g. eliminating the still persistent de facto discrimination against women in the United States. As a result of local lobbying, two American cities have passed ordinances requiring implementation of the Convention in their own laws and policies. A most significant accomplishment was the Convention's adoption as a city ordinance in San Francisco in 1998. With the Convention adopted as local law, two city departments undertook analyses of their operations and policies according to the Convention's norms and made significant changes. The City Council of Los Angeles, California, has also adopted the Convention as a city ordinance but has not yet followed up with policy reviews. When the United States finally ratifies the CEDAW Convention, it will be as a result of efforts at every level, from grassroots groups to state governments to citizen-driven Washington lobbying.

SUBSTANCE OF THE CONVENTION

The Convention is an innovative human rights treaty. It expanded the understanding of international law at the time of its adoption in 1979. First, it is the first and only human rights convention that obliges States Parties to modify and abolish social attitudes and cultural patterns and practices that are based on the idea of the inferiority or superiority of either sex. Second, it explicitly prescribes States Parties' obligations to eliminate discrimination against women not only by State agents, but also by private individuals, organizations, or enterprises. Third, it integrates women's civil and political rights and economic, social, and cultural rights under the normative framework of nondiscrimination and equality. Fourth, the Convention also covers the guarantee to respect, protect, and fulfill women's human rights in the private sphere of the family. Discrimination against women in marriage and family life is not only a human rights violation in itself but often the basis for their discrimination in other areas of their lives. Fifth, the Convention, in addition to using a nondiscrimination and protection approach, also allows for the correction of former practices of discrimination through the application of temporary special measures (sometimes known as affirmative action) for women (Hevener 1986, 70-88).

The Convention consists of a preamble and thirty articles. The Preamble clearly establishes that all forms and manifestations of discrimination against women violate "the principles of equality of rights and respect for human dignity." It puts the fulfillment of the norms of nondiscrimination and women's equality with men in the wider context of political and economic issues of the late 1970s, such as the striving for peace and development, a new international economic order, disarmament, eradication of apartheid and of (neo)colonialism. The Preamble also considers women as active individuals, but less with respect to their own empowerment—a notion that was to be developed later especially in the Beijing Declaration and Platform for Action—but rather in the support of and service for others, e.g. family, country, and humanity. However, the recognition that "the full and complete development of a country, the welfare of the world and the cause of peace require the maximum participation of women on equal terms with men in all fields" establishes—together with the substantive articles of the Convention a legal basis for the inclusion of women not only in a country's national development plan but also in the area of international conflict resolution. This norm was to be developed further some fifteen to twenty years later in the Beijing Platform for Action (1995) and in Security Council Resolution 1325 on Women, Peace, and Security (2000).[9] Lastly, the Preamble also sets an innovative tone in international law by pointing to the need for change "in the traditional role of men as well as the role of women in society and in the family," which includes the notion that the "upbringing of children requires a sharing of responsibility between men and women and society as a whole." These concepts reemerge in several articles of the Convention.

Articles 1 to 5, and Article 24 of the Convention are so-called framework articles. Their content, as expressed in the form of definitions and State obligations, is important not only in itself but also informs the remaining substantive Articles 6 to 16 in that these definitions and obligations need to be applied by States Parties each time they make efforts to implement any of them. Articles 17 to 23 and Articles 25 to 30 cover procedural issues, e.g. the parameters for the creation of the monitoring Committee and its work; the reporting obligation of States Parties; the issue of reservations to the Convention; and the conditions for solving disputes among States Parties as to the interpretation and application of the Convention. The following short overview of the most salient features of the six framework articles highlights the Convention's innovative and encompassing character.

The Nature of Discrimination

Article 1 of the Convention goes beyond the concept of discrimination used in many national and international legal standards and norms. While these prohibit discrimination on the grounds of *sex* and protect both women and men from treatment based on arbitrary, unfair, or unjustifiable distinctions, exclusions, or restrictions, the Convention focuses on discrimination against *women*, emphasizing that they have suffered and continue to suffer from various forms of discrimination *because* they are women. It also defines discrimination both as an intentional and an unintentional act, the latter being discriminatory in its *effect*. Such discrimination of effect or indirect discrimination against women occurs where laws, policies, and programs—based on apparently gender-neutral criteria—actually have a more disadvantageous impact on women than on men because such criteria may be inadvertently modeled on male lifestyles and thus fail to take into account aspects of women's life experiences that may differ from those of men. These differences result from the real biological differences of women's birthing and nursing capacities, or they may exist because of stereotypical expectations, attitudes, and behavior directed toward women. Such criteria may also fail to recognize the consequences of past discrimination against women including unequal power relations between men and women.

Discrimination against women differs from discrimination on other grounds in both quantitative and qualitative ways. Women form approximately half of the world's population. They are thus not one "vulnerable group" simply to be placed next to other vulnerable groups as defined by ethnicity, race, age, disability, and other grounds, because they are always members of such groups and may suffer discrimination both within and outside of these groups. In fact, women often suffer from multiple forms of discrimination based on their intersecting identities as women and as members of another group, which compounds their disadvantageous situation. In addition, the relationship between oppressor and victim is, for women, uniquely and universally intimate, in that the majority of women live with men in nuclear and extended families. Women suffer discrimination within male-oriented structures, manifested in laws, policies, institutions, and programs. They also frequently experience discrimination on the basis of their status as unmarried daughter, wife, common-law spouse, or widow. It is therefore an important step forward that Article 1 prohibits discrimination against women "irrespective of their marital status."

The Nature of Equality

The Convention stipulates different forms of equality. First, it demands the achievement of purely formal equality, e.g. equality of women with men in and before the law with respect to formal opportunities and treatment. Second, the Convention stipulates de facto or substantive equality, meaning that women enjoy equality with men in practice. The Convention explicitly and implicitly recognizes both biological and socially constructed differences between women and men. It addresses biological difference by requiring protective measures such as maternity leave without penalty. It provides for corrective measures such as the application of temporary special measures to *accelerate* the achievement of substantive equality. Achievement of substantive equality also requires a redistribution of resources and power between women and men as well as changes in the public and private environments to provide for equality of results. Lastly, the Convention specifically addresses diversity among women by alluding to the special needs of rural women, for example, who are the majority of women in the world (Article 14). The Convention, therefore, must also be interpreted as covering the needs of other specific groups of women not explicitly mentioned in its text, including women with disabilities, the girl child, and elderly women.

The Convention clearly names equality and not equity as the human rights norm to be respected, protected, and fulfilled. In a legal context, equity means fairness. The term was introduced by conservative forces at the Fourth UN World Conference on Women in Beijing (1995) as a substitute for equality. In other discussions, the term is used to describe men and women as equal in dignity but different in life and tasks. In this context the concepts complement each other, and thus equality becomes irrelevant. In the last decade, some feminists have adopted "equity" as encompassing substantive equality for diverse groups of women. However, there is a danger that this interpretation will be confused with the meaning of the term as used by conservative opponents to the Convention.

Sex and Gender

The Convention clearly forbids discrimination against women on the basis of sex. When the Convention was drafted, the term "gender" had not yet moved from social science research into a broader application, including its application in legal discourse.

> Gender is defined as the social meanings given to biological sex differences. It is an ideological and cultural construct . . . [that] affects the distribution of resources, wealth, work, decision-making and political power, and the enjoyment of rights and entitlements within the family as well as in public life. Despite variations across cultures and over time, gender relations throughout the world entail an asymmetry of power between men and women as a pervasive trait. Thus, gender is a social stratifier, and in this sense it is similar to other stratifiers such as race, class, ethnicity, and age. The social construction of gender clarifies the unequal structure of power that underlies the relationship between the sexes. (United Nations 1999, ix)

Although the terminology of gender was not part of the drafting discussions of the Convention, the concept is stated quite clearly in Article 5 (a), articulating States Parties' obligation to eliminate prejudices and practices based on the notion of the inferiority or superiority of either sex or on stereotyped roles ascribed to them. The content of Article 5 (a) thus adds to the definition of discrimination in Article 1. Unfortunately, "gender" has become a loaded term both inside and outside the United Nations. Religious fundamentalists of all denominations denounce it, inaccurately, as signifying and permitting nonheterosexual orientation. Others who are more well meaning—including States Parties, UN staff, and NGOs—sometimes confuse the issue by using the term interchangeably and inaccurately with the terms "sex," "women," or even "men."

Arguably, discrimination against women on the ground of their sexual orientation, which is not covered in explicit language, is prohibited by the Convention. However, Committee members may not always find consensus on this, depending on their national or cultural backgrounds. There has been at least one instance, though, when the Committee has been concerned about legal and practical discrimination against and victimization of women who are lesbians, and it has formulated recommendations in its concluding comments to the respective State Party to decriminalize the practice (CEDAW 1999, 18, paras. 127 and 128).

The Nature of State Obligations

State obligations to respect, protect, and fulfill women's human rights to nondiscrimination and equality are clearly defined in all articles of the Convention, but most important and in an overarching sense in Article 2, which defines them foremost as the obligations of States Parties to condemn and eliminate discrimination against women through legal and other steps. Scholars of international law differentiate between States' obligations of means or conduct, which are obligations "to act by specified means toward the achievement of aspirational goals," and obligations of ends or results, which are obligations "to achieve certain results by whatever means are determined to be appropriate" (Cook 1994, 231–32). This differentiation also applies to the CEDAW Convention, which gives States Parties the discretion to select their means within the context of "all appropriate measures" including legal ones. Thus, while it is up to States Parties to decide on the kinds of measures for implementing, for example, "maternity leave with pay or with comparable social benefits without loss of former employment, seniority or social allowances" (Article 11 [2] [b]), the Convention clearly also imposes that some form of paid maternity leave must be installed.

In Article 2 (a–g), general obligations of results encompass the duties of States Parties to eliminate "discrimination in all its forms," which not only entails the task to "embody the principle of the equality of men and women" in national constitutions and other legislation, but to ensure "the practical realization of this principle." All forms of discrimination— whether they are committed by state agents or by private organizations, enterprises and persons—must be prohibited by legislation and must be punished with "sanctions where appropriate" through "competent national tribunals and other public institutions." In addition, "existing laws, regulations, customs and practices which constitute discrimination against women" must be modified and abolished (also Article 5 [a]).

Acting Without Delay

Of great importance is the fact that States, by ratifying or acceding to the Convention, agree to pursue such a policy of eliminating discrimination *without delay*. It is not always fully understood by them that not only discriminatory action but also the omission of "positive" action to end discrimination falls under the prohibition of the Convention. Many States Parties move very slowly even to change existing legal discrimination against women in their countries, not to mention their drafting new laws against domestic violence or for equal opportunities. Others work in incremental steps or do nothing at all to end discrimination in such areas as marriage and family relations. While the Committee is aware that it takes time to completely eradicate discrimination in practice—as manifested in attitudes, behavior, and institutions—it does understand the obligation to act without delay as stipulating the need for immediate action by States Parties to repeal discriminatory laws, adopt policies, institutional arrangements, and programs to overcome previous discrimination against women and affect long-term cultural change.[10]

Institutions and Procedures

Articles 3 and 24, in particular, allow for a dynamic interpretation of the Convention, since they enjoin States Parties to take "all appropriate measures, including legislation, to ensure the full development and advancement of women, for the purpose of guaranteeing them the exercise and enjoyment of human rights and fundamental freedoms on a basis of equality with men" as well as "all necessary measures at the national level" to achieve "the full realization of the rights" contained in the Convention. In the Committee's view, Article 3 obliges governments first to establish a "national machinery," e.g. a specific governmental institution dealing with women's human rights. This institution must have a clear mandate, adequate resources, and authority. Second, the obligation to pursue the practice of gender mainstreaming also is embodied in this Article. Such a procedure guides all governmental institutions to aim at identifying potentially more negative effects of a law, policy, or program on women (or on men) before these are adopted. Such an analysis, based on the recognition of the variations in life circumstances of women and men due to biological differences and socially constructed roles, allows for modifications of the intended law, policy, or program in order to avoid disparate impact. From an institutional perspective, this involves the training of government officials, including high-level ones, and establishing gender focal points with authority and accountability in all parts and at all levels of government for monitoring purposes. Third, Article 3 also covers the obligation of "gender budgeting." This involves an analysis of the governmental budget according to the needs of women and men and should result in an improved allocation of resources to women. Lastly, and more recently, the Committee has been engaging States Parties' attention to their obligations under Articles 3 and 24 as to the need for gender sensitivity in asylum laws, policies of migration, development cooperation and responsibilities in supranational organizations.

Special Measures

As mentioned before, women's capacity for childbearing and nursing warrants special protection. The Convention clearly enunciates in Article 4 (2) that such special measures of protection are not to be considered discriminatory. Other articles spell out the nature of such measures to protect women's maternity functions within the context of their employment rights and in their right to substantively equal access to and treatment in health care, including family planning and "appropriate services in connection with pregnancy, confinement and the post-natal period" (Articles 11 [2], 12 [1], [2]). It is important to note that the Convention drafters also saw a potential need for revision, repeal, or extension of many protective measures for women in employment on the grounds of pregnancy and maternity and asked for their periodic review in the light of new scientific and technological developments (Article 11 [3]).

Temporary special measures in their various forms are also not to be considered discriminatory and the Committee deems their application a necessary strategy for States Parties. In contrast to the measures under Article 4 (2), they have a corrective function to make up for the disadvantages of past discrimination against women and to accelerate the achievement of their substantive equality—not only with respect to opportunities and treatment in comparison with men, as explicitly mentioned in Article 4 (1), but also to results such as overcoming women's underrepresentation in all fields and achieving a redistribution of power and resources. States Parties often do not recognize the distinct features of each of the two measures under Article 4, nor do they sufficiently differentiate between general policies for the advancement of women and specific temporary special measures as the Committee explained in its General Recommendation No. 25. [11]

Culture

The Convention also notes that culture (including religious precepts) and tradition often reinforce the notion of women being generally different from and even inferior to men, thus allowing not only for the application of restrictive stereotypes but also severe physical, psychological, material, and legal forms of discrimination in such areas as health, education, employment, property or land rights, decision-making, and others. Both Articles 2 (f) and 5 (a) define States Parties' obligations in this respect. Thus, States Parties must carry out a modification or abolition of such traditions in general and as they relate to specific forms of discrimination prohibited under each substantive article. UN member States at the 1993 UN World Conference on Human Rights in Vienna reaffirmed that cultural traditions may not be used as an excuse for avoiding the promotion and protection of all human rights and fundamental freedoms (United Nations 1993b, para. 5).

Characterization of Substantive Articles 6–16 of the Convention

All obligations of States Parties under the six framework articles are relevant for the implementation of each of the remaining ten substantive Articles 6–16 and need to be taken into consideration by them when addressing the elimination of women's discrimination in specific areas of their lives. Articles 6-16 cover the suppression of traffic in women and of the exploitation of prostitution of women (Article 6); the abolition of discrimination against women in political and public life, including at the international level (Articles 7 and 8); in nationality laws and regulations (Article 9); in education (Article 10); in employment and work in the formal and informal labor market sectors (Article 11); in health care (Article 12); in all areas of economic and social life (Article 13); in women's legal capacity (Article 15); and in marriage and family relations (Article 16). Given the fact that the majority of the world's women live in rural areas, it is important to note that the various aspects of their lives, often characterized by multiple forms of discrimination, are highlighted in a specific article (Article 14).

Eliminating restrictive cultural norms, traditions, and practices is of particular importance when considering women's legal and factual equality in marriage and family relations. A major obstacle to women's exercise and enjoyment of their human rights in this field and all other fields of life has been the "public/private divide" in society and, for a long time, in international law, which divides human activities into two spheres and relegates women to the private sphere of the family with fewer rights, powers, and resources, and—with variations throughout history and world regions—subordinates them to their fathers, brothers, guardians, and husbands (Romany 1994, 85–115). More than any other provisions in any human rights instrument dealing with the institution of the family, Article 16 spells out in detail what the norm of equality of rights and responsibilities of spouses "as to marriage, during marriage and its dissolution" means, as stipulated in the UDHR and the ICCPR.[12] In addition to this principle and other rights already contained in these treaties, such as entering marriage at a "marriageable age" with free and full consent, Article 16 of CEDAW specifies equality between women and men in this area as also including the prohibition of child betrothal or marriage; the right to choose a spouse freely; the obligation of a State Party to determine a minimum age for marriage, to make marriage registration in an official registry compulsory; and to guarantee equal parental rights including "guardianship, wardship, trusteeship and adoption of children, or similar institutions"; the right to choose "a family name, a profession and an occupation"; and the right to "ownership, acquisition, management, administration, enjoyment and disposition of property." The Committee's General Recommendation No. 21 points to other forms of discrimination implicit in Article 16, including domestic violence.

Of particular importance—and to be recognized as a victory gained after a long struggle by women's movements and women inside the United Nations—is Article 16 (1) (e), which obliges States Parties to give women the "same rights to decide freely and responsibly on the number and spacing of their children and to have access to the information, education, and means to enable them to exercise these rights." These rights are further elaborated in Articles 10 (h) and 12 (1). Other articles of the Convention also need to be seen in conjunction with the equality norm in marriage and the family, such as the common responsibility of men and women and society for childrearing (Preamble, Articles 5 [b] and 11 [2] [c]); women's rights to equality before the law and to exercise equal legal capacity, regardless of marital status (Articles 1 and 15); and women's equal rights to "acquire, change or retain their nationality" and transmit nationality to their children (Article 9). Equal recognition of legal personhood and of full status as a citizen in relation to the State are fundamental for women's exercise and enjoyment of all their other rights. If not recognized as fully competent human beings, women can be—and, in fact, are—easily prevented by state agents, private employers, a parent, sibling, or spouse from realizing their human rights in practice. The language of Articles 9 and

15 is unique in the Convention in that it demands immediate and direct application, whereas the obligations under other articles allow States Parties considerable flexibility in policy implementation, although they also have to pursue the initiation of such policy development without delay and with the obligation to achieve results.

Resistance to the equal rights of women with men in marriage and family relations is widespread among States Parties due to cultural, including religious, beliefs and precepts as to the alleged "nature" of women and their roles in the family and in society. While States Parties are obliged to modify attitudes and practices deriving from such beliefs, the Committee often finds them reluctant to do so. Many States Parties enter reservations to these articles in order to be exempt from changing their personal status laws. Perceiving women's equality with men in the exercise and enjoyment of rights in the family as a prerequisite for enjoying their human rights in other areas of their lives, the Committee, in various statements and most clearly in its contribution to the fiftieth anniversary of the UDHR in 1998, has defined reservations on Articles 2 and 16, in particular when they are of a general nature, as incompatible with the Convention (Schöpp-Schilling 2004, 12–29).

The Scope of the Convention: General Recommendations

Article 1 also defines the Convention as a dynamic instrument. By using the term "*all* forms of discrimination" and by adding "or *any other* field" to the ones clearly specified, it opens the way for an interpretation of its articles, including when new "forms" or "fields" of discrimination are identified (my emphasis). Such interpretations are permitted through Article 21 (1) of the Convention, which allows the Committee to "make suggestions and general recommendations based on the examination of reports and information" received from States Parties. General recommendations or general comments as they are called by some human rights treaty bodies, are considered "soft law," e.g. not legally binding, although the CEDAW Committee—in unison with other treaty bodies—expects States Parties to accept and implement them in good faith.

Between 1986 and 2004, the Committee adopted twenty-five such general recommendations, some covering specific articles such as the application of temporary special measures (Article 4 [1]); the elimination of prejudices and practices based on socio-cultural factors (Article 5); equality in marriage and family relations (Article 16); equality in political and public life (Articles 7 and 8); equal remuneration for work of equal value and unpaid women workers in rural and urban family enterprises

(Article 11); and women's equality in healthcare (Article 12). Expanding the scope of the Convention in an even more innovative way are those general recommendations that highlight forms of discrimination against women not explicitly referred to in its text. These include such important statements as declaring violence against women a form of discrimination; addressing the issue of "female circumcision," which today is identified as female genital mutilation (FGM); discrimination against disabled women; discrimination against women with HIV/AIDS; and discrimination against women doing unremunerated domestic work. One general recommendation recommends the creation of national machinery for women by each State Party. However, many articles of the Convention and many forms of discrimination in a variety of areas, including the nature of multiple or intersectional discrimination, have not yet been fully elaborated. Other general recommendations refer to topics in procedural articles, such as resources of the Committee, its location, and the amount of its working time (Article 17); reporting obligation of States Parties, including provision of statistical information (Article 18); and reservations (Article 28) (see the "Summary List of General Recommendations," included at the close of this book).

PROGRESS AND CHALLENGES

Criticism of the CEDAW Convention has ranged from concern about its vague language as compared to other human rights treaties, its originally restricted power to have its implementation monitored to questions by feminists of the southern hemisphere about the value of individual human rights entitlements versus entitlements to general economic empowerment. In the more than twenty-five years since the adoption of the Convention some of these questions have been answered in part through various UN world conferences. The adoption of the Optional Protocol to the Convention in 1999 added two monitoring instruments—the communication and inquiry procedures—to the review process of States Parties' reports.

Additional progress with regard to the respect for, and the protection and fulfillment of women's human rights can be seen at many levels in many States Parties. In addition, new regional instruments in Latin America and Africa addressing the human rights of women support the Convention's impact. The four UN World Conferences on Women have been pivotal for strengthening it as has been the 1993 UN World Conference on Human Rights in Vienna, which altered perceptions of the Convention and repositioned it as a human rights rather than a development instrument. The Millennium Development Goals include gender equality as one goal along with indicators under other goals also pertaining to women's human rights. It is self-evident that these goals cannot be achieved unless States Parties build their implementation on a detailed implementation of the Convention (UNIFEM et al. 2005).

Other challenges remain and new ones have emerged. These include the reluctance of some States Parties to implement the Convention due to lack of political will or resources. Even with political will and resources, the complexity of States Parties' federal political structures, may make it difficult to achieve consistent implementation, although the Convention requires this. The legal status of the Convention in a specific State Party is another question: Is the Convention, through ratification or accession, directly valid as domestic law and applicable by domestic courts; does it need to be incorporated as a whole or in individual legal provisions into domestic law; or does it remain a human rights treaty that serves only as a guiding principle and that cannot be invoked in courts? These questions complicate its implementation and thus women's exercise and enjoyment of their human rights. The coexistence of international law, statutory law—often influenced by former colonial powers—customary, and religious law (with the last three systems most likely containing provisions discriminating against women) also compose considerable challenges for States Parties to deal with.

Implementation of the Convention has contributed to considerable progress in legal and sometimes substantive equality of women with men in many countries. Still, such new developments as economic globalization; the rising importance of supranational organizations that claim not to be bound by the human rights treaties; the emergence of new or expanding patterns of women's exploitation in trafficking and migration; the re-emergence of old and new forms of nationalism, ethnic strife and religious fundamentalism—all threaten women's human rights and subordinate them to other claims.[13]

NOTES

I am grateful to Marsha Freeman for research and language on the section dealing with the Convention and the United States and to Cees Flinterman for editorial comments.

1. Asbjørn Eide, then Special Rapporteur of the Sub-Commission on Prevention of Discrimination and Protection of Minorities promoted these three categories of State obligations in 1989 (Eide 1989).

2. These are the Convention for the Suppression of the Traffic in Persons and of the Exploitation of the Prostitution of Others (1949); the following Conventions of the International Labour Organization (ILO): Convention (No. 100) concerning Equal Remuneration for Men and Women Workers for Work of Equal Value (1951), Convention (No. 111)

concerning Discrimination in respect of Employment and Occupation (1958), and the Convention (No. 103) on Maternity Protection (1952); also the United Nations Educational, Scientific and Cultural Organization (UNESCO) Convention against Discrimination in Education (1960).

3. Signing a convention indicates that a State supports the purposes of a convention; ratification is the legal act by which a State that has signed a convention agrees to be bound by its provisions; accession is the act whereby a State becomes a party to a treaty without previous signature.

4. The late Angela King from 1997 to 2004 and Rachel N. Mayanja since 2004.

5. As of December 2006, the following States have not ratified or acceded to CEDAW: Islamic Republic of Iran; Nauru; Palau; Qatar; Somalia; Sudan; Tonga; and the United States (although it signed the Convention in July 1980). The Holy See, which as a State Party holds the status of an observer to the United Nations and which ratified the CRC, is also not a State Party to the Convention. There are currently 192 UN member States (http://www.un.org/members/list.shtml). The potential number of States Parties is thus 193.

6. So far, the United States only ratified the ICCPR (in 1992), the Convention against Torture and Other Cruel, Inhuman or Degrading Treatment or Punishment (CAT, in 1994), and the ICERD (in 1994), but it did so with a number of reservations, declarations, and "understandings" (RDUs).

7. The Heritage Foundation has been particularly active in misconstruing the Convention and the work of its Committee as have been a number of anti-abortion groups (see the 2001 comprehensive report by the Heritage Foundation, http://heritage.org/Research/InternationalOrganizations/BG1407.cfm and its 2002 statement, http://www.heritage.org/Press/commentary/ed082802.cfm).

8. Halberstam describes the ratification efforts under Presidents Carter and Clinton and the evaluation by the State Department, which proposed four reservations, two declarations, and three "understandings" (RDUs), which are discussed by Mayer (Halberstam 1997, 54–62; Mayer 1996, 799–819). It is noteworthy that in 1994 the goal to ratify the Convention was almost reached when the Senate Foreign Relations Committee sent its resolution on ratification to the floor of the Senate. By then, however, the political winds had shifted sharply in the United States. The Republicans sensed that they were about to gain the majority in both houses of Congress, and they used a procedural maneuver to place a "hold" on all pending legislation in both houses, denying passage to bills supported by the Democrats and leaving all issues under discussion to be considered anew in a post-election, Republican-controlled Congress. Consideration of CEDAW ratification died with all the other legislation at that point and has been taken up only once since that time. With a change in control of Congress after the 2006 elections, Convention supporters are renewing their efforts and considering the best strategies to promote ratification. But the Democratic majority in the Senate is slim, and many senators on both sides of the aisle are unfamiliar with the treaty. Moreover, the RDUs drafted by the Clinton State Department remain under "study" by the second Bush administration and may even be reformulated to be more limiting.

9. The Beijing Platform for Action contains a section "women and armed conflict" and lists a number of strategic objectives and steps to be taken to achieve them (United Nations 1995a, paras. 131-49). This section laid the basis for the UN Security Council Resolution 1325 on Women, Peace, and Security (2000) the implementation of which is reviewed by the UN Security Council at regular intervals. The resolution can be easily linked with States Parties' obligations under Articles 7 (women's equal representation in political and public life), 8 (women's equal representation at the international level) and 4 (1) (application of temporary

special measures to accelerate the achievement of equality of women with men, including equal representation). It would be desirable if the Committee could make this linkage explicit in a new general recommendation.

10. This threefold approach to the implementation of the Convention was developed by Dutch Feminists (Groenman et al. 1997).

11. Temporary special measures, depending on the context and on the specific goal, may comprise a wide variety of legislative, executive, administrative and other regulatory instruments, policies and practices, such as outreach or support programs; allocation and/or reallocation of resources; preferential treatment; targeted recruitment, hiring and promotion; numerical goals connected with time frames; and quota systems as explained in General Recommendation No. 25. Also, different measures may need to be applied in the field of employment as compared to the field of public or political representation. Employment is connected to qualification and merit, though these criteria may embody a culturally determined gender bias, but in appointment, selection, or election to public and political office, other criteria than qualification and merit may also be influential, including democratic fairness and electoral choice.

12. Article 23 of the ICCPR (1966), in elaborating on Article 16 of the UDHR, recognizes the right to marry and found a family; the right not to be forced into a marriage; and the right to enjoy equality of rights and responsibilities of spouses as to marriage, during marriage, and its dissolution. However, it does not give any further details.

13. The most extensive and annotated bibliography on the Convention and its Committee can be found at Bora Laskin (2004).

PERSONAL REFLECTION:

INTERPRETING THE CONVENTION

SILVIA ROSE CARTWRIGHT, NEW ZEALAND

The CEDAW Convention was the product of a determined bid by the women's movement to ensure a comprehensive code setting out the major principles of women's human rights and the obstacles to achieving them throughout the world. It was a notable piece of work, ranging across a huge canvas, but it was a work constrained by opposition to a new human rights instrument, particularly one devoted to women's human rights, and by the limitations in understanding the full spectrum of abuses of women's rights at the time of the completion of the draft in 1979. So there was no reference to the major issue of violence against women, a subject that, since the coming into force of the Convention, has increasingly become a challenge for governments across the world.

This issue was the first to stimulate detailed attention by the CEDAW Committee to the mechanisms in the Convention that might be used to alleviate critical human rights abuses faced by women. The Committee identified the provision, giving it the power, under Article 21 (1), to "make suggestions and recommendations based on the examination of reports and information received from the States Parties," as a means of addressing the issue of violence against women.

Until General Recommendation No. 19 on violence against women was adopted by the Committee in its eleventh session in 1992, previous general recommendations had largely been brief, and had lacked the explanation and detail that might persuade States Parties to pay attention. The earliest work of the Committee had been devoted to setting out the manner in which States Parties should report, but a more confident approach had begun to emerge by the sixth session in 1987, in which the Committee in its General Recommendation No. 3 noted that the thirty-four reports considered up to that time "present features in varying degrees showing the existence of stereotyped conceptions of women, owing to sociocultural factors, that perpetuate discrimination based on sex and hinder the implementation of article 5 of the Convention."

EARLY DEVELOPMENTS

The Committee then began elaborating general recommendations on such issues as temporary special measures to promote de facto equality between women and men, the perennial issue of resources for the Committee's work, and equal remuneration for work of equal value. But brevity remained a characteristic. In General Recommendation No. 8, for example, adopted in the seventh session in 1988, the Committee noted that it had considered the States Parties' reports and recommended that States Parties "take further direct measures in accordance with article 4 . . . to ensure the full implementation of article 8 . . . to ensure to women on equal terms with men and without any discrimination the opportunities to represent their Government at the international level and to participate in the work of international organizations."

There was no evaluation of the material in the reports considered, no comment on how States Parties might move forward in this specific area, and no assessment of the harm done to women by excluding them—or of the advantages of including them—in the public life of their countries.

However, by 1989, and after considering Economic and Social Council (ECOSOC) Resolution 1988/27, the Committee for the first time required States Parties to provide it with information concerning the incidence of violence against women in that country and the measures taken to combat it. The Committee's accumulated knowledge of this human rights violation was not articulated; it seemed that the Committee chose rather to reflect ECOSOC's call for action to be taken.

The first signs of an independent evaluation of a women's human rights issue came with General Recommendation No. 14 on female circumcision, adopted in 1990 at the ninth session. Although no reference was made to material presented in previous reports, the Committee required States Parties to include a broad range of information about the issue in future reports. This was a pattern repeated in General Recommendation No. 15 on the issue of HIV/AIDS, also adopted at the ninth session. No reference was made to any information in States Parties' reports, but note was taken of the reports and materials that the World Health Organization (WHO) and other UN organizations provided. Clearly the Committee was beginning to build on the work of other agencies, and to lend its support where it considered this appropriate.

ISSUES AND CHALLENGES

However, by far the most significant, reasoned work was the 1992 General Recommendation No. 19 on violence against women. In it, the Committee noted that it had decided in anticipation of the 1993 UN World Conference on Human Rights to allocate part of the eleventh session in 1992 to a study of Article 6 and other relevant articles "relating to violence against women."

This was a strong indication that, although violence against women was not overtly included in the Convention as a violation of women's rights, the Committee was ready to read that provision into it. Since that time, the Committee has routinely required and usually received information from States Parties concerning the way in which General Recommendation No. 19 is being implemented in the domestic sphere.

Following the successful development of that General Recommendation, the Committee determined to systematically review a number of articles in the Convention, to summarize its views of the information being gained through examination of States' reports, and to take advantage of the wide range of expertise represented on the Committee. It decided that the issues affecting women in the family needed analysis and comment and began the elaboration of Articles 9, 15, and 16. The method of collating material relevant to these articles was discussed in detail at the twelfth session held in Vienna in 1993, and from this time the work of the Committee routinely included discussion of a new general recommendation, or examination of a draft prepared by one or more experts between sessions.

The Committee recognized immediately that resource issues would have an impact on the drafting of new general recommendations. There was insufficient time during the scheduled sessions, and that posed real problems for the translation of discussion. Eventually, in order to encapsulate the views and expertise of all members of the Committee, it was decided to break into small working groups, and to assign a part of Articles 9, 15, and 16 to each. Interpreters were occasionally available, but often translation was undertaken by individual experts. Virtually no secretarial assistance was provided, but one expert took responsibility for collating the views of the whole Committee, and that work formed the nucleus of General Recommendation No. 21 on equality in marriage and family relations, ultimately adopted by the Committee at its thirteenth session in 1994.

For practical and other reasons, this was a difficult exercise. Most experts were of the view that it was important to articulate the issues but not to set out exhaustively the means by which States Parties might comply. There was also intense discussion around several substantive issues. For example, it was the view of one expert that polygamy ought not to be condemned, particularly for women in whose societies marriage offered social and financial security. The vast majority, however, considered that the attitudes that underpinned polygamy should be changed, rather than to give even tacit support to the practice.

Observations in General Recommendation No. 21 on women's roles in public and private life and on the emergence of various forms of family have provided a useful commentary, often reflected in States' reports. Reference was made also to two major concerns of the Committee: the issue of violence against women and the provisions of General Recommendation No. 19; and the serious problem of reservations to Articles 2 and 16. This pattern of reinforcing previous work of the Committee was later followed in General Recommendation No. 23, for example, on the impact on women of their confinement historically to the private sphere of life and the stereotyping of their roles. And in General Recommendation No. 24, the Committee linked the issue of women's right to health to issues already discussed in earlier general recommendations, such as HIV/AIDS and a woman's right to decide the number and spacing of children.

At the sixteenth session, a major General Recommendation, No. 23 on women in public and political life (Articles 7 and 8), was adopted, but the Committee felt that more could be done to include the expertise of nongovernmental organizations (NGOs). Until this point, all consideration of general recommendations had been in closed session but, increasingly, interested NGOs were offering comments or assistance in framing and drafting.

The Committee's decision to take up Article 12 of the Convention and prepare a general recommendation on health provided an ideal opportunity to harness the knowledge and interest of NGOs. Before a scheduled session, some experts met with NGO experts in issues around women's health. That resulted in a comprehensive draft for consideration by the Committee as a whole. However, the majority of the Committee, while acknowledging the scholarship involved, felt that it was better to set out broad principles rather than to formulate a very detailed general recommendation that might date quickly.

For many, women's health was an area that was changing rapidly in most parts of the world. Issues such as the impact of violence on health, female genital mutilation (FGM), and HIV/AIDS on women were increasingly being identified as threats, but other diseases and practices might also become as difficult to combat or even to diagnose and cure. So the original draft was modified to set out basic principles of human rights in relation to women's health with reference to the Convention. In this way, it was hoped that the general recommendation would be a more useful document in the longer term. All agreed that no general recommendation should be exhaustive, given the potential length of such a document and the difficulty then faced by States Parties already working hard to report on the many issues raised by the Convention.

By this time, a significant part of the Committee's work, usually outside of the regular sessions at which interpreters assisted, was devoted to general recommendations. The work itself was made more difficult by the lack of resources such as secretarial support, but increasingly the Secretariat became engaged and accepted its importance. There was often debate about which articles in the Convention should be subjected to the scrutiny of the Committee in the process of drafting a general recommendation. Other pressing issues—such as the need to encourage amendment of Article 20 (1), which limited the Committee's meeting time—often encroached on what little time the Committee had to spare from its routine work of examining the reports of States Parties. Generally, however, the Committee found the work associated with analyzing, conferring, and utilizing its combined expertise, drawn from individual knowledge and skills and from the experience of examining many States' reports, to be satisfying and even stimulating.

SUGGESTIONS

During this period of rapid development of the analytical and interpretive work of the Committee, it was decided to make a clear distinction between the elaboration of general recommendations and of suggestions. The Committee agreed that general recommendations were interpretations of the Convention to assist States Parties in reporting and in their domestic work implementing the Convention, while suggestions were to be confined to areas where the Committee wished to make a contribution to the work of the United Nations and its organs. A classic example of this was Suggestion No. 7, adopted in the Committee's fourteenth session in 1995 and directed to the Commission on the Status of Women (CSW). It discussed the rationale for elements that, in the Committee's view, ought to be included in an Optional Protocol to the Convention. This instrument was intended to provide communication and inquiry procedures for those who had suffered violations of rights under the Convention and—for the communication procedure—had exhausted their domestic remedies. The suggestion provided the foundation for the work of the CSW, which ultimately submitted the text of an Optional Protocol for adoption by the General Assembly in 1999.

CONCLUSION

The years 1993–2000, during which I was a member of the Committee, were a period of rapid development of its work. There were many constraints on the Committee's time, such as more complex periodic reports, increasing ratifications resulting in more reports, contributions to world conferences, and the consideration of the Optional Protocol. Resources *were always a problem, though increasingly the Secretariat provided good professional support and found ways to assist the Committee in its work. However, the added work of developing general recommendations and suggestions may not be sustainable in the longer term without increased meeting time and more Secretariat support.*

RELATIONSHIPS WITH UN CONFERENCES, SPECIALIZED AGENCIES, PROGRAMS, AND FUNDS

IVANKA CORTI, *ITALY*

The adoption of the Convention on the Elimination of All Forms of Discrimination against Women was a historical event for women of the world and the recognition of their human rights. Nevertheless, its implementation was faced with various difficulties: the CEDAW Committee had only one monitoring instrument—the reporting procedure with the only "power" of making recommendations to the States Parties. The Convention also allowed reservations to its articles. In the 1980s CEDAW had the highest number of reservations among all human rights treaties, all of which challenged the universality of its norms.

Moreover, the Convention's article 20 (1) restricted the Committee's meeting time, thus obstructing the Committee's timely and successful scrutiny of States Parties' reports. Lastly but most important the Committee was administratively and geographically separated from the other human rights treaty bodies. I joined the Committee in 1987, after having been involved in the struggle for women's human rights both in my own country, Italy, and at international levels mainly through the Socialist International as well as the Socialist International Women, where I had also served as Vice-President from 1980–1986. From 1993–1996, I served as Chairperson of the Committee. When the other experts elected me for the first time, I told myself that I would have to "repay" their trust by doing something for the Committee. Since 1987, I had always been disturbed by the fact that so few people—both inside the UN system and also among the large community of NGOs—knew about the Convention and the Committee. I cannot recall how many times in numerous meetings I had to explain both, including what exactly the Committee was and how it worked. Thus, I decided to use the skills gained from my lifelong political experience to move the Convention and the Committee from the margins of the human rights framework to a place of high visibility. In the following sections I will describe the steps taken by the Committee to create links with the various UN World Conferences, with UN specialized agencies, programs, and funds, and with NGOs, and try to show how such links contributed to a strengthening of both the Convention and the Committee.

LINKS BETWEEN CEDAW AND THE FIRST THREE UN WORLD CONFERENCES ON WOMEN

With respect to its formulation as well as to its acceptance by States as a legally binding instrument, CEDAW benefited from a close link with the first two UN World Conferences on Women. The first, held in Mexico City in 1975, had called for a legally binding convention for the elimination of discrimination against women and urged the Commission on the Status of Women (CSW) to accelerate the compilation of its final text to ensure equality between men and women in all fields of public life as well as family relations.[1] Bearing in mind that the Mexico Conference took place during the Cold War, and that many States were reluctant to have a document that would oblige them to address the issue of discrimination against women in their territories, this was a great success. The fact that a consensus was finally reached was mostly the product of the determined work of many women engaged in the CSW, the intergovernmental body of the United Nations responsible for the first draft of the Convention. It also showed the strength of the women's movement and its leadership, including those women involved in different UN forums, who had used every opportunity to urge the adoption of such a document, and who managed to overcome the major political differences of the time.

The CEDAW Convention was adopted by the General Assembly in December 1979, and on July 17, 1980, at a special ceremony during the Second UN World Conference on Women in Copenhagen, fifty-one States signed it, including the United States. Two States submitted their instruments of ratification on that same date.[2] In 1981, the Convention entered into force after the twentieth State had ratified it.

While both the Mexico and Copenhagen Conferences had been important stepping-stones for bringing the Convention into existence, neither one of them had paid due attention to the actual recognition and improvement of women's right to equality as a *human right*. Delegates at the two Conferences had viewed the disadvantages experienced by women as *social problems* and had concentrated their discussions and decisions in particular on women's role in the development process. They had thus focused on women's education; their access to adequate health care, the labor force, and decision-making processes; and on their role and their contributions in agriculture. Due to the Cold War conflict and the different emphases the conflicting States placed on civil and political versus economic, social, and cultural rights, human rights in general remained a delicate political problem, giving rise to many difficult and unresolved discussions in the UN system.[3]

The Third UN World Conference on Women, which also marked the end of the UN Decade for Women, was held in Nairobi in 1985. Desirée Bernard, the Chairperson of the Committee in 1985 delivered the Committee's report on its activities on the implementation of the Convention since 1982, but neither the Convention nor the Committee attracted much attention from the official Conference (United Nations 1985), which continued to attribute most forms of women's inequality with men to their general backwardness rather than to a failure of governments to recognize and implement universal principles and standards of justice (Timothy and Freeman 2000, 5). At the parallel Nairobi Forum, however, convened by women from national and international NGOs, a group of feminist and human rights leaders initiated workshops on the Convention and explained its importance and its potential as a legally binding instrument to assist women in their achievement of equality. The nature and function of the Convention as international law stimulated increasing interest among the audience, particularly when it became clear that women might be able to invoke the Convention before their domestic courts once their governments had ratified it. A group of visionary women from different continents, and from the United States, under the leadership of the American activist Arvonne Fraser, decided to form the first international NGO to support the Convention: the International Women's Rights Action Watch (IWRAW).

Based in the United States, IWRAW became a very important organization for the Convention and the Committee. It published and distributed the text of the Convention in different languages on a global scale; tutored different NGOs and individual women in advocacy vis-à-vis their governments and in the use of the Convention in assessing discriminatory elements in laws and policies; provided the Committee with extensive and informative so-called "alternative" or "shadow" reports on the women's human rights performance of countries to be discussed in the respective sessions; organized workshops during the Committee's sessions for members and NGOs on subjects of interest, particularly on the preparation of new general recommendations interpreting the Convention; promoted a better understanding of the content and importance of the Convention through short essays in its newsletter; and, at the same time, helped the ever-growing number of NGOs to become interested in and knowledgeable about the Convention, giving them the confidence to utilize it (IWRAW 2006).

Nonetheless, both the Convention itself and the excellent work that the Committee accomplished over several years in monitoring its implementation, despite the inadequate servicing by the Division for the Advancement of Women (DAW) in Vienna, which lacked sufficient budget and staff for this purpose, remained largely unknown among women at the national level in different countries. On the one hand, this was due to lack of information provided to their wider public by governments about their policies for the implementation of the Convention, including any visibility of their reports to the Committee. On the other hand, the isolation of the Committee from other human rights treaty bodies made it difficult, even for potentially interested audiences, to locate information on the Committee's work, including its own extensive reports on its discussions with governments. This, of course, was the time before the Internet!

EMERGING RELEVANCE

The UN World Conference on Human Rights, held in Vienna in June 1993 at a time of general enthusiasm about human rights—given that the Cold War and its concomitant conflict about human rights had ended—proved to be an important opportunity to promote the relevance of the Convention for women throughout the world. The Vienna Declaration and Programme of Action reaffirmed the universality, indivisibility, interdependence, and interrelatedness of human rights in general and asserted that the "human rights of women and of the girl-child are an inalienable, integral and indivisible part of universal human rights" (United Nations 1993b, para. 18). The document also asserted that implementation of the human rights of women and girls was a priority for the member States of the United Nations and for the UN system itself.

My election as Chairperson of the Committee happened in January 1993, at the time of the general preparation within the UN system for this Conference. Both the Committee and the CSW wanted to have an input into the Conference and had put it on their agendas. On my request to participate in the respective CSW session, however, I was told by DAW that such participation had not been foreseen in the Division's budget and thus there were no funds to pay for travel and other costs. When I consulted with the Committee members on this issue, everybody agreed on the necessity of participation in order to establish contacts and promote the recognition and inclusion of the Convention in the CSW's deliberations. Thus, I went at my own expense but was allowed to speak in this forum only after many difficulties. My name had not been inscribed in the list of speakers because neither the bureau of the CSW nor the staff of DAW had seen a necessity for the Committee's presence and my speech. Following this experience, the Committee learned its lesson and asked DAW to include representation by the Committee's Chairperson in the next session of the CSW in the relevant budget. This is now normal practice. The presence of the Committee's respective Chairpersons in the CSW sessions later also permitted us to promote decisions by the Committee to be adopted as resolutions by the CSW, which ultimately allowed us to meet twice a year instead of only once in order to cope with our increasing backlog of reports.

The Vienna Conference attracted an enormous audience from all parts of the world, including more than three thousand representatives of international and national NGOs. The NGOs active in the field of women's human rights succeeded in making their concerns a matter of priority in the agenda and outcome of the Conference through their "Forum," held parallel to the official World Conference. In a plenary session of the Conference, held on the day dedicated to "Women and Human Rights," the results of the NGO "Global Tribunal on Violations of Women's Human Rights"—including more than one hundred and thirty thousand signatures to a worldwide petition entitled "Women's Rights are Human Rights"—were presented to a visibly moved audience of delegations from UN member States and formally accredited NGOs. The UN Development Fund for Women (UNIFEM), in cooperation with a number of NGOs, acted as the host of a daily women's caucus. It invited me in my capacity as Chairperson of the Committee to participate in these meetings, thus giving me the opportunity to discuss the Convention and point to its importance for the promotion and protection of women's human rights, for the elimination of the various and multiple forms of discrimination against women, and for the achievement of equality. This initiative contributed greatly to a more general acknowledgment of the importance of the Convention and compensated for the shock I had experienced on arriving at the World Conference to represent the Committee. When I had wanted to take my seat together with the Chairpersons of the other human rights treaty bodies, I found that no place had been assigned there for me. I lost a lot of time trying to find "my seat," and finally discovered it among the group of representatives of national human rights committees and accredited NGOs. This incident served as another example of the then-reigning conviction that the Committee was not as important as the other UN human rights treaty bodies. Although I felt frustrated, I was not discouraged, and during the very first break of the meeting I was attending, I changed my seat, placing the CEDAW flag located on my desk among the other treaty bodies!

The Vienna Declaration and Programme of Action is unambiguous in its call for the "full and equal participation of women in political, civil, economic, social and cultural life, at the national, regional and international levels, and the eradication of all forms of discrimination on the ground of sex." In addition, it states that "[G]ender-based violence and all forms of sexual harassment and exploitation, including those from cultural prejudice and international trafficking, are incompatible with the dignity and worth of the human person, and must be eliminated" (United Nations 1993b, para. 18). Although this paragraph makes no reference to the Convention it is completely in keeping with its spirit, particularly in view of the fact that in 1992 the Committee had adopted General Recommendation No. 19, which defined violence against women as a form of discrimination. The Conference also included the wording of the Committee's Suggestion No. 4 on the removal of reservations to the Convention in its final document. Furthermore, it underlined the necessity of increased cooperation among UN entities and, in particular, of their interaction with the Committee. Lastly, it requested the formulation of an additional monitoring mechanism for the Committee, the right of petition. Thus, the Vienna Conference put CEDAW on the world's human rights agenda and further strengthened it. The Committee was given universal recognition as a human rights treaty body, and the doors of the manifold UN entities, other than the CSW, were finally thrown open to begin a new and productive period of cooperation.

COOPERATION WITH UN SPECIALIZED AGENCIES, PROGRAMS, AND FUNDS

The Committee immediately responded to the positive outcome of the Vienna Conference, and in its first session in 1994 it successfully examined fifteen State Parties' reports in a period of three weeks. In addition, it prepared itself to adopt new general recommendations elucidating articles of the Convention. It also started the procedure of formulating so-called concluding comments on States Parties' implementation of the Convention to be included in its final report of each session (CEDAW 1994, 144, paras. 812–17). Realizing that support for its work, such as had been received through the world conferences, was invaluable, it decided to initiate an active cooperation with different UN entities as well as NGOs from all continents, and to establish contacts with "friendly" governments.

As a consequence of this decision, we started active cooperation with different UN specialized agencies, programs, and funds, in particular with UNIFEM, the United Nations Development Programme (UNDP), the United Nations Population Fund (UNFPA), United Nations Educational, Scientific and Cultural Organization (UNESCO), and United Nations Children's Fund (UNICEF). With respect to UNIFEM, I took the initiative, supported by the Committee, to suggest to its executive director that UNIFEM should become a kind of "sponsor" to the Convention and its Committee in the way UNICEF had been sponsoring the Committee on the Rights of the Child. UNIFEM replied positively to this request and "challenge," created a CEDAW-UNIFEM task force, and subsequently integrated the Convention into its work. This step greatly contributed to the Committee's visibility and impact among national NGOs in particular, helping them to develop the concept of the empowerment of women. As the Committee recognized in its statement for the Fourth UN World Conference on Women in Beijing, "nongovernmental organizations and individual women have turned to the Convention as the framework for equality, using it to campaign for women's rights at all levels" (United Nations 1995b, para. 44).

The Committee also proceeded with the analysis of different articles of the Convention in new general recommendations that were much more elaborate than the early ones, clarifying the meaning of these articles and indicating specific steps that States Parties should take to fulfill their obligations under the Convention. The very important General Recommendation No. 21 on nationality, legal capacity, and family relations (Articles 9, 15, and 16) was prepared during 1993 and adopted at the beginning of 1994.

In 1994, UNFPA invited me as the Committee's Chairperson and sponsored my stay at the UN Conference on Population and Development, held in Cairo. I was asked to explain the Committee's Suggestion No. 6 on these topics to the plenary. This noted in particular both the "vicious circle of women's illiteracy, poverty, high fertility rates and discrimination in formal and informal employment, as well as an interrelation of these issues with population and development issues" and the need to give "due attention . . . to this interdependence in any population and development policies" as well as allowing women's access to decision-making processes (CEDAW 1994, 11, para. 4). At the same time, at the Forum of NGOs that was convened in parallel, I chaired the "Tribunal," modeled on the one held in Vienna, at which many women testified to the terribly negative consequences of various forms of discrimination, such as the lack of adequate health protection and the detrimental impact of various traditional practices, including female genital mutilation (FGM), to their bodies and health. Already in its ninth session in 1990, the Committee had, as the very first voice within the UN system, condemned the practice of what it then called "genital circumcision" as a form of discrimination against women in its General Recommendation No. 14. My in-depth participation in the Cairo Conference gave me, as Chairperson of the Committee, an invaluable opportunity to establish new contacts with numerous NGOs, particularly from the developing world. They were dedicated to the issues of reproductive health and family planning, and they acknowledged the importance of the Convention as a legal framework and support for their activities.

The final document of the Cairo Conference emphasized that education is the main instrument for empowering women and underlined the need to reduce maternal and infant mortality, associated with high-risk pregnancy, as a prerequisite of development and population policy. It further recognized that reproductive health implies the right of women and men to be informed about and have access to the widest possible range of "safe, effective, affordable and acceptable methods of family planning of their choice, as well as other methods of their choice for regulation of fertility which are not against the law" to enable "all couples and individuals to decide freely and responsibly the number, spacing and timing of their children" (United Nations 1994, paras. 7 [2], [3]). These statements reflect, sometimes even verbatim, formulations contained in the Convention. In 1995 they were repeated in the Beijing Platform for Action of the Fourth UN World Conference on Women (United Nations 1995a, paras. 94 and 95).

As a direct consequence of the Cairo Conference, and at the initiative of the Committee, the Glen Cove Round Table on "Human Rights Approaches to Women's Health with a Focus on Sexual and Reproductive Rights" was held in December 1996. The idea had been agreed to by UNFPA. The High Commissioner for Human Rights and DAW had joined as supporters. All human rights treaty bodies were called on to examine this issue from the perspective of their treaty and were asked to begin a process of developing cross-sectoral and interdisciplinary collaboration. It was the first meeting ever of members of all human rights treaty bodies on one thematic issue, and various UN agencies, NGOs dealing with the issue of women's reproductive health. Some representatives of academia were also active participants.

In September 1994, following the recommendation of the Vienna Programme of Action that an optional protocol to the Convention be developed, a meeting took place at the University of Limburg in The Netherlands sponsored by the Governments of Australia and The Netherlands and the Women In the Law Project (WILP) of the International Human Rights Law Group. Three experts from the Committee were among the participants in this meeting, which prepared a "Draft Optional Protocol to the Convention." This draft could not be adopted by the meeting in a formal way because, institutionally, only the CSW was entitled to prepare such a document. Nonetheless, it served as the reference point for many of the drafting proposals put forward in future negotiations. In addition, at its fourteenth session in 1995 the Committee prepared Suggestion No. 7, "Elements for an optional protocol to the Convention," which was adopted by an overwhelming majority of Committee members (CEDAW 1995, 8–11, paras. 1–29). As a result, when the first meeting of the CSW Working Group on an optional protocol to CEDAW met in 1996, it not only requested the presence of a Committee member as a resource person, but also based its initial discussion on this document. The final text of the Optional Protocol to CEDAW, adopted by the General Assembly in December 1999, incorporated many of the elements of the Committee's Suggestion.

PREPARATIONS FOR THE FOURTH UN WORLD CONFERENCE ON WOMEN

Preparations for the Fourth UN World Conference on Women started in late 1993 when the first regional conferences were convened. In 1994, the Committee—together with the CSW and DAW—was asked to move to New York, which it did rather reluctantly, since it had expressed a desire, through a resolution to join the other human rights committees in Geneva. In New York the same difficulties continued: still limited working time, lack of resources, and separation from the mainstream human rights system of the United Nations in Geneva. The move to New York gave the opportunity for new contacts and initiatives contributing to the greater visibility of the Committee and helped to spread knowledge about the Convention as a basic framework for the human rights of women.

In January 1995, at its fourteenth session, the Committee faced an ever-growing number of States Parties' reports waiting to be examined. We thus issued General Recommendation No. 22, which proposed an amendment to Article 20, deleting the restriction on our meeting time, a recommendation fully supported by the CSW in its subsequent (thirty-ninth) session. However, we were aware that such an amendment depended on a decision by States Parties to promote its adoption in the General

Assembly. Going against the "instructions" of DAW I frankly informed these States Parties at their meeting in May, to which I had been invited as the first Chairperson ever of CEDAW, that we needed at least two sessions a year. Our "friendly relationships" with States Parties, which later were further enhanced through invitations extended to me to visit a number of countries and speak at conferences,[4] led to the endorsement of an amendment to Article 20 (1).[5]

Our ongoing cooperation with UN specialized agencies, programs, and funds—as well as NGOs—showed positive results in the preparation for the Beijing Conference. UNIFEM, UNESCO, and UNFPA undertook a number of concrete actions. UNICEF joined UNIFEM in the publication of a kit on CEDAW, which included the full text of the Convention and a detailed explanation of its articles. UNIFEM also made a very important decision to enable a group of NGO representatives from the Asia Pacific region to attend a session of the Committee so that they could familiarize themselves with the Convention, the work of the Committee, and the presentation and discussion of States Parties' reports.

Active cooperation with UNESCO also took place, when UNESCO representatives, with the cooperation of a number of CEDAW experts, prepared a joint manifesto entitled, "Toward a Gender-Inclusive Culture through Education" in Paris in late 1994, which was adopted both by the CEDAW Committee and UNESCO in 1995 (CEDAW 1995, Annex, 132–34, para. 1–14; UNESCO 1995). UNESCO also accepted Article 10 of the Convention as the basic principle of women's fundamental human right to education. The manifesto, printed as a booklet in different languages, was officially launched at the Fourth UN World Conference on Women in Beijing in the presence of the High Commissioner for Human Rights, the Director General of UNESCO, and all the Committee members.[6]

These developments required the Committee's presence at the Beijing Conference, where it would have to inform the delegates about its work and to demonstrate the necessity to build the achievement of equality for women on the Convention. To help the Committee prepare such a report, the Government of Spain offered to organize and fund a one-week informal meeting in Madrid in the spring of 1995. Only after weeks of consultation with the various legal sections of the United Nations, however, did we receive permission to hold this "non-official" meeting.

The meeting in Madrid enabled the Committee to prepare a comprehensive and informative report, "Progress Achieved in the Implementation of the Convention," which became an official conference document in all UN languages and in which the Convention was characterized as the "definitive international human rights instrument requiring respect for and observance of the human rights of women . . . universal in reach, comprehensive in scope and legally binding in character" (United Nations 1995b, para. 15). While this achievement showed the Committee's ability to overcome certain bureaucratic obstacles, we were soon confronted with new ones. Given the importance of the Fourth UN World Conference on Women for its work, the Committee had adopted a formal decision in its fourteenth session (Decision No.14/III in CEDAW 1995) to request funds for the participation of all Committee members in the Conference.

THE FOURTH UN WORLD CONFERENCE ON WOMEN AND THE CONVENTION

The Fourth UN World Conference on Women in Beijing turned out to be "a major human rights accomplishment for women. . . . The Conference Declaration and Platform for Action is built on a rights framework, invoking the substance and the language of human rights in every section, and referring specifically to the [CEDAW] Convention . . . as well as to the other human rights treaties" (Timothy and Freeman 2000, 1). I need to emphasize the words *rights framework*, because they highlight the Committee's opinion that the *legally binding* Convention is reinforced by the extensive programmatic document of the Beijing Declaration and Platform for Action, which, though it postulates concrete goals and strategies to be implemented by UN member States, NGOs, and the UN system, is *not* legally binding. However, all twelve "areas of concern" in the Platform can—and should—be linked to specific articles of the Convention, thus giving the Platform a human rights basis even in those sections in which human rights are not explicitly mentioned.

Major references in the Beijing Platform with respect to the Convention and its Committee served to strengthen both. While noting that three quarters of the members of the United Nations had become States Parties to the Convention, the Platform urged the remaining member States to achieve universal ratification by the year 2000 (United Nations 1995a, para. 230 [b]). It is with a great sense of achievement that in 2006 we can say that almost all member States have now ratified the Convention. In addition, the Platform strengthened the Committee in a particular way. While it made clear that the CSW "should have a central role in monitoring, within the UN system, the implementation of the Platform for Action," it also called on the Committee to take into account "within its mandate . . . the Platform for Action when considering the reports" submitted by States Parties (United Nations 1995a, paras. 318, 322).

Thus, the Platform at least partially endorsed the declaration to that effect made by the Committee in its Decision No.14/III. The Beijing Conference followed the Vienna Conference in highlighting the elaboration of an optional protocol to the Convention, urging the earliest adoption of the right of a petition procedure (United Nations 1995a, para. 230 [k]). These statements turned out to be a very important contribution to the recognition of the human rights of women guaranteed under the Convention. Since December 2000, when the Optional Protocol entered into force, the Convention now has two additional monitoring procedures: the communication and the inquiry procedures.

As with all the previous world conferences, the official Conference in Beijing was accompanied by an NGO Forum. At the last minute, the Chinese Government moved the Forum from Beijing to the small city of Huairou, where the conference site was still under construction when the more than thirty thousand participants arrived from all continents. UNIFEM, together with IWRAW, sponsored the stay of ten CEDAW experts at the Forum, which gave them the opportunity to speak at various workshops and to familiarize many women from all parts of the world with the Convention. I do not know how many workshops on CEDAW took place at the Forum! I only recall that when going through the small streets of Huairou between some newly built buildings, I could see numerous posters that mentioned the Convention and drew attention to meetings on it. Many of the NGOs told me that they participated in workshops on CEDAW, discussing the content of its articles and its value for human rights education. Grassroots women participated in these meetings, listened and made their voices heard, after having made huge financial and personal sacrifices to travel to China and having overcome the lack of organized transportation between Beijing and Huairou as well as numerous language difficulties. It was of utmost importance to them that they were able to learn about the Convention as a valid treaty in international law, to which they could refer in their struggles to obtain respect for their human rights. One of the NGOs, the Peoples' Movement for Human Rights Education, published the Convention text with the title "Passport for Dignity."

The Beijing Conference and the Forum proved to be unique in their historic importance for women's human rights. From both locations, women and men issued the most powerful, peaceful, but determined "call for change" for women at the end of the last century. Immediately after the Conference, the Committee updated its guidelines for reporting by States Parties, including questions as to their efforts toward the implementation and follow-up of the Platform for Action. Since 1996, the CSW, as an intergovernmental body, has been monitoring the implementation of selected recommendations contained in the Platform by UN member States. The Committee, however, in its ongoing examination of States Parties' reports, regularly monitors overall progress in achieving results by each country on the basis of the country's political commitment expressed in Beijing and by linking this commitment to the legally binding articles of the Convention.[7]

CONCLUSION

Have women achieved the goals that were formulated at the various UN World Conferences on Women? To me this seems to be a logical question to ask in 2006. If we look back over the last thirty years or more, I must give a positive response. The United Nations has done much to support a powerful international women's movement. In an important interplay with national and international women's movements, it has furthered social change, giving women an opportunity to demand from their governments recognition and respect as human beings endowed with dignity and for their full rights of citizenship as well. Because of its legally binding nature, CEDAW is undoubtedly one of the United Nations' most important achievements for the women of the world.

When we speak of the outcome documents of each of the UN World Conferences, we must not, however, overlook the preparatory meetings to each Conference in which these documents were formulated and prepared for adoption. In countless discussions many different proposals were placed on the table; substitutions, often one by one, for numerous words or sentences were requested; disagreements resulted in numerous brackets around words, sentences, or even large portions of the text. These brackets, which often remained in the documents up to the last day of the respective UN World Conference itself, could only be solved in many night or Sunday sessions. Women everywhere, diplomats as well as NGO representatives, deplored the loss of time and finances and feared for the UN's budget. Personally, I recall in particular the tensions provoked by religious fundamentalists of both Muslim and Christian faiths before and during the Cairo Conference, and the way in which the media presented this Conference as a "proabortion" world gathering. The final document of the Cairo Conference proved to be exactly the opposite of that media message. Through carefully chosen wording, it only pointed to the need to reduce maternal mortality caused by unsafe abortions. Again, there were many similar difficulties and bureaucratic obstacles obstructing the Beijing Conference.

I cannot forget the dire forebodings we all had one month or so before the Conference date with respect to the sudden change of the site of the NGO Forum. And yet, despite of all these obstructions, the moment of success always came: In the marathon sessions, the final documents were adopted by consensus.

I cannot answer the question that spontaneously arises as to the real motivation and causes for these obstacles. Is it fear of change? Fear of loss of power through the demolition of patriarchal culture? Even if we have the satisfaction of saying that much has changed for the better for women, we still have a long way to go until the full recognition of the human rights of women around the world is achieved. But despite the many and persisting social, cultural, economic, and political kinds of discrimination against women, the public opinion of the world has been awakened to the fact that one of the major political problems of our times is the existing imbalance between the rights of women and men in law and in practice, and that achieving a balance—i.e. equality between the sexes in the enjoyment of their human rights—is a prerequisite for the development, progress, and well-being of both women and men, and their countries, in our turbulent times.

What gives hope—and what I have tried to show—is that engaged women, working as teams, are able to introduce new ways to overcome what is sometimes called "existing rules" and "established procedures." These, in reality, are nothing but a façade for holding on to power and not granting it to women. Today, a great part of the women's community in the world knows the Convention well. The Committee's authority has been enhanced through new monitoring procedures under the Optional Protocol, through improved mechanisms of work, and through better servicing support provided by DAW. However, this success did not come easily. It would not have been achieved without a steady belief in the Convention, a serious commitment to its implementation, and the equally serious work of the Committee's members, mostly going long into the night both in sessions and in individual preparation. If the UN World Conferences have greatly contributed to the visibility of the Committee, the parallel immense efforts deployed by the Committee's members, by its Chairpersons, and by numerous "friends" of the women's human rights movement from governments, NGOs, and UN specialized agencies, funds, and programs have also done their share. In 2006, the Committee is no longer being "discriminated" against. It is considered with great respect and is highly appreciated, which is totally justified considering that it is monitoring the human rights of half of the population of the globe.

The sixteen years I have spent as a CEDAW expert, particularly the four years as the Committee's Chairperson, are memorable years of my long experience and activity in political life. In summing up, it seems that my conviction has proven accurate. Women, when united and committed to a common goal, are able to promote change, modernity, and innovation even in institutions in which rigid concepts of "existing rules" dominate. The world's political leaders must understand that all remaining resistance must be overcome, and that the human rights of women cannot remain absent from any political agenda at national or international levels. We will have to continue to contribute to one of the most important developments of our times, the "cultural revolution" of gaining equality between women and men, in order to tap into and utilize the enormous human potential of women's talents that currently still often go unrecognized.

NOTES

1. The World Plan of Action dedicated paragraph 198 to the acceleration of the preparation and successive adoption of the Convention, including "effective procedures for its implementation" (United Nations 1976, para. 198).

2. The two States submitting their instruments of ratification on that date were Cuba and Guyana, while Sweden (July 2) and the German Democratic Republic (July 9) had already ratified the Convention. The United States also signed the Convention on that date; unfortunately, however, as mentioned earlier in this volume, it still has not ratified, making it the only Western and industrialized member State of the United Nations not to have done so.

3. For a detailed history on the formulation of the Convention and the role played by several important women committed to the promotion of equality who fought against the many forms of discrimination women are still subjected to, consult Fraser and Tinker 2004, xvi, paras. 11–12 and 31–33. For a general overview of the *travaux préparatoires* of the Convention, see Rehof 1993.

4. I will only mention two country visits. In Argentina, I spoke in the meeting of the national parliament in favor of the introduction of a quota system for female and male electoral candidates into the new Constitution, arguing on the basis of the text of the Convention. The Government of Japan organized many meetings and conferences for me with local and high-level bodies in 1994 and 19955 at which I spoke on equality for women, the legal ramifications of the Convention, and the obligations of States Parties.

5. Thanks to the initiative of the Scandinavian countries the Meeting of States Parties endorsed the amendment, which was noted with approval later in the year by the General Assembly, also asking States Parties to accept this amendment as early as possible (United Nations 1996a).

6. This is available at http://unesdoc.unesco.org/images/0010/001036/103643Eb.pdf.

7. The Committee also added a standard paragraph to its concluding comments to a State Party, requesting additional detailed information in the State Party's next report about measures undertaken to comply with the Platform for Action and expressing appreciation or criticism with respect to its efforts.

HUMAN RIGHTS I: OVERARCHING CHALLENGES

UNIVERSALIZING WOMEN'S HUMAN RIGHTS THROUGH CEDAW

SAVITRI GOONESEKERE, *SRI LANKA*

The Convention on the Elimination of All Forms of Discrimination against Women (CEDAW) was one of the first human rights treaties that incorporated the concepts of universality, indivisibility, and interdependence of human rights. The Convention's norms of equality and non-discrimination on the ground of sex are elaborated in specific provisions on the civil, political, socioeconomic, and cultural rights of women, which are all considered on par with each other. These concepts were reaffirmed much later at the UN World Conference on Human Rights in Vienna (1993) by the community of UN member States as was the key issue of violence against women as being linked to infringement of the human rights to bodily security and freedom from gender-based discrimination. Again, already in 1992, the CEDAW Committee, in its General Recommendation No. 19, had identified these rights as being covered by the Convention. Thus, the consensus of UN member States on these issues in Vienna gave the Convention a new global relevance. As we come to the twenty-fifth anniversary of the Committee's work, it is important to reflect on how the Convention and its Committee have contributed to the women's rights movement regionally and across countries, by reinforcing the universality and indivisibility of women's human rights.

I was privileged to serve as a member of the CEDAW Committee in the years 1999 to 2002. Women's human rights issues had become central to my research and teaching as a university academic and lawyer. The subject of human rights in my generation had not been part of the law school curriculum. International human rights law and women's rights were therefore areas I had to learn about on my own, and they gave a new perspective to my work. My experience as a member of the Committee enriched my understanding of comparative law and of the relevance and meaning of harmonizing international human rights norms at the domestic level. This essay will therefore reflect on that experience and on the contributions made by the CEDAW Committee on human rights issues of special relevance to women in developing countries.

THE NORM OF UNIVERSALITY, RESERVATIONS, AND DIVERSITY

The Convention's concept of the universality of women's rights is reflected in its preamble and content. Most important, the definition of discrimination on the basis of sex as both de jure and de facto denial of women's rights in Article 1—and the State's responsibility to eliminate it in all fields including the political, social, economic, and cultural in Article 3—set a comprehensive and common standard of equality for the enjoyment of human rights. The State's responsibility to intervene and take steps to eliminate discrimination by both state agents and nonstate persons, enterprises and organizations, in the family and community, is emphasized in Article 2 and Articles 5 and 16, the latter dealing with social and cultural practices and attitudes in the family that endorse gender-based discrimination. This approach to the universality of women's rights has generated much debate, with cultural relativists arguing that this is an imposition of "Western" standards on countries in the South. Universality is perceived as a patronizing attitude that "infantilizes" developing countries, and removes their right to achieve progress in harmony with their own cultures. Some feminists have also suggested that the adversarial and individualistic approach to rights reflected in CEDAW, focusing exclusively on equality between women and men, undermines an ethic of care and a sense of community, reinforcing the State's power to intrude on privacy (Robinson 1998; Steiner and Alston 2000).

Since the Convention follows international treaty law in permitting reservations, States Parties have in fact tried to modify the applications of these universal norms in their country's context. States Parties from developing countries in particular have entered reservations or declarations to important articles, especially Articles 5 and 16. CEDAW is the treaty with the highest number of reservations, some of which should not have been permitted, for they undermine the very object and purpose of the Convention.

Though the Convention has not given it a mandate to review reservations, the CEDAW Committee has addressed the practice of reservations and justifications in general and, when based on ethnic and religious diversity, has consistently promoted the Convention's concept of "all rights for all women." It has used its general powers while scrutinizing reports to raise these issues with States Parties and has developed a quasi-jurisprudence on reservations and universal norms through a number of general recommendations and statements.[1] Its consistent approach to reservations has enabled the Committee to question States Parties on a country's context relating to reservations, often on the basis of information received from independent sources or materials outside the State Party's report. Concluding comments frequently refer to reservations and declarations, and encourage a State Party to withdraw them.

Some countries have withdrawn their reservations to the Convention after ratification. Among them are Fiji, Jamaica, Liechtenstein, and Thailand, which reported during my membership on the Committee. The dialogue with a State Party on reservations, as well as an uncompromising insistence on the universal validity of CEDAW norms, has contributed to the review of reservations. It has also stimulated initiatives on law and policy reform that usually accompany the withdrawal of a reservation or declaration.

The concept of universal women's rights and the need for consistency across countries in achieving common standards have influenced the Committee's approach to cultural and religious diversity. States Parties often use arguments based on culture and religion, as well as reservations, to justify their failure to fulfill commitments made to CEDAW. Concluding comments consistently use the human rights framework and underscore the need to eliminate *all* traditional practices that conflict with the Convention. General Recommendation No. 21 on equality in marriage and family relations also reflects this approach. Cultural diversity has not been accepted as a justification for perpetuating inequality and the infringement of women's human rights. Concluding comments refer to the contradiction between traditional practices and CEDAW norms and call on States Parties to intervene and eliminate them and withdraw reservations that seek to perpetuate or justify them. The Committee has also encouraged States Parties to revisit their own national experience through broad-based consultation with women's groups, religious groups, and the community. Improving women's access to remedies under national constitutions that set aspirational standards on equality and human rights has also been recommended in concluding comments, encouraging women to test the validity of these customs against local constitutional standards on women's rights. This has been done recently in Nepal, where a women's group filed public interest litigation and the Supreme Court directed the government to ban a custom that required women to live outside the house in a cowshed during menstruation (*Sharmila Parajuli v. HMG Nepal* 2004). The Committee's approach has encouraged other treaty bodies to address practices such as "honor crimes" as an infringement of human rights that comes within the scope of their mandates (Connors 2005, 22–41).

The most dramatic influence of the Committee's work in the context of ethnic and religious diversity in plural societies is seen in the recently adopted regional instrument, the African Protocol on Women's Rights (2003). Described as the "African CEDAW" (Banda 2004), it introduces the concept of women's right to live in a positive cultural environment and actively participate in its creation. This reinforces the Committee's viewpoint that negative traditional practices reflecting gender bias must not be fostered by a State Party on the rationale of "culture." This Protocol endorses CEDAW standards, without diluting them on the basis of cultural diversity and regionalism.

The CEDAW Committee's attitude to the diversity of approaches to women's rights within common religious or legal traditions also strengthens the notion of universality. Thus Islamic countries like Maldives, and countries like Singapore and Sri Lanka with Muslim communities, have been encouraged by the Committee to engage in consultation with women's groups in an initiative that can help to harmonize CEDAW commitments with the norms of Islamic law that promote women's rights. The subsequent discussion with these States Parties shows that they have not perceived such comments as an intrusion on State sovereignty. The concluding comments of the Committee have also strengthened the ability of local women's groups and policy makers sympathetic to gender equality to initiate reform. The Committee has often highlighted the importance of reforming nationality laws and eliminating practices like "honor" crimes that women's groups in Islamic countries have themselves described as contrary to Islamic religious tradition. The Committee has also encouraged these countries to use comparative experiences from other Islamic countries that have engaged in a reform process on family law. The discussions in this essay on legislative reform in some of these countries and the emerging case law in their domestic courts demonstrate that the Committee's work has helped countries with a common heritage of colonial law to review received law and to harmonize legislation and case law with CEDAW.

REINFORCING THE INDIVISIBILITY OF HUMAN RIGHTS AND THE RIGHT TO PERSONAL SECURITY

The focus on implementing socioeconomic rights for women and eliminating violence against women has also increased the opportunities for lobbying and advocacy by women's groups at the local level to eliminate customary laws, social practices, and State policies that reinforce or foster gender bias and the infringement of women's rights.[2] Thus a constructive dialogue on the articles of the Convention on health (Article 12) and education (Article 10), and on General Recommendation No. 24 on health, have provided an opportunity for the Committee to make recommendations on cultural practices that reflect gender bias. Traditional practices such as child marriage (Article 16 [2]), expulsion of girls from school due to teenage pregnancy (Article 10 [f]), genital mutilation (General Recommendation No. 14), and seclusion that denies or prevents women's access to health care come within the scrutiny of the Committee in relation to articles on health and education. The links between these practices, socioeconomic rights, and the infringement of bodily security by violence have made it easier for the Committee to move into areas of local custom that would otherwise be controversial. It becomes more difficult to sustain the argument of State sovereignty in preserving national cultures and traditions when the Committee demonstrates in its work that these customs also deny basic rights in health, education, and personal security. Similarly, Article 6 on trafficking in women and the exploitation of prostitution of women has provided an opportunity to question a State Party on traditional practices that force women into prostitution.[3]

THE IMPACT OF INTERNATIONAL HUMAN RIGHTS AND CEDAW IN UNIVERSALIZING NORMS

The majority of countries that have ratified CEDAW adopt a dualist approach to international law. This means that standards of a human rights treaty do not apply within countries unless constitutions, domestic legislation, and case law incorporate these standards. A few examples of such legislative reform and jurisprudence in the courts demonstrate how the Convention and other human rights treaties have helped to consolidate domestic efforts to achieve a universal norm of nondiscrimination and gender equality.

Legislation is an important source of rights. If legislation is not in place, there is generally no basis for exercising legal rights. At the same time, putting the law in place without effective enforcement is undoubtedly a sterile exercise. While emphasizing implementation, the Committee has taken the view that legislative intervention is an initial and essential first step in achieving harmony with the Convention. Many countries that reported in the period 1999–2002 had clearly initiated efforts to "put the law in place" through legislative reform. I recall, in particular, the efforts of countries from diverse geographical regions—including Burundi, Egypt, Fiji, Jamaica, Maldives, Sri Lanka, Thailand, and Uzbekistan—that took place due to the ratification of CEDAW or as a consequence of constructive dialogue with the Committee. Legislative reform in some key areas has reinforced the universal relevance of CEDAW and has sometimes resulted in the withdrawal of reservations that, in the opinion of other States Parties and of the Committee, undermined the Convention.

Nationality

CEDAW incorporates the concept of equality in transmission of citizenship (Article 9) and in the proof of domicile or the permanent home of an individual (Article 15 [4]). The Committee highlighted the link between discriminatory nationality law and discrimination in the family in General Recommendation No. 21, which includes a few paragraphs on nationality (paras. 5–6). Nationality or citizenship within a country provides the very foundation of rights. Yet nationality laws in many countries have entrenched discrimination against women. This has often been justified on the basis of local culture, tradition and custom, family values, or religion.

The English common law and civil law (based on Roman law) denied women equal rights with regard to nationality because of patriarchal ideology and the concept of a single male head of household and breadwinner, with women and children placed under his protective marital power or "coverture," described in common law as a "wing of protection." Domicile (permanent home) in these legal systems was dependent on the permanent residence of the husband or father. Nationality laws in colonized countries derived from English common law or civil law were based on *jus soli* (birth within the territory), or *jus sanguinis* (birth and descent) and the concept of domicile. They undervalued the biological link of children to the birth mother. These colonial legal values were assimilated without question because they harmonized with the patriarchal and male-dominated bias in these societies. Colonialism in Asia and Africa invariably reinforced patriarchy and undermined positive local values on the status of women. Former colonies that have gained independence have been slow to change nationality laws, which continue to be seen as a reflection of customary law and tradition (*Attorney General of Botswana v. Unity Dow* 1992; Goonesekere 1997). Even when countries like Jamaica and Singapore reformed their laws on nationality, the concluding comments of the Committee to the States Parties indicate that vestiges of discrimination against women remain in some respects, as, for example, with regard to the status of foreign spouses or in passport laws.

Some Islamic countries also have discriminatory nationality laws and have entered reservations to Article 9. Egypt, which introduced significant reforms in its family law in harmony with CEDAW, nevertheless had discriminatory nationality laws that were the subject of the CEDAW Committee's concluding comments. Algeria, Bangladesh, and Jordan, which have a strong base of Islamic law, have similar discriminatory nationality laws. Maldives, on the other hand, which has an Islamic legal system, harmonized nationality laws with CEDAW. Islamic legal values on the child's link to the mother, and women's property rights and other rights in the family, support the view that women originally had a right to nationality that was not dependent on the males in the family. Research on legal systems in the Maghrebi states of Algeria, Morocco, and Tunisia illustrates how the jurisprudence of the *Maliki* school[4] and the legal system assimilated the patriarchal legal values of the French civil law. A similar assimilation of common law values of nationality took place in British colonies that had a prior foundation of Islamic law (Ali 2004; Mayer 1995). The reservations to CEDAW's article on nationality and discriminatory nationality laws are therefore often based on a received colonial legal tradition derived from English common law or civil law or interpretations of Islamic law that are inconsistent with some basic tenets of Islam.

The Committee's articulate voice on nondiscrimination in nationality laws has promoted review and withdrawal of reservations to Article 9 and reformist legislation. Fiji, Jamaica, Liechtenstein, and Thailand withdrew their reservations and introduced nondiscriminatory nationality legislation. Burundi, India, and Sri Lanka also harmonized their nationality laws with CEDAW. Reports by States Parties show that there is a near consensus among them with regard to gender equality in nationality laws. The Committee's continued insistence on a State Party's reviewing nationality laws and harmonizing them with CEDAW will motivate further review and reform. For example, the Islamabad Declaration of the Fifth South Asian Ministerial Meeting of May 2005, which celebrated the review of the implementation of the Beijing Platform for Action (Beijing +10), identified inadequate progress in commitments under CEDAW Article 9 as a priority area for eliminating discrimination in South Asia within a two-year period.

Family Relations

States Parties' reports also reveal how colonial legal values with regard to family relations, a single male breadwinner, and the marital power of the husband have profoundly influenced the family law of developing countries. Customary laws in Asia and Africa reflect a great deal of diversity.

However, they focus in general on the concept of family affiliation and assistance in an extended family. Though women were considered members of a patriarchal extended family, most customary laws did not distinguish between legitimate and illegitimate children. Children born out of wedlock were not considered *filius nullius*, or children with only a link to the mother, as in both English common law and civil law. Marriages could be dissolved by mutual consent on the basis of breakdown of the marriage, rather than matrimonial fault. Duties of support and maintenance were also owed to members of the family. Women had specified rights related to use of and access to land and resources in the community under customary laws, while land rights of male members were linked to duties of support and assistance to women and children in the family. The English common law on family support evolved from a very different value system, which focused on very limited obligations imposed to prevent poverty, vagrancy, and destitution in the community. The Judeo-Christian ethic on the indissolubility of marriage, and on the father as exclusive guardian of minor children, was reflected in the English common law and civil law on marriage and divorce.

Both the British and French colonial regimes adopted a selective approach to local customary laws. They recognized some customary laws but rejected others when they came into conflict with European values. The English colonial administration used the concept of "equity and good conscience" in Asian and African countries to abolish customary laws as part of the legal system. They also recognized the concept of choice and the capacity of individuals to opt out of customary legal regimes. The inevitable interaction and assimilation between the dominant colonial systems and the local laws transformed the context of customary law and even religious regimes like Islamic law (Ali 2004; Alston 1994; Cotran 1968; Goonesekere 1990; Mayer 1995; Mbote 2002).

Custom and tradition are never static but evolve and assimilate ideas in response to political, social, and economic change. Colonialism resulted in the entrenchment of legal values regarding marital power, illegitimacy, property, inheritance, family support, and marriage that reinforced aspects of indigenous patriarchy and undermined certain positive norms of family obligations that benefited women. Practices such as bride price, widow inheritance, *bulubulu*,[5] which are justified as "local custom" in States Parties' reports, are inconsistent with these positive customary norms on marriage and children.

This transformation has not been recognized adequately by States Parties to CEDAW with a colonial legal heritage and systems of personal law that determine the principles of family law. The concluding comments in the Committee's reports during the period of 1999 to 2002 reveal that discriminatory legal values affecting family relations, derived from English common law and civil law but now rejected in Europe and the United Kingdom, nevertheless continue to thrive in the legal systems of African, Asia Pacific, and Caribbean countries.

Some countries—including Burundi, Fiji, Maldives, Tunisia, Uzbekistan, and Vietnam—responded to the need for harmony and introduced a wholesale review of family law after ratification of the Convention. Egypt introduced reforms to permit no-fault divorce under Islamic law in 2001. The Committee's very specific concluding comments to the States Parties on the importance of enacting legislation without delay helped local women's groups to lobby successfully for Nepal's Eleventh Amendment to the Country Code (2003) regarding inheritance, the Hindu Succession Amendment Act in India (2005), and the Family Law Act 2003 in Fiji (Jalal 2005; Muthu 2001; UNIFEM South Asia Regional Office 2002; UNIFEM and Institute of Social Sciences Trust 2005). Maldives enacted a comprehensive Family Code in 2001 and adopted a new Multi Sector Action Plan based on CEDAW in response to the CEDAW monitoring process. The Maldivian Family Code introduced provisions on the rights of women in polygamous marriages and controls on the procedure in the *talaq* form of divorce by the husband's unilateral repudiation of his wife. The Committee's concluding comments on the need for a holistic review of family law, and its critique of discrimination, have clearly provided an impetus for many countries to repeal received colonial law, transform customary laws, and initiate a process of local law reform based on commitments to CEDAW.

Concluding comments on the initial reports of India (CEDAW 2000, 10, paras. 60–61) and Singapore (CEDAW 2001, 53–54, para. 74), and the third and fourth periodic report of Sri Lanka (CEDAW 2002, 43, paras. 274–75) referred to the importance of introducing a common or uniform family law applicable to all women in harmony with CEDAW. However, some States Parties with plural societies have expanded the concept of choice to opt out of a system of personal law and encouraged harmony with CEDAW in each separate system. This has been done in India, Indonesia, and Malaysia. In Malaysia, Islamic Family Law was expanded to give more rights to women, and the Law Reform Marriage and Divorce Act was extended to non-Muslim women who chose to register their marriages under this Act. Introducing a uniform single state law is often resisted even by women's groups since it comes into conflict with the identity politics of ethnicity and religion in postcolonial societies. Implementing CEDAW norms in the area of family law thus poses special challenges in plural societies, but it also presents important opportunities to deconstruct customary or religious legal traditions, thereby also expanding the areas of choice in determining family relations according to uniformly applicable laws. The CEDAW Committee's concluding comments on universality assist women's groups, activists, and governments in their efforts to minimize—if not eliminate—discriminatory diversity in family laws and policies.

Criminal Law and Violence against Women

The same process of entrenchment of colonial legal values and the reinforcement of patriarchy surfaces in the criminal justice systems of former colonies. Many States Parties' reports have revealed criminal laws that legalize violence against women. The defense of "reasonable chastisement" or killing when adultery or a clandestine relationship is discovered by a husband and the forced marriage of a woman to a rapist or in a case of pregnancy were both legalized in penal codes in countries as far apart as Estonia and Uruguay. Vagrancy and "offences against the person" legislation in Asian, African, and Caribbean countries have criminalized the conduct of women who engage in prostitution and, at the same time, exempted the conduct of male clients.

Penal codes derived from British colonial law in African and Asian countries reflected the same norms on the need for the corroboration of a rape victim's allegation and the need to prove bodily injuries or resistance. The concept of proof that sexual intercourse was "against the will" of the victim is found in these penal codes, when rape should be defined simply as absence of consent, encouraging lawyers and judges to acquit an accused when there are no signs of injuries on the woman's body. Incest is also not recognized as an offense in many penal codes, because British colonial law considered this to be a matter for the ecclesiastical courts that dealt with issues of marriage.

Domestic violence, when recognized as an offense, is a category of general crime such as murder and causing grievous hurt. Other forms of violent and degrading treatment have not been criminalized. Marital rape is legalized by a definition of rape in penal codes in countries of Asia, the Pacific, Africa, and even Thailand that has been derived from the nineteenth-century Penal Code of India, enacted by the British colonial administration. This provision reflects the early English common law concept that a prosecution for rape (i.e. sexual intercourse without consent) cannot be brought against a husband. An exception is found in penal codes in the Indian subcontinent and Sri Lanka, where a man who marries a girl under the legal age of marriage can be prosecuted for rape. Such legislation, however, has never been enforced as a deterrent to child marriages, which are celebrated in some of these countries as customary unions (Goonesekere 2004).

The CEDAW Committee's work has not yet stimulated a broad-based review of criminal law. But domestic violence legislation has been enacted in Caribbean countries and in many countries in South East Asia and the Pacific. Interventions such as "no-drop" policies on prosecution and "one-stop" centers for the delivery of service to victims have been established in many of these countries. Jordan's revision of its Penal Code coincided with its report to CEDAW in this period. India amended its legislation prohibiting sex-selective abortions in 2002 to strengthen its capacity for implementation. A Bill on domestic violence is in preparation in Nepal, after this country submitted its reports to the CEDAW Committee. Pakistan, which is due to submit its initial report, has enacted some limited legislation to prohibit "honor" crimes. Sri Lanka and India enacted domestic violence legislation in 2005 and 2006 respectively, after reporting to CEDAW. Bangladesh has strengthened its criminal legislation on sexual violence and the phenomenon of acid attacks on women in 2000 and 2002 and established one-stop crisis centers.

These initiatives indicate that it is possible to change the normative framework of criminal justice and harmonize domestic law with CEDAW norms, if the State can be made accountable and responsive to the need for change. While the Committee's work may not have been the only motivation for legislative reform, an articulate voice in the form of concluding comments helped to promote political will and the campaigns of gender advocates and women's groups who lobbied the State to initiate a reform process introducing the universal norms on violence into domestic law and policy.

INCORPORATING CEDAW STANDARDS IN DOMESTIC COURTS

CEDAW and the Committee's work have had a limited impact on jurisprudence in national courts of developing countries (Emerton et al. 2005; Goonesekere 2004). Isolated and celebrated cases on nationality in Botswana and Nepal (*Attorney General of Botswana v. Unity Dow* 1992; *Meera Gurung v. Dept. of Immigration Nepal* 1991; *Mani Sharma v. Office of Prime Minister, Nepal* 2005), inheritance in Nepal and Tanzania (*Meera Dhungana v. Minister of Law and Justice* 1995; *Ephrahim v. Pastory* 1990), sexual harassment in India and marital rape, and employment practice in Nepal (*Vishaka v. State of Rajasthan* 1997; *Apparel Exports Promotion Council v. A.K. Chopra* 1999; *FWLD v. Nepal Ministry of Law* 2002, *Rina Bajracharya v. H M's Government S.C. Nepal* 2000), and guardianship in India (*Gita Hariharan v. Reserve Bank of India* 1999) constitute a jurisprudence that has cited the Convention in court decisions. Judicial decisions of the Superior Courts in Africa, Asia, and the Pacific have challenged gender-discriminating norms of received colonial law in the area of criminal justice. The publication of case law on human rights in the Pacific in particular shows how CEDAW is being integrated into domestic jurisdiction in common law-based jurisdictions in the Pacific islands (*Bandara v. State* 2001; *Ranjit Hazarika v. State of Assam* 1998; *Balelah v. State, Republic of Kiribati v. Timiti and Robuti* 2005—corrobation; *Noel v. Toto* 2005—customary land rights; *State v. Bechu* 2005—sexual violence).

In this respect, CEDAW is in contrast to the growing quasi-jurisprudence on human rights under the International Covenant on Civil and Political Rights (ICCPR) and the Convention against Torture and Other Cruel, Inhuman or Degrading Treatment or Punishment (CAT) that has strengthened women's human rights. The State's accountability for inaction or failure to conform to a standard of due diligence in preventing infringements of fundamental rights, recognized in the celebrated Velásquez Rodríguez Case,[6] has been developed through many cases in domestic jurisprudence, and impacts positively on women's rights (Goonesekere 2004; *Yogalingam Vijitha v. Wijesekere* 2001; *Sriyani Silva v. Iddamalgoda* 2003). "A right to life" as a civil liberty has been interpreted in India to recognize a woman's right to freedom from sexual violence (*Vishaka v. State of Rajasthan* 1997; *Apparel Exports Promotion Council v. A.K. Chopra* 1999). Similarly the right to freedom from torture has been interpreted in Sri Lanka in many cases as a right to freedom from sexual abuse, and more recently, a right to life (*Yogalingam Vijitha v. Wijesekere* 2001; *Sriyani Silva v. Iddamalgoda* 2003). South Africa's constitutional guarantees on socioeconomic rights have been interpreted so as to confer rights in the areas of shelter and health (*Soobramany v. Minister of Health* 1998—emergency health care; *Minister of Health v. Treatment Action Campaign* 2002—HIV/AIDS drugs; *Government of RSA v. Grootboom & Others* 2000—shelter). The recent jurisprudence on international criminal law and sexual violence in the ad hoc tribunals for Rwanda and Yugoslavia may have an impact on domestic jurisdictions in the area of criminal justice and violence against women.

The jurisprudence of constitutional courts on women's rights that has developed through reference to other human rights treaties is important. The CEDAW Committee in its concluding comments for a specific State Party should also seek more information on its national case law, and reflect further on the potential for both women victims of discrimination and their lawyers and judges to use the Convention and the Committee's general recommendations in the domestic Courts. The concluding comments often focus on gaps in constitutions regarding the definition of discrimination, as well as on the lack of remedies and enforcement procedures. However, reforming a constitution is a difficult task. Judicial interpretation is a much easier path to reinforcing CEDAW standards. The Committee's concluding comments on India referred positively to jurisprudence in gender equality and nondiscrimination of the Supreme Court. Specific reference to case law in concluding comments can help to expand the scope for integrating CEDAW standards in domestic courts, as well as legislation and policy, and stimulate a "traveling jurisprudence" on women's rights that can fertilize domestic law in other jurisdictions of States Parties to the Convention.

CONCLUSIONS

CEDAW has been described as the "poor relation" of the treaty bodies, and its concluding comments as the "most visible output of the Committee" (Bustelo 2000, 98; 94). From the perspective of women's rights lobbies in *developing* countries, however, I think that the Committee has become an important treaty mechanism, strengthening advocacy and local initiatives to integrate all women's human rights at the domestic level. In preparation of the UN World Conference on Human Rights in Vienna, the Bangkok Declaration of the Asia Preparatory Conference showed how developing countries in Asia created a separation between human rights and development by critiquing the concept of human rights as an ideology of *civil liberties* that failed to address basic socioeconomic needs and poverty elimination. The post-Vienna focus on the indivisibility of human rights brought these into the development discourse. The *Human Development Report 2000* of the United Nations Development Programme (UNDP), and other UN documents concerning a human rights-based approach to development, helped to create greater interest in the CEDAW Convention, which had already incorporated the concept of the indivisibility of human rights. Meeting CEDAW obligations on women's health, education, and employment and recognizing violence against women as part of human rights came to be perceived as part of the development agenda. Its new relevance helped to widen ratification of

CEDAW. With over 90 percent of the UN's member States having ratified the Convention, it may even be argued that gender-based discrimination has, through that process, become part of *jus cogens* (absolute norms of international law) or customary international law.

More recently, other development agendas have emerged on the international scene. The Millennium Development Goals (MDGs) have become the new mantra in the development discourse. Women's empowerment is defined as one of the goals but is elaborated in very limiting terms that refer to eliminating the gender gap in education and increasing women's employment in the formal sector and political participation in national parliaments (United Nations 2000a). In 2005, proposals were made to expand this concept at the World Summit, but even these proposals do not reflect or incorporate the wide sweep of CEDAW (United Nations 2005a, paras. 58–59). Current initiatives on reforming the treaty bodies system can pose new challenges for the work of the CEDAW Committee. A disturbing reality, and another danger to the Convention and its Committee, is that fundamentalist religious lobbies that attack the Convention as antifamily, proabortion, and proprostitution are becoming more vocal than before in all parts of the world.

It is still too early to predict whether the Optional Protocol to CEDAW, which came into force in December 2000, will have an impact on promoting and strengthening a universal concept of women's human rights. Bangladesh and Sri Lanka are two countries in South Asia that have ratified the Optional Protocol, though Bangladesh opted out of the inquiry procedure on ratification. Both countries recognize social and religious practices that do not conform with CEDAW. A recent controversial decision of the Supreme Court of Sri Lanka has questioned the validity of Sri Lanka's ratification of the Optional Protocol to the ICCPR (*Singarasa v. Attorney General* 2006). The judgment can be questioned on various grounds and may not be a binding precedent. Several communications under the Optional Protocol to the ICCPR have been initiated successfully by Sri Lankans before the Covenant's monitoring body, the Human Rights Committee, though no action has been taken by the Government on its recommendations. The ratification by States Parties of CEDAW's Optional Protocol—despite the limitations on enforcement—can provide an important opportunity for women to challenge the continued recognition of those practices that infringe upon women's human rights. At a minimum this is an opportunity to give international publicity to and promote scrutiny of governments' action in implementing the Convention.

I was on the Committee at a time when the rules of procedures and the working methods had been strengthened, and we had access to the information and support necessary for effectively monitoring State Party performance. The services of the Women's Rights Section of the Division for the Advancement of Women headed by Jane Connors gave us professional support, with high quality documentation, including reports on the work of other treaty bodies. The United Nations Development Fund for Women (UNIFEM) provided opportunities for many nongovernmental organizations (NGOs) and gender advocates from developing countries to interact with the Committee. It also supported women's groups working on and with CEDAW at the national and regional levels, through its excellent information and data base, publications, and regular meetings in South Asia to share country experiences in integrating accountability and commitments under both CEDAW and the Beijing Platform for Action.

Moreover, the United Nations Children's Fund (UNICEF) and the International Labour Organization (ILO) provided their own evaluations on countries reporting to the Committee at each session. The presence of several senior experts sustained institutional continuity within the Committee, which, I believe, benefited from the range of members' professional backgrounds and commitment. Most important, women's groups were free to access the Committee in a nonadversarial and transparent environment. The constructive dialogue and concluding comments of the Committee on NGO participation in the review and implementation process gave legitimacy to their work nationally, regionally, and internationally, on what might have been considered politically "sensitive" issues. I was "country rapporteur" for the Committee with respect to various States Parties on several occasions, and it gives me a sense of satisfaction to see how these States Parties have responded to the Committee's concluding comments and introduced law reforms in the areas that I have discussed in this paper. The specificity of the comments and the concrete proposals helped to nurture an environment for the kind of follow-up the Committee envisaged. It was an exciting time to be on the Committee.

The human rights-based approach to women's issues must be sustained and not diluted by other UN agendas and proposals for reform of treaty bodies that currently are under discussion. "Gender mainstreaming" has not served women well, often undervaluing the importance of maintaining a balance between leadership and partnership on women's issues, joint accountability, and participation of governments, international agencies, and women's groups that the CEDAW Committee has helped to promote, especially in the developing countries of the world. A twenty-fifth anniversary is surely an occasion to declare successes, recognize limitations, and create new spaces for performing even better on women's human rights.

NOTES

1. General Recommendation No. 4 (1987) is on a State Party's responsibility under the Convention to review reservations, with a view to withdrawing those that are incompatible with the object and purpose of the Convention. General Recommendation No. 20 (1992) suggests that States consider introducing into the Convention a more restrictive procedure on reservations, comparable to that in other human rights treaties (para. 2 [c]). The Committee's statement on the fiftieth anniversary of the Universal Declaration of Human Rights (CEDAW 1998, 47–50, paras. 1–25) was also on reservations. General Recommendation No. 21 on marriage and family relations, adopted in 1994, is particularly significant since it relates to several Articles, such as 9, 15, and 16, on which many countries have entered reservations (paras. 6–8 and 1–47).

2. Unwritten customary laws sometimes incorporate patriarchal norms or are interpreted in a manner resulting in the deprivation of women's rights as proscribed under the Convention.

3. One example is the Indian *devadasi* practice that still operates in parts of southern India. Under this system young girls—usually before they reach puberty—are "married" to a deity or a temple. The girl eventually becomes a prostitute. The CEDAW Committee urged the Government of India to prohibit this and other such practices (CEDAW 2000, 11, paras. 68 and 69). A similar practice exists in Nepal under the *deuki* system, which the Committee also recommended eliminating (CEDAW 1999, 62, paras. 153 and 154).

4. The *Maliki* school is one of the four schools within Sunni Islam being the third largest, followed by approximately 15 percent of Muslims, mostly in North and West Africa. For their derivation of rulings, all four schools use the Qur'an as primary source, followed by the *sunnah* of the prophet Muhammad transmitted as *hadith* (sayings), *ijma* (consensus of believers) and *qiyas* (analogy); the *Maliki* school, in addition, uses the practice of the people of Medina as a source.

5. *Bulubulu* (or *bulu bulu*) is a traditional, community-based form of apology, reconciliation, and recompense that is used to force a girl who is raped to marry the rapist. Activists criticize its application in cases of rape of women or sexual assault, as it may lead to a nonconviction of the perpetrators by courts. The Committee has voiced its concern about the application of the custom to such crimes of violence against women (CEDAW 2002, 14, paras. 58–59).

6. This case involved the disappearance of a person in Honduras caused by nonstate persons. The judgment of the Inter-American Court of Human Rights was that a State has a positive duty to prevent human rights violations occurring in territory subject to its effective control, even if such violations are carried out by non-State people (*Velásquez Rodríguez v. Honduras* 1988).

CULTURE, RELIGION, AND CEDAW'S ARTICLE 5 (A)

FRANCES RADAY, *ISRAEL*

The clash between culture, religion, and women's equality with men has become a major issue in the global arena. Such conflicts arise in the context of almost all orthodox religions and traditionalist cultures and result in barriers to women's rights that vary in form and severity. My interest in this topic goes back to 1974, when, as a young lecturer, I introduced the first course in feminist studies at the Hebrew University of Jerusalem. I quickly discovered—and at that time there was no general awareness of the fact—that the three monotheisms, Judaism, Christianity, and Islam, whose religious courts have jurisdiction over marriage and divorce in Israel, all impose patriarchal institutions and norms—both religious and secular—on the women of the three communities. I became convinced that, without a transformation of religious patriarchy by decree of the constitutional system, women could not gain full equality. Furthermore, with time, I came to understand that, without the dismantling of patriarchy within the religions, traditionalist women would have no right to equal religious personhood. I was convinced that the importance of religion to a significant section of society and the movement of religious principles into general political discourse would remain a hard core of patriarchal politics so long as this transformation did not take place. In research, teaching, and feminist lobbying and litigation, I have attempted to contribute to this transformation in Israel. From the early 1990s, I represented the Women of the Wall in their petitions before the Supreme Court of Israel, asking for the right to worship in an egalitarian way: to pray from the Torah scroll, draped in prayer shawls, in group prayer in the prayer plaza of the Western Wall—all against violent objections of ultra-Orthodox worshipers.

In 2000, I joined the CEDAW Committee and was energized by the expansion of these issues to a global scale. The energy came from meeting and working with women from different regions, cultures, and religions, all of whom shared a dedication to women's equality. It also came from the women of nongovernmental organizations (NGOs) who, in their "shadow reports" and expert evidence, exposed the barriers to women's equality within their own countries. Some of these women take personal risks in order to fight for women's equality, especially those from countries whose legal systems include criminal penalties based on patriarchal religious law, as in some Muslim states. The energy also grew from the fact that the CEDAW Convention contains a unique provision requiring States Parties to modify cultural patterns of conduct which prejudice the advancement of women's equality. In this essay, I will examine the solution that is provided by the CEDAW Convention, by other instruments of international law, and by national constitutions, in cases where equality rights clash with cultural practices or religious norms. The cultural clash is expressly cited in CEDAW, which requires modification of "cultural patterns of conduct" in its Article 5 (a) and of "customs" and "customary . . . practices" in Articles 2 (f) and 5 (a) that prejudice women's equality. The religious clash is also referred to in Article 18 (3) of the International Covenant on Civil and Political Rights (ICCPR), which regulates possible conflict between the "[f]reedom to manifest one's religion or beliefs" and "the fundamental rights and freedoms of others," including implicitly the right to gender equality.

CONCEPT OF GENDER

Unlike sexual identity, which results from the differing physiological makeup of women and men, gender identity results from the norms of behavior imposed on women and men by culture and religion. The story of gender in traditionalist cultures and religions is that of the systematic domination of women by men, of women's exclusion from public power, and of their subjection to patriarchal power within the family. This is, of course, not surprising, since it was not until the Enlightenment that the human rights basis for the subsequent recognition of women's right to equal citizenship was established and not until the twentieth century that women's right to equality began gradually to gain momentum; the ethos of traditionalist cultures and the monotheistic religions was, of course, developed long before that. Hence, at the start of the twenty-first century, traditionalist culture and orthodox religion remain bastions of patriarchal values and practices. Claims to protect traditional culture and to practice religious freedom are still employed as means to stem the tide of women's equality.

CONCEPT OF CULTURE

Culture is a macroconcept, definitive of human society. Anthropologists commonly use the term "culture" to refer to a society or group in which many or all people live and think in the same ways, and it is "[in] its most general sense . . . simply a way of talking about collective identities" (Kuper 1999, 2). The coexistence of different cultures may be viewed from three different perspectives: ethnicity or religion; institutional subcultures varying at the levels of family, workplace, church, and state; and the developing international or global culture, which includes the human rights culture.[1] Gender equality may be accepted conceptually in some cultures or subcultures, while patriarchy prevails in others. In its regulation of the clash between gender equality and "cultural patterns of conduct," CEDAW must be understood as referring to traditionalist cultural norms that are at variance with the human rights culture and to the maintenance of patriarchal norms that conflict with and resist gender equality.[2] These traditionalist cultures accord with a perception of culture as a relatively static and homogenous system, bounded, isolated, and stubbornly resistant (Comaroff and Comaroff 1991; 1997). The contrasting view regards culture as adaptive, in a state of constant change, and rife with internal conflicts and inconsistencies. Where an adaptive culture accepts the human rights demand for gender equality, there will be a process of interactive development rather than a confrontation.[3]

Many of the practices defended in the name of culture that impinge on human rights are gender specific; they preserve patriarchy at the expense of women's rights. Such practices include a preference for sons, leading to female infanticide; female genital mutilation (FGM); the sale of daughters in marriage, including giving them in forced marriage as child brides; paying to acquire husbands for daughters through the dowry system; patriarchal inheritance systems in which daughters inherit less than sons; marriage arrangements allowing the husband control over land, finances, and freedom of movement; a husband's right to obedience and power to discipline or commit acts of violence against his wife, including marital rape; family "honor" killings by the shamed father or brothers of an unmarried girl who has had consensual sexual relations or been raped; witch-hunting; compulsory restrictive dress codes; customary division of food, which produces female malnutrition; and restriction of women to the lives of housewives or mothers, without a balanced view of women as autonomous and productive members of society.[4] Many of these practices have been the subjects of criticism in the concluding comments by the CEDAW Committee on reports from States Parties as different as Algeria, Cameroon, China, Democratic Republic of Congo, Guinea, India, Indonesia, Jordan, Maldives, and Uganda, to name only a few examples.[5]

Of the harmful cultural practices that have been defended against human rights challenges, some are geoculturally pervasive, if not universal, and some specific to regions. The most globally pervasive of the harmful cultural practices mentioned above is the stereotyping of women exclusively as mothers and housewives in a way that limits their opportunities to participate in public life, whether political or economic.[6] The continuing prevalence of this stereotypical approach was made evident in the virulent reaction of the Heritage Foundation in the United States to the CEDAW Committee's Reports, which it condemned on the grounds that they were "pushing an agenda that counters traditional moral and social norms regarding the family, marriage, motherhood, and religion" (Fagan 2001). Other patriarchal practices that were widely prevalent in the past have been eliminated in some societies but have survived in others.[7] Some have always been peculiar to certain areas.[8]

CONCEPT OF RELIGION

Culture and religion are frequently treated as different categories, yet religion is a part of culture in its wider sense. It might even be said that it is an integral part of culture.[9] What exactly constitutes religion remains a conundrum. One classic work on the subject enumerated forty-eight different definitions (Cohn 1997–1998). Usually such definitions include some transcendental belief in or service to the divine.[10] In practice, most religious claims against gender equality have been made under one of the monotheistic religions—Judaism, Christianity, or Islam, which, taken in conjunction, are the world's most widely observed religions—and I will therefore concentrate on them. The distinctive marks of monotheistic scriptural religions are clear: They have a canonical text with authoritative interpretations and applications, a class of officials to preserve and propagate the faith, a defined legal structure, and ethical norms for the regulation of the daily lives of individuals and communities. Religion is, hence, an institutionalized aspect of culture, with bureaucratic institutions that are focal points for economic and political power within the society. Indeed, religion forms, both theoretically and empirically, the core of cultural resistance to human rights and gender equality. Religions, not cultures, have codified custom into binding source books that predate the whole concept of gender equality and have both the legal and the institutional structures to enforce their principles.[11] These characteristics render religion less amenable to adaptive pressures from without. Change must be wrought within the religious hierarchy of the community and must be shown to conform to the religious dogmas of the written sources. Within secular states, religious sects are "often a haven against social and cultural change; they preserve ethnic loyalties, the authority of the family and act as a barrier against rationalized education and scientific explanation" (Fenn 1978).

The fundamental tenets of monotheistic religions are at odds with the basis of human rights doctrine. Monotheistic religion is based on the subjection of the individual and the community to the will of God and on a transcendental morality. Human rights doctrine is human-centric; it is based on the autonomy and rights of the individual (individualism) and systemic-rational principles (rationalism) (Parsons 1963). The doctrine takes as its premise the authority of the state (secularism) (Arieli 1999, 44) and, as its goal, the prevention of abuse of the state's power over the individual.[12] Within some branches of monotheism, there has been a movement to reform and to close the gap with human rights doctrine, e.g. in Protestantism and Reform Judaism. There are also interpretations of Catholicism and Islam, issued by individual religious leaders, which are more consonant with a human rights approach. However, this hermeneutical endeavor is far from complete, in the best of cases, and is demonstratively absent in those cases where the religious community is asserting a defense against human rights claims.[13]

Religious norms impose patriarchal regimes that disadvantage women. It has often been said that the three monotheistic religions recognized from their inception the full humanity of woman, and that woman was created in *imago dei* (the image of God).[14] However, the argument has been made that attribution of *imago dei* to women resulted from gradual inculturation in Judaism and Christianity and did not occur in Islam at all (Borresen 1995). Furthermore, even if women's equal personhood were to be regarded as accepted by religion as a spiritual matter, monotheistic religions have promulgated patriarchal gender relations. Women have been excluded from the hierarchies of canonical power and subjected to male domination within the family.[15] In accordance with the source books of the monotheistic religions, women are not entitled to equality in inheritance, guardianship, custody of children, or division of matrimonial property, and they are not eligible for religious office. In some, they are limited in their freedom to participate in public life, whether political or economic.

There has been much variety among different monotheistic religions, and among the branches within each of them, concerning the nature of their patriarchal norms and their adaptation to changes in women's roles. Judaism originally allowed polygamy (though it was prohibited from the sixth century and formally prohibited from the eleventh century), reserved to the husband absolute power over the woman's right of divorce, and imposed on women harsher penalties for adultery in the law of divorce and *mamzerut* (bastardy). However, it also prohibited marital rape and allowed abortion in circumstances where the mother's health was threatened. Christianity, from the outset, established monogamy and a fair measure of symmetry between women and men in regard to chastity and adultery. On the other hand, it abandoned the prohibition on marital rape, and Catholicism adopted and retains a prohibitive attitude toward abortion and contraception (Pope John Paul II 1995). Some branches of Christianity (Lutheran, Episcopal, and Protestant) and Judaism (Reform, Reconstructionist, and Conservative) have shown a readiness to abandon formal patriarchal rules regarding women's eligibility for religious office and have ordained women as religious leaders. Islam has remained more closely attached to its sources, and, in many forms of Islam and in many of the countries that have Islamic regimes, it has retained Sharia law, polygamy, harsh penalties for the offense of adultery by married women (including, in some systems, the possibility of stoning),[16] unequal inheritance rights, and the husband's power of unilateral divorce. The outstanding example of an Islamic country that has prohibited polygamy is Tunisia. Other than that, gender equality as an accepted norm in Islam is still at the level of individual religious leaders, intellectuals, and women's NGOs and has certainly not been accepted at normative institutional levels.

CLASH OF NORMS

The clash with which we are dealing is between those norms of culture or religion that inculcate patriarchal values and demand perpetuation of these patterns of behavior and the norm of gender equality. The conflict with women's rights may arise with regard to a majority culture in a constitutional framework or a cultural or religious subgroup within the constitutional society. Patriarchal claims by cultural or religious subgroups may range from negative demands for privacy and nonintervention to positive demands for autonomous control of their own social institutions and active support by the state.[17] In theocratic regimes, they require state imposition of patriarchal religious norms. Deference to any of these would result in infringement of women's right to equality.

International conventions and UN declarations protect the human rights to freedom of religion or belief, including its manifestation individually or in community with others, and to enjoy one's culture.[18] The guarantee of freedom of religion is far reaching in its scope, with regard to both the protection of religion in all societal contexts and the protection of all behaviors implicated in the freedom of religion. The Declaration on the Elimination of All Forms of Intolerance and of Discrimination Based on Religion or Belief details the rights to freedom of thought, conscience, and religion for adults and children, some of which may prove at odds with women's rights (United Nations 1981).[19] For instance, the right "[t]o train, appoint, elect or designate by succession appropriate leaders called for by the requirements and standards of any religion or belief" (Article 6 [g]) may involve the exclusion of women from religious leadership. In contrast, the right to enjoy one's culture is primarily concerned with the protection of ethnic, religious, and linguistic minorities (ICCPR, Article 27; Convention on the Rights of the Child (CRC), Article 30. The Vienna Declaration adds further protection for the cultural and religious rights of minorities (United Nations 1993b, para. 19).[20]

Women's right to equality is also expressly protected in international conventions and other instruments, starting from the Universal Declaration of Human Rights, continuing with the ICCPR, the International Covenant on Economic, Social and Cultural Rights (ICESCR), and culminating in CEDAW, which is considered to be the international bill of women's human rights. The clash between culture and gender equality is expressly regulated in CEDAW. Article 5 (a) imposes a positive obligation on States Parties to modify social and cultural practices in the case of a clash: "States Parties shall take all appropriate measures . . . [t]o modify the social and cultural patterns of conduct of men and women, with a view to achieving the elimination of prejudices and customary and all other practices which are based on the idea of the inferiority or the superiority of either of the sexes or on stereotyped roles for men and women." Additional CEDAW articles can be regarded as supporting a strong application of Article 5 (a). Article 2 (f) imposes an obligation to "modify or abolish . . . customs and practices" that discriminate against women, while all measures required of States Parties under the Convention, including those under Articles 5 (a) and 2 (f) must proceed without delay according to Article 2 (Steiner and Alston 2000, 179).[21] Custom is the way in which the traditionalist cultural norms are sustained in a society. It is clear, then, that the combination of Article 5 (a) and Article 2 (f) gives superior force to the right to women's equality with men in the case of a clash with cultural practices or customs, including religious norms, thus creating a clear hierarchy of values. Furthermore, Article 5 (b) strikes at what I have described above as the most universal traditionalist cultural norm that disadvantages women, which is the stereotypical assignment of sole or major responsibility for child care to women. It requires States Parties to take all appropriate measures "[t]o ensure that family education includes a proper understanding of maternity as a social function and the recognition of the common responsibility of men and women in the upbringing and development of their children."

VIEWS OF TREATY BODIES AND WITHIN THE UN SYSTEM

Culture, as noted above, is a macroconcept, definitive of human society, and the concept of "cultural practices" thus subsumes the religious norms of societies. Interpretation of Article 5 (a) to include religion within its purview is further legitimized and reinforced by ICCPR's Article 18 (3), which provides that the right "to manifest one's religion or beliefs may be subject only to such limitations as are . . . necessary to protect public safety, order, health, or morals, or the fundamental rights and freedoms of others." Article 18 (3) thus provides an exception to the right to the freedom to manifest one's religion, should a confrontation with the fundamental rights and freedoms of others arise, including, by clear implication, the right to gender equality, which is itself protected in Article 3 of the ICCPR. Thus the ICCPR limits the right to manifest religion when this infringes on women's human rights. While both the ICCPR and CEDAW recognize the need for protecting women's human rights, the conception of a mandatory hierarchy of values in Article 5 (a) of CEDAW (imposing a positive obligation on States Parties) is not matched by a similar edict in Article 18 (3) of the ICCPR. Article 18 (3) merely provides an exception to a human rights standard and, as such, the Human Rights Committee (HRC) has said it must be strictly interpreted (Human Rights Committee 1993, para. 8). Nevertheless, ICCPR's Article 18 (3) does legitimize limitations on the right to manifest one's religion where such manifestation infringes on women's human rights. Indeed, the Article, in providing an exception for such limitations as may be "necessary" to protect fundamental rights, may be read to imply that there will be an obligation on States Parties to impose them. This seems to be the reading implicit in the HRC's General Comment on the equality of rights between men and women, which, although not expressly referring to Article 18 (3), holds that the right to religion does not allow any state, group, or person to violate women's rights to equality (Human Rights Committee 2000, paras. 5 and 32). This reading is also apparent from country reports in which the HRC has called on States Parties to prohibit polygamy, even where it is a religious and not only a cultural practice.[22]

Use of the construct of culture in CEDAW as a macroconcept under which religion is included gives the widest possible range of protection to the human rights of women. The use of the term "culture" without express reference to religion, which is a more rigidly defended construct than culture, appears to have resulted in a readiness by States to accept the hierarchical preference given to women's equality in Article 5 (a). This is clear from an analysis of the reservations of States Parties. There are at least twenty reservations that clearly indicate that a State Party wishes to conserve religious law principles either for its entire population or for minority communities. These reservations are made primarily under Article 16 of the Convention dealing with women's rights to equality within the family,[23] yet only four countries—India, Malaysia, Niger, and the Cook Islands—have entered reservations to Article 5 (a).

In international forums, cultural practices have been taken to include religious norms. The interwoven nature of culture and religion, insofar as they affect women's rights, has resulted in a merging of the two within the UN system as well as bodies involved with the application and enforcement of the human rights treaties.[24] It is in this spirit that the committees of experts, charged with monitoring compliance by the States Parties to the two treaties, have applied Article 5 (a) and Article 18 (3) (Bayefsky 2001). Where the CEDAW Committee has, in its concluding comments, recommended that States Parties enact laws making cultural practices discriminatory against women illegal or enforce existing laws aimed at ending such practices, it has included religious practices that are prejudicial to women (e.g. Jordan, CEDAW Report 2000, 19, para. 167; Guinea, CEDAW Report 2001, 58, paras. 122–23; Singapore, CEDAW Report 2001, 53–54, para. 74). The Committee has not only held purely cultural practices, such as the practice of FGM, to be in violation of the Convention in its General Recommendation No. 14. It has also consistently expressed its concern about the continuing authorization of polygamy, whether or not based on religious belief, and has asked governments—including those of Egypt, Indonesia, and Jordan—to take measures to prevent its practice (CEDAW Report 2001, 37, paras. 354–55; CEDAW Report 2000, 19, paras. 174–75; CEDAW Report 1998, 26, para. 284 [a]). The HRC has also stated its policy on the relationship between culture, religion, and gender in the General Comment on the equality of rights between men and women mentioned above:

> Inequality in the enjoyment of rights by women throughout the world is deeply embedded in tradition, history and culture, including religious attitudes. . . . States parties should ensure that traditional, historical, religious or cultural attitudes are not used to justify violations of women's right to equality before the law and to equal enjoyment of all Covenant rights. . . .

The rights which persons belonging to minorities enjoy under Article 27 of the Covenant in respect of their language, culture and religion do not authorize any State, group or person to violate the right to the equal enjoyment by women of any Covenant rights, including the right to equal protection of the law. (Human Rights Committee 2000, paras. 5 and 32)

NATIONAL AND INTERNATIONAL CASE LAW

This overview clearly shows that practices injurious to women are regarded as outlawed under the UN human rights system, whether or not they are claimed to be justified by cultural or religious considerations. The cultural defense and the right to religious freedom have, as noted, been raised in opposition to women's claims to gender equality both in constitutional courts and in quasi-judicial and judicial procedures of various bodies.

I have, elsewhere, analyzed the rhetoric and the outcome of constitutional judgments in different countries as they relate to the hierarchy of values between culture, religion, and gender (Raday 2003). This analysis may also shed some light on the possible interpretations and application of the CEDAW Convention. However, such analyses of the decisions in different constitutional cases must be tentative, both because of the limited number of cases and because key variables not considered, such as the constitutional framework for the court's jurisdiction, may have been crucial to the outcome. Nonetheless, a few indicators, intended to promote further inquiry, are in order. Certain variables, for example, prove inconclusive as guides to the hierarchy of values adopted by constitutional courts. First, the constitutional courts examined do not seem to be more consistently deferential to claims of religious freedom than to cultural defense claims. Second, constitutional courts in different countries having apparently similar religious or cultural rules have sometimes ruled in contrary ways. Third, there does not seem to be a clear and consistent distinction in the ways constitutional courts treat majority vis-à-vis minority claims to a cultural or religious defense. In contrast, the secular or nonsecular nature of the State seems to be a constantly relevant factor; in secular States, the courts cite the national secular character of the state as justifying the insistence on the right of women to equality, while religious law is a barrier to intervention.[25] One other theme appears to be constant. Decisions in which constitutional courts have ruled against the popular sentiment of a religious majority or large minority, without the backing of the government, are rare. But when they do occur, they are usually ineffectual. It seems that, although constitutional courts may have been no more circumspect on religious than cultural issues, their decisions have been more vulnerable to popular opposition aroused about religion. In such circumstances, without strong governmental support, the constitutional courts have generally not prevailed in their championing of gender equality. At the level of international quasi-judicial and judicial bodies, there have been very few cases and therefore they cannot be used to produce a principle. Anecdotally, however, it is worthy of note that in all such cases, human rights and women's equality were preferred in the result, and the religious and cultural defenses were rejected. A number of examples follow.

In 1977, Sandra Lovelace submitted a communication to the HRC contesting the decision by the Canadian Supreme Court to reject her petition to cancel the Indian Act's provisions, which authorized her loss of Indian status as the result of marrying a non-Indian. The HRC held that the Indian Act unreasonably deprived Sandra Lovelace of her right to belong to the Indian minority and to live on the Indian reserve (*Sandra Lovelace v. Canada* 1980). This was an unjustifiable denial of her right to enjoy her culture under Article 27 of the ICCPR. It is notable that, in contrast with the high courts of Canada and the United States, which had upheld tribal autonomy, the HRC was very clear that minority tribal discrimination against women was an unjustifiable denial of women's right to equality.

In 1981, the HRC considered a communication in which a number of Mauritian women alleged that Mauritius immigration law discriminated against women in violation of Articles 2 (1) and 3 of the ICCPR (*Aumeeruddy-Cziffra et al. v. Mauritius* 1981). The Government of Mauritius had adopted an immigration law providing that, if a Mauritian woman married a man from another country, the husband must apply for residence and permission might be refused. If, however, a Mauritian man married a foreign woman, the foreign woman was automatically entitled to residence. The HRC held that Mauritius had violated the Covenant by discriminating between women and men without adequate justification (1981).

In 1983, the European Commission on Human Rights considered the complaint of a devout member of the Jewish faith that an order of the French Court of Appeals infringed his freedom of conscience and religion under Article 9 of the European Convention of Human Rights.[26] The court had ordered the complainant to pay damages to his former wife for his refusal, subsequent to their civil divorce, to provide a letter of repudiation of the marriage (*ghet*), as required under Jewish law to complete the religious divorce allowing the spouses to remarry. The Commission held that there was no infringement of Article 9. The argument used by the Commission was that the refusal to hand over the letter of repudiation was not a manifestation of religious observance or practice. In so deciding, the Commission accepted the holding of the French Court of Appeals that "under Hebrew law it is customary to hand over the letter of repudiation after the civil divorce has been pronounced, and that no man with genuine religious convictions would contemplate delaying the remittance of this letter to his ex-wife" (*D. v. France* 1983).

In 1993, the European Commission on Human Rights upheld the decisions of the Turkish courts regarding the prohibition of the wearing of Muslim head scarves on university campuses: "The Commission takes the view that by choosing to pursue her higher education in a secular university a student submits to those university rules, which may make the freedom of students to manifest religion subject to restrictions as to place and manner intended to ensure harmonious coexistence between students of different beliefs. Especially in countries where the great majority of the population owe allegiance to one particular religion, manifestations of observance and symbols of that religion without restriction as to place and manner may constitute pressure on students who do not practice that religion or those who adhere to another religion" (*Senay Karaduman v. Turkey* 1993). Although no direct reference was made to the issue of women's equality, this issue has been seen as intrinsic to questions of women's dress and modesty.

In 2004, however, the issue of women's right to equality *was* material to the decision: In *Leyla Sahin v. Turkey*, the European Court of Human Rights (ECHR) upheld the Turkish ban on Muslim head scarves on university campuses. The Court held unanimously that there was interference in the right of Muslims to manifest their religion, but the interference was prescribed by law and, being based on the principles of secularism and equality of women and men, was legitimate (2004 and 2005).

In 2001, the ECHR rejected a petition to strike down a ruling of Turkey's Constitutional Court disqualifying the political party Refah from participating in the elections. The Constitutional Court had held that Refah had become a "centre of activities contrary to the principle of secularism, encouraging the wearing of Islamic headscarves in public and educational establishments." It had held that manifesting one's religion in such a manner amounted to exerting pressure on persons who did not follow that practice and created discrimination on the grounds of religion or beliefs. The European Court of Human Rights held: "It is difficult to declare one's respect for democracy and human rights while at the same time supporting a regime based on Sharia, which clearly diverges from Convention values, particularly with regard to its criminal law and criminal procedure, its rules on the legal status of women and the way it intervenes in all spheres of private and public life in accordance with religious precepts." Expressing concern about use of "divine rules in order to define the political regime" and Sharia's compatibility "with the democratic ideal," the ECHR held by four votes to three that, because the limitation imposed on the freedom was justified, there was no violation of Article 11 of the Convention, which guarantees freedom of association (*Refah Partisi* [*Welfare Party*] *and Others v. Turkey* 2003).

CONCLUSION

In conclusion, the intersection between traditionalist culture, religious norms, and gender clearly does not support women's human rights. The communitarian arguments of multiculturalist ethics and social consensus, used to justify a "defense" against women's equality, marginalize and silence women's voices in the process of deferring to community norms. Only when individual women choose to consent to live under patriarchal norms must their autonomy be respected, since only at the individual level can the systemic impact of patriarchal authority in the community be avoided. But consent cannot be taken to validate any practice that denies women the most basic of their human rights and that undermines their very personhood and their capability for dissent; such practices are repugnant and invalid. As for lesser infringements of their human right to equality, women's autonomy must be respected but women's individual consent to inequality in a strongly patriarchal environment is suspect. Constitutional authorities cannot remain indifferent to the quality of women's consent, and it is incumbent on them to establish the conditions for genuine, free, and informed consent. This entails putting into place a spectrum of measures to create an educational and economic infrastructure that will augment women's autonomy; indeed, that will offer autonomy as an alternative. Furthermore, women who do dissent must have access to constitutionally guaranteed social equality. This might be achieved, in some cases, by allowing women a right of exit into a civil framework that provides them with the option of an egalitarian position in life or, where possible, by enforcing their rights to equal personhood within their own traditional communities.

Thus, where there is a clash between cultural practices or religious norms and the right to gender equality, it is the right to gender equality that must have normative hegemony. At the international level, this hierarchy of values has been adopted in international treaties, in case law of international courts, and in views of international treaty bodies and commissions, thereby establishing state obligations. At the constitutional level, this principle is only patchily applied, whether as regards majority or minority cultures or religions. The application depends on political will. Some constitutional courts have attempted to implement gender equality in the face of religious resistance, but such efforts have usually been transient or ineffectual where the government has not supported them. The courts in municipal systems cannot be left with the sole burden of securing the human rights of women. It is the duty of legislatures and governments to implement the gender equality obligations that States Parties have undertaken in ratifying CEDAW. In order to further assist legislatures, governments, and courts to implement the gender equality obligations that States Parties have undertaken in ratifying CEDAW's Article 5, it would certainly be helpful if the CEDAW Committee were to formulate a new general recommendation on this issue.[27]

NOTES

I want to thank my CEDAW Committee friends and colleagues for the wonderful interaction, across borders and boundaries, that led me to think as a CEDAW person. I want to thank Maya Seon, Trudy Deutsch, and Julie Asila for excellent research assistance and bibliographical help. Responsibility for the contents of this essay remains, of course, mine alone.

1. The human rights culture has been called "a particular cultural system . . . rooted in a secular transnational modernity" (Merry 2003). This global culture is, on the one hand, generated by States and, on the other, is increasingly determinative of the limits of state power and of States' constitutional culture.

2. A wider definition of culture would clearly not be helpful as it would include the gender equality norms themselves.

3. The cultural defense is often asserted at a rather abstract level. Thus, it has been argued that the imposition of universal human rights regimes is a Western concept, undermining African or Asian culture (Pannikar 1982), often in the context of postcolonialism (Ibhawoh 2001), or as antithetical to the claims of indigenous peoples (Sjørslev 2001). An anthropological perspective is often used to base claims for nondiscrimination against subcultures and for the protection of cultural identity as expressed in language, dress, or communal institutions. This view is unproblematic. The problem arises when anthropologists, as ethical relativists (Hatch 1998, 8), insist on a cultural defense that demands the preservation of practices infringing human rights (Nussbaum 1999, 35–39).

4. For a fuller description of these cultural practices see Cerna and Wallace 1999, 630–40); also United Nations 2002b, 70–81 (preference for sons), 12–20 (FGM), 55–64 (marriage), 45–48 (witch-hunting), 38–44 (the pledging of girls for economic and cultural appeasement), 21–37 ("honor" killings), 89–95 (practices that violate women's reproductive rights), and 85–88 (restrictive practices).

5. Algeria still contains many discriminatory provisions denying women their basic rights, such as free consent to marriage, equal rights with husbands in parenting, the right to dignity and self-respect and, above all, the elimination of polygamy (CEDAW Report 1999, 14–15, paras. 68–92); Cameroon still allows discriminating cultural practices relating to FGM, levirate, inheritance, early and forced marriage, and polygamy (CEDAW Report 2000, 55, para. 54); China still permits "illegal practices of sex-selective abortions, female infanticide, and the nonregistration and abandonment of female children" (CEDAW Report 1999, 31, para. 299); in the rural parts of the Democratic Republic of Congo women are prevented from inheriting or gaining ownership of land and from certain foods because of "food taboos" (CEDAW 2000, 24, paras. 230 and 232); Guinea widely accepts and lacks sanctions for practices such as FGM, polygamy, and forced marriage (including levirate and sororate) (CEDAW Report 2001, 59, paras. 134); India's customary practices include dowry, *sati*, and the *devadasi* system (CEDAW Report 2000, 11, para. 68); laws in Indonesia discriminate against women regarding family and marriage, including polygamy, age of marriage, divorce, the requirement that a wife obtain her husband's consent for a passport, and sterilization or abortion, even when the woman's life is in danger (CEDAW Report 1998, 26, para. 284); Jordan's Article 340 of the Penal Code excuses a man who kills or injures his wife or his female kin caught in the act of adultery (CEDAW Report 2000, 20, para. 178). The Committee's concluding comments call on the Government of Maldives to obtain information on the causes of maternal morality, malnutrition and morbidity, and the mortality rate of girls under the age of five years, and to develop programs to address those problems (CEDAW Report 2001, 18, para. 143). Uganda perpetuates domestic violence and discriminates against women in the field of inheritance (CEDAW Report 1995, 69, para. 332). Most CEDAW Reports are available at http://www.un.org/womenwatch/daw/cedaw.

6. Examples are criticicism of the prevalence of stereotypes controlling women's lives in Georgia in government policies, in the family, and in public life (CEDAW Report 1999, 57, para. 99; 58, para. 105), or great concern about existing social, religious, and cultural norms in Indonesia that recognize men as the head of the family and breadwinner and confine women to the roles of wife and mother and that are reflected in various laws, government policies, and guidelines (CEDAW Report 1998, 26, para. 289).

7. Patriarchal control over land, finances, or freedom of movement were prevalent throughout the world, but they were removed at the end of the nineteenth century in Europe and the United States with married women's property and capacity legislation. They currently remain a part of women's lives in many African, Asian, and Latin American cultures, though change is occurring. The legitimacy of patriarchal spousal violence has gradually been disappearing, and many countries and cultures now prohibit domestic violence. Nevertheless, light sentences for domestic violence by a husband and recognition of a defense of provocation in cases of what are, euphemistically, called "crimes of passion" reveal continued cultural tolerance for such forms of violence. While in most parts of the Americas and Europe, marital rape has been criminalized, this is not the case in the majority of countries (United Nations 2002b, para. 62). Persecution of witches was common in sixteenth- and seventeenth-century Europe and up until the Salem Witch Trials in 1692 in the United States; it is still a cultural practice found in some Asian and African communities (United Nations 2002b, paras. 45–48).

8. Radhika Coomaraswamy, then UN Special Rapporteur on violence against women, lists the countries in which family "honor" killings are reported: Egypt, Iran, Jordan, Lebanon, Morocco, Pakistan, Syria, Turkey, and Yemen. It should be added that in many of these countries such behavior is regarded with extreme latitude under the criminal law, and

either immunity or reduced sentences are prescribed by statute. For instance, Coomaraswamy points out that an attempt to outlaw "crimes of honor" was stalled in the Pakistani parliament (United Nations 2002b, 22 and 37). FGM is believed to have started in Egypt about two thousand years ago. It is practiced in many African countries. It entails short- and long-term health hazards, an ongoing cycle of pain in sexual relations and childbirth, and a reduction of women's capacity for sensual pleasure. Although not restricted to Muslim communities, Islamic religious grounds are given for its continuation in some societies (United Nations 2002b, 14). China is regarded as a major culprit for female infanticide in the wake of its one-child policy. However, while female infanticide is practiced in rural areas, it is not condoned by the central authorities (Shalev 2001).

9. Walter Burkert comments that there has never been a society without religion (Burkert 1996).

10. Natan Lerner claims that all dictionary definitions of religion incorporate recognition of a supreme being, usually called God (Lerner 2000, 4). However, many modern commentators regard the concept as also including nontheistic and even atheistic beliefs (Cohn 1997–1998). In international documents, such as the ICCPR Article 18, the protection of freedom of "belief" is specifically added to the protection of religious freedom.

11. This religious institutional power is much in evidence at the United Nations: The Holy See has the status of a nonmember State Permanent Observer, and the Organization of Islamic Conferences, which represents fifty-three nations, has considerable influence on UN policy-making.

12. The confrontation between monotheistic religion and modern human rights is clearly evidenced in the gap between the concept of religious duty and human right (Cover 1987); in the clash between the religious prohibition of apostasy or heresy and freedom of speech, conscience, and religion (Cohn 2000); and, as discussed here, in the patriarchal, religious opposition to women's right to equality.

13. There is a rich literature on such hermeneutical efforts. See, for example, in Islam (An-Na'im 1990).

14. The Old Testament, the source book of the three monotheistic religions, forcefully frames gender as a patriarchal construct in the story of creation, which constitutes a paradigmatic expression of the "otherness" of woman, as recounted by Simone de Beauvoir (de Beauvoir 1952). The patriarchal version of the story of creation and original sin, while not present in the Qur'an, was later included in Islamic tradition.

15. Much has been written in defense of the humanism of the Bible's treatment of women in the context of biblical times (see Berger and Lipstadt 1996, 310). Indeed, women were in some respects protected by biblical law against abuse. However, protections for women were paternalistic, given to them as unequals like those given to slaves or children, as in the case of protection against excesses of physical violence by husbands exercising their right of chastisement. Such protections did not bestow autonomy or power.

16. Islamic courts in Northern Nigeria have twice sentenced women to death by stoning in 2002, on the grounds that this is the Sharia punishment (Isaacs 2002). Courts in Pakistan (Mydans 2002, 2) and Iran (United Nations 1997) have acted similarly.

17. Jack T. Levy establishes a useful typology for the rights claims of subgroups, such as immunity from unfairly burdensome laws; assistance; self-government; external rules limiting freedom of nonmembers; internal rules limiting the freedom of members; recognition and enforcement of autonomous legal practices; guaranteed representation in government bodies; and symbolic claims (Levy 1997).

18. These include Article 18 of the Universal Declaration of Human Rights (UDHR); the Declaration on the Elimination of All Forms of Intolerance and of Discrimination

Based on Religion or Belief; Articles 18 and 27 of the ICCPR; Article 13 (3) of the International Covenant on Economic, Social and Cultural Rights (ICESCR) on religious freedom in the education of children; and Articles 14 and 30 of the Convention on the Rights of the Child (CRC). For discussion, see Lerner (1966).

19. Although not a treaty, the Declaration on the Elimination of All Forms of Intolerance and of Discrimination Based on Religion or Belief carries the weight of UN authority and may be seen as stating rules of customary international law (Lerner 1996, 123).

20. The Vienna Declaration and Programme of Action provides: "The persons belonging to minorities have the right to enjoy their own culture, to profess and practise their own religion and to use their own language in private and in public, freely and without interference or any form of discrimination" (United Nations 1993b, para. 19).

21. The effect of Article 2, which requires States Parties to proceed without delay, combined with Articles 5 (a) and 2 (f) of the Convention to eliminate discriminatory cultural practices and stereotypes, is to establish an *immediate* obligation and not an obligation merely to take steps with a view to achieving progressively the full realization of rights, as in the ICESCR (Steiner and Alston 2000, 179).

22. In relation to polygamy, see, for example, concluding observations regarding Nigeria (Human Rights Committee 1996, 291) and Yemen (2005, 9). Notwithstanding the Human Rights Committee's approach, Natan Lerner, writing on ICCPR, Article 18 (3), remarks that "there are virtually no problems regarding the religious practices of the major, well established religions" (Lerner 1996, 92). This is a rather remarkable conclusion. Indeed, the references by Lerner to difficulties with ritual slaughter in the Jewish tradition and the wearing of turbans, skull caps, and veils, alongside his omission in this context of any mention of polygamy, *agunot* (women refused a divorce), contraception, abortion, or exclusion of women from religious office underlines the invisibility of religious patriarchy or discrimination against women among many of even those academics who deal with the topic (see Raday 1992 for more on this topic). In contrast, Donna Sullivan, although not commenting directly on Article 18 (3), reaches the conclusion that: "A major area of conflict between religious law and human rights law is that of women's rights" (Sullivan 1988).

23. In many cases, the State Party expressly indicates that the reason for the reservation is in order to apply the Sharia. See the reservations of Algeria, Bangladesh, Egypt, Iraq, Jordan, Kuwait, Lebanon, Libya, Malaysia, Maldives, Mauritius, Morocco, Saudi Arabia, Tunisia, and Turkey. A few of the reservations were in order to allow continued application of various different religious laws (for example, see reservations of India, Israel, and Singapore).

24. The CEDAW Committee clearly states in its General Recommendation No. 21 on equality in marriage and family relations that whatever the form and concept of family and whatever "the legal system, religion, custom or tradition within the country" the legal treatment of women in public and private must be according to Article 2 of the Convention. Similar statements can be found in the UN Declaration on the Elimination of Violence against Women (1993) (United Nations 1993a, Article 4) and in the Beijing Platform for Action (United Nations 1995a, paras. 9 and 24).

The UN Secretary-General, in a 2001 Report, included polygamy, a religious as well as cultural norm, among the traditional practices and cultural norms prejudicial to women that create an obstacle to implementation of the Beijing Platform (United Nations 2001b, para. 30). And Mary Robinson, then UN High Commissioner for Human Rights, in a general overview of developments regarding the human rights of women and the girl child in the Beijing +5 Review Conference, referred to the fact that certain States still refuse to recognize marital rape, "honor" killings and domestic violence as violations of these rights (Robinson 2000).

25. The Court's reliance on secular civil authority for intervention was made clear in *Bavli v. Rabbinical Court of Appeals* 1994, and in *Shakdiel v. Minister of Religions* 1998.

26. The European Convention norms are similar to the provisions of the ICCPR in Article 9.

27. Thanks go to the editors for the suggestion, made on the basis of the commentary in the article, that CEDAW write a general recommendation.

PERSONAL REFLECTIONS:

IN THE MUSLIM WORLD

EMNA AOUIJ, *TUNISIA*

Elected for three terms as a member of the CEDAW Committee, I am offering a few thoughts on my experiences in this important institution. As experts within the Committee, we understood very early on that our main counterparts, although not the only ones, were the States Parties. We needed to establish trust and a constructive dialogue with them, not to judge them but to inspire them to negotiate and thus to improve the status of women in the country concerned, to us the measurement of success. If a State Party recognizes its deficiencies and commits itself to take the necessary steps to bring about change, it is our belief that we have helped the women of a given country on the road to progress. This also means a gain for all women everywhere.

As the first woman magistrate in Tunisia and belonging to the Arab-Muslim culture, I was especially interested as a Committee member in promoting legal implementation measures by States Parties in general and by the Muslim States Parties in particular. Of particular interest to me, therefore, was the removal of legal barriers under the Articles 2 (general obligations by the State) and 16 (equality in marriage and family). Legal provisions that are favorable to women act as catalysts to progress and evolution of the whole society. Sometimes, however, States promulgate laws that appear to be positive for women but actually conceal an undeniably perverse effect. A discussion comes to mind that occurred during the presentation of one report of a State Party concerning the personal status of a married woman who could be divorced by her husband—in a manner that seemed more like a repudiation—by his simply giving her a "present." I reacted immediately by saying: "Mr. Representative, women need justice and dignity, not a sweetener or a gift!" When reports of States Parties are examined, members of the Committee try to help the (often male) State representatives to see and act on responsibilities with regard to the other half of their country's population.

My cultural background led me to be interested in the evolution of women's rights in Muslim countries, each of which refers to the Sharia in its own fashion. The religious text recommends that men reflect on the paths they take; it urges them to use reason, and exhorts them to move toward progress. The best example of an enlightened reading of the religious text concerns polygamy. It is important to emphasize that Islam did not invent polygamy, which was already widespread in many societies and civilizations. It simply restricted it and set the fundamental condition that the husband pledge completely equal conduct toward his wives, which is actually an impossible requirement to maintain. In Islam polygamy is not a dogma, and nothing prevents governments from renouncing or forbidding it (as Tunisia and Turkey have done). On the other hand, a positive aspect, birth control was never proscribed by the Texts. Such fructuous debate between the Committee and the State Party is an incentive to make reforms and changes and could lead to move away from the status-quo attitude.

Improving the lives of women is a "parameter" by which one may measure the degree of development in any country. Muslim nations understand the extraordinary resource that women represent for humanity. They also understand that any progress or modernization of their countries must inevitably pass through the emancipation of women. Many Muslim countries have joined the Convention, a fact applauded by members of the CEDAW Committee, myself included. Although many laws do not yet conform to the Convention's provisions, these States recognize the essential point: that the text of the Convention is a working tool and a means of pressure that will undeniably have a positive impact on improving the situation of women in their countries.

Setting up the Convention is directly linked to governments' willingness and political decisions. That is why, we, as a Committee, have decided to develop some general recommendations which offer States Parties clear guidance on the application of the Convention in particular situations. Observing these general rules regarding women's rights is very important, especially in countries where religious fundamentalism is increasing dramatically. Women should always be protected from any kind of ideological thoughts or economic instability that could generate discrimination against them.

What reassures me is that in Tunisia, my country, much progress has been made in achieving equality for women. I am always using this as an example when I underline that the status of women can, indeed, be improved if the political will is there to demand it, beyond any religious or sectarian extremism.

FROM THE ARAB REGION

NAELA GABR, *EGYPT*

I would like to focus on my personal experience as an Egyptian expert belonging to an ancient civilization and culture that has been open to contacts with the outside world for thousands of years and has thus produced a unique national character. As an Egyptian Muslim, I am also joined to the Islamic world with its religious and cultural specificities; to the African continent burdened by its developmental problems and by the legitimate aspirations of its peoples; and last, but not least, to the Middle East region with all its political perplexities.

I wish to share a specific experience that I had a couple of years ago during a short visit to Sudan. This experience symbolizes for me the extent of my personal commitment to CEDAW, and the importance of this Convention as a legally binding instrument of human rights. Despite my extensive engagements as a Permanent Representative of my country's mission to the United Nations in Geneva at the time, I managed to find time for this trip, which was made.in response to an invitation from the Human Rights Commission in Sudan and a nongovernmental organization (NGO) based in Geneva. When I arrived in Sudan, a country that has not yet ratified CEDAW, I was not expecting the enormous challenge that awaited me. I had been expecting lively discussions relating to Islamic Sharia law, but what I found was a unified front opposed to any discussion of the issue. This group was comprised entirely of women, mainly from the Sudanese judiciary. I stood out in contrast to them, not only in my views, but also in physical appearance. I was not wearing a veil, and was dressed in a Western style women's suit, while they were all dressed in very traditional Sudanese attire (the tob, *or wraparound cloth).*

Nevertheless, the challenge I faced brought out immense energy in me. I was supported by an Islamic scholar from Jordan, who based her arguments on verses from the Qur'an, and by a Lebanese professor, and all three of us stood firm in the face of that front. We held extensive discussions and raised strong arguments and counterarguments by providing examples of numerous Islamic countries that had ratified the Convention, while at the same time explaining the categories of reservations some of them had expressed on a few of its articles (mainly dealing with personal status matters in the family, Article 16). We also offered an analysis of the different interpretations of the Convention and emphasized the impact of complying with human rights norms on the credibility of a country and of improving the role of women according to UN standards, especially in the developmental process.

In my assessment, this experience in its entirety was constructive. It demonstrated that while my physical presence stood out in contrast to most of the Arab women present, no one could deny that—as an Egyptian—I was one of them. My presence as a Muslim mother, grandmother, ambassador, and diplomat was a message in itself: that my country and other Islamic countries do not have a problem with the Convention.

The experience also provided me with an opportunity to become acquainted with some of the positive developments related to the enhancement of women's lives in Sudan, in particular with regard to their political involvement and participation. I would like to highlight the helpful actions of women of the Sudanese civil society, the Sudanese Foreign Affairs representatives, and especially H.E. Sadek El Mahdy, former Prime Minister of Sudan, whose presence—coupled with the views expressed by some of the Islamic and Christian clerics—provided support and offered a deep understanding of the internal political scene in the country.

Moreover, this experience encouraged me to initiate a marathon of studying the variations in the implementation of the Convention in the countries of my region and of speaking about their different experiences in the Committee to many audiences. In the future, I will continue to raise awareness in my own country and my region about such pressing issues as women's illiteracy, female genital mutilation (FGM), the threat of HIV/ AIDS, and the need for women's economic and political empowerment. I believe firmly that discussions, exchanges of expertise, and the study of stories of success and failure constitute useful paths to solving many of the legal and practical problems facing implementation of the Convention.

EDUCATION AND LEGAL LITERACY

SILVIA PIMENTEL, *BRAZIL*

For more than twenty years the CEDAW Convention has been part of my life. I lectured on it as a professor of law, I used it as an activist and since 2005 I monitor its implementation as a CEDAW Committee member. This essay will focus on the meaning and scope of Article 10 of the Convention providing for the right to education. I will also consider women's literacy, women's equality, and their equality in education as challenges for the field of education and provide key information on these issues in Latin America and the Caribbean. Finally, I will discuss women's legal literacy, highlighting the experiences of Brazilian women's groups in legal capacity-building projects to empower women's community leadership and to train law professionals in national and international women's human rights law and mechanisms.

THE MEANING AND SCOPE OF ARTICLE 10 OF THE CEDAW CONVENTION

Article 10 provides that States Parties are obliged to take all appropriate measures to eliminate discrimination against women to ensure equal rights between women and men in education. It establishes in particular the obligation of States Parties to ensure equal access to studies and the achievement of diplomas at all levels and in all sectors of education, in rural as well as urban areas; the elimination of stereotypes in textbooks and teaching methods; equal opportunities for scholarships and grants; equal access to continuing education and literacy programs; and the reduction of female student dropout rates and the organization of programs for girls and women who have left school prematurely. It also establishes the right of women and men to have the same opportunities to participate actively in sports and physical education, as well as to have equal access to information that contributes to the health and well-being of families, including advice on family planning.

In a number of general recommendations, the Committee has further substantiated the obligations of States under Article 10. These general recommendations also link women's right to education with States Parties' obligations under other articles of the Convention, thus emphasizing the central role education plays for the implementation of the rights contained therein. In both General Recommendations Nos. 5 (1988) and 25 (2004) on Article 4 (1) the Committee strongly recommended the application of temporary special measures to accelerate the full integration of girls and women into education on an equal basis with men. In General Recommendations Nos. 3 (1987) on Article 5 (a) and 19 (1992) on violence against women as a form of discrimination that seriously inhibits women's ability to enjoy rights and freedom on a basis of equality with men, the Committee urged States Parties to pursue the elimination of all stereotyped concepts of male and female roles through education and public information programs. It concluded that traditional attitudes by which women are seen as subordinate to men "perpetuate widespread practices involving violence or coercion . . . [that] help to maintain women in subordinate roles," thus contributing to their lower educational levels and expressly affirmed that information programs "will help eliminate prejudices and current practices that hinder the full operation of the principle of the social equality of women."[1] General Recommendations Nos. 14 and 15 (1990) emphasized how specific health issues affecting women such as female genital mutilation (FGM) and HIV/AIDS must be linked with the right to education and the right to equal access to health care (Article 12), recommending that States Parties introduce "appropriate educational and training programs and seminars based on research findings about the problems arising from female circumcision [FGM]" and also "take measures to enhance [women's] role . . . as educators in the prevention of infection with HIV."

In General Recommendation No. 21 (1994) on equality in marriage and family relations (Article 16), the Committee emphasized the importance for women to have access to information and education in order to decide freely and responsibly on the number of their children, highlighting how deeply women's capacity for bearing children and traditional responsibility for raising them affect their right of equal access to education, employment, and other activities related to their personal development. The Committee also underlined women's fundamental need for access to sex education and inspired by the findings of the World Health Organization (WHO), it affirmed the negative effects on girls' health, education and economic autonomy, when they marry and have children. The theme of family planning and sex education was repeated in General Recommendation No. 24 (1999) on women and health (Article 12), in which the Committee established that States Parties have an obligation to ensure—on a basis of equality between women and men—access to health-care services, information, and education. They should guarantee without prejudice and discrimination the right of all girls and women to information, education, and services related to sexual health, including girls and women who have been trafficked, even if they are not legally resident in the country. In particular, States Parties should ensure the right of female and male adolescents to sexual and reproductive health education by properly trained personnel in specially designed programs that respect their rights to privacy and confidentiality. The Committee also recommended that States Parties should prioritize sex education and ensure that training curricula of health-care workers include comprehensive, mandatory, gender-sensitive courses on women's health and human rights, particularly on gender-based violence.

Lastly, in General Recommendation No. 23 (1997) on political and public life (Article 7) the Committee pointed out that women frequently have less access than men to information about electoral candidates, political platforms of parties and voting procedures, and that this lack of political education is a factor that impedes the full exercise of their political rights.

GLOBAL AND REGIONAL CHALLENGES FOR EDUCATION

The right to education for all—women and men—has been increasingly recognized by the international community as a strategic issue for achieving equality, development, and peace. The Platform for Action from the Fourth UN World Conference on Women in Beijing (1995) was a landmark, emphasizing once more that education is a human right and an indispensable tool in order to achieve other goals. Subsequently, the Regional Program of Action for Women of Latin America and the Caribbean (1995–2001), adopted at the VII Regional Conference on Latin American Women (Mar de Plata, 1994), pointed to areas in which States need to intervene: (a) to create legislation that guarantees the equality of conditions in the access of women to education; (b) to ensure the access and parity of female students at all levels and in all types of studies; (c) to establish educational centers without sex segregation; (d) to adopt a curriculum composed of a balanced set of knowledge and values that support equality at all levels; (e) to introduce nondiscriminatory textbooks that promote equality; (f) to eliminate practices in the educational system implicitly containing values and attitudes that strengthen inequality; (g) to eliminate sexist language; (h) to include women in sports activities; and (i) to establish parity of the teaching staff (Subirats 1998).

At the World Education Forum held in Dakar, Senegal, in 2000, 164 States adopted six major goals for education. Two of these goals were also adopted as part of the Millennium Development Goals in the same year.[2] The six Education for All (EFA) goals include the attainment of universal primary education and gender equality in education; the improvement of adult literacy and the general quality of education; the promotion of equitable access to appropriate learning and life-skills programs for all young people and adults; and the expansion of early childhood education. All goals were supposed to be achieved within fifteen years. However, in the words of Koïchiro Matsuura, Director-General of the United Nations Educational, Scientific and Cultural Organization (UNESCO), the "gender goal was judged to be particularly urgent—requiring the achievement of parity in enrollments for girls and boys at primary and secondary levels by 2005, and of full equality throughout education by 2015" (UNESCO 2003a). In order to assess global progress toward achieving the EFA goals, the UNESCO periodically produces editions of the *EFA Global Monitoring Report*, in which progress by States in relation to each one of the EFA goals is measured.[3] Every edition of the reports also selects a specific theme, and in this essay, I will draw attention to two that focus on gender and education for all: *The Leap to Equality* (UNESCO 2003a) and *Literacy for Life* (UNESCO 2006).

Gender parity is merely a numerical concept. Its achievement would imply, for instance, that the same proportion of girls and boys—relative to their respective age groups—enter the education system and participate in the full primary and secondary cycles. Gender equality is a more complex concept and a more ambitious goal and also more difficult to measure. Full gender equality implies that girls and boys have the same opportunities to go to school and to receive education of high quality and that they "enjoy teaching methods and curricula free of stereotypes and academic orientation and counseling unaffected by gender bias" (UNESCO 2003a). It also implies equality of outcomes in terms of length of schooling, learning achievements, and academic qualifications and, more broadly, equal job opportunities and earnings for similar qualifications and experience. Gender parity is fundamental but not enough; the currently available indicators on educational outcomes and learning achievement allow only a partial assessment of gender equality. Educational inequality, according to the EFA Report, is caused by deeper structural forces in society that extend well beyond the boundaries of educational systems, institutions, and processes.

UNESCO has also initiated a Latin American and Caribbean Regional Project of Education (PRELAC), 2002–2017, which is based on four principles: (1) from goods and structures to persons; (2) from the mere transmission of knowledge to the integral development of persons; (3) from homogeneity to diversity; and (4) from school education to a society of educators. The PRELAC conception of an education model puts people at the center of its actions and further defines five strategic priority areas for intervention and change: (1) in the content and practice of education in order to understand ourselves, others, and the world in which we live; (2) among teachers in order to strengthen their role as protagonists of educational change, so that they may respond to the learning needs of students; (3) in the culture of schools, so that they convert themselves into communities of learning and participation; (4) in the management and flexibility of educational systems, to offer opportunities for effective learning throughout life; and (5) in the responsibility of society for education, in order to generate commitments to its development and outcomes (UNESCO 2002).[4]

The PRELAC perspective brings interesting approaches and valuable additional elements toward the creation of a more favorable environment for achieving gender equality in education. In fact, there is a demand for intervening in traditional models of education in a way that incorporates new paradigms based on more critical and creative teaching-learning processes that open new opportunities for girls and boys to develop their talents without restrictions from sex-role stereotypes as required by the CEDAW Convention.

In light of the importance of education for human rights and of the size of the problem in different regions of the world, in 1998 the UN Commission on Human Rights created the mandate of a Special Rapporteur on the right to education. The first Special Rapporteur was the late Katarina Tomaševski , from Croatia, and since 2004 Vernor Muñoz Villalobos from Costa Rica is implementing the mandate. They have both addressed aspects of gender inequality in education in their last reports (United Nations 2004, 2005b, and 2006c), specially emphasizing the need and relevance of the States' obligation in providing access to sex education, in accordance to the CEDAW General Recommendations Nos. 21 and 24.

Literacy

As a basic principle, gender equality is not possible without women's literacy. Literacy has been considered by UNESCO as one of the most neglected EFA goals, since it is a basis not only for learning and for achieving education for all but also for reaching the overarching goal of reducing human poverty. The United Nations therefore established the Literacy Decade (2003–2012). While the EFA Report of 2003/2004 focuses on gender equality, its 2006 edition highlights literacy and clearly underlines that women's literacy is of crucial importance in addressing wider issues of gender inequality (UNESCO 2006).

Taking the nine most populated developing countries (the E9 group) together, e.g. Bangladesh, Brazil, China, Egypt, India, Indonesia, Mexico, Nigeria, and Pakistan, women still make up the majority of adult illiterates in them although some countries have significant gender disparities. Among them, only Brazil has reached gender parity in adult literacy, while Mexico is close to achieving it.[5] The EFA Report's regional overview of Latin America and the Caribbean shows that the lowest adult-literacy rates in the region are found in El Salvador, Guatemala, Haiti, Honduras, and Nicaragua (UNESCO 2003b). This regional overview also offers four additional observations. First, while on average there are almost no gender disparities in adult literacy in the region, in some countries (Bolivia and Guatemala) there are less than eighty literate women for every 100 literate men. Second, some countries with significant gender disparities in literacy are also among those with the lowest overall literacy rates—Guatemala, for example. Third, in some countries (Bolivia and the Dominican Republic), the literacy gap between the poorest and wealthiest strata of society is about 30 percent, and the gap is greater for women than for men. Fourth, the higher the levels of participation in education, the higher the adult-literacy rates, as, for example, in Argentina and Cuba.

In Latin America girls have been expelled from educational institutions for displaying any kind of affection for other students of the same sex. Punishments have been meted out based more on the prejudices of school authorities than on explicit rule-breaking behavior. Human rights mechanisms emphasize that States are obliged to develop and execute programs on sexuality in both formal and informal education that promote respect for girls' and women's rights. This is not an easy challenge, especially in times of growing political conservatism and religious fundamentalism around the world.

A range of other factors connect higher or lower levels of literacy with gender disparities and inequalities. For example, in countries where overall literacy rates are comparatively low, urban/rural disparities tend to be high. Because of economic, social, cultural, and political prejudices and various forms of discrimination based on them, certain population groups—like migrants, people of African descent, indigenous groups, people with disabilities, and people belonging to various minorities—are often excluded from mainstream society, resulting in their reduced access to formal education and literacy programs. Women in these groups, again, are more disadvantaged than men.

The right to literacy is a fundamental dimension of the right to education. It is a powerful tool for the enjoyment of other human rights. It has implications for the quality of life of women and men in all groups and benefits individuals, families, and communities in relation to their access to health, educational, economic, political, and cultural opportunities. There is an urgent need to increase the literacy of women as a right in itself and as a means to access other rights.

The EFA Reports reveal that: (1) women who participate in literacy programs have a better knowledge of health and family planning and are more likely to adopt preventive health measures such as immunization or to seek medical help for themselves and their children; (2) mothers who are educated themselves are more likely to send their children, particularly girls, to school; (3) participation in adult-literacy programs enables women to gain access to and challenge male domains, for example, by learning the official language of a country or managing household finances; (4) literacy programs in minority languages enhance cultural diversity, which improves people's ability to engage with their own culture; and (5) economic returns of education increase individual income and national economic growth (UNESCO 2003a and 2006). In Latin America and the Caribbean some literacy—and legal literacy—programs also take on gender issues at the community level.

THE CEDAW COMMITTEE'S CONCLUDING COMMENTS ON EDUCATION FOR LATIN AMERICA AND THE CARIBBEAN

A reading of the CEDAW Committee's concluding comments on country reports of Latin America and the Caribbean offers relevant information and valuable insights into the educational reality of women in the region. While expressing deep concern about acute social and economic disparities in the region, the Committee has highlighted the high rates of illiteracy among rural and, in particular, indigenous women and has recommended to States Parties that all their policies and programs should explicitly address this problem. In order to improve the situation of indigenous girls and women, it has stressed the need for implementing bilingual programs at all levels of education and for ensuring indigenous women's access to education and health care, as mechanisms to fight social, cultural, and economic factors that cause high dropout rates and illiteracy.

The Committee has also expressed its concern about the persistence of gender stereotypes in the family, in the educational system, and in the society in general; about discrimination against girls and women in education due to pregnancy, including nonreadmission to school of teenage mothers due to the practices of educational institutions run by churches. It has further indicated concern about the lack of correlation between the high level of education reached by some women and the low level of their incomes. Its recommendations to States Parties include implementation of curricular reforms and revision of textbooks; improvements in the collection and analysis of general statistical data disaggregated by sex, age, race, and ethnicity and in those statistics relating to education, teachers, and students; recommendations for broad training programs for lawyers and all public officials,—in particular law enforcement officials, the judiciary, health-care providers, and social workers—on gender-based violence as socially and morally unacceptable and a violation of women's human rights. Lastly, the Committee has increasingly and continuously requested that the communication media help modify cultural patterns of conduct to ensure the elimination of stereotypes associated with women's traditional roles in the family, workplace, politics, and society in general.

LEGAL LITERACY AND PROMISING PRACTICES IN BRAZIL

The law and the legal system often speak a language that is incomprehensible to women because it is technical and male-biased. Learning that language and understanding how the system works empowers women to know and defend their own rights and those of their communities. Such programs provide women with information about the law, legal language, and legal procedures. Legal literacy thus implies the recognition and protection of the right to understand the law and how it is applied. Translating the information on rights and meanings of the legal system for people with limited literacy skills requires that law professionals clearly understand the dual nature of legal literacy: the ability to read and familiarity with the legal and social contexts. The legal system can and must be translated into common language and interpreted by governments, legal and educational institutions, and individuals through the lenses of nondiscrimination, gender equality and respect for diversity. The legal system needs to become a mechanism that can be used by women, even by those with a low level of education, for the defense of their citizenship rights.

Legal literacy programs for women around the world have used a participatory methodology, based on appropriate pedagogical methods for human rights education with young and adult women. The program beneficiaries not only increase their knowledge and awareness of their rights through information acquisition but also develop their individual and collective skills to move from information to analysis and action. For these women legal literacy is more than simply knowing about their rights; it is also about understanding and enjoying their rights, as well as spreading their knowledge of these rights, so that they can intervene in their community and help other women discover and make use of their rights. Some of the goals and outcomes of these programs include the training of a large number of female community leaders, the creation of centers for support, the expansion of the program initiative at the national level, and the active involvement of women in improving their communities.

In Brazil, strategic projects aimed at "rethinking" the law have been developed with a special focus on justice for women. One remarkable project on legal literacy for women community leaders educates women to become qualified community-based legal advisers, the *Promotoras Legais Populares* (PLPs). It is impossible to discuss the PLPs project without referring to CEDAW. In fact, CEDAW has been a source of inspiration and a key instrument for educating women about their rights. In contrast to most law professionals, the PLPs learn about and how to use CEDAW.

In 1992, the Latin American and Caribbean Committee for the Defense of Women's Rights (CLADEM) held a Regional Seminar on Criminal Law in Brazil that among other issues focused on the presentation and sharing of experiences of the legal education of women in Argentina, Chile, Costa Rica, Mexico, and Peru. This seminar proved to be very influential and became an entry point for the development of projects in the area of women's legal literacy in Brazil. Subsequently, the NGO Themis–Legal Consultancy and Gender Studies developed a PLPs project in the Brazilian state of Rio Grande do Sul to train women of all ages and enable them to act as community-based legal advisers, thereby multiplying knowledge and skills on women's rights and intervening, if necessary, in defense of women's human rights as community agents of justice. The strategic tool is the training of women in the understanding and use of CEDAW. Each course is attended by thirty participants who have been living at least for one year in the area where the program takes place, who are recognized as community leaders, and who can fulfill the demands of the program (which takes from four to six months). Participants are educated in such concepts as law and citizenship; the organization and function of state powers, especially the judiciary; national and international women's human rights laws and its monitoring mechanisms; and other legal and public policies issues. After being trained, the PLPs spread awareness and information on women's rights as volunteers in their communities as well as through the Women's Information Service (SIM), e.g. resource centers created by the PLPs in some communities due to the lack of state legal services in poor regions and the high public demand for the prevention of violations of women's rights.

An evaluation of the project found that the courses significantly affect the lives of participants, the communities in which they live, and society at large. These results also attest to the effectiveness of the methodology of using CEDAW in informal education programs. Through more than a decade of experience in training the PLPs who then work with women from low-income backgrounds, Themis can see the project's impact. The empowerment of women may take the form of small personal transformations, such as taking better care of themselves, returning to school, or investing in personal projects. In addition, the political vision and the world vision of these women have broadened and deepened so that they can take on public responsibilities and participate actively as citizens. Because of the success of the Themis methodology, other states of Brazil have adopted it. Themis has also been recognized and awarded for its contribution to human rights education.

The PLPs project in the state of São Paulo, also inspired by the CLADEM seminar, was launched in 1994 by the NGO Union of Women of São Paulo and set up in partnership with the Brazilian Institute of Public Advocacy and the Movement of the Democratic Public Prosecution Service. The program has involved women of different ages over the age of fourteen, of diverse ethnic-racial groups and origin, and of different levels of education.

The program provides legal education for women community leaders in basically the same way and with the same success as the Themis experience. The PLPs learn about human rights, help mobilize other women around their rights, and also interact with different public services (e.g. police, health, education), in particular with public bodies that promote and provide access to justice (e.g. public defenders, public prosecution service, judiciary). In more than ten years, the project has educated two thousand community leaders in the state of São Paulo; has created a center for women victims of violence; has presented two cases of women's murder to the Inter-American Commission on Human Rights of the Organization of American States (OAS), in partnership with CLADEM and the Center for Justice and International Law (CEJIL); and has been a pioneer for establishing the recognition of rape in the workplace as a responsibility of the employer.[6]

The PLPs projects developed by Themis and the Union of Women were the first experiences in Brazil of informal legal education for women. From these two successful projects, the concept and methodology of the PLPs have spread through the five regions of the country, adopted by different groups. Some of these focus on specific issues, as for instance, race and ethnic issues emphasized in PLPs courses developed by black women's organizations, and environmental issues, sexual and reproductive rights, by other groups. The PLPs are considered a model for legal literacy programs and are now also studied by educators and scholars in education, law, and social sciences. The impact of these programs can also be charted through the testimonies of the PLPs themselves. As one participant stated: "The course reinvented my life. It woke me up. Being a PLP means taking hope, information, and self-esteem to communities without hope. Being a PLP helps our rights to prevail."[7]

Law and social reality have, unfortunately, often been part of two distinct universes. This is particularly true when referring to women's rights and gender relations. In this respect, law professionals also have a responsibility to defend such rights. But in Brazil, very few of them have made use of human rights treaties, both global (e.g. CEDAW) and regional (e.g. the Convention of Belém do Pará). Law schools, as well as the public examinations and professional courses for different legal careers, do not include international human rights law in their programs. While this is a very recent field of study, things finally are changing little by little.

Since Brazil is a country of continental dimensions, it is necessary to train law professionals throughout its different regions. The national section of CLADEM in Brazil and the Institute for the Promotion of Equity, in collaboration with various organizations and with Ford Foundation support, developed a pilot project of four three-day regional seminars. Carried out between 1999 and 2000, these trained a hundred law professionals in international human rights law. The aim of the project was to sensitize law professionals about the stereotypes, prejudices, and forms of discrimination still present in the legal arena. It also aimed at developing the skills of law professionals in using instruments and mechanisms of international human rights law focusing on gender, race/ethnicity, and social and economic inequalities issues and at prioritizing in particular discrimination and violence against women and their sexual and reproductive rights. The project was designed to enable and encourage law professionals to formulate their own strategies on how to apply international human rights instruments, such as CEDAW, at different levels of their legal practice. A key feature of this program was its interactive methodology, mixing traditional lectures with individual and working group dynamics. The teaching-learning process engaged not only the participants' legal, formal, and technical knowledge and rational understanding of women's human rights, but also and especially their emotional attitudes. Participants' evaluations of the program indicated that its impact was extremely positive.

FINAL CONSIDERATIONS

Certain progress has been made under CEDAW obligations, and it is important to recognize the efforts some governments have taken to seriously implement women's right to education. However, the application of gender mainstreaming strategies in educational systems is only still modest, and many goals on gender parity and gender equality in education will not be achieved in the millennium decade by a large number of countries, especially the poorest ones. Further, a large number of States are violating CEDAW provisions and Committee recommendations by not providing access to sex education, in particular for girls, due to the influence of fundamentalist sectors of religious groups within official politics. A comprehensive strategy is needed in order to create conditions for the elimination of gender discrimination with regard to the right to education, as well as for enhancing the exercise and enjoyment of all rights and freedoms through education.

In addition, a gender-sensitive educational strategy is needed to bring international human rights law, in particular CEDAW, to local government levels, as, for example, in the 1992 Paulista Convention on the Elimination of All Forms of Discrimination against Women, adopted and implemented by the State of São Paulo and the governments of the municipalities. Even though it has not yet been fully implemented, this initiative may serve as an interesting strategy to be replicated and further developed. It may also serve as a source of inspiration for other local governments in the country, in the region, and in the world.

The CEDAW Convention and especially its Article 10 are clearly linked to the idea that education is a key tool for personal empowerment, more specifically for the personal empowerment of women. In this sense, literacy as well as legal literacy are crucial dimensions of the right of women to education. Legal literacy programs, like the PLPs' project presented in this essay, have the role of ensuring women's awareness and exercise of their rights.

"Before the Law stands a doorkeeper," says Franz Kafka's parable (Kafka 1925). Legal literacy is a crucial tool that empowers women to get past all the "doorkeepers" standing in their way, so that they can finally reach and move through the "gate" of law. The CEDAW Convention and its Committee provide key concepts and tools for women, in any part of the world, to pass the "doorkeepers" and go through the "gate" to enjoy their rights.

As a human rights activist, I believe in education. I believe in the role of CEDAW to ensure the rights of women to education. I believe in a fairer world for women and men. Even in difficult times, we should not silence our voices. On the contrary, we must intensify them. It is what all of us who have contributed to this book are seeking to do. Finally, I invoke the revolutionary wisdom of the Brazilian educator, Paulo Freire, and his pedagogy of freedom: "Education does not make us educable. It is our awareness of being unfinished that makes us educable. . . . It is in our incompleteness, of which we are aware, that education as a permanent process is grounded. Women and men are capable of being educated only to the extent that they are capable of recognizing themselves as unfinished" (Freire 2001, 58).

NOTES

I would like to thank Valéria Pandjiarjian for the translation of this essay and for her input to the text; I would also like to thank Flávia Piovesan and my sisters from the women's movement at national, regional, and international levels with whom, for the last three decades, I have had the privilege of developing joint feminist activities

1. When CEDAW was adopted in 1979, it was not yet possible for it to have an explicit reference to violence against women. As a cofounder of the International Women's Rights Action Watch (IWRAW) I used to enthusiastically advocate for the Convention's "immediate amendment" to include this issue. Some colleagues with more experience, however, explained the difficulties and risks inherent in the process of amending the Convention. Regarding the Latin American and Caribbean region, it is relevant to mention the existence of the Inter-American Convention on the Prevention, Punishment and Eradication of Violence against Women (Convention of Belém do Pará) of 1994, in which education is seen here as the main tool for avoiding gender-based violence, which impedes equality (Article 8 [b]).

2. Goal 2. Achieve universal primary education. Target 3. Ensure that, by 2015, children everywhere, boys and girls alike, will be able to complete a full course of primary schooling; Goal 3. Promote gender equality and empower women. Target 4. Eliminate gender disparity in primary and secondary education, preferably by 2005, and at all levels of education no later than 2015. See UNESCO (2000).

3. The EFA Global Monitoring Report is produced by an independent team based at UNESCO (Paris), with technical support from the Institute for Statistics (Montreal). See UNESCO (1995).

4. PRELAC seems to be influenced and inspired by the ideas of Paulo Freire, the famous Brazilian educator.

5. Through the initiative of the E-9 countries, which together account for half of the world's population and 70 percent of the world's illiterates, specific efforts have been made to achieve education for all, with priority on the education of women and girls.

6. The proposal of considering rape in the workplace *also* as an accident at work was accepted by a Court in São Paulo in a case where the employee was raped by the son of her employer in their workplace.

7. See *Promotoras Legais Populares*, http://www.promotoraslegaispopulares.org.br for the testimony of Roseli Aparecida Pavan from the ninth edition of the PLPs in São Paulo, 2003.

PERSONAL REFLECTION:

PERSISTENT DISCRIMINATION

CHRISTINE KAPALATA, UNITED REPUBLIC OF TANZANIA

I joined the CEDAW Committee in January 2002 after the Tanzanian expert, Dr. Asha Rose Migiro, who had been elected to the Committee in August 2000, resigned by virtue of being appointed Minister of Community Development, Gender and Children. The Committee accepted my nomination as a replacement, and I was expected to serve the remaining two years of her term. I was sworn in as a member of the Committee at its twenty-sixth session. Taking the oath that all new members are required to take, I knew that I had undertaken a commitment as an independent expert that required me to put the human rights of women above any feelings I might have about my own government or the government of the reporting State.

I soon found out that serving on the Committee requires a lot of reading and understanding of the political, social, as well as economic systems of the States Parties. During the first few days of my membership, I burned a lot of midnight oil trying to catch up with a rigorous examination of the reports. I later found out that, because members of the Committee come from different disciplines, it is possible for each expert to concentrate on her or his area of expertise in the examination of States Parties' reports while at the same time acquiring general knowledge of the country. This "unofficial distribution of expertise" enriched the debate and produced a comprehensive examination of the reports before the Committee.

It was a veritable revelation to learn that from north to south and from east to west, discrimination against women existed. Women in poor countries often die because they do not have access to medical facilities, and conversely, women in developed countries may be denied positions in some professions or denied equal pay for work of equal value. Forms of discrimination are found in both poor and wealthy countries, in developed and developing countries alike. I was particularly perturbed at the discrimination in developed countries where people were no longer struggling for the bare basics of life, as they are in developing countries. For example, France to me (naïvely, I now know) was the land of Liberty, Equality, and Fraternity, and so I was surprised to discover that women could not vote until 1944. Canada and Japan, to cite two other examples, also surprised me when I learned of their discrimination against Inuit women and the women of the social minority group "buraku," respectively. Clearly, levels of development were not necessarily synonymous with respect for human rights, particularly those of women.

When the Committee took up the examination of the third and fourth periodic report of Tunisia, I learned that Tunisia has been able to harmonize the provisions of Islam with human rights tenets. In order to improve the situation of women in the family, Tunisia first prohibited polygamy by law and later introduced the concept of partnership in marriage. To me, these were brave and practical steps.

In January 2003 after a year's experience, I became Rapporteur *in the Bureau of the Committee. My assignment was to take notes faithfully of the discussions of the Committee to be summarized in the concluding comments to each State Party. While this task somewhat limited my participation in the debate, I never missed an opportunity to make an intervention when seized by an issue.*

Serving on the Committee is both a privilege and a service. The long hours spent discussing States Parties' reports are rewarded by the fact that delegations return enlightened, if not totally determined to implement the recommendations coming from the Committee's concluding comments. Tanzania, my country, has, for example, amended provisions of its Constitution to increase the number of women members of parliament from 15 percent in 1995 to 20 percent in 2000. While this is not the optimum, it has nonetheless been possible because of a combination of pressures, in part from the Committee, in part from the Beijing Platform for Action and other international documents.

As the Committee celebrates its twenty-five years of existence, it is heartwarming—particularly for anyone who has served on the Committee—to see the number of amendments that countries are making in their laws to bring them in line with respect for women's rights, which are indeed human rights, required under the Convention. The crowning glory comes from the celebration by African countries in general and Liberia in particular, of the first democratically elected woman president in Africa's oldest republic. Women have cause to celebrate; the struggle, however, continues!

PRIVATE GLOBAL ENTERPRISES, INTERNATIONAL TRADE, AND FINANCE

ELIZABETH EVATT, *AUSTRALIA*

When I was a member of the CEDAW Committee in the mid-1980s, my colleagues and I spent much energy on the struggle between competing ideologies. Members from the Soviet Union and the Eastern bloc countries, which dominated the Committee, insisted that women could achieve equality only under their centrally controlled socialist economies. Members from Western countries did not agree. This led to many hotly contested debates. Now, however, that struggle between competing ideologies is over. It is no longer a question of which national economic system delivers the best outcomes. The new issue, of which we were hardly aware in those early days, is that of the impact of globalization on the implementation of the CEDAW Convention.

The ability of some States, particularly developing countries, to improve the situation of women has been seriously affected by the expansion of private global enterprises with the strength and resources to challenge the power of governments and by the power and policies of international trade and finance organizations. These forces have led the CEDAW Committee to call for codes of ethics for multinationals and for corporate responsibility toward women workers (CEDAW 2002, 70, para. 429 [g]). The Committee has also confronted international organizations with questions about how their economic policies affect women. These are the themes considered in this essay.

THE IMPACT OF PRIVATE GLOBAL ENTERPRISES ON WOMEN'S RIGHTS

Under the CEDAW Convention, States must not only prohibit discrimination by public acts, policies, and laws, but also must prevent discrimination by private perpetrators in employment, education, delivery of health services, and the provision of credits and loans. Some States have found it difficult to fulfill these obligations under the Convention because of the operations of powerful private global enterprises, or "multinationals." These enterprises have extensive resources that enable them to operate in a number of countries and to move their investments and operations from country to country to seek advantages such as tax concessions, cheap labor, and open markets. Their operations can have a huge effect on the economies of developing countries and on their people (Habbard 2001). Although nominally subject to the laws and regulations of the countries in which they operate, their financial power may be so great that they are effectively beyond the control of a single developing country. These factors can often cause particular disadvantages to women.

Some developing countries have established export processing zones (EPZs or *maquiladoras*) in order to attract foreign investment by providing tariff concessions and cheap labor. Recent studies have shown that the areas set aside as EPZs in developing countries are dominated by foreign companies (IWRAW Asia Pacific 2004). The majority of the labor force in these zones are usually women. Although the EPZs provide opportunities for employment that might not otherwise be available, this has to be set against the apparent unwillingness or inability of the home State to enforce its antidiscrimination laws and other labor standards on the enterprise. The result can be increased discrimination against women, combined with poor working conditions and low remuneration. In many cases, women are subject to pregnancy tests. They are also exposed to hazardous chemicals and other risks. The resort by multinationals to casual employment, outworking, and homeworking is another factor that leaves many women without the protection of labor standards (UNDAW 2001, paras. 23–42).

The CEDAW Committee has condemned the practice of compulsory pregnancy tests and the violence and sexual harassment commonly experienced by women in the EPZs and *maquiladoras*. It has been critical of those States that have permitted women's rights, and in particular their rights to safety and health, to be violated in these zones. The Committee considers that States must take responsibility for combating discrimination in their jurisdiction, despite the difficulties in ensuring that global enterprises meet the necessary standards. It has recommended that States strictly enforce labor legislation and health and industrial safety regulations in *maquila* industries to protect the women working there or has asked for laws to be amended. States where these issues have arisen include the Dominican Republic (CEDAW 2004a, 146, 147, paras. 306; 307), El Salvador (CEDAW 2003, 44, paras. 269; 270), Guatemala (CEDAW 2002, 174, paras. 186–87), Mauritius (CEDAW 1995, 49, 52, paras. 191; 216), and Nicaragua (CEDAW 2001, 76, paras. 314–15).

In 2002 Human Rights Watch drew the Committee's attention to the pregnancy-based sex discrimination endured by women workers in the *maquila* sector in Guatemala and the obstacles they were encountering in gaining access to reproductive health care. CEDAW later asked Guatemala to "promote stronger private sector codes of conduct" in order to comply with its Convention obligations (CEDAW 2002, 174, paras. 186–87). Similarly, reports on Mexico by Human Rights Watch revealed that women applying for work in the *maquiladora* sector along the Mexico-United States border were obliged to undergo mandatory, employment-related pregnancy testing as a condition for employment. Women who became pregnant soon after being hired risked mistreatment and forced resignation. The Committee recommended to Mexico that the imposition of pregnancy tests on *maquiladora* workers be prohibited (CEDAW 2002, 210, paras. 441–42). It later investigated and reported on the dire situation of women in Mexico's *maquiladoras* under the Optional Protocol, following reports of sexual violence, murder, abductions, and disappearances of women workers (CEDAW 2005a).

These examples suggest that developing countries are reluctant to enforce their labor laws or to insist on minimum standards in the EPZs. This may be due to fear that the investment will be shifted elsewhere, where fewer questions are asked. Even where the principles of CEDAW are part of domestic law, it appears that they can be disregarded with impunity, along with international labor standards. As a consequence, the employment opportunities created by allowing multinationals to operate in the EPZs have a serious downside in terms of the exploitation of vulnerable women workers.

Regrettably, the emphasis of globalization has been on the expansion of trade and commerce, while the free movement of people is not encouraged. Multinational enterprises can move their activities from country to country to take advantage of cheap labor and other inducements, while the workers cannot move freely to countries where there are better wages and conditions. Those who want to improve their position may therefore be tempted to undertake illegal migration. For women this can bring the added risk of trafficking. Women thus have the choice of exploitation in their home country or exploitation as a result of attempts at illegal migration. This has been recognized by the Committee. For example, in 2001 it asked Nicaragua to provide further information on the reasons for the migration of women and girls and the extent to which they became vulnerable to sexual exploitation, including trafficking, prostitution, and sex tourism (CEDAW 2001, 76, para. 315). The fact remains that if women are forced by lack of other opportunities to accept employment in EPZs where they do not enjoy the same wages and conditions as other workers in the country, the State's obligations under CEDAW are being disregarded.

CAN GLOBAL ENTERPRISES BE MADE DIRECTLY ACCOUNTABLE?

Attempts have been made in recent years to find ways of ensuring that powerful multinationals are held directly accountable for human rights violations. Multinationals might, for example, be made liable under the law of their State of incorporation for their activities elsewhere in the world. An example is the United States Alien Tort Claims Act, under which U.S. courts can hear claims by foreign citizens for injuries caused by actions in violation of the law of nations or a U.S. treaty. This Act could be used against multinationals that are complicit in serious international crimes such as genocide, crimes against humanity, torture, slavery, and forced labor.

The concept could be extended to make corporations accountable for failure to respect a range of human rights, including the provisions of CEDAW, in both their own and other countries. Under the Convention, especially under Article 2, the obligation of States to prohibit discrimination by private entities is not necessarily confined to the boundaries of the State. There is no such restriction as found in the International Covenant on Civil and Political Rights (ICCPR), under which rights are to be ensured to *persons within the territory and under the jurisdiction of the State* (Article 2).[1] If an enterprise that is under the jurisdiction of the State carries on activities outside the borders of that State that violate the equality rights of women in other countries, the home State could—some would say should—take preventive or remedial action in respect of that enterprise. Where the Committee has information that a particular multinational is contributing to discrimination against women in developing countries, it could raise this issue in its dialogue with the State in which that enterprise is incorporated. It could recommend that the State take action to ensure that all multinationals incorporated under the law of that State respect the principles of the Convention wherever they operate and introduce appropriate legislation allowing for enforcement action or for private litigation to make them accountable for violations. This approach could be developed as an alternative option for securing compliance with CEDAW.

While the Committee looks to the States Parties as bearing the main obligation to ensure that the Convention is implemented, it has also considered alternatives that would make multinationals directly responsible for respecting international human rights. In its statement to the Conference on Sustainable Development in 2002, the Committee asked that codes of ethics be developed for multinationals operating in EPZs; it also asked that a concept of corporate responsibility to women workers be developed, so that they are offered equitable employment conditions with adequate safeguards for occupational health (CEDAW 2002, 70, para. 429 [g]). Several international mechanisms aim to ensure that multinationals respect and are accountable for human rights. What is their potential for the implementation by CEDAW?

The ILO Tripartite Declaration

One of the earliest steps toward making multinational enterprises accountable for human rights standards was taken in 1977 by the International Labour Organization (ILO), when the Governing Body adopted a Tripartite Declaration of Principles concerning Multinational Enterprises and Social Policy. The Declaration calls on all parties, including multinationals, to respect the ILO Labour Standards and other international standards related to workers' rights. It refers expressly to the ILO Conventions No. 100 on equal remuneration for men and women workers and No. 111 on nondiscrimination in employment and occupation (International Labour Organization 1977).

The Declaration is a guidance document, and it is purely voluntary for businesses. It has been followed up by ILO initiatives to monitor labor standards as a condition of market access. The special role of the ILO, under Article 22 of CEDAW, gives this Declaration particular significance.[2] The ILO could be brought into the dialogue with States Parties where the Declaration appears relevant to an issue of compliance with the Convention by multinational enterprises.

The OECD Guidelines

The member countries of the Organisation for Economic Co-operation and Development (OECD) are the source of most of the world's foreign direct investment and are home to most major multinational enterprises.[3] In response to the problem of regulating the operations of multinational enterprises, the OECD adopted Guidelines for Multinational Enterprises in 1976, with the aim of promoting responsible business conduct. The Guidelines cover human rights and core labor standards. They recommend that businesses "respect the human rights of those affected by their activities consistent with the host government's international obligations and commitments." The labor standards in the Guidelines include the elimination of all forms of forced or compulsory labor and nondiscrimination in employment and occupation.

Although the OECD Guidelines are not legally binding on enterprises, adhering States are committed to promoting them among multinational enterprises operating in or from their territories. Since 2000, National Contact Points (NCPs) have been appointed by each State, from within their public service, to promote the Guidelines and to resolve specific issues arising in their implementation. These NCPs can receive specific complaints against enterprises established or operating in the relevant State and contribute to the resolution of issues relating to the implementation of the Guidelines through a mediation process. Most of the cases considered have dealt with company conduct in non-OECD countries. The role of NCPs is limited to clarifying issues; their interventions do not bind the parties (Habbard 2001). The process itself is confidential, although the outcome can be published. Despite these shortcomings, the adoption of the OECD Guidelines means that OECD States have actually accepted a degree of responsibility for ensuring that enterprises based in their countries respect human rights wherever they operate. And the multinationals themselves can be brought into a process.

The CEDAW Committee could build on the principles of the OECD Guidelines in its dealings with those States Parties to the Convention that also adhere to the OECD Guidelines. Those States could be asked about the steps they have taken to ensure that multinationals incorporated in their countries comply with equality standards in their operations in developing countries. As mentioned earlier, the obligations of States under CEDAW are not limited to their own territory. The Guidelines also provide opportunities for nongovernmental organizations (NGOs) to approach the relevant NCP of the home State of a multinational to complain about noncompliance with standards by that multinational. In cases where a State Party has been unable or unwilling to ensure that a multinational operating in its territory (e.g. in an EPZ) complies with CEDAW standards, the OECD Guidelines may provide an alternative recourse if the multinational is incorporated in one of the OECD adhering States. It is a further practical step toward making multinationals accountable.

The UN Global Compact

In 2000 the Secretary-General launched the United Nations Global Compact (http://www.unglobalcompact.org). It is a voluntary initiative that asks participating business organizations to support a set of core values in the areas of human rights, labor standards, the environment, and anticorruption. There are over 1,700 formal participants in the Global Compact, including business organizations, UN agencies, labor, academia, and civil society. The principles of the Global Compact are based on key international human rights instruments. The labor standards include the elimination of all forms of discrimination in employment and occupation. This means that participating business entities have made a commitment to eliminate discrimination against women employees. While the commitment is valuable, however, the scheme is purely voluntary and lacks effective supervisory or monitoring mechanisms. Participants are asked to report on progress annually. A new Governance Framework introduced in 2005 asks businesses to use indicators of progress. The only sanction for failure to respect the principles or to report progress is denial of the right to use the Global Compact name and logo.

The Global Compact is indicative of a wider interest in the concept of corporate accountability for human rights. It could be a tool for NGOs or others in drawing attention to a corporation's failure to participate or to respect the principles it has agreed to accept. NGOs, with the support of the CEDAW Committee, should seek to ensure that the Global Compact and other voluntary mechanisms include appropriate principles to protect women's interests. However, it is unlikely to provide assistance to the Committee in dealing with States Parties to the Convention or in seeking action against multinationals that fail to respect women's equality rights in developing countries.

The UN Sub-Commission

In 2003, the UN Sub-Commission on the Promotion and Protection of Human Rights drafted Norms on the Responsibilities of Transnational Corporations and Other Business Enterprises with Regard to Human Rights.[4] These Norms are based on the principle that transnational corporations and other business enterprises should respect and protect human rights—including, inter alia, ensuring equality and elimination of discrimination, refraining from forced or compulsory labor, respecting the rights of children, and providing a safe and healthy working environment and adequate remuneration. The Norms recognize that States have the primary responsibility to ensure respect for human rights and should have a legal and administrative framework to ensure implementation of the Norms by transnational corporations. Transnationals are asked to disseminate the Norms, to take steps to implement them, to evaluate their implementation, and to report periodically. The Norms are to be incorporated in contracts, and companies should deal only with others that follow the Norms. In addition, there is provision for independent monitoring and verification of the application of the Norms by United Nations and other mechanisms. The detailed provisions of the Norms on implementation, monitoring, verification, reporting, and stakeholder involvement go well beyond earlier initiatives. These provisions make them exciting and interesting to the NGO community but have attracted hostility and opposition from within the business community (Nolan 2005) and are considered by some to be divisive.

Opposition from some quarters has prevented action to give the Norms any legal status, and they have not been formally adopted by any UN body. Nevertheless their existence has led to further developments. The United Nations High Commissioner for Human Rights (UNHCHR) prepared a major report on the responsibilities of multinationals for human rights in February 2005 (UNHCHR 2005). In July 2005, Professor John Ruggie was appointed as Special Representative of the Secretary-General (SRSG) on the issue of human rights and transnational corporations. In his interim report of February 22, 2006, the SRSG defined his challenge as to make "the promotion and protection of human rights a more standard and uniform corporate practice" (Ruggie 2006, 14, para. 53). He identified certain areas of concern, which included abuses of labor rights in the apparel and footwear industries, particularly in low-income countries with weak governance. The interim report is critical of the legal basis claimed for the Norms. The SRSG appears to favor "the possible extension in the extraterritorial application of some home countries' jurisdiction for the worst human rights abuses committed by their firms abroad" (Ruggie 2006, 18, para. 71). This would hold companies to similar standards as in the areas of money laundering, bribery, and corruption. The final report of the SRSG, seeking a one year extension of mandate, was presented to the Human Rights Council in February 2007 (Ruggie 2007).

The appointment of the SRSG has created an opportunity for the CEDAW Committee and for NGOs supporting the Convention to raise their concerns about the neglect of women's rights by transnationals in EPZs and other situations and to put forward proposals to deal with the situation. An area of potential interest for the Committee in the work of the SRSG is that of impact assessment, which the SRSG considers to be an important part of the ability of companies to meet their human rights obligations. His interim report notes the lack of standard tools for undertaking human rights impact assessments and refers to his lack of resources to develop these (Ruggie 2006, 19, para. 76). The Committee should engage in consultation with the SRSG to ensure that Convention issues are adequately covered. It should seize the initiative, provide information to the SRSG, and seek a meeting with him or his representative to discuss issues such as impact assessment where it may be able to make a contribution.

Ethical Trading Initiatives

Both the UNHCHR, in the February 2005 Report, and the SRSG in his interim report discussed ethical trading initiatives. An example is the Fair Labor Association, which endorses an industry-wide code of conduct in the footwear and apparel industries and provides for independent monitoring. There are also a number of certification schemes such as Worldwide Responsible Apparel Production (WRAP) and SA8000, established by Social Accountability International, a nonprofit organization based in the United States. Some of these have independent procedures to monitor compliance with international labor standards.

These options do not involve States and would therefore be difficult for the CEDAW Committee to take up directly, but they could be pursued further by NGOs with particular concerns about women workers in the industries covered. A goal could be to ensure that the codes developed for the industries include those principles of the Convention that are of special relevance to women workers (Nolan 2005, 591).

This brief survey shows that there are situations where the State in which a multinational operates is unwilling or unable to protect human rights due, for example, to lack of political will, lack of appropriate laws, weak institutions, or corruption. There is growing interest in proposals that business enterprises, including multinationals, should respect and comply with human rights standards in their activities, and that they should be held accountable for this either under the law of their home State or directly under international law. Various options are under consideration, which are also relevant for the Committee to consider in its work. The Convention's standards of nondiscrimination and equality of rights should be respected in all the models discussed here. A possible avenue for the Committee to pursue is that of regulation of multinational operations by the home State (State of incorporation), since its engagement under the Convention is with the States Parties, who bear primary responsibility for enforcing compliance with international human rights standards. The Committee's close cooperation with NGOs that could become active within the framework of the Global Compact or the OECD Guidelines could also lead to a better protection of women.

It has been suggested that the UN Convention against Corruption provides a model for the extension of State responsibility to act in respect of multinationals violating human rights principles. That Convention is directed to private sector corruption as well as public corruption, and it provides for international cooperation in dealing with corporate violations of rights. It has a particular focus on preventive measures. Persons who have suffered damage from corruption can initiate legal proceedings against responsible parties (Vogl 2004). More recent proposals to develop UN Norms on universal human rights standards applicable to business, and to make multinationals directly accountable under international human rights law, may offer better outcomes in the long run, but there are many issues concerning jurisdiction and accountability to be resolved.

The Committee should undertake or encourage further study of the extent to which implementation of the Convention is frustrated by the actions of multinationals and consider in each case whether any of the options discussed here would help toward a resolution of the problem. It could use the information already gathered from States and NGOs, and seek additional information from the ILO. Such a study could be the basis of a general recommendation on this issue, insisting that States do not permit the working conditions of women in EPZs to fall below those of the general population. The Committee should also insist that States accept responsibility for controlling the actions of multinational enterprises based in their jurisdiction and make them accountable for violations. If employment conditions provided by multinationals, whether in EPZs or elsewhere, are different to those in other parts of the State, or if the ordinary standards and conditions are not adequately enforced by the State, there may be grounds for a complaint under the Optional Protocol to the Convention.

IMPACT OF INTERNATIONAL FINANCE AND TRADE ORGANIZATIONS ON DISCRIMINATION

It is generally accepted that women have less access to resources and to education and have lower incomes and higher levels of poverty than men. States therefore need to allocate additional resources in order to achieve equality (United Nations 1995a, para. 5). Some argue, however, that the ability of States to do this has been threatened by the policies pursued by international institutions.

There are several aspects to this. The resources of developing countries have been limited by debt burdens and by the adverse terms of international trade. Particular criticism has been directed to structural adjustment programs that require countries to privatize services such as energy, health, and water; to reduce social spending; and to introduce user fees. These factors have led to diminished public resources available for poverty reduction and have thus reduced the capacity of the State to help women achieve equality and enjoy the full scope of their rights, especially their economic, social, and cultural rights (IWRAW Asia Pacific 2004, 2). When developing countries are pressured to move health services from the public to the private sector, in order to relieve the public burden, women and their infant children are disadvantaged, as they are the most vulnerable and least able to pay. When food subsidies are removed, the higher costs may lead to women reducing their own food intake in favor of their children (AWID 2002, 3).

The liberalization of trade is believed by many to benefit the rich, developed nations because trade barriers continue to prevent developing countries from accessing world markets with their agricultural products. They are, in this way, hindered in the alleviation of poverty. A recent study shows that the liberalization of trade in services under the General Agreement on Trade in Services (GATS) has led to an expansion of private health services; as a result, the public sector has been forced to charge fees to the consumer to make up for declining revenues—leading to fewer women having access to health care (IWRAW Asia Pacific 2004, 23–24; Wintersteen 1999). The recognition and protection of "ownership" rights in plant varieties and seeds under the Trade-Related Aspects of Intellectual Property Rights (TRIPS) in 1995 have imposed additional costly burdens on third world farmers, and threatened traditional food production methods and food security (Donohoe 1999). The TRIPS rules can also increase the cost of patented drugs and delay the introduction of cheaper generic drugs. This limits women's access to protection against HIV/AIDS (IWRAW Asia Pacific 2004, 12–19).

When women are faced with increasing poverty and lack of employment opportunities, they may be pushed to seek work far from home—in the city, in other regions, or in other countries. This, in turn, places many women at risk of economic and sexual exploitation or trafficking. At least one State has reported to CEDAW that globalization is a cause of the increase in trafficking in human beings and sexual exploitation (CEDAW 2003, 46, para. 286).

It appears that the goals of expanding trade and economic development have been pursued without regard to the obligations of States under CEDAW or other human rights instruments, or to the effect that the agreed policies may have on the human rights of individuals especially their economic and social rights. The overall result has been to limit the resources available to developing countries and to make it more difficult for them to lift poor women out of the poverty trap. In 1995, the Beijing Platform for Action noted that economic globalization had contributed to inequalities between women and men (United Nations 1995a, paras. 157 and 158). The Outcome Document of the follow-up conference, Beijing +5, noted in 2000 that globalization had contributed to the feminization of poverty and increased gender inequality, including often deteriorating work conditions and unsafe working environments (United Nations 2000b, paras. 35 and 41). Both the Beijing Platform for Action (United Nations 1995a, paras. 342 and 354) and Beijing +5 (United Nations 2000b, paras. 49 and 101) called for the equal participation of women in macroeconomic decision-making and for action to reduce the feminization of poverty. The UN Millennium Development Goals have given further impetus to programs to eradicate poverty and promote women's equality (United Nations 2000a; United Nations 2000d).

The CEDAW Committee has observed that the trend to globalization and the liberalization of trade policies are having an adverse effect on the poorest of the poor, especially women in rural areas (Bangladesh, CEDAW 1997, 121,122, paras. 444; 453). It has asked governments of developing countries to take measures to combat the negative effect that structural adjustment programs or free trade agreements have on the high incidence of poverty and on women in particular (Trinidad and Tobago, CEDAW 2002, 28, paras. 155; 156; Costa Rica, CEDAW 2003, 91, para. 63). It invited Eritrea to emphasize the promotion and protection of women's rights in all development cooperation programs with international organizations and bilateral donors (CEDAW 2006, 19, para. 85).

The Committee has recognized that developing countries may lack the power to change their own situation, and it has, in fact, carried the issues into the international arena. In its 2002 statement to the Conference on Sustainable Development, the Committee drew attention to the problem in these terms:

> Women are also disproportionately affected by the negative impact of external debt, the implementation of structural adjustment programmes, the decrease in the price of local produce, the decline in levels of development assistance and growing disparities in the distribution of wealth. (CEDAW 2002, 69, para. 428)

In that statement, the Committee asked the international organizations responsible to give greater priority to the effect of their international trade and finance policies on the implementation of women's rights. It asked that policies be gender-sensitive and that they improve the quality of life of women. It also commended international programs designed to lift women out of poverty, such as microfinancing for low-income women's entrepreneurial activities (CEDAW 2002, 70-71, para. 429; see also Bisnath 2001).

The World Bank

Responding to NGO criticism, the World Bank accepted that gender inequality tends to slow economic growth and make the rise from poverty more difficult. Its 2002 gender mainstreaming strategy, "Integrating Gender into the World Bank's Work: A Strategy for Action," calls for Country Gender Assessments from each client country, analyzing the gender dimensions of development, and for priority policies to be developed in response to the Assessments. Critics have pointed out, however, that the strategy does not provide for rights-based targets, nor does it make achieving equality and nondiscrimination a specific goal (AWID 2002, 4–5; Global Policy Forum 2002; Brodnig 2001). It is argued that there should be monitoring and evaluation mechanisms to assess the impact of the Bank's programs on human rights and gender equality. For example, have they increased the level of education of women and girls, raised the earning level of women, or lifted more women out of the poverty trap?

In recent years NGOs have tried to establish a solid basis for the evaluation of the policies, programs, and activities of international organizations for their compatibility with human rights principles and with the achievement of equality for women. This is a project to which the CEDAW Committee could contribute, by exploring with States Parties the most appropriate means of evaluating Bank programs in particular countries. The development of indicators measuring progress in achieving the goals of CEDAW would be a practical contribution to the assessment process.

International Trade and the WTO

The economic well-being and the resources of a State are vitally affected by the terms of international trade. As noted above, international trade agreements under the World Trade Organization (WTO) have been much criticized as being skewed in favor of rich Western countries, mainly because they maintain agricultural subsidies and import restrictions. The effect, it is argued, is to limit the ability of developing countries to relieve poverty and disadvantage. Yet, most WTO members are in fact developing countries. In 2001, the Doha Development Agenda was launched to give development a more prominent role in WTO's work and to give greater market access to developing countries for their agricultural products. The negotiations are still proceeding, and benefits have not yet been realized. The WTO does not have any specific policy framework for considering the impact of its policies on human rights or for considering gender issues. Some NGOs have proposed that the WTO terms of trade should include a social clause, to protect labor standards such as freedom of association, the right to organize and collectively bargain, nondiscrimination, and prohibition of forced or child labor. The advantage of this approach is said to be that the WTO enforces its trade rules strictly. However, little progress appears to have been made in this direction.

Another approach that has been suggested is to persuade the member States of the WTO to attend to their accountability for human rights in their trade negotiations. In such cases, States would oppose proposals that are incompatible with human rights in their own and in their trading partners' countries, on the basis that those human rights are nonderogable (Canadian Feminist Alliance for International Action 1999). For example, if trade agreements directly impact health services, their implementation should be compatible with the protections provided by such instruments as CEDAW and the International Covenant on Economic, Social and Cultural Rights (ICESCR). If States approached trade negotiations on this basis, it is argued, they could help to ensure that economic and trade goals are not pursued at the expense of women, who are the majority of the poor (IWRAW Asia Pacific 2004, 55). Mary Robinson, then UN High Commissioner for Human Rights, described the proposal for national governments to consider human rights in trade negotiations in these terms: "In the WTO, for example, this means negotiating trade rules bearing in mind their responsibilities to protect human rights, not only of their own citizens but of all who may be affected" (Robinson 2001).

I suggested above that the CEDAW Committee could take up with States their responsibility to regulate the overseas activities of multinationals to ensure respect for women's rights. The Committee would take State responsibility under the Convention a step further were it to ask States Parties how they have taken into account their obligations to women in developing countries in formulating their trade negotiation policies. They could be asked to institute the same commitment respecting the rights of women in their trading partners as in their domestic jurisdiction. Such a commitment could give human rights a significant responsibility in the WTO negotiation process. While it cannot be predicted with any confidence that member States of the WTO would be willing to accept obligations to respect the rights of women in other jurisdictions, this is nevertheless an issue that the Committee should take up with States in the reporting process, because the economic progress of States is of vital importance to women's rights. It is necessary to overcome poverty and to improve women's access to health and education, if the goals of CEDAW are to be achieved in developing countries. The Committee should continue to engage with organizations such as the World Bank and the WTO to ensure that issues vital to women's rights are given proper attention.

ARE STATES WILLING TO COOPERATE?

The need for international cooperation and assistance to ensure the full enjoyment of economic and social rights is expressly recognized in Article 2 (1) of the ICESCR. It is also recognized in the Official Development Assistance (ODA) targets set for the developed world and in the mandate of the World Bank. The UN General Assembly (UNGA) High Level Plenary Session in September 2005 made many commitments to eradicate poverty, to promote development, and to increase aid. It called on the World Bank and the International Monetary Fund (IMF) to consider ways to overcome the debt burden, and it supported trade liberalization and called for the full participation of developing countries in the world trading system. But despite these commitments, the rich, developed States are still far from meeting their ODA targets. In 2004, the only five countries to exceed the UN target for ODA of 0.7 percent of gross national income (GNI) were Denmark, Luxembourg, The Netherlands, Norway, and Sweden. The situation of people, and especially women, in the least developed countries does not appear to be a high priority of most nations.

The commitment to overcome poverty should be compared or contrasted with another commitment of the UNGA High Level Plenary. It agreed in general terms that the international community has a responsibility to take collective action to protect populations from genocide, war crimes, ethnic cleansing, and crimes against humanity, when the resort to peaceful means and national authorities has failed to ensure protection (United Nations 2005a, paras. 138–40). But is there not a comparable responsibility to protect populations from famine and disease (such as HIV/AIDS) and to protect women from the life-threatening effects of long-term gender inequalities, when national authorities have failed in this, and where the causes and the means of alleviation are to a large extent influenced by external factors under the control of States with powerful economies? The willingness of States to cooperate in this way could be an important factor in improving the situation of women.

CONCLUSIONS

A common thread that runs through this brief review is that, at a time when we are approaching almost universal ratification of CEDAW (185 States), international forces are making it more difficult to secure effective implementation of the Convention's principles. These forces, lumped together under the name of "globalization," require new approaches by all concerned with advancing women's equality.

Key issues for States are their responsibilities for the overseas actions of multinationals incorporated in their State and their responsibilities to take their obligations under CEDAW (and other human rights instruments) into account in their trade negotiations and in the exercise of functions they may have in the World Bank and other international organizations. International trade, finance, and investment organizations need to take stock of their guiding principles to ensure that the obligations of States Parties under human rights instruments (including CEDAW) are given relevance in negotiations. The CEDAW Committee and the NGOs which support its work should make use of new developments relating to the accountability of multinationals.

NOTES

I would like to express thanks to Justine Nolan for providing material and suggestions about mechanisms being developed for the accountability of multinationals and about the relevance of the UN Convention against Corruption.

1. My emphasis.

2. Article 22 of the Convention permits UN specialized agencies to be invited to submit reports on the implementation of such provisions of the Convention that fall within the scope of their activities and to be represented at the consideration of the States Parties' reports by the Committee.

3. In October 2006 the OECD comprised thirty countries: Australia, Austria, Belgium, Canada, Czech Republic, Denmark, Finland, France, Germany, Greece, Hungary, Iceland, Ireland, Italy, Japan, Korea, Luxembourg, Mexico, The Netherlands, New Zealand, Norway, Poland, Portugal, Slovak Republic, Spain, Sweden, Switzerland, Turkey, United Kingdom, and United States. In addition, nine nonmember States adhere to the Guidelines: Argentina, Brazil, Chile, Estonia, Israel, Latvia, Lithuania, Romania, and Slovenia.

4. The Sub-Commission—called the UN Sub-Commission on Prevention of Discrimination and Protection of Minorities until 1999—was established in 1947 to assist the work of the UN Commission on Human Rights, an intergovernmental body. It is comprised of twenty-six independent experts in the field of human rights who are elected by the Commission. In 2006 the Commission on Human Rights was replaced by the Human Rights Council. The Council will have to discuss whether the work of the Sub-Commission will be continued and in what form. For the Human Rights Council, see http://www.ohchr.org/english/bodies/hrcouncil.

HUMAN RIGHTS II: SPECIFIC CHALLENGES

POVERTY, PROSTITUTION, AND TRAFFICKING

ELVIRA NOVIKOVA, *RUSSIAN FEDERATION*

In 1986, I was a professional researcher at the Trade Union Research Center in Moscow, responsible, as Chief of the Section, for studying issues concerning working women. In that capacity I had prepared a variety of documents for the United Nations and the International Labour Organization (ILO); I had taken part in the Second and Third UN World Conferences on Women in Copenhagen (1980) and Nairobi (1985), as well as the ILO Session (1981), which adopted the Workers with Family Responsibilities Convention.[1] When the Ministry of Foreign Affairs approached me to propose that I be nominated for membership in the CEDAW Committee, I was quite surprised but also interested. Thus, I became a CEDAW member in 1987.

During my four years of work in the Committee, I often asked myself a question to which I still have no real answer even today: Do we discuss the country report of the respective State Party or the real status of women in that country? Clearly, governments always try to present the best picture. But understanding the actual situation is more important, and, in my experience, the Committee always tried to make a real impact on the situation of women in the country under discussion. One of the means through which this can be achieved is to study additional materials provided by various organizations and specialized UN agencies and by nongovernmental organizations (NGOs). Such information was and is particularly helpful with regard to the exploitation of women in prostitution and the trafficking of women, both prohibited by Article 6 of the CEDAW Convention.

In this essay I want to explore these topics, which are of an international nature, from a Russian point of view. I will first point out the negative impact on women of the economic reforms in Russia, which have forced them legally and illegally to migrate for work, often falling prey to trafficking, mostly in the sex industry. Second, I will highlight the elements of the recruitment processes and the trade routes for trafficked women. Third, I will discuss legal measures to deal with these criminal phenomena. Lastly, I will make some recommendations to the CEDAW

Committee on dealing with the issues of women's exploitation in prostitution and trafficking under Article 6 of the Convention.

GENDER DIMENSIONS OF RUSSIAN REFORMS: CREATING CONDITIONS FOR HUMAN TRAFFICKING

Since the dissolution of the USSR in late 1991 and the establishment of a new state—the Russian Federation—radical changes have taken place in the country. These have strongly affected the daily routine of people's lives, their moral values, common perceptions, and life strategies, as well as social norms in general (Russian Academy of Sciences 2002). The evolution of market relationships, privatization of property, economic restructuring, and changes in the social sphere, as well as other changes associated with the transition period, have affected the status of women and men in different ways. They have also generated a variety of acute problems, including the sexual exploitation of women and human trafficking—phenomena that are strongly contextualized, i.e. dependent upon the general social and economic situation (International Labour Organization 2005, 74–78). Studying the context allows for a better understanding of the genesis and evolution of these phenomena in modern times, their incorporation into the existing economic and social order, and the potential implications of their escalation. It also permits the development of effective measures to combat them. In analyzing the transformations in Russia as they affect women (who make up 53 percent of the population), one can make the generalization that women's adaptation to the new realities is fraught with disproportionately high cost (Pachi 2003, XIV). These realities include low pay, unemployment, and increasing poverty; rising crime; violence and the threat of violence; immigration and prostitution; and illegal migration and international human trafficking.

Poverty

Following radical changes in the employment structure, Russian women (whose share in the labor force amounts to 49 percent) now prevail in the lowest-paid sectors of the economy (textile and food industries, health care, and education). Reforms have increased the gap in growth rates between salaries in the so-called "nonproductive" female-dominated spheres of the economy and average growth rates of salaries in the economy at large. Horizontal (interdepartmental) gender segregation adds to predominant vertical (intradepartmental) employment practices; women receive lower wages in all sectors of the economy, both in those where they are underrepresented and those where they dominate (Rzhanytsyna 2002,

147). According to data from the State Committee of the Russian Federation on Statistics (Rosstat), in 1999 women's monthly wages amounted to 65 percent of men's, and in 2003 to 64 percent (Rosstat 2000, 65; 110). Other survey data testify to an even bigger gap of up to 50 percent (Zdravomyslova 2003, 27). It is noteworthy that the minimum wages received by one third of employees in the Russian Federation are below the subsistence level. Thus, a large cohort of the so-called "working poor" has emerged, a disproportionate share of them being women (Rzhanytsyna 2002, 157). Another major phenomenon contributing to poverty, including women's poverty, is the widespread problem of wage arrears in various sectors, at factories, and in institutions with both state and private forms of ownership.

The phenomenon of unemployment was officially recognized in Russia after 1991. At the start of the economic reforms, massive labor force releases affected women primarily. Within nine years, eight million women had lost their jobs compared to four million men. In 1992, women's share among the unemployed was 72 percent. By 1994, this had declined slightly to 65.1 percent. Russia's labor market is notable for the high educational level of unemployed women. Women now make up 70.1 percent of the unemployed with university education, and 69.5 percent of the unemployed with secondary education. Job placement is most problematic for women belonging to the 16–28 and 45–55 age groups. The combination of gender and age seriously affects women's position in the labor market at the beginning and end of their working careers.

There is an evident decline in families' standard of living with a resulting feminization of poverty. In 1990, 2.3 million people (1.6 percent of the population) lived below the poverty line (Rzhanytsyna 2002, 204). Between 1991 and 1995, the gross domestic product dropped by over 50 percent, while annual per capita income averaged $3,400 ($4,000 in 2004). In 1999, according to World Bank data, among the people who lived on $2.15 per day, there were 32 million women and 24.5 million men (Pachi 2003, 8). In late 2001, when the subsistence level was 1,500 rubles per month (approx. $50), about 30 percent of the population (44 million people) lived below this line. When these numbers are added to those who are just balancing on the poverty line, the overall number encompasses up to two thirds of the population. Half of the poor were children and young people under the age of thirty.

During the reform years, this sharp polarization of society continued and even worsened. Many people lost their savings twice—in 1992 and 1998. Those in the top 10 percent income bracket earned fourteen times more than those in the lowest income bracket (Rzhanytsyna 2002, 203). The disintegration of social protection systems and the social infrastructure, along with galloping prices and taxes, deprived citizens of the benefits of free education, health care, and cultural services. Rising costs of housing and public utilities increased the expansion of poverty and the marginalization of large populations. Another disturbing aftermath is the growth of the number of homeless and neglected children, including girl children, now nearly 1.3 million (*Population Review* 2002, 4, 13).

The Russian experience clearly demonstrates that macroeconomic and structural reforms are gender neutral only in theory. In practice they affect women and men differently and turn the former into hostages and victims of reform. Such an assessment is corroborated by a gender analysis of the 2002 budget of the Russian Federation. Women and children, who make up 64 percent of the population, have access to only 38 percent of state resources and experience a declining share of social expenditure (Rzhanytsyna 2002, 118). The national budget disregards gender dimensions while preserving and aggravating gender asymmetry.[2]

Rising Crime

A major feature of modern Russian life is the high level of criminalization in economic activities. Crimes are most acute in the informal sector of the economy, where state laws and guarantees have little effect and where violence or its threat serves as a key tool of coercion and exploitation of hired laborers. High crime rates on the one hand, and corruption of bureaucrats on the other, build barriers to the creation of legal small- and medium-sized businesses. They also restrain sustainable economic growth and foster economic activities such as drug dealing, theft, smuggling, bribery, fraudulent business schemes (made possible by bribery and intimidation), and human trafficking. By modest estimations, the scope of the informal and shadow economy is as high as 22.4 percent of the gross national product (GNP) (Tyuryukanova 2004, 57).

Poverty, unemployment, and economic and social instability, as well as the erosion of public morale and family values, are conducive to deviant behavior. The absence of facilities for leisure and public activities adds to the idleness of young people and raises the risk for criminal activities. The number of young girls who are arrested keeps growing, up 2.5 times in 1998 as compared to 1993. The number of girls aged 14 to 17 who are alcoholics and drug addicts is also on the rise. In 2004, 54.2 thousand women were held in prisons and correctional labor facilities (8 percent of all convicts), and 89 percent of women in minimum-security correctional labor facilities were under the age of 25. Since 2000, the number of convicts has not changed, but the degree of their criminality has intensified. One in four women is in jail for murder or for inflicting heavy injuries, and one in every five for theft. Nearly one in three is convicted of crimes related to illegal drug trafficking. The average term of imprisonment for women is 7.8 years, and their average age is 32.5. About 70 percent were convicted for the first time, 21.5 percent for the second time, and nearly 9 percent for the third time or more (Ministry for Social Development 2005, 59).

Violence

Women's difficult social situation seriously affects their attitudes and mental outlook. Opinion poll data testify that 60 percent of women are worried, pessimistic, and afraid of the future due to the growth in aggression, crime, and violence (UNICEF 1999, 90–91). Violence and the threat of violence have become routine, manifested as street offenses, domestic violence, violence at the workplace, and even violence exerted by law-enforcement bodies. According to data of the Ministry of Internal Affairs, over 546,000 crimes were registered in 2003, affecting over 184,000 women (Council of Europe 2005, 51). Currently, statistics do demonstrate a drop in the number of reported rapes (from 15,500 in 1993 to 8,100 in 2003) (Rosstat 2004, 185), as well as in the number of deaths from domestic violence (from fourteen thousand women who perished in 1994 to twelve thousand in 2001) (UNICEF 1999, 93). Still, it is no secret that not all cases of violence against women are reported to the police, especially considering the growing public distrust of law-enforcement bodies (UNICEF 1999, 104).

Public surveys corroborate the spread of various types of domestic violence. Thus, over half of women responding said that they had suffered physical violence from a male relative at least once; 79 percent of respondents suffered from emotional abuse and threats; and 16 percent constantly suffered from psychological pressure from their husbands. Over half of the respondents faced various forms of economic violence. One in every four women was subjected to at least one type of sexual violence (Polenina 2005, 164). Poverty and the low probability of gaining a job constrain women's ability to break up painful relationships. Recently, the problem of sexual safety in the workplace has become acute. In a majority of cases (and especially with migrant women), sexual harassment serves as a precondition for hiring, promotion, and even for holding the job. One in every four women in the provinces and one in every three women in

Moscow and St. Petersburg face this problem. Again, it is very likely that the actual figures are much higher, because most women understand sexual harassment only when it consists of an actual sexual assault (Polenina 2005, 67).

Both alcoholism and drug addiction, which have risen greatly between 1991 to 2006, present an increased risk for domestic as well as street violence. The number of women being addicted is on the rise (Rzhanytsyna 2002, 175). Lastly, it is the fact that many women do not see a way to prevent violence and consider themselves unprotected by the law, which increases their insecurity (ROSSPEN 2002, 83).

Migration and Prostitution

The grave upheavals of the transition period provoked a rapid growth in the scope and intensity of migration. The movement of huge masses of population in the post-Soviet territories since 1993 gave rise to a variety of concurrent problems, including illegal labor migration. Russia is still an attractive destination for migrants from parts of the former USSR. According to the Federal Migration Service, in 2005 the number of illegal migrants from the Commonwealth of Independent States (CIS) and South East Asia amounted to fourteen million people, among whom only 750,000 had work permits.[3] According to Goskomstat data from 2001 and 2003, women made up 13 percent of foreign workers in Russia—15 percent of them aged 18–29 years, and 17 percent (2001) and 19 percent (2003) aged 16–17 years.

Migrant women work as saleswomen in markets, as domestics, in public services, and in the entertainment sector, including sex services and related spheres (dancing, striptease, prostitution, escort services, the fashion business). In general, women's labor migration presents an "increased risk zone," as most work is in informal, criminalized, and socially unprotected sectors of the economy, of which the sex industry is the prime example. An ILO survey of 2003 highlighted that the sexual exploitation of female migrants "on a mass scale occurs in an open social space, not only in the entertainment and sex sectors, but also across other sectors of female-dominated labor markets" (Tyuryukanova 2004, 66).

An inability to find a decent job, combined with fear of poverty, domestic and sexual violence, and the lure of easy money attracts some young women, especially those without educational and professional experience, to prostitution. Prostitution did exist in the USSR previously but was not officially recognized until the middle of the 1980s. Nowadays it is a diverse and extensive economic sphere. Women prostitutes differ in their workplaces (railway station, street, hotels, etc.), level of payment, degree of business organization (presence of a pimp, infrastructure, facilities for meeting clients), and age (from schoolgirls to middle-aged women). The scope of this phenomenon may be assessed by the following figures: In Moscow there are 80,000 to 130,000 prostitutes, 90 percent of them from CIS countries. The annual receipts from the sex industry in the Russian Federation are estimated at half a billion dollars.

Prostitution is often legalized when presented as dating services, communal services, massage parlors, saunas, beauty parlors, etc., which are broadly advertised in the mass media. The replacement of moral principles by economic expediency, and the infiltration of a mass culture aimed at youth and adolescents and based on permissiveness and deriding traditional values, have resulted in the emergence of certain groups of the population who are vulnerable with respect to this activity. They supply sex dealers with potential victims, ready to risk any hopeless adventure as long as it gives them the illusive hope of achieving financial well-being. These conclusions are corroborated by the results of an inquiry conducted among adolescent girls in the small town of Balakovo (Saratov region). Every fourth girl surveyed considered prostitution to be prestigious, and half of the respondents did not blame prostitutes. Moreover, adolescent girls treated prostitution as a chance to make good money and build a better life (*Population Review* 2002, 4, 35).

There is also a visible change in public attitudes showing more tolerance toward prostitutes: 15.9 percent of female respondents denounce prostitutes' behavior, and 8.4 percent despise them; while 30.8 percent feel sorry for them, 41.9 percent treat them indifferently, and 2 percent are envious of them (ROSSPEN 2002, 48). The proportion of those disapproving of prostitutes depends on the age of the respondents—from 16. 4 percent among the youngest age group (17–18 years) to 32.3 percent among women aged 41–50. The indifferent attitudes toward prostitutes of most respondents suggest a shift in fundamental moral norms, manifested in a concern for one's own behavior but without a sense of societal responsibility of the general welfare. Such an attitude ("every person for oneself") is most vividly displayed by the younger generation, i.e. women who grew up in the post-Soviet period.

Human Trafficking

Another social process, which is also connected to the negative aftermath of liberalization, is Russia's involvement in illegal migration and international human trafficking. Before the 1990s, the problem of illegal export of Russian women abroad for sexual exploitation did not exist. The collapse of the Iron Curtain, open borders, broader opportunities for travel across the world in search of pleasure or jobs, the internationalization of the shadow economy, the establishment of international criminal groups, the corruption of public officials (even judicial loyalty to prostitution in many countries) provide pimps and others who live off the earnings of prostitutes with a secure base for the recruitment of young women.

Trafficking in women is closely related to prostitution and women's exploitation in the national commercial sex sector, but these are different problems. It is important to differentiate between prostitution and forced prostitution, and between voluntary prostitution and exploitation of prostitution by third parties. With this in view, I would like to support the opinion of specialists concerning women's ostensibly voluntary departures abroad for their involvement in the sex industry (Tyuryukanova et al. 2001). The equation of trafficking in women with coercion into prostitution not only limits the contingent of migrant women in need of protection of their rights, but, more important, relieves those States from which these women come and those that are the recipients of the migrant workforce of their responsibility for the results of illegal and semilegal exits and entrances. Among migrant workers, including female migrant workers, many could not earn a decent living in their home country. Only under extremes of poverty would someone decide to go to a foreign country without knowing that country's language and laws and without possessing the necessary documents for accommodation and work. For this reason, one must speak about so-called "voluntary exits" with great reservation; in fact, the alleged voluntary nature of this kind of migration is equal to compulsory participation for those who are without real economic choices. Dealers in human slaves receive similar profits from the sale of "voluntary" sex workers as they do from the exploitation of those kept by force.

Given the feminization of unemployment and poverty in Russia, therefore, one cannot assume that women go abroad voluntarily to work in the sex industry. The new interpretations of international human rights law, highlighted after the Fourth UN World Conference on Women in Beijing (1995), is vitally important here. These judge the passivity or reluctance of governments to protect women's economic, social, or cultural rights in their country as violations of human rights. In short, women go abroad to escape from their difficult situation, then fall into the hands of pimps and brothel-owners, and are subjected to further coercions that can be categorized as crimes. These individual acts of violence are thus preceded by violations of human rights by the State. Neither sending nor receiving countries should avoid responsibility for the consequences of human trafficking.

RECRUITMENT OF HUMAN SLAVES—AND TRAFFICKING ROUTES

Migrant workers are trafficked to Russia from the former USSR republics and from South East Asia (where standards of living are lower). Russia is also a transit country and a supplier (mostly of women of its own nation) to more developed countries or to centers of sex tourism. The mass influx of women from former Soviet republics—Byelorussia, Latvia, Russia, and Ukraine—into the global sex industry may be called the "fourth wave" of criminal human trafficking in women, following earlier waves of women for sex work from Brazil, Colombia, the Philippines, and Thailand, and later from Bulgaria, Poland, and Romania. Moscow and Kiev are the largest sites for the transit of women from Central Asia, the Balkan countries, and from Russian and Ukrainian provinces. From these places, women are transported to Europe and the Middle East.

Middlemen use several transit routes. The Baltic route via Lithuania is most often used by illegal migrants going to Germany, Scandinavia, and the United States. The Georgian route has grown in importance due to Georgia's policy of open borders with Turkey. Large numbers of women and children have been transported via Georgia to Greece, Turkey, and other Mediterranean countries. Since the 1992 Russian-Chinese agreement to increase the number of tourists and establish neighborly relations has expanded opportunities, the Chinese-Siberian route for trafficking has emerged.

It is hard to verify data on the number of Russian women sold into sexual slavery. With the secrecy surrounding this trade, women's voices are silenced, and court prosecution is rare. The available figures should be considered as preliminary, since the actual figures are likely to be several times higher. The scanty information available shows that in 1997, some 175,000 young girls from Eastern and Central Europe and CIS countries were sold to developed European states. In this region, the sex industry is well developed in the metropolitan areas of many countries and leads to a demand for regular supply. According to data from the International Organization for Migration (IOM), there are currently over half a million foreign prostitutes in Europe, including an unknown number of Russian women (Global Survival Network 1999, 5). According to official data, fifty thousand women leave Russia annually for permanent residence abroad, but without their destinations being ascertained. It is known, however, that Russian women—victims of the sex industry—now reside in over forty countries of the world, including Bosnia and Herzegovina, Canada, China, Croatia, Cyprus, Czech Republic, Germany, Greece, Hungary, Italy, Japan, The Netherlands, Spain, Syria, Turkey, United Arab Emirates, the United States, and Yugoslavia (Global Survival Network 1999, 32–33).

The majority of women victims of trafficking are younger than 25 years of age. Data collected in Israel helps to shed light on their education and family status. The majority of these victims of trafficking (70 percent of them Russian) had secondary education, and 10 percent had university diplomas. In addition, 71 percent of these women were single, 15 percent were divorced or widowed, 6 percent were married, and 25 percent had children. There is evidence that the slave dealers prefer women with children as they are more dependent and thus more obedient. They need to send money home to support their families and are afraid to endanger their children by escaping or cooperating with the authorities. Many shared with the interviewers that their fathers had deserted their families when they themselves were small girls, which left their mothers with the task to bring them up alone. Only 9 percent of the women had prior experience as prostitutes, 29 percent had previously been unemployed, while those who had been employed had worked as secretaries, shop assistants, teachers, dressmakers, etc. Their average wages back home had amounted to $38 per month. It is no surprise that the promise of $1,000 per month had captured their imagination (Pachi 2003, 87).

The transfer of recruited women to countries of transit or destination is not necessarily linked to illegal migration. Authentic documents and visas are sometimes used to enter countries. Dealers arrange invitations for work, study, tourist trips, or even invitation as guests. Ninety percent of migrants begin to work under guest or tourist visas (which forbid paid jobs); thus, in reality these women become illegal migrants.

The process of supplying female slaves has several key elements that are closely linked. The promoters place advertisements to attract clients, then organize the travel of those recruited to the countries of destination. Usually the suppliers are citizens of the same regions as their victims, and as a rule they cooperate with brothel owners in other countries. Second, there are middlemen, also "compatriots," who act as couriers and company on the route. They are in charge of documentation or, if documentation is not available, of smuggling the victims. Since they are often linked to the drug mafia, they actively introduce women to drug addiction. Third, there are "masters," usually foreigners, who maintain authority over the victims. The key figure, the customer, subsidizes the whole process from the background.

Thus, the first link in the chain of trafficking is the company that deals in organizing leisure tours, tours of dancers and theater groups, dating services—anything that involves travel abroad. Women are tempted by alluring promises, their documents are duly processed, and they are even provided with travel money. But once they arrive abroad, their passports are nearly always withdrawn (ostensibly for registration purposes); then they are informed about an alleged change of the originally promised work situation and the necessity to modify their contract provisions. Ending up in a strange country in the hands of professional swindlers, without documents, without knowledge of the language spoken, and without any connections, women are inevitably trapped into sexual slavery. They have no other option. Thus, their vulnerability to violence grows not only due to their work but also to their illegal status.

According to surveys, about 60 percent of potential migrants assume that it is next to impossible for young women without a university education to find jobs unrelated to the sex industry. Nearly one fourth of young women under the age of 30 looking for jobs abroad indicate readiness to work in the sex industry (Tyuryukanova et al. 2001, 33). Thus, one cannot say that women who are allegedly going abroad to work in "show business" are unaware of the nature and scope of the risk. Mostly, however, they hope to be able to control the situation; some count on their luck that nothing will happen to them, and still others know that even at home they would need to run the same risks for less money.

In reality, the behavior of these women is controlled by human dealers through constant emotional and physical manipulations: by withdrawing their passports; confining them to a place of residence or work; depriving them of legal, medical, and social support; imposing penalties and debt bondage; blackmailing them or threatening their families; or subjecting them to violence. By its very nature, women's migration is a sphere rife with social risks that are not addressed by current migration policies or practices. One analyst has commented, "One may speak about deliberate alienation of politicians from specificities of women's migration due to negative attitudes toward some types of female employment and due to hypocrisy. In reality, this alienation results in the spread of repressions against migrant women and potential migrants" (Tyuryukanova et al. 2001, 134).

LEGISLATIVE AND OTHER MEASURES

The Criminal Code of the Russian Federation condemns as criminal actions the encroachment on sexual autonomy and sexual freedom of individuals, as well as recruitment into prostitution and distribution of pornography.[4] The articles relating to recruitment into prostitution and its organization were modified in December 2004, fortifying the criminal liability of the organizer. However, as officials from the Ministry of Internal Affairs have admitted, neither the original nor the reformed provisions of the Code affect the real situation of prostitution or the forced recruitment of women and minors into such activities. This admission is corroborated by the occasional, sparse information that appears in the media. Voluntary prostitution is not a *corpus delicti*, and the key tool of the police for combating prostitution as such consists of unsatisfactory administrative measures. Under the current legislation, the documents necessary to institute proceedings against those engaged in prostitution must be delivered to administrative bodies responsible for their place of residence. The majority of prostitution perpetrators, however, reside neither in their homes nor at the places of their registration. Thus, even when such administrative proceedings are initiated they rarely lead to criminal prosecutions.

Prior to 2003, the laws of the Russian Federation contained no provisions concerning slavery and the slave trade, despite the increased number of cases of slavery and human trafficking, both open and latent, including women's sale and purchase. Relevant international agreements signed and ratified by the Russian Federation are mentioned in Article 15 of the Constitution, but have not been acted upon.

One reason for the poor results and ineffective work of law enforcement bodies is the negligible number of appeals from victims and the difficulties in their being examined abroad, since prostitution and sexual exploitation are closely linked to illegal migration. In 2000, for example, only 102 applications were submitted to Russian consulates from women who were victims of sexual exploitation requesting help to return home. The victims' appeals included seventy in Germany, twenty in China, five in the Czech Republic, four in Bosnia and Herzegovina, and three in Hungary. The same year, only thirty-seven criminal prosecutions were initiated in Russia for trafficking in minors.

In most cases the authorities in countries of destination treat victims of the slave trade as criminals, subjecting them to prosecution, detainment, and/or deportation. In addition, their fear of revenge from slave traders deters women victims from cooperating with law enforcement bodies in these countries. Inadequate knowledge of their legal rights is compounded by cultural and language barriers as well as a lack of support mechanisms. These complicate the legal ambiguities of the women's status and prevent them from pursuing justice.

In Russia, the problem of human trafficking was first raised by NGOs, who initiated the first Round Table in the national parliament of the Russian Federation, the Duma. In December 1997, working together with the Global Survival Network and the International League for Human Rights, NGOs also organized an international conference in Moscow on the illegal exit of women from CIS countries for the sex trade (Global Survival Network 1999). Before this conference, neither trafficking in women nor their sexual exploitation had been recognized or discussed at the government level. Now these issues are brought to the public's attention principally through the actions of NGOs who oppose human trafficking and who have been conducting preventive information campaigns and providing assistance to victims with support from international organizations and foundations.

After the Istanbul Organization for Security and Co-operation in Europe (OSCE) Summit (1999) and the OSCE Foreign Ministers Meeting in Vienna (2000), at which OSCE countries committed to combat human trafficking, the situation changed. In December 2000, Russia signed the UN Convention against Transnational Organized Crime (2000) and its Protocol against the Smuggling of Migrants by Land, Sea and Air (2000) and ratified both documents in 2004 (Polenina 2005, 70). The Protocol highlights the gender dimensions of this issue and recommends that States Parties enact national legislation to criminalize it, protect victims' rights, prevent human exploitation (primarily women's and children's), and combat their treatment as human slaves. The Optional Protocol to CEDAW, which allows for a communication or inquiry procedure, regarding the implementation of Article 6 of the Convention, was also ratified by the Duma on June 19, 2004.

In December 2003, new provisions were introduced into the Russian Federation's Criminal Code on "human trafficking" and "use of slave labor." The first interprets human trafficking as "buying-selling of a person . . . or such person's exploitation in the form of recruitment, transportation, transfer, harboring or receipt of such person," while the second defines exploitation as "use of prostitution by others or other forms of sexploitation, slavery or services, or servitude." These offenses are punishable by a term of up to 15 years imprisonment (Tyuryukanova 2004, 111–112).

Now, with all legal provisions in place, much needs to be done to translate the legislation into implementation and practice. As repeatedly indicated by President V. Putin, this is vitally important for Russia's international image. According to UN standards, Russia remains in the third category of countries: those that have failed to observe minimal standards to combat human trafficking and have taken inadequate steps for their implementation (Pachi 2003, 89). One can only hope that the active intent to change this situation demonstrated by recognized international organizations and Russian NGO activists will encourage the Government to adopt and implement the adequate measures so urgently needed.

The three areas generally accepted as key to combating human trafficking are prevention, protection, and prosecution. Russian NGOs and crisis centers have accumulated broad experience in preventing human trafficking and assisting its victims. The largest of them conduct programs focused on trafficking victims and manage networks of professional lawyers and psychologists to support them. NGOs also work to raise awareness about the dangers and scale of human trafficking, and they define specific legislative proposals.

In January 2004, the First All-Russian Assembly of Nongovernmental Organizations on Combating Human Trafficking was held, with President Putin sending greetings to participants. The Assembly adopted a special appeal, which recommended that the following actions be taken:

1. Government authorities, public associations, nongovernmental and international organizations should cooperate in developing, coordinating, and implementing measures against human trafficking;
2. State support for NGO programs must be ensured, while aiming at increasing public awareness in general and of high-risk groups in particular about the dangers inherent in human trafficking and the need for assistance to its victims;
3. Effective machinery to fund and support human rights public associations and nongovernmental and international organizations should be created;
4. Public control mechanisms of the activities of government authorities and self-governance bodies should be established, including public discussion of relevant state proposals at the preparatory stage;
5. Participation of NGOs and public associations in government social policies should be ensured.

Somewhat later, in December 2004, an international seminar on "Prevention and Combating Trafficking of People" was held in Moscow at the initiative of the Department on Equality–Directorate General of Human Rights of the Council of Europe together with the Russian Association of Women's Crisis Centers called "Stop the Violence." Participants drafted recommendations for a prospective national Plan of Action against human trafficking (Council of Europe 2005, 110–15).

The work of NGOs has become a major factor in designing effective steps aimed at preventing and combating trafficking in women. These steps envisage special programs aimed at protecting high-risk populations against unemployment, homelessness, poverty, forced migration, corruption, organized crime, and legalization of criminal gains. Overcoming these destructive phenomena will require strong political will. Primary efforts should be focused on social prevention, as addressing the effects of trafficking in women and their exploitation in prostitution through criminal measures brings only partial results. For visible change to be achieved, well-coordinated, multilateral, and well-funded approaches are necessary, based on specific, long-term strategies of sending and receiving States within a framework of international cooperation. Prostitution, illegal migration, and human trafficking present global challenges that cannot be resolved in traditional national liberal-democratic frameworks. The search for new and effective social and legal tools and solutions is under way around the world, and Russia is more and more actively involved in this process.

CONCLUSION

The CEDAW Committee should also take still more responsibility for this issue when pursuing its activities, including discussing the reports of the currently 185 States Parties to the Convention. By way of conclusion, I would like to present several proposals both for the Committee and to other human rights agents in the field:

1. Rather than discussing each article of the Convention at length at the review of a State Party's *periodic* report, the Committee should focus on specific articles only, in this case, Article 6 if warranted. In the constructive dialogue, the Committee should then not concentrate merely on the list of legal and policy measures to address these phenomena, but should give special consideration to the provision of resources (primarily financial), to control measures, and to the practical results of the antitrafficking activities of the State Party.

2. The Committee should reflect in greater detail the global restructuring of the world economy, which widens the gap between the female and male employment sectors and supports labor migration, particularly of women. Female labor migrants often are relegated to the status of second-rate, low qualified workers (mostly in the service sector), a process, which may be rightly qualified as a global violation of CEDAW.

3. International political and gender strategies must concentrate on:
   - creating greater visibility of the Optional Protocol to CEDAW so that more States Parties to the Convention will also ratify or accede to it;
   - raising awareness among individuals and groups at the national and international levels to utilize the communication procedure under the Optional Protocol to CEDAW and other international human rights treaties as instruments to tackle human rights violations of women in prostitution and trafficking of women that can be considered both as grave or systematic and a result of States not guaranteeing economic and social rights.

The CEDAW Committee's concluding comments on the fifth periodic report of Russia are still valid (CEDAW 2002, 56–60, paras. 373–405). The lack of systematic and targeted activities of my country toward the advancement of the status of women—and the guarantee of their human rights by the authorized agency at the federal level in charge of these activities and equipped with necessary legal power and material and financial resources—clearly indicate that the substantive provision of equal rights and equal opportunities for women and men has not yet become a priority for the Russian Federation.

Twenty-five years of the CEDAW Committee's activities have created a body of active former members. They should still cooperate with the CEDAW Committee and help it with its comprehensive and intense work.

NOTES

The original version of this essay was written in Russian and translated in Moscow. The editors do not have any means of checking the accuracy of quotations.

1. The Convention concerning Equal Opportunities and Equal Treatment for Men and Women Workers: Workers with Family Responsibilities (No. 156) was adopted by the General Conference of the ILO at its 67th Session (Geneva, June 1981) and came into force in August 1983.

2. In practice, gender analysis of budgets has been introduced in several regions. Since 2003, such activities have been under way in the Komi Republic with support from the United Nations Development Programme (UNDP) and United Nations Development Fund for Women (UNIFEM).

3. After the dissolution of the USSR, fifteen former republics turned into independent States. Twelve of them (Armenia, Azerbaijan, Byelorussia, Kazakhstan, Kyrgyzstan, Georgia, Moldova, Russian Federation, Tajikistan, Turkmenistan, Ukraine, and Uzbekistan) joined the Commonwealth of Independent States (CIS) in December 1991. Latvia, Lithuania, and Estonia did not join this union.

4. Various articles of the Russian Federation Criminal Code cover the following crimes: murder; rape; violent actions of a sexual nature; coercion to sexual actions; sexual intercourse and other sexual dealings with minors; debauchery; involvement of minors in antisocial activities, including prostitution; organization of prostitution; manufacture and distribution of materials or objects with pornographic depictions of minors.

PERSONAL REFLECTION:

RETHINKING PROSTITUTION AND TRAFFICKING

KRISZTINA MORVAI, HUNGARY

I shall never forget my first CEDAW session in January 2003 and how enthusiastically I prepared for it. As I read one of the first government reports as a member of the Committee, I did not want to believe my eyes at one point. The report of a not-to-be-named Western European State proudly declared that it had a very pro-woman migration policy. The report "proved" it by pointing to the fact that the State granted a privileged visa status to female entertainers, i.e. "cabaret dancers." I had not realized prior to this that some governments, which appear to be in the forefront of the fight against trafficking in and sexual exploitation of women, in fact indirectly encourage these severe forms of sex discrimination. They do so, inter alia, through the provision of easier, more flexible migration options for "exotic" women of other regions, colors, and races. In other words, they provide these options for poor women from poor countries, who are promised a brighter future in exchange for selling their sexual attractiveness—and often also their sexuality—in the more fortunate countries of the world. In my very first question ever as a CEDAW member, I tried to address the members of the reporting government in a very diplomatic way. It went something like this: "May I ask the distinguished delegation, why, of all professions, did you identify and choose 'cabaret dancing' as a basis for a special visa status for women? Why not brain surgery, civil engineering, or opera singing, for example?" The delegation members looked embarrassed, and the representatives of nongovernmental organizations (NGOs) in the room were laughing. It was obvious that the government spokespersons had never before considered this issue as problematic from a sex-equality point of view. I hope that they did consider it so from that moment on.

But at this very first session I came to realize that the use of women in the local and global sex trades was generally not viewed as a fundamentally discriminatory practice. In particular, most governments did not look at prostitution itself as a phenomenon that in and of itself discriminates against women. What astonished and hurt me even more was the fact that some Committee members did not appear to look at it in this way either. Some experts and even some of the Committee's concluding comments used the word "sex worker" to refer to women in prostitution. I was aware that this was meant to give some dignity to these women, so the intentions were good. Still, I knew from my previous research and fieldwork that the expression did not give any dignity to the women concerned. The kind of "work" they do is anything but dignifying. Allowing dozens of completely unknown, often disgusting or abusive men to touch their most private body parts and penetrate them, and performing oral sex on dozens of different men five minutes after they first meet, would not make any woman feel dignified, whatever the activity is called. It is the "dignity" of the sex industry *that is achieved by using the expression "sex work." Pimps and brothel keepers are transformed into "entrepreneurs," and clients who make women in prostitution do these things for them are transformed into "service customers" through this "magic" expression. What is called "work" in the context of prostitution would be called sexual abuse in the context of other relationships between the sexes—if we think about the ugly words, the verbal abuse that clients are free to use with prostitutes before, during, and after the "work" done for them. The "work" would be called sexual violence, because we are talking about acts of sex that are not wanted by the woman concerned.*

As feminists, we fight hard for the right of any girl or woman to say "no" if she does not want to have sex, whether due to lack of attraction to the particular man, due to loving somebody else, due to a headache—whatever reason, or no reason at all. Prostitutes are obviously considered an exception. In their case, we call the unwanted sex "sex work" and not sexual abuse. Because the expression is false and does not reflect the realities of prostitution and of the women in it, I protested the use of it from the time I joined the Committee, and I am proud that I could contribute to basically deleting it from our vocabulary while I was there.

Similarly, I was sad and frustrated by the artificial separation of trafficking in women and prostitution both in the dialogue conducted by the Committee with States Parties and in the laws and policies of States Parties themselves. I enthusiastically tried to point to and explain the clear link between these two phenomena. Without prostitution, there would be no trafficking in women for the purpose of prostitution. It follows that one can effectively suppress trafficking only by effectively suppressing prostitution. Not *prostitutes, but* prostitution. *The function of the 1949 Convention for the Suppression of the Traffic in Persons and of the Exploitation of the Prostitution of Others was to prevent the criminalization of prostitutes. That is why both that Convention and the CEDAW Convention talk about the suppression of the exploitation of* prostitution—*as opposed to the suppression of prostitution. These Conventions limit any suppressing actions of the State to the exploiters of prostitution, such as pimps, procurers, and brothel owners. I wanted—often passionately—for the Committee to understand that this expression did not prevent us from looking at prostitution as such in States Parties and to consider it a fundamentally discriminatory practice that should be eliminated at some point in the future.*

This ambitious aim is the leading philosophy behind the so-called Swedish model, which considers prostitution a social evil and a form of oppression of women by men that is, therefore, fundamentally discriminatory and should be eliminated. Current Swedish law (in force as of 1999) shifts the focus (finally!) to the demand *side of prostitution and thus puts the blame for its existence on the clients, who are criminalized and punished. This attitude, in and of itself, is an excellent way of achieving justice vis-à-vis the discrimination and labeling inherent in prostitution for so many centuries. It is not the women in prostitution who cause this particular form of social evil and sex-based abuse. The fundamental cause is the male demand for exercising power over women through having unwanted sex with them. In other words, prostitution is mainly about men's rights and opportunities to pay for not treating women as equal human beings who have pasts, feelings, and wishes of their own and who suffer pains and enjoy pleasures. They give money, and in exchange they expect the woman to behave as if she was an object that was meant to please men who do not want to take the trouble of finding a human and/or sexual relationship that is based on mutual respect and equality.*

This close and complex relationship between prostitution and sex discrimination was so clear to me that I probably did not feel the need and did not have the patience to explain it to all the experts on the Committee in the course of my first few sessions. I had no idea about their general openness and flexibility toward rethinking their views on the relationship between trafficking and prostitution, the evil of legalizing prostitution, the false distinction between "voluntary" and "forced" prostitution, and all other matters related to Article 6. I became very pleasantly surprised as soon as I started a new strategy at some point in my second year of membership.

I organized lunchtime workshops for Committee members and staff of our Secretariat regarding topics covered by Article 6. I researched the Committee's past concluding comments and gave a talk on my findings, namely that there was no consistency in the interpretation of this important article. The concluding comments contained both pro- and anti-legalization messages, and the philosophy behind the interpretation of Article 6 of the Convention was neither clear nor predictable and certain in the way that States Parties should expect to hear from the Committee in the interpretation of the Convention, which is a legal instrument. Thus, we started to work out a philosophy and coherent interpretation that was in line with the Convention as a whole. I invited two guest speakers, who were leading experts in the field of State responses to trafficking in women and prostitution. One was Melissa Farley from the United States, a clinical and research psychologist and author of several groundbreaking books and articles on the psychological aspects of prostitution, in particular on the traumatic experiences most prostitutes suffer prior to entering prostitution and during their years of sexual exploitation. On another occasion, Gunilla Ekberg, Special Adviser to the Swedish Government on Issues Regarding Prostitution and Trafficking in Human Beings, visited the Committee for a lunchtime seminar in New York. Her talk on the urgent need to reform laws and policies regarding prostitution was very convincing, especially her call for shifting the focus to the demand side and criminalizing male clients, as well as the need to support women who want to move out of prostitution. She also showed us, during the following day's lunchtime, the heartbreaking film about a young woman in prostitution titled Lilja Forever. *When the camera was focusing on the rotating faces of lots of men "doing their thing" inside the almost paralyzed body of Lilja (who originally entered prostitution without any explicit force), I looked around the room, saw the shock and sadness of the CEDAW experts who were present, and knew I had won a large victory: The views of the Committee would not remain unchanged on what prostitution is all about and what it has to do with discrimination in general and our Convention in particular.*

Unfortunately, after four challenging but wonderful years on the Committee, I had to say good-bye to the other members, many of whom had become friends and also allies in my "Article 6 fight." I am grateful to them all for their patience toward my impatience, for their openness in understanding new views and perspectives, and for their strong commitment to the dignity and rights of all women in the world.

UNFINISHED BATTLES: POLITICAL AND PUBLIC LIFE

FRANÇOISE GASPARD, *FRANCE*

This essay is the product of three different experiences. First, there is my experience as a historian. Like many students and academics of my generation I discovered, with the help of the feminist movement of the sixties, that history—as it was then written and taught—ignored women almost completely. Thus, I learned in school that universal suffrage had been introduced in France in 1848, when in fact this was the date when *male* suffrage was instituted. French women had to wait until 1944 before they could vote and run for office.

Second there is my experience as an elected official. I have been a mayor, a deputy in the French National Assembly, and a member of the European Parliament. When I was elected mayor in 1977, only 1 percent of the mayors of roughly thirty-six thousand French municipalities were women, and there were only two of us who headed a town with a population larger than thirty thousand. In the European Parliament, where I held a seat from 1979 to 1981, the situation was less unsatisfactory (16 percent women). Progress has continued there, and in 2004 women made up 30.7 percent of those elected. This is so undoubtedly because the European Parliament still has little power, and those with seats often enjoy only minor visibility in their respective countries. In contrast, the French National Assembly remains a male bastion: There were just 5.4 percent women in 1981 when I was elected for the first time, and only 12 percent were elected to the Assembly in 2002. Carrying out these different mandates—especially that of deputy in a chamber that had close to 95 percent men—showed me how difficult it is for elected women to press for the rights of women when they are such a small minority.

Third and last, there is my experience as a member of the CEDAW Committee where, together with my colleagues, I have had the opportunity to appraise the situation of women all over the world. I have been able to note their marginalization almost everywhere in decision-making proceedings, whether these be political, administrative, judicial, economic, social, or cultural.

For women, gaining the vote and the right to run for office was the fruit of a battle that is almost completed today. With the exception of just one nation (Saudi Arabia), in 2006 all the world's countries that have parliamentary representation and elected territorial assemblies grant women political citizenship. However, having the right to vote and being eligible for office does not ensure women's effective participation in political and public life—far from it. And women do not yet have equal access to all the different jobs available on the market or in public service, nor to positions of responsibility whether in the private or the public sector.

FROM THE VOTE TO RUNNING FOR OFFICE

Universal suffrage is one of the hallmarks of democracy. At the time of their founding, the modern Western democracies generally had only male suffrage. In many countries, even this was not universal; it depended on property or other wealth, or on race or ethnicity.[1] Women were excluded on the basis of their sex, and in many countries they remained so for a long time.[2]

"Men make laws, women make mores," wrote the French philosopher Jean-Jacques Rousseau, who had a profound influence on the revolutionaries of the eighteenth century. The exclusion of women from political citizenship, and more generally from the public arena, is the result of stereotyping that presumes a natural difference between the two sexes—their complementarity rather than their equality. Even if they occur differently in different societies and vary over time, these stereotypes have led almost everywhere to differences in function, role, and status, confining women to domestic and maternal roles. States are committed to fighting these stereotypes when they ratify the CEDAW Convention.[3]

Women's demand for participation in the public arena in the nineteenth and twentieth centuries was seen by many political leaders as a threat to the order that men had established among themselves. Sir Winston Churchill, for example, said in 1897 that "If you give women votes, you must ultimately allow women to sit as members of Parliament. . . . [O]nce you give votes to the vast numbers of women who form the majority of the community, all power passes to their hands" (Churchill 1966, 194). This viewpoint deserves our attention. It assumes that women are an undifferentiated group, while men are individuals capable of representing all political differences and varieties of social life. Another way of disqualifying the "second sex" from public life is even more perverse: It is the suggestion that women are not interested in politics. Even today, in the reports that States submit to the Committee and in the dialogue between the experts and the national delegations, this idea is regularly put forward to explain why women are underrepresented in elected assemblies. Similarly, it is claimed that women prefer not to vote for women, something that many studies have proven wrong.

As late as the eve of World War I (WWI), parliamentary democracies that had recognized women's right to vote and run for office were the exceptions. Only New Zealand (in 1893), Australia (in 1902, although not for Aborigines), and the Russian Grand Duchy of Finland (in 1906) had granted women the same civil rights as men. During the war, Danish and Icelandic women became citizens. Between the two world wars, the movement widened and touched every continent. But the male politicians of many countries, including the old parliamentary democracies, continued to resist. While the women of the Dominican Republic, Mongolia, Poland, Sri Lanka, and Turkey were allowed to vote, French women were still denied official citizenship. The issue was debated by the French Parliament on several occasions but rejected each time. Some countries granted citizenship to certain women but not to all, or else to all women but not in every election. When it became impossible to resist the suffragist pressure, the question became how to limit and slow down the inevitable.

Sometimes governments adopted a one-step-at-a-time policy. Thus, female property owners in Great Britain were able to vote on the local level before WWI. In 1919, some Belgian women were admitted to the ranks of voters because they were widows or mothers of soldiers who had died in the war, or they themselves had been prisoners of war. At the same time, Canadian women who enlisted in the army gained the right to vote. In Great Britain, women over the age of thirty became voters in 1918, although men could vote when they were twenty-one. This age-based difference was not abolished until 1928. In several Latin American countries and in Portugal, there was a requirement of a minimum level of schooling that only applied to women. In 1944, the fear of the fact that women were a majority of the electorate was clearly expressed when French political leaders haggled over the terms of suffrage after the liberation. Some of them wanted to wait for the return of all prisoners of war before granting women the vote—in order, they said, not to create an imbalance in the electorate. Moreover, women's vote did not mean that they could participate in every ballot. It was only prudent, said the male politicians, that women practice their citizenship first on the local level and only in municipal council elections. The right to vote in all elections would come later.

In 1945, when the United Nations was born, more than half of the fifty-one nations that had ratified the Charter did not allow women to vote in the same way men did; their suffrage was most often restricted to local elections.[4] Moreover, it was quite rare at the time to find women holding leadership positions in national administrations or seats on international bodies. Even today, in many founding member nations, diplomatic jobs and positions are not yet open to women or, if they are, women are the exception.

One of the first tasks of the UN Commission on the Status of Women (CSW), created in 1946 and spurred on by women's movements, especially in Latin America and the Caribbean, was to write the Convention on the Political Rights of Women, adopted in 1952.[5] The CEDAW Convention, adopted in 1979 by the UN General Assembly, builds on all previous Conventions.[6] It thus constitutes a true global charter of women's rights. Article 7 is specifically concerned with women's access to decision-making in the political and public domains. At the present time almost all UN member States recognize women's equality in the field of political rights but, in many of them, including my own, women still constitute a tiny number in elected assemblies and even fewer in governments. Some jobs in various administrations are still closed to women.

States that ratify the Convention or accede to it may do so with reservations. Those that refuse to follow Article 7 are rare, especially where it concerns the right to vote. Nevertheless, Kuwait did exactly that when it acceded to the Convention in 1994. Following the CEDAW Committee's examination of an initial report, and of a second one during its thirtieth session in January 2004 (CEDAW 2004a, 17, paras. 60–61), Kuwait finally granted women their political rights. It did not do so until supporters of these rights, which included nongovernmental organizations (NGOs), pointed to the Committee's conclusions and urged the national parliament to act on its commitment, which it finally did in 2005. On December 9, 2005, the Government of Kuwait informed the Secretary-General of its decision to withdraw its reservation in respect of Article 7 (a), made upon accession to the Convention.

Still, the right to vote can be a mere formality. The absence of any elections or of free elections, violations of freedom of expression, or lack of security limit its practice in different regions of the world for women and men alike. But here, too, the situation can be different for women. Although granted political rights they may feel reluctant to use them, or they may face obstacles that prevent them from voting. In many countries women cannot register to vote because they are missing a birth certificate or identity papers that are issued only to men. Registering Afghan women in the 2005 elections, for example, required the help of the international community and was a very difficult task. Once registered, women do not always manage to make it to the voting booth. They lack the education or access to the information they need in order to familiarize themselves with the political state of affairs and make autonomous choices. Sometimes they are discouraged from expressing themselves, or they are intimidated into not voting. This was the case in Algeria in 1992. Husbands were authorized to vote on behalf of their wives without needing power of attorney. In Saudi Arabia women were allowed to participate for the first time in local elections in 2005.[7] However, even though some women announced their candidacies, they were excluded from the proceedings. "Technical" reasons were cited by those in power to oust women from the electoral process, not only as candidates but as voters as well: "The problems in setting up voting sites for women, the lack of experience with democracy, the identity papers that women do not have, all served to justify the time the government needed to integrate women in the democratic process" (Jabre and Samouillier 2006, 594).

EQUALITY IN POLITICAL REPRESENTATION

From the nineteenth century on, suffragists thought that the right to vote and run for office would put them on an equal footing with men. This was not the case even when, generally speaking, women acquired the right to vote and the right to be elected at the same time.[8] States agree under Article 7 of the Convention not only to ensure equality in voting but also that women be "on equal terms with men . . . eligible for election to all publicly elected bodies," and can "participate in the formulation of government policy and the implementation thereof."

Beginning in the early 1990s, the Inter-Parliamentary Union (IPU) helped make women's underrepresentation in parliaments visible by its strong support of the Convention's Article 7.[9] It contributed to the elaboration of global statistics of women in parliaments and in political parties and disseminated the results of the first large inquiry dealing with the composition of the sexes in national parliaments in 150 countries (Inter-Parliamentary Union 1995). Christine Pintat drew the following conclusions:

What is striking is the immense time-lapse one notes in most of the European and North American countries between four dates: the one when the parliamentary institution was established, the one when women realized they were given the right to vote and be elected, the one when they entered the Parliament as a parliamentarian rather than as secretary or assistant, and finally the one when, in some countries, a woman could have access to the presidency of the Assembly. Let us cite a few examples of the most significant ones. If the archives faithfully reflect reality, it took 486 years for a Swedish woman to be elected to the Parliament (in the modern sense of the term) established in 1435 in the nation that is recognized today as the most egalitarian in the world. It took 156 years for a woman to become a member of the French Parliament although it was founded in 1789 to the revolutionary cry of "Liberty, Equality, Fraternity." In Switzerland, 123 years went by between the creation of the Parliament and the election of a woman, in Spain it took 121 years, in Portugal 113 years, in Greece 108 years, in Italy 98 years, and in the United States 76 years. (Pintat 1997, 799)

After they had been admitted to vote and were eligible to be candidates, the demand for women's active representation was late in coming. Other than in the Nordic countries in Europe, the women's movements of the 1970s rarely claimed the right to participation in formulating laws and managing nations. In the Western European countries, activists had other priorities. If it had not yet been obtained, they were asking for civil equality and personal rights (contraception, medically supervised abortion, sharing of household tasks, criminalization of domestic violence) that were perceived as the conditions for the establishment of women's autonomy. They barely noticed the almost all-male character of the political scene, which passed for "natural" or inevitable. At the time there were very few models of women in politics, and the link was rarely made between discriminatory legislation based on sex and the fact that on the national level it was men for the most part who were writing laws and deciding policies for everyone.

In 2006, the global average of women present in the parliaments of 187 nations was 16 percent (Inter-Parliamentary Union 2006). The ranking that the IPU provides on a regular basis shows that no connections can be made between the length of time since universal suffrage was established in a given country, the level of economic development, and the feminization of the legislative body. The country that heads the list is Rwanda with 48.8 percent women elected to its lower chamber, coming even before Sweden (45.3 percent). Globally, the United States ranks 67th, France 81st, Japan 102nd, all of which are vastly outdistanced by less-developed nations that came to the democratic system much later.

The case of Rwanda is especially interesting and demonstrates the role that the Convention can play. In this regard, my missions to Rwanda will always remain an exceptional experience for me. At the time of this country's democratic transition and on the occasion of the drafting of its new Constitution, in 2000, the IPU was asked by the Forum of Parliamentary Rwandan Women to organize several missions to help with the process of integrating gender into the basic law of the country. These missions, which I conducted, led to the explicit inclusion of a reference to the Convention in the Preamble to the Constitution and of an article that guarantees the presence of at least 30 percent women in all decision-making bodies. The electoral laws adopted ensure this. In the lower chamber, 30 percent of the seats are reserved for women in a final stage of the process. The fact that this percentage was greatly surpassed attests to the social and political mobilization of Rwandan women during the period that followed the genocide. In 1994, women represented close to 70 percent of the population due to the large numbers of men who had been killed or had gone into exile. For several years, in a nation where women until then had had almost no access to public responsibilities, Rwandan women were obliged to ensure the country's survival. It is believed that at the time of the election of 2003, the demographic situation changed and that women made up 54 percent of the population, notably because of the return of the exiles. Against all expectations, however, women still gained seats where the competition was open—that is to say, where they were in a race against men.

Creating women's parties has been one strategy to increase women's participation in political life. In different countries this has been a way of protesting against the machismo of partisan political groups. It should be noted that in Iceland in 1906 (even before universal suffrage was established), in Luxembourg in the 1920s, in the Philippines in the 1950s, and in South Africa during the 1994 elections, such groups were formed with mixed success.

Sometimes the results were positive, as in Sweden, where the threat of forming women's parties was utilized to overcome the resistance of party leaders to including women among the candidates. When the 1991 elections brought about, together with the defeat of the Social Democrats, a decrease in the number of elected women on the national level and a change for the worse in social policies important to women, women of all parties reacted and threatened to form a political party with the slogan "a full salary and half the power." On the eve of the 1994 elections, this threat was taken seriously: A poll showed that the women's party could well obtain 40 percent of the vote (Edwards 1995, 56). This frightened the regular parties, which included more women on their lists. The results of this strategy are striking: Today female parliamentarians have surpassed the 40 percent mark, and the Swedish Government now has the same number of women and men ministers. When women's parties do exist, however, they are often difficult to sustain.

Another strategy consists of asking female voters to vote massively for women candidates. This is what happened in the municipal elections of 1971 in Norway, when political activists and members of women's groups, angered by the slim number of female candidates on the ballots, called on voters to scratch out the names of male candidates and vote only for women, even if they belonged to a different party. In three of the large cities of Norway, including Oslo, a majority of women was elected (Skjeie 1991).[10] After that Norwegian parties took women into account as full-fledged politicians.

Yet another strategy involves voluntary adoption of quotas for candidates of either sex. Such quotas were originally adopted in northern Europe by the Social Democrats and in Germany and The Netherlands by the Green Party. This often led to other parties, including conservative ones, paying attention to the need for female candidates for fear of losing women's votes.

A more forceful method of increasing female representation involves compelling political parties by law to either reserve a certain number of seats for women or to include a certain percentage of women candidates. Reports submitted to the Committee suggest that such legislation can concern all ballots or only some of them. The quota level, too, is variable. Sometimes it is no more than symbolic (5 percent, as in Nepal), but most often it is 30 percent (International Institute for Democracy and Electoral Assistance 1995). Quotas can be more or less restrictive. There is not always a punishment for failure to comply. Also, the number of female candidates does not necessarily guarantee the same number being elected.

The French law of June 2000 (usually referred to as the Parity Law) offers a revealing case of the limits of legal pressure on political parties. The French Constitution was revised in 1999 to allow for the adoption of legislation requiring equal numbers of women and men as candidates. The laws were passed almost unanimously by both chambers because pressure from women's organizations was very strong and the idea of parity was popular with the public. The Parity Law went into effect in 2000 and has different requirements for different elections: proportional and single candidate. In proportional elections where the voting is for a list— municipal, regional, European, and some Senate seats—each list must have an equal number of male and female candidates listed alternately. In the elections where this law applied—towns with a population of more than 3,500, in regional elections and in those for the French delegation to the European Parliament—parity has been achieved, or almost: 48 to 49 percent of those elected are women. Still, since the law refers only to seats in the assemblies, executive positions in these bodies (mayors, presidents of regional councils) continue to be primarily male.[11] In the local assemblies that are not affected by these provisions—where the voting is not based on a ballot list—the number of women remains unchanged. The same holds true for the National Assembly, where deputies are elected by voting for a single candidate. The Parity Law stipulates that parties that do not present 50 percent female candidates will lose a fraction of their public financing. But political parties have sometimes chosen to forgo the funding rather than comply with this (as happened in 2002 during the general elections to the National Assembly).

In almost every country that has ratified the Convention, there is no legal bar to the eligibility of women. There are reservations by some States Parties regarding Article 7 (b), limiting access to specific political or public functions, but these are the exceptions. The Committee addresses these reservations and asks for their withdrawal in its concluding comments on the States Parties' reports. This was the case for Maldives, where legislation forbids women to stand for the presidency or vice-presidency (CEDAW 2001, 17, paras. 130–31). It was also the case for the Grand Duchy of Luxembourg, where the crown is passed on through the male line. Based on the recommendations of several of the Committee's concluding comments (CEDAW 2000, 41, paras. 400–01; CEDAW 2003, 48, paras. 300–01), Luxembourg's government has begun to discuss measures that would no longer exclude women from succession to the throne.[12]

Even when States endorse Article 7 fully, they do not necessarily provide equal access for women's political representation. The Committee has had to be especially vigilant about this by checking the number of women, the distribution of their positions, and the prerequisites for their holding office. The case of Samoa, which acceded to the Convention in 1992, illustrates this clearly. The Committee expressed its concern about the fact that only those women who had the status of head of an extended family could be candidates, since women who hold this title are few (CEDAW 2005b, 13, paras. 52–53).[13] In its concluding comments, the Committee refers to General Recommendation No. 23, explaining Articles 7 and 8, and General Recommendation No. 25 on the application of temporary special measures according to Article 4 (1), when urging States

Parties to accelerate women's equality in political and public life. As noted above, some States have adopted measures such as quotas or a reserved number of seats for each sex. But this is not an ideal solution because quotas are not always respected or else, when they are, they can function as a ceiling. Also, quotas have been overturned either by parliaments or constitutional courts on the grounds that they were considered discriminatory—without any reference to the Convention or to the obligations it places on the States Parties.[14] Reserving seats for women in parliaments can certainly be seen as a "special temporary measure." But for this to work, women must have the same legitimacy as their male colleagues. For this reason, the Committee is deeply concerned about procedures in Bangladesh, where in order to ensure a female presence in parliament, the existing members (overwhelmingly male) are those who choose which women will gain such a seat (CEDAW 2004a, 139, paras. 255–56).

The Committee is increasingly attentive to women's participation in all bodies of political decision-making, especially in local and national assemblies. It asks the States to provide relevant statistics and, on this basis, may record in its concluding comments that the underrepresentation of women in places where decisions are made that affect the daily life of individuals is evidence of discrimination.

TOWARD EQUALITY IN ALL OF PUBLIC LIFE

The presence of women in substantial numbers in elected assemblies is not sufficient to guarantee equal participation of the two sexes in every sector of political, public, economic, social, and cultural life. Women should be true participants everywhere in decision-making, and their decision-making ought not to be confined to their concerns in the private realm. The Convention on the Political Rights of Women (1952) not only made the right to vote and to be eligible for office a condition of equality, but it stipulated in Article 3 that women "shall be entitled to hold public office and to exercise all public functions, established by national law, on equal terms with men, without any discrimination." The Declaration of Mexico, adopted at the end of the First UN World Conference on Women (held in Mexico City in 1975), indicated that a "greater and equal participation of women at all levels of decision-making" would promote development and peace (United Nations 1976, para. 9 [unnumbered]). The CEDAW Convention picked up this theme again in Article 7. General Recommendation No. 23 insists on this point, showing how the road led from the battle for suffrage to a more general demand for women's participation on all levels of collective life. It states:

The political and public life of a country is a broad concept. It refers to the exercise of political power, in particular the exercise of legislative, judicial, executive and administrative powers. The term covers all aspects of public administration and the formulation and implementation of policy at the international, national, regional, and local levels. The concept also includes many aspects of civil society, including public boards and local councils and the activities of organizations such as political parties, trade unions, professional or industry associations, women's organizations, community-based organizations and other organizations concerned with public and political life. (para. 5)

In response to questions contained in the list of issues sent by the Committee to States Parties before the oral dialogue with the national delegations begins, the States Parties are invited to provide in their reports all information available—preferably in statistics—on the situation of women in political and public life, not only in all elected assemblies, but also at the various levels of administration, in advisory councils and committees, as well as in organizations of civil society. At the same time the Committee expects information concerning measures taken or envisaged to ensure equality of the sexes in accordance with Article 7 (b).

In all countries, including those that appear to be the most advanced concerning equality between the sexes, men continue to outnumber women in decision-making positions, sometimes very heavily so. This is so in governments as well as in the highest posts of the judicial and administrative branches and also in advisory councils and committees. Furthermore, in all these structures—on the local, national, and international levels—women still find that they are rarely assigned tasks that are traditionally considered to be male (defense, security, foreign affairs, finance, urban planning), while social and educational affairs are far more regularly entrusted to them.

Article 8 of the Convention deals specifically with diplomacy. Since before WWI, international women's movements had called for an international organization that had the aim of preserving peace and regulating and settling conflicts peacefully. In 1919, after much struggle, feminist activists obtained the right to be seated in the new League of Nations as representatives of their countries and to occupy posts on every level. It was an important victory at a time when, in many member nations, women not only did not have any political rights but also were prohibited from working in many professions, particularly in public functions. Thus, it is not surprising that, when the members of the CSW (the majority of the diplomats on which have always been women) formulated the CEDAW Convention, they were particularly concerned with women's equal participation in the public arena, including the diplomatic service.

Supranational organizations play a considerable role in prescribing norms that member countries must respect. Here again, men greatly outnumber women. This was true in the 1950s and still is today. It is enough to walk through the hallways of the UN headquarters in New York and enter the conference halls to see this in action. In many countries diplomatic careers were opened to women quite late. In France, for example, it took a legal battle for a woman to enter the Ministry of Foreign Affairs in the late 1930s. Moreover, her career was a modest one, and she was never posted abroad. In 1988, the Committee in a first general recommendation on this issue—General Recommendation No. 8—asked States Parties to make sure that Article 8 of the Convention was fully complied with. Furthermore, General Recommendation No. 23 asks States to furnish statistics, broken down by sex, of their diplomatic services and to provide information on the measures taken to promote the presence of women in this sector. Nevertheless, the Committee notices that States frequently explain the meager presence of women as due to women's hesitancy to become involved in a diplomatic career when they are married and have children. They rarely analyze the situation in terms of discrimination or take measures toward its elimination.

Article 7 (c) of the Convention also refers to women's participation on equal terms with men "in non-governmental organizations and associations concerned with the public and political life of the country." If women continue to be underrepresented in political life it is because there are generally fewer women than men who are involved in political parties, either because they are not encouraged to do so or because they cannot surmount difficulties that include lack of time, lack of money, and discriminatory political "rituals" in force in their culture. When they are present they do not often hold positions of leadership. Since the early 1970s, political parties in different countries have also adopted quotas (sometimes progressive ones with an expiration date, as the Social Democrats in Germany have done) to avoid the systematic exclusion of women from party responsibilities. Other measures are possible, such as financial aid for a political party's women's organization, or training programs intended to encourage women to present themselves as candidates.

Still, in all organizations—and especially those in civil society, such as labor unions and NGOs—women should not only be present but should also be able to make decisions. Women's movements, in their reaction against women's subordination, can and do work together in order to struggle against discrimination based on sex and gender. These associations ought to be recognized and supported, especially financially. During the Committee's sessions, the oral information presented by NGOs and their written "shadow" reports make an immense contribution. They correct the States' tendency to present an idyllic picture of the rights situation of women in their territory or to conceal the various forms of discrimination that it is the Convention's goal to fight.

CONCLUSION

In the nineteenth century, feminists debated the question of which should come first: civic equality or civil equality—that is, equality for women with men in political rights or equality in all other fields of women's lives such as education, marriage, and employment. It was a difficult decision then and resonates even today, especially in countries where laws do not recognize civil equality. Yet as long as women cannot contribute in large numbers to the formulation and reformulation of the law and the rules that govern all levels of community life, many inequalities between the sexes will continue to be invisible. When they are invisible, direct and indirect forms of discrimination cannot be the object of policies intended to eliminate them, and this will ensure their de facto permanence. Discrimination affects all women. While its specific aspects appear in different guises depending on the world's regions, in each of these it is women—women in all their diversity—who continue to be the victims. Decision-making bodies obviously cannot represent all of society in every aspect of its diversity, but they must become more representative if inequality is to be recognized and corrected.

NOTES

I would like to thank Joan Wallach Scott for improving the original translation of my essay from French into English.

1. This was the case for male African Americans, who had no political rights until 1865 (black women, like all American women, only won the vote after WWI). It was equally the case for Jews and Muslims in French Algeria, where suffrage was granted in 1848, but only to French men. Algerian Jewish men (but not women) became citizens and also eligible for office in 1871; Muslim men became citizens in 1946. It is important to note that male

Algerian Muslims won their political rights after French women in France, and that female Algerian Muslims were granted full citizenship only in 1958.

2. Stranger yet, some women who were first granted citizenship at the dawn of the modern democracies were deprived of it later. Thus in Canada, where female property owners in the State of Quebec were able to vote locally from 1791 until 1849, the word "male" was later introduced into the electoral law.

3. Article 5 of the Convention.

4. Argentina,* Australia,* Belgium,* Bolivia,* Brazil, Byelorussia, Canada,* Chile,* China,* Colombia, Costa Rica,* Cuba, Czechoslovakia, Denmark, Dominican Republic, Ecuador,* Egypt,* El Salvador, Ethiopia, France, Greece,* Guatemala,* Haiti,* Honduras,* India,* Iran,* Iraq,* Lebanon,* Liberia, Luxembourg, Mexico,* The Netherlands, New Zealand, Nicaragua,* Norway, Panama, Paraguay,* Peru,* Philippines, Poland, Saudi Arabia,* South Africa,* Syrian Arab Republic, Turkey, Ukraine, Union of Soviet Socialist Republics, United Kingdom of Great Britain and Northern Ireland, United States of America, Uruguay, Venezuela,* Yugoslavia. http://www.un.org/Overview/growth.htm. The asterisk indicates those States that in 1945 did not recognize the full equality of women to have the right to vote or be eligible for office, according to the IPU: http://www.ipu.org/wmn-e/suffrage.htm.

5. The Convention on the Political Rights of Women, which came into force on July 7, 1954, did not have a monitoring body. Article 7 of the CEDAW Convention builds on its provisions. http://www.unhchr.ch/html/menu3/b/22.htm.

6. In addition to the Convention on the Political Rights of Women, these notably include the Convention of 1957 on the Nationality of Married Women and the Convention of 1962 on Consent to Marriages, Minimum Age for Marriage, and Registration of Marriage.

7. Saudi Arabia ratified the Convention in 2000, accompanying it with a general reservation.

8. It should be noted, however, that in several countries women were eligible for office before they could vote. This is true for Belgium and Norway, for example.

9. The Inter-Parliamentary Union (IPU) was founded in 1889 by two backbench members of parliament: Frederic Passy from France and William Randal Cremer from the United Kingdom. It is a worldwide organization of parliamentarians working for peace and cooperation among peoples and the firm establishment of representative institutions.

10. Norway is not a member of the European Union, but the case deserves to be mentioned because it influenced the Nordic countries as a whole.

11. In the communities affected by the law, there are just 7.5 percent female mayors, and only one Regional Council of the twenty-two metropolitan French regions is presided over by a woman.

12. However, the Constitution has not yet been revised and the clause remains on the books. Belgium introduced a similar clause on ratification of the Convention in 1985, for its Constitution reserved the exercise of royal powers for males alone. The Constitution was later revised, which in 1998 led to the removal of the clause.

13. The combined initial, second and third periodic report from Samoa was examined by the Committee at its thirty-second session in January 2005 (CEDAW 2005b, 9–16, paras. 27–70).

14. See specifically the Committee's concluding comments concerning the initial report from Jordan (CEDAW 2000, 20, paras. 182–83), whose Parliament rejected a petition asking that 20 percent of the seats in the National Assembly be reserved for women.

IMPEDIMENTS TO PROGRESS: THE FORMAL LABOR MARKET

HANNA BEATE SCHÖPP-SCHILLING, *GERMANY*

When I started my work as an expert on the Committee on the Elimination of Discrimination against Women (the Committee) in 1989, I held the political position of Director General for Women's Affairs of the newly established Department of that name in the traditional Federal Ministry of Family, Youth and Health in the Federal Republic of Germany (FRG). At the time, I had hardly any knowledge of international law and human rights and was only barely acquainted with the Convention, which had not played a driving role in the Federal Ministry when we drafted the "Ten-Point-Plan for Women" in 1987. In fact, my original academic training in German and American literature and cultural history had not included any knowledge of or training in law per se. However, due to a number of factors, which had influenced my professional development in the late 1970s and 1980s, I had gained insight into various aspects of antidiscrimination and labor law and had become an ardent proponent of the American practice of affirmative action (temporary special measures according to Convention Article 4 [1]), when I started serving on the Committee. In addition, international conferences on emerging feminist issues related to women's work, which I had conceptualized and convened for academic circles, elite groups of public figures as well as the general public, had introduced me to different policy models promoting women's employment and striving for compatibility of work in the family and the labor market. These included the innovative Swedish policy of the *dual* roles of men and women and the contrasting approaches of the FRG and the German Democratic Republic (GDR), which were based on very different principles of political, legal, economic, and social organization and pursued almost opposite ideologies with respect to the lives and work of women living under their respective jurisdictions. Having lived, studied and worked in West Berlin since 1962, I had not only been confronted with the reality of the Berlin Wall on a daily basis, but also with the practical impact of these ideologies on women's lives in the two Germanies.

The conferences also introduced me to the world of politics and ultimately led to my political appointment as the first Director General for

Women's Affairs at the federal level in 1987. In this position I became engaged in the formulation or amendment of a number of laws in various areas, including the amendment of the nondiscrimination provision on the basis of sex of the Civil Code as requested by the European Court of Justice (ECJ) on the basis of the European Union Directives of 1975 and 1976 as well as a new equal opportunities law for the public sector.

Once I joined the Committee in 1989, my government work suddenly confronted me with unforeseen challenges. On November 9, 1989, the Berlin Wall came down. In early 1990, the GDR held its first free and democratic election, but in the course of subsequent events, including a mass exodus of its population into the FRG, it could not survive as an independent State. On October 3, 1990, the two German States unified; the GDR acceded to the FRG. From November 1989 and until I left my government position in early 1992, I had to deal with some of the consequences of the transformation of the socialist political and economic system. My position allowed me to identify and utilize many opportunities, policies, and strategies to obviate or counteract at least some aspects of the economic changes, which impacted negatively on both women and men of the GDR on a massive scale, but, in particular on its women. Among other measures, the inclusion of a quota provision in the German Labor Promotion Act to guarantee unemployed women places according to their percentage among the unemployed population in programs of retraining, further training, and public job placements proved to be one of the more important and to some extent successful strategies to maintain economic opportunities for them (Schöpp-Schilling 1995, 27–40).

These and other experiences of a more personal nature gave me a keen interest in Articles 11 (women's equality in employment) and 4 (1) (temporary special measures) of the Convention. While I raised questions regarding the implementation of many articles of the Convention during eighteen years on the Committee, these two have remained at the center of my scrutiny of States Parties' efforts and accountability. My interest includes the manner in which various industrialized European countries of different political and economic systems have pursued contrasting strategies to implement women's substantive equality in employment; and how they have addressed the traditional division of labor among men and women in the family, the abolition of which, according to the Convention, is a prerequisite for achieving equality between the sexes in the labor market.

CHARACTERISTICS OF ARTICLE 11

Work is a basic element of the human condition and an organizing principle of human societies. The right to work is a human right based on the dignity of each person as already expressed in the Universal Declaration of Human Rights (UDHR) and later in the International Covenant on Economic, Social and Cultural Rights (ICESCR, 1966).[1] Economic empowerment of persons usually derives from the fruit of their labor. Throughout history and in all regions of the world, women have always *worked*, but their efforts have been obstructed, exploited, nonrecognized, or undervalued both in the "productive" and in the "reproductive" spheres of the formal/informal labor markets and the family (Bullock 1994, 2). The primary assignment of women to work in the private sphere of the family has usually resulted in severe consequences for them with respect to their equality with men in access to opportunities and treatment in the formal and informal labor markets, including income. Even today, such discrimination has not been overcome in practice. In addition, women's work in the family remains largely invisible, is not accounted for in gross national products, and does *not* give women economic empowerment. Even when women are economically active in the labor market they are expected also to fulfill family obligations.

Article 11 of the CEDAW Convention specifically clarifies women's human right to nondiscrimination and equality in the area of employment. In doing so it incorporates some of the nondiscrimination and protection provisions of the Conventions of the International Labour Organization (ILO), which were in force at the time when the CEDAW Convention was drafted.[2] In a detailed way, Article 11 gives a clear picture of many forms of work-related discrimination against women, which should be eliminated by States Parties through "all appropriate measures." Thus, women are to exercise and enjoy equally with men the right to work in general and to choose a profession or a specific employment in particular. Women have a right to equal employment opportunities in training and retraining; to equal criteria with regard to recruitment, pay, promotion, job conditions and security, and benefits. Women should be able to exercise rights to aspects of social security and of health and safety protection in working conditions, including the "safeguarding of the function of reproduction" (Article 11 [1] [a–f]). Of great importance is that equal pay is guaranteed for "work of equal value," and that "equality of treatment in the evaluation of the quality of work" must be ensured (Article 11 [1] [d]), thus pointing to the fact that sex-segregated labor markets cause indirect wage discrimination against women in female-dominated sectors, because their work is valued less than work in male-dominated sectors.

The concept of women's equality encompasses both identical treatment or opportunities and *nonidentical* treatment and opportunities due to reasons of women's pregnancy and maternity (Article 11 [2] [a–b, d]). Protective legislation, however, must not become an obstacle and, therefore, must be reviewed on a regular basis in order to have it "revised, repealed or extended as necessary" (Article 11 [3]). Article 11 must also be seen in relation with almost all other parts and articles of the Convention. For example, it builds on the Preamble of the Convention and on Articles 5 (a) and (b) by referring to *parents'*—not solely women's—need to balance family obligations with work responsibilities and participation in public life and to receive support from society, so that States Parties are "encouraged" to provide such relevant social support services as child-care facilities (Article 11 [2] [c]). Read in conjunction with Articles 1–3 and 24, it is obvious that Article 11 prohibits both direct and indirect discrimination in employment by public and private employers. Such discrimination must be punished and remedied through competent tribunals and public institutions. Provisions for pregnancy/maternity protection are reinforced by Article 4 (2). Nonidentical treatment of women encompasses also *corrective* measures of assistance (Article 4 [1], General Recommendations Nos. 5, 23, and 25) and implies the adoption of preferential treatment and enabling conditions on a temporary basis as *necessary* strategies for States Parties to *accelerate* the achievement of this goal and to overcome the effect of past discrimination against women as a group (Schöpp-Schilling 2003, 17–18).[3]

So far, the Committee has not produced a full interpretation of Article 11. Only four short general recommendations relate to specific aspects of its norms (General Recommendations Nos. 9, 13, 16, 17), while at least five others address additional facets.[4] The Beijing Platform for Action's section on "women and the economy" spells out detailed steps to be undertaken by States in the implementation of Article 11 (United Nations 1995a, paras. 178–80), and Goal No. 3 of the Millennium Development Goals engages UN member States' commitment to gender equality and women's empowerment, through increasing women's share in wage employment in the nonagricultural sector (United Nations 2000a).

IMPLEMENTATION OF ARTICLE 11 IN SOCIALIST COUNTRIES IN CENTRAL AND EASTERN EUROPE

The socialist model of emancipation according to Marx and Engels saw women's subordination as a subcontradiction of the major contradiction between capital and labor. Once the latter was solved through socialism, women's emancipation would automatically follow. Thus, from a philosophical and human rights point of view, women's equal rights with men did not seem to have a status of their own, but their achievement was connected to and dependent on the abolition of the exploitation of labor. In the twentieth century, various socialist countries of Eastern and Central Europe—the former Union of Soviet Socialist Republics (USSR) and those forced by her directly or indirectly into socialism after World War II—pursued a centrally-planned economy within a socialist political, economic, and social framework of "peoples' democracies" controlled by their respective communist parties.[5]

The Cold War also included an ideological conflict among its opponents—with practical implications for the peoples of the respective countries—about what human rights to emphasize and to implement. Thus, socialist countries pointed to their achievements in the guarantee and fulfillment of the economic, social, and cultural rights of their populations, and tended to be silent about their sometimes also formal, but mostly practical lack of respect—in various forms and to different degrees—for the civil and political rights of their peoples. Or, if they acknowledged that lack at all, they tended to justify it by different interpretations of such rights within the socialist ideology or by unfortunate developmental steps in the achievement of socialism. In 1993, after the demise of socialism in Europe and in reacting to such notions, the UN World Conference on Human Rights in Vienna reaffirmed the universality, indivisibility, and interdependence of all human rights, which should be treated in a fair and equal manner so that one set of rights could not be implemented without the others (United Nations 1993b, 30, para. 5).

States Parties' reports from socialist countries dominated in the early years of the Committee's work, since those countries rapidly ratified the CEDAW Convention. Not only did those countries believe that they fully complied with the Convention—which they undoubtedly did in almost all aspects of women's *formal* equality with men; they also were convinced, as were the Committee's experts coming from these countries, that their laws and equality policies as well as the nature of their reports under Article 18 of the Convention could serve as "models" for other countries (United Nations 1989b).[6]

In the area of education girls and women enjoyed equal access to and equal opportunities at all levels with boys and men. With national variations, women in these countries were totally or almost totally integrated into the paid labor force within contexts of full employment policies, planned, executed, and controlled by the state. While women did not reach economic decision-making powers at the same rate as men, their numbers were often higher than in nonsocialist industrialized countries in Western Europe. If *direct* discrimination against women occurred, women had access to tribunals, labor inspectorates, and courts, and trade unions were supposed to support them in the submission of their complaints.

Nevertheless, in most countries a sharp gender-based segmentation in vocational, technical, and academic training, and consequently in the labor market persisted. Women dominated in the administrative, health, and cultural employment sectors, in light industry, and in certain agricultural tasks, though they could also be found in high numbers in the judiciary. While women and men received the same wages and benefits when working in the same sector, women (and the few men) in employment sectors dominated by women received lower wages than men (and the few women), who worked in those sectors dominated by men. States never analyzed the productive value of the work done in male and female dominated sectors and never raised questions about whether gender-based assumptions might underlie wage structures.

The integration of women into the productive sector was closely allied with a focus on protecting employed women who were *mothers*. But laws and policies as well as beliefs, attitudes, and behavior, as manifested in institutions and expressed by individuals, lacked equivalent attention on employed men who were *fathers*, although this is stipulated by several articles of the Convention. Women's biological birthing and nursing required protection. In addition, these biological factors allegedly translated into certain psychological characteristics, and thus into sex-segregated roles, which also needed to be recognized. Women continued to be viewed as primary caretakers of children and the elderly in the family. Thus, protective measures went far beyond the special protection needed by women "during pregnancy in types of work proved to be harmful to them" and in the form of maternity leave "with pay or with comparable social benefits without loss of former employment, seniority or social allowances" as requested in Article 11 (2) (d, b). Protective measures also covered mothers of small children with respect to termination, overtime work, and business trips. Women also enjoyed earlier retirement ages than men due to a recognition of their double or even triple burden of work in employment, the family, and in the community and an expectation that, in their later years, they would take over the needs of younger women in their families for child care. At the same time, an extensive network of social and educational services for children, including full-day or all-week-day crèches, kindergartens, after-school care facilities, and organized vacations were created in order to allow employed mothers full commitment to employment activities.

These policies of socialist countries clearly influenced the formulation of several provisions of the Convention. While it was the USSR, to whom credit must be given for introducing an extensive list of rights to be covered under Article 11 supported by other socialist countries, the USSR also insisted on detailed protective provisions for women throughout the discussion of the various drafts of the Preamble and this Article (Rehof 1993, 32–36, 124–26).

THE GERMAN DEMOCRATIC REPUBLIC

The initial report of the GDR—the country second to ratify the Convention in 1980—was delivered on time and was the first report ever discussed by the Committee. The discussion clearly demonstrated all the aspects outlined above (United Nations 1989b, 72–79 and 115–22).

With respect to women's access to paid employment, the GDR could show in 1983 that 87 percent of all women of working age were gainfully employed; 99.2 percent of women, who had left school early and had not gone on to higher educational institutions, underwent vocational training. Vocational training for women was possible up until the age of thirty-five, even at the workplace; 79.4 percent of rural women, all working in collective farms, had completed vocational training. Girls constituted over 70 percent of the enrollments in technical and engineering schools. Almost 50 percent of the participants in adult education were women. Women held approximately half of the managerial posts in all sectors of society and one sixth of such posts in industry and agriculture, though at the highest levels, they were far less visible.[7]

The GDR did not aim merely at "meeting the formal statistical requirements of equality for women by establishing certain quotas," but wanted to "to create the conditions necessary for enabling women, through education and training, to do the same work as men and to achieve the same or better results" (United Nations 1989b, 115). For the government representative quality did not mean giving preference to one sex or the other, but to entrust a given task to the person who could perform it best. In contrast to this denial of preferential treatment according to Article 4 (1), the head of the GDR delegation nevertheless pointed out that the promotion of women was ensured through respective plans at factories and institutions. Such plans were part of collective agreements, drawn up on an annual basis between trade unions and management. A special plan existed to train one thousand female college graduates for managerial positions by 1990, with precisely defined promotion schedules and the support of a mentorship system.

Extensive protection existed for employed pregnant women and for mothers. A pregnant woman was not permitted to do work that could be detrimental to her health or that of the fetus. Transfer to another job, due to her condition, guaranteed her former pay; night work and overtime work were forbidden to her. Expectant mothers and mothers of small children could not be refused access to employment, nor could they be dismissed until a child was one year old; single mothers and fathers could not be dismissed until a child was three years old. Additional legislation protected women from health hazards and jobs involving lifting or carrying heavy objects.

In Committee discussion, it became obvious that existing ideology, legislation, and practice identified working women as being responsible also for family work. As such they were specially protected through the Constitution and through the Labor Code. Working fathers received similar attention only in some instances when they had no wives. The representative acknowledged that women's emancipation in the home ultimately was possible only through the emancipation of both sexes and that remaining traditions would need to be examined in this respect.

Existing measures designed to alleviate the double burden of working mothers included one day of paid leave per month for all married women, mothers with young children, and single women over the age of forty, to enable them to do their domestic chores; and a reduction of the weekly working-time at full pay for employed mothers with two or more young children. After the biological maternity leave, mothers could take unpaid leave until a child's first birthday; in the case of a second or subsequent child the leave would be supported by 75 to 90 percent of the net average wage. If the leave was extended, there was a job guarantee until the third birthday of a child. Since the representative repeatedly stressed the rising birthrate, one Committee member inquired whether such policies friendly to women were motivated by population considerations rather than equality concerns. Mothers also were supported by an extensive network of child care. Sixty-one percent of children spent their days in a crèche, while almost all young children attended all-day kindergartens.

Committee members' questions about equal pay for work of equal value were not answered. However, Committee members from nonsocialist countries weren't responded to either when they pointed to the contradiction between existing legislation and practices protecting employed mothers and the Convention's goals of having men share family responsibilities in order to achieve the basis for women's substantive equality.

The discussion of the GDR's second periodic report in 1989 highlighted progress in some areas covered under Article 11, both with respect to infrastructure support to employed mothers and a first legal recognition of the responsibilities of all working fathers in childrearing (United Nations 1989d, 1-12). The percentage of women of working age in employment, training, or studying had increased to 91 percent. A *paid* maternity leave of one year with job guarantee, following the biologically induced maternity leave, had been introduced, which could now also be taken by the *husband* or grandmother. Eighty-one percent of children under the age of three could find places in crèches, and all children of pre-school age could go to kindergarten, with 94 percent of parents taking advantage of these facilities.

While the division of labor within the family was still predominantly sex-specific with women spending more time on domestic work than men, there was an increase in time spent in joint childrearing activities, and fathers were more inclined to take paid leave to care for their sick child(ren). The State recognized the persistence of "ideological barriers and outdated family traditions and customs" which, together with deficiencies in the service sector to support working mothers, also translated into women holding only one in three executive positions. This was seen both as an achievement and a problem. At the same time, it was pointed out that problems with respect to looking after children, which arose in families with both spouses in such positions, "were personal and individual and could not be solved by government decree."

While occupational segregation and the wage gap still existed, the representative claimed that it should be credited to the strenuous nature of physical labor. Women were encouraged to study microelectronics and computer science in the form of in-service training with full pay, accounting for 40 percent of those undergoing such training, in order to upgrade their work in female-dominated sectors. Great efforts were being made to increase the number of male students in the educational sciences, since teaching, while currently dominated by women, was considered a responsibility of both sexes. The right to equal pay for work of equal value was considered a basic right, laid down by the Constitution. However, it was not fully implemented as had been recognized by the GDR Supreme Court and trade unions. The delegation was eager to receive advice from the Committee in this respect (United Nations 1989d, 3, para. 9; 7, para. 31; 11, paras. 51-52; 11-12, para. 58).

IMPLEMENTATION OF ARTICLE 11 IN WESTERN INDUSTRIALIZED COUNTRIES

After WWII, industrialized countries in Western Europe followed either liberal or welfare-oriented market economies within the context of democratic parliamentary political systems that allowed for a plurality of political parties of all orientations, including conservative, liberal, social democratic, socialist, and communist parties. The European Convention for the Protection of Human Rights and Fundamental Freedoms, a regional manifestation of the civil and political rights as expressed in the UDHR, had been adopted as early as 1950 by the Council of Europe and signed by its member States, including Sweden and the FRG, to be discussed in this essay.[8] Constitutions and other legislation guaranteed equal rights to men and women and prohibited discrimination. Usually no legal obligation demanded that women work outside the home; however, for many years and with national variations, married middle-class women were strongly expected to become homemakers at least when they became mothers. Such expectations also controlled their educational aspirations. In the FRG this perspective on women also manifested itself in an insufficient number of child-care institutions. However, as the Committee learned from the various reports of these countries and the ensuing discussions with government delegations, their responses were sometimes based on a commitment to equality goals per se, or they were driven by respective party ideologies, or by economic or population needs.

Sweden

Sweden, the first country to ratify the Convention in 1980, was the subject of discussion at the Committee's second session in 1983. Committee members then learned about a concept of equality that differed decisively in one aspect from those encountered in discussions with socialist countries: this one involved men as well as women.

During the first part of the twentieth century in Sweden, formal legal equality between men and women in the labor market and as spouses and parents had been more or less established. In the 1960s, however, women's right to pursue paid employment in practice still depended, as elsewhere, on their willingness and ability to carry the double burden of work and family. In addition, the labor market was heavily sex-segregated. In 1959, a woman journalist had posed the question, radical at that time, why this double burden was not being carried by men, too. The ensuing discussion about sex roles in general and men's roles in particular, including the one-sided socialization of boys and girls respectively, led to a paradigm shift in the thinking of women's groups, trade unions and political parties. In 1968, when responding to a UN request to report on the status of women, Sweden presented its concept of the dual roles for both sexes and stated the need "to abolish the conditions which tend to assign certain privileges, obligations or rights to men. No decisive change in the distribution of functions and status as between the sexes can be achieved if the duties of the male in society are assumed *a priori* to be unaltered" (Dahlström 1971, 213). A holistic approach toward achieving equality of women and men in practice would pursue legal and policy changes in the areas of education, family, support services to families, social insurance, taxation, and the labor market (Dahlström 1971, 211–302).

Consequently, during the discussion of the various drafts of the Convention text, Sweden, together with the other Scandinavian countries, continuously emphasized the need for changes also in men's lives, the mutual responsibility of spouses for sharing family obligations and the protection against health hazards for both sexes. [9] Following this line of thought, the Swedish representatives criticized the CEDAW Convention in its initial report as confining itself to the elimination of discrimination against women only and not including a wider approach to sexual equality with measures affecting forms of discrimination against men as well, which still existed in Sweden and elsewhere (United Nations 1989b, 134). In her introduction to the discussion with the Committee, the Swedish Government representative stated that "equality between the sexes, which meant that men and women enjoyed the same rights and the same opportunities for personal development, affected all aspects of social life and was based on the practice of a profession and financial independence" (United Nations 1989b, 127). Since the late 1970s, in Sweden, various components of a national machinery, at ministerial levels, had been created in order to ensure the implementation of the Convention in practice. An Equal Opportunities Commission had been established and mandated to examine complaints regarding discrimination. Equality policies were also pursued through a special Equal Opportunities Act and a corresponding comprehensive Equality Plan.[10] The persistence of sex-role stereotypes in all forms and at all levels of education was countered through mandatory equal curricula for both sexes, textbook revision, and teacher training. Regarding the labor market, the Equality Plan aimed to address the sex-specific segmentation through the abolition of male and female job classifications, measures geared to both sexes with respect to their career choices, and preferential vocational training of the underrepresented sex. Furthermore, the Plan was directed toward eliminating wage differences; shortening of working hours; improving the conditions of part-time workers; and encouraging women homemakers to take up employment. Women's currently higher unemployment rate was countered with training and retraining. Regional development assistance with respect to the creation of new jobs had been coupled with quota regulations of 40 percent for either sex.

An innovative approach concerning the sharing of family responsibilities through the introduction of a paid *parental* leave after the birth of a child was not only connected with efforts directed at changing male attitudes and behavior as well as with new patterns of working structures and working time in paid employment, but also with policies for equalizing wages between men and women. The latter goal had been more or less achieved by raising the lower wage and salary scales, which included predominantly women. Parental leave was available for either parent with 90 percent of his or her salary for the first nine months and a fixed allowance for the last three months. The representative admitted that, although a survey had revealed that both Swedish men and women felt that men should devote more time to their children and to household chores, only 10 percent of fathers had availed themselves of parental leave in 1980. After its expiration, either parent could request a shortening of the work day to six hours until a child reached the age of eight. A parent who stayed home to care for a child until the age of three remained eligible to participate in pension schemes. While child-care institutions were considered an important part of equality policies and plans existed to expand them, currently available facilities did not meet the demand. In general, the Swedish representative concluded that, although the right equality policy was in place, it still had a long way to go to be fully implemented.

A number of Committee members pointed out that some forms of discrimination obviously still existed in Sweden in practice, and a few were dissatisfied with a lack of data. More information on men availing themselves of the privileges now available to both sexes was requested in future reports (United Nations 1989b, 133–39, 148).

In the presentation of its second periodic report in 1988 (United Nations 1988a, 2–10, paras. 2–46; United Nations 1988b, 3–4, paras. 8–15), the government representative pointed out that while the State aimed at providing a policy framework for equality, which would allow each man and woman to make his or her own choices as to education, profession, and division of work in the home, the framework also included a recognition of the labor market as one of the most important paths to women's equality. At the same time, policies directed toward the labor market, the family, and equality had to be viewed as being closely interrelated.

Since the initial report, additional progress in implementing the Convention could be noticed, while in some areas not much change had taken place. In 1987, 90 percent of women between the ages of twenty-five and fifty-five were in the labor force as compared to 93 percent of men within a context of a full-employment policy for both sexes. Wage differentials had been further decreased through trade union activism, in which women had increased their participation. A problem, however, was the increasing number of women as compared to men, who worked part-time on an involuntary basis, though those employed part-time for at least seventeen hours enjoyed the same labor rights as a full-time employee. Sex-segregation in the study of certain university disciplines, in vocational training, and in the labor market persisted and translated into a remaining wage gap. Sexual harassment at the workplace had been studied and was now considered a work environment issue, for which employers were to provide appropriate physical and psychological safeguards. Parental leave would be extended from twelve to eighteen months at the beginning of the 1990s, and as of 1991, child-care facilities were planned to cover all children from eighteen months of age whose parents worked or studied. Nevertheless, the representative admitted that despite all policy efforts to engage men in family work, women still bore the main burden though they had some relief in the form of supportive institutions.

Federal Republic of Germany

The Basic Law (Constitution) of the FRG of 1949 had stipulated the equality of men and women and the prohibition of discrimination on the basis of sex. However, amendments to laws took place incrementally and with delay due to a long-term reign of conservative parties and the influence of the Catholic Church. In 1959 the Constitutional Court declared the law giving fathers the last word in matters relating to their children as unconstitutional. This right had been upheld in the First Equal Opportunities Act only two years earlier after a heated discussion. While unmarried women, war widows, and working class women pursued employment because of financial necessity, the dominant ideology of women as homemakers, in particular when they became mothers, persisted for the middle class. This ideology manifested itself in a school system with irregular school hours for younger children ending generally at noon when children would expect to be served their main meal of the day at home and supervised by their mothers as they did homework. It also translated into a tax system favoring married couples with only one spouse employed, whether or not there were children.

By 1985, when the FRG ratified the Convention with one reserva-tion,[11] a strong autonomous women's movement that had been active since 1968 questioned the traditional division of labor and lobbied for new equality policies and institutions. Equal opportunity institutions at the federal, the *Länder*, and the municipal levels had been created, although only in one *Land* out of eleven had municipal offices of equality been for-mally instituted. In addition, some political parties had successfully intro-duced a quota system to increase the number of women in parliaments at the three governmental levels. All political parties were exerting some effort to raise the number of women in political representation.

For a number of reasons, the FRG's initial report had not been pre-pared until 1988. The Committee discussed it in January 1990 as well as an amendment that had become necessary due to the availability of new census data and the fact that the country was dealing with the impact of the fall of the Berlin Wall. The Federal Minister for Women's Affairs explained that while legal equality between men and women existed, many examples of discrimination against women could be found in prac-tice. Women constituted 39 percent of the employed population, most of them in the service sector and almost one third part-time. Part-time workers enjoyed the same benefits as full-time workers if they worked above a specified number of hours per week. Unemployment affected women more than men, due to the large number of women re-entering the labor market and their request for part-time employment.

The nondiscrimination provisions of the employment contract law in the Civil Code, which had been introduced on the basis of the 1975 and 1976 European Union Directives, were to be amended following the court verdicts of the ECJ that such remedies, which women were to receive in cases of discrimination, had to be higher than the original law had foreseen in order to make the law effective. Protective legislation for women was under review and would be repealed, revised, or extended to both sexes so that only six occupations would remain closed to women for reasons of health. Women's average gross income was lower than men's. Indirect wage discrimination possibly still existed in those categories of work predominantly performed by women that had be characterized as "light work." A court verdict that *all* factors, not only the amount of physical strength required, had to be taken into account when evaluating work and setting wages needed to be translated into the wage structure by the autonomous employers' associations and trade unions. The high-level representative of the FRG expressed her skepticism with respect to quota regulations in the labor market and in politics, despite the low number of women in higher positions. Still, the government encouraged private employers to apply temporary special measures on a voluntary basis, while in the federal public sector, binding guidelines on such measures had been introduced, and in some *Länder* a legal basis had been created for preferential treatment of women in the public sector.

A child-rearing leave of ten months with job guarantee had been introduced in 1985 for employed mothers *or* fathers and extended in 1988. During that period a child-rearing allowance conceived as a flat fee was paid to the parent taking the leave, which became means-tested after the seventh month. Only 2 percent of fathers availed themselves of the leave. Part-time work was permitted during the leave. Crèches and kindergartens existed in insufficient numbers, availability varied in the regions, and kindergartens rarely offered full-time places.

Various legal provisions recognized women's work in the family, including the payment of the child-rearing allowance also to women who were homemakers at the birth of the child; the recognition of child-rearing and home-nursing years in the statutory pension schemes; [12] employed women's right to earlier retirement than men, as justified by a Constitutional Court verdict about women's double burden; re-entry programs for women into the labor market after a child-rearing phase with recognition of these years in their legal claim for special retraining opportunities under the Employment Promotion Act; reflection of the value of homemakers' work in national statistics. Committee members noted the frankness of the report, and also their concerns about the low representation of women in decision-making positions in politics, the absence of men sharing family work, the traditional career choices of young girls, and the low number of child-care facilities (United Nations 1990a, 2–14, paras. 2–85; United Nations 1990b, 8–24, paras. 54–142).

IMPACT OF THE TRANSFORMATION OF SOCIALIST SOCIETIES ON WOMEN'S EMPLOYMENT

The political, economic, and social transformations of the former socialist countries in Central and Eastern Europe following 1989 had a severe impact on women's exercise and enjoyment of their human rights in employment. Globalization created additional difficulties. Jobs disappeared as a number of heavy and light industries closed, as agriculture became more mechanized, and as overemployment in public administration could no longer be maintained. The fact that these countries had never officially questioned the traditional division of labor between men and women in the family and that protective legislation for working women and mothers remained strong now became major negative influences on women's equal opportunities in the newly emerging private labor markets under neoliberal or welfare-state oriented governments.

States Parties' reports to the CEDAW Committee, submitted by these countries and alternative reports provided by nongovernmental organizations (NGOs) in the 1990s and in the first years of the twenty-first century have indicated, that, while both men and women have been affected by unemployment, usually young women of child-bearing age have especially experienced difficulties in finding work and have remained unemployed for longer periods than men. Prejudices have also turned against older women in labor markets, for whom retraining opportunities are not sufficiently available. While nondiscriminatory legal systems are still in place, they are not adhered to by newly emerging private employers, and women, whose rights have been violated, no longer turn to courts. Support structures, including child-care facilities, have either decreased or become expensive. Pensions are low in general and for women, due to their earlier retirement age and their concentration in lower wage sectors, even lower, and women's previous opportunities to keep on working while drawing pensions no longer exist.

Developments in the territory of the former GDR, which, after unification of the two German States, now exists as five "new" *Länder* of the FRG, took a slightly different turn. Several factors modified the negative impact of the economic transition on women. First, the systems of social welfare, labor market promotion, health care, and pensions of the FRG immediately functioned in the new *Länder*, supported with funds from the old *Länder*. In addition, economic transformation and development were heavily subsidized through West German funds. Second, the GDR in its last months of existence had adopted the institutional equal opportunities machinery at all political levels, which had also existed in the FRG. Some of the existing or newly emerging political parties had followed their West German counterparts in adopting numerical goals or quota systems for women's political representation, thus achieving a fairly good political representation of women in parliaments at all levels. The newly established regional and local labor market boards also had to institute equal opportunities officers since they also existed in such boards in the old *Länder*.

All these factors contributed to an effective monitoring of the implementation of the quota regulations in training, retraining, and allocation to public work job schemes for unemployed women as well as of a number of other issues, including the maintenance of child-care facilities, financed by the federal German budget for five months, as agreed in the Unification Act. In addition, this Act stipulated that the German State was to develop equal opportunity legislation as well as legislation to improve the compatibility of employment and family work. As a result, women in unified Germany fought for and achieved an amendment to the German Constitution that can be interpreted as an obligation for the application of temporary special measures. In addition, a legal claim for a child-care place when children reach the age of three years was introduced, as well as improved equal opportunities legislation covering the public labor market sector (Schöpp-Schilling 1995, 27–40).[13]

Thus, the realization in practice of certain economic and social rights by women in the GDR within the context of the socialist economy described above undoubtedly influenced new law and policy formulation in the economic and social sphere for *all* German women during the unification process itself and in the resulting unified Germany. While unification gave women of the former GDR gains in the real exercise of their civil and political rights, these new laws and policies in the economic and social fields as well as their practical implementation fell short of what they had previously experienced, while for women in the old *Länder* of the FRG they certainly led to an improved situation. Also, by adapting to the FRG's tax and school systems, former GDR women now had to accept institutions that reinforced sex-role stereotypes. At the same time, the negative impact of the transformation from a socialist to a free market economy, which women in all former socialist countries had to face, was softened for East German women by the fact that the FRG market economy has strong welfare-state features and by the establishment of new equal-opportunity structures in the new *Länder*. The CEDAW Committee, when considering the second and third combined periodic report of Germany as well as its fourth and fifth reports in 2000 and 2004 voiced concerns about a persistent wage gap; women's higher unemployment rate particularly in the new *Länder*; women's higher participation in part-time jobs in general; and about a lack of temporary special measures in the private labor market. The Committee also clearly and repeatedly questioned Germany about the persistence of sex-role stereotypes, their manifestations in women's significantly higher participation in (unprotected) part-time jobs; in the allocation of school hours; the lack of child-care facilities in the old *Länder*; and the design of parental leave with little pay, which actually discouraged fathers from taking it. The Committee also requested the government to analyze the impact on women of new health, pension, and labor market reforms, which did not seem to take into account the realities of women's lives as expressed in their patchwork employment careers due to family obligations (CEDAW 2000, 31, para. 307 ; 32–33, paras. 311–16; CEDAW 2004a, 65, para. 384; 66, paras. 388, 392).

CONCLUSION

The countries discussed above show *models* for a typology that contains different ideologies, policies, and strategies used by different governmental, political, and economic systems to create a nondiscriminatory framework for women's work inside and outside the home. Undoubtedly, other variations might be found in other parts of the world. But as the CEDAW Committee's review process over time demonstrates, what does not vary is the persistence and longevity of sex-role stereotypes for women and men. Closely connected to women's biological potential for birthing and nursing, such stereotypes continue to create unequal opportunities, treatment, and results for women's activities in the labor market. Modern methods of contraception theoretically, and in Western Europe also in practice, allow European women to decide "freely and responsibly on the number and spacing of their children" (Article 16 [1] [e]). This new reproductive freedom, however, has not yet fully translated into the sharing of family work as required by the Convention, which is a prerequisite for women's equality with men in the labor market. In the three types of countries considered here, sex segregation of the labor market both horizontally and vertically as well as between the public and private sectors has persisted. Wage gaps have continued to be a problem based on hidden value factors influencing setting wages for women's labor.

The transformations of socialist countries exposed the persistence of patriarchal role models and power systems, despite much progressive legislation and the implementation of women's economic and social rights. States Parties' reports from Sweden and other Nordic countries testify to the intransigence of traditional sex-role aspirations and behavior, as well as to the durability of power relations between men and women even when an official dual role policy is in place with important changes in family law, taxation, education, employment, and the creation of a service infrastructure.

The FRG, despite having instituted a legal and institutional framework for equality, continues to struggle even more with the remnants of the traditional image of women as homemakers, manifested in welfare and tax systems, school hours, and lack of child-care institutions, although the majority of younger women of all social strata want to combine employment and rearing children without any or only brief interruptions of their careers. The sixth periodic report of the FRG to CEDAW, due in 2006, will show new policies regarding parental leave arrangements including payments as a proportion of the *real* income of fathers or mothers, and the creation of child-care institutions for children under the age of three.

The innovative feature of the CEDAW Convention requesting the modification of "social and cultural patterns of conduct of men and women" based on "the idea of the inferiority or the superiority of either of the sexes" or on "stereotyped roles" for them, and stipulating "recognition of the common responsibility of men and women in the upbringing and development of their children" (Article 5 [a] and [b]) has proven most difficult to implement, although that goal is imperative not only with respect to the implementation of the Convention as a whole, but also with respect to women's employment rights under Article 11. It is high time for the Committee to address itself to the interpretation of these articles in general recommendations.[14] At the same time, individual women as well as women's human rights organizations should explore opportunities under the communication and inquiry procedures of the Convention's Optional Protocol to bring to the Committee's attention violations of women's rights in the labor market in general as well as because of institutional manifestations of sex-role stereotyping.

NOTES

I thank Dörte Doering and Heiner Bielefeldt for commenting on an earlier version of this essay.

1. Article 23 of the UDHR, which can be considered legally binding from the point of view of international customary law, is formulated in male language and from a predominantly male point of view, identifying *men* as breadwinners. The Declaration gives everyone the right to work; to free choice of employment; to just and favorable conditions of work and protection against unemployment; the right to equal pay for equal work without discrimination; to just and favorable remuneration to ensure for "himself and his family" an existence worthy of human dignity, and supplemented by means of social protection, if necessary; the right to form and join trade unions for the protection of "his" interests. Articles 6 and 7 of the ICESCR made the provisions of the UDHR, related to the right to work, legally binding as a human rights treaty and enforced the norm that all such rights must be exercised and enjoyed without discrimination on any grounds, including sex, in two additional articles.

2. No. 103, Maternity Protection Convention (1952, revised the earlier Convention of 1919); Equal Remuneration Convention No. 100 (equal remuneration of men and women workers for work of equal value, 1951); Discrimination (Employment and Occupation) Convention No. 111 (forbidding discrimination in respect to employment and occupation, 1958). In addition, there were a number of Conventions protecting women workers.

3. Obligations of States Parties under additional articles also contain the basis for overcoming the public/private divide in work allocation for both sexes. Of particular importance is the Convention's call for the elimination of women's subordination to men and their discrimination in decision-making in family planning and public and political life.

Women's equal rights with men to nationality rights; education; access to health care services and economic and social life; in the rural areas, before the law as well as in all other family matters are relevant, too, for the exercise of their rights under Article 11 (Articles 5 [a]) and 5 [b], 16 [e]), 7–16).

4. General Recommendations Nos. 9, 13, 16, and 17 highlight the need for sex-segregated data, implementation of the principle of equal pay for work of equal value, recognition of the unpaid work of women in rural and urban family enterprises, recognition and quantification of women's unpaid family work in the gross national product. General Recommendations Nos. 24, 12, 19, 21, 23 elaborate on such aspects as safety in working conditions, including sexual harassment; and women's economic dependence on men due to their relegation to the domestic sphere, which also results in their lack of influence in the political sphere.

5. I am aware of the variations among socialist realities and practices, due to national or cultural characteristics (religion), previous status of economic and political development and other factors. However, they do not affect the main theses of my argumentation in a major way.

6. Rehof recounts that during the drafting process of the Convention socialist countries pointed out that "discrimination against women had been eliminated in their countries" (Rehof 1993, 36). In addition, numerous examples of the same view can be found in the summary records of the second session both in the discussion of the various States Parties' reports and in the Committee's discussion of its own report for that session (United Nations 1989b, 61–228).

7. It has to be pointed out today, that, according to the Constitution of the GDR, everybody was obliged to be engaged in paid work. The necessity of rebuilding the country after WWII as well as of compensating for the constant population drain to the FRG before the Wall was built, reinforced this requirement and the commitment of every able-bodied person, male or female. The 1968 Constitution of the GDR contained the stipulation that the advancement of women, in particular their occupational qualification, was an obligation of society and state.

8. Article 14 of this Convention prohibits discrimination based on sex and a number of other grounds in relation to the rights contained in the Convention .

9. Sweden introduced paragraph 14 of the Preamble that points to the need for role changes for both sexes in society and the family (Rehof 1993, 40).

10. The equality plan covered the following areas: institutional mechanisms for promoting equality between the sexes; education and training; working life; family policy and law; housing and community planning; health and social problems; representation; shaping public opinion; international cooperation (United Nations 1989b, 128–32).

11. The FRG had signed the Convention in 1980 in Copenhagen. Due to a change of government in 1982, the process of ratification was delayed until 1985, when it took place with one reservation, concerning Article 7 (b), because the Basic Law (Constitution) of the FRG prohibited women to carry arms in the Federal Armed Forces. This provision was later challenged by a woman in court. When the ECJ decided in her favor, the FRG changed its Basic Law and withdrew the reservation.

12. This provision was valid for men, too, who performed these tasks.

13. The Unification Act also stipulated the adoption of a uniform abortion law, which turned out to be more progressive than the previous one of the former FRG, while it restricted the abortion rights women had enjoyed in the GDR.

14. A Dutch academic, Rikki Holtmaat, laid the ground for an interpretation of Article 5 (a) in her study commissioned by the Dutch Ministry of Social Affairs and Employment (Holtmaat 2004).

PERSONAL REFLECTION:

OPPORTUNITIES AND TRAPS—THE INFORMAL LABOR MARKET

PRAMILA PATTEN, MAURITIUS

It was not long after I joined the Committee in 2003 that I realized that I had earned the reputation of an "Article 11 fanatic." That was mainly because during the examination of States Parties' reports, I regularly posed questions on the situation of women in the informal sector and expressed my concerns about the increase of females in the global workforce in the informal economy and the plight of women who are outside the world of full-time, stable, and protected employment. As a Committee member from the African region, I am very sensitive to the significant number of African women who sustain themselves in a variety of largely traditional activities because they are unable to get "proper" work. Their work in the informal sector is a much larger source of their income security than this sector is for men, and they are numerous in the lowest-paid and most exploited categories of work, namely in small enterprises, in the simplest types of self-employment, as outworkers, in domestic work, and as unpaid family workers. Work in the informal sector comprises 48 percent of non-agricultural work in North Africa, 84 percent in sub-Saharan Africa, and as much as 90 percent of total employment in those countries that include agriculture in their estimates of informal employment (International Labour Organization 2002).

While globalization has created some new job opportunities for women in the formal labor market, it has also led to an expansion of the informal labor sector. Although both men and women work in the informal sector and are both affected by the slow or even negative growth of formal sector employment opportunities, the detrimental effects have been more severe on women. Within the informal economy, women are more often found in work associated with low and unstable earnings and with high risks of poverty. Women in informal work are also often excluded from formal social protection programs.

The concept of the "informal sector" continues to evolve, and its definition also has become more sophisticated, as scholars and international organizations express renewed interest in it. In recent years, a broader definition has been adopted to incorporate the whole dimension of informality, including both enterprise and employment relations

(International Labour Organization 1999). Thus, the informal sector may be described as very small-scale units owned and operated by largely independent, self-employed persons, sometimes also employing family labor or a few hired workers and apprentices. These units produce and distribute goods and services with very little capital and a low level of technology. Work in these enterprises is highly unstable and incomes are generally if not low, certainly irregular.

Although data remain somewhat unreliable, there is consensus that the informal sector is steadily growing in almost all developing countries with women significantly dominating the two largest subgroups of the informal workforce, namely home-based work and street vending. Sixty percent or more women in the developing world work in this informal sector outside agriculture, while in sub-Saharan Africa, the statistic is 84 percent (International Labour Organization 2002). There is also reason to believe that the actual figures are much higher, since women often take on multiple activities, especially in rural areas.

The Committee has not remained indifferent to the situation of women in the informal sector: Its written lists of issues and questions sent to States Parties before consideration of their reports; the oral dialogue with States Parties in the examination of reports; and its concluding comments testify to its concern for the welfare of women in the informal sector. But States Parties' reports often contain very little information about women in the informal sector. States Parties invoke the nonformal organizational structures as well as the diverse activities and modes of operation within them as major impediments to data collection. Traditionally, therefore, informal sector activities in the national accounts of many developing countries are underestimated, based on assumptions of low productivity and income.

Just as Article 10 of the Convention on education, which does not explicitly refer to "informal education," covers both formal and informal education, Article 11, which prohibits discrimination against women in the field of employment, also covers both formal employment and work in the informal sector, although it does not explicitly mention the latter. In addressing the scope of the Convention to protect women in the informal sector, Article 11 must be read in conjunction with other articles of the Convention, including Articles 1 to 5 and 24, which form the general interpretative framework for all of the Convention's substantive articles; Articles 13 and 14, which are key provisions for the promotion of women's economic independence in urban and rural areas; and General Recommendations Nos. 16 and 17 (1991) on the situation of unpaid women workers in rural and urban family enterprises and on the measurement and quantification of the unremunerated domestic activities of women. The concluding comments of the Committee also offer useful guidance on the interpretation of the Convention. Since the mid-1990s, the Committee has regularly addressed the question of women in the informal sector, has demanded statistical data from States Parties, and has made both specific and general recommendations. Nevertheless, there is still room for improvement.

Questions could be raised, for example, about the particular vulnerability of different categories of female informal workers, on social protection entitlements, and on public policy to cover various aspects of their activities. Labor market behavior can never be understood if a major segment of the total workforce is not adequately assessed and measured. Since regulating the informal sector is not an easy task for most States Parties, the Committee could improve its constructive dialogue by highlighting the importance of improved statistics disaggregated by sex and by emphasizing that the informal workforce needs to be recognized by policy makers and government planners to ensure that appropriate policies, institutions, and services are put into place. States Parties should also be questioned about their efforts to create policies that aim to increase economic opportunities for women, to formalize informal work opportunities, and to expand formal employment opportunities.

Finally, the Committee should offer more specific recommendations and improved guidance to States Parties concerning the situation of women working in the informal sector. Although several previous concluding comments contain references to very specific concerns and some recommendations, most of the concerns expressed by the Committee have been of a general nature, namely the concentration and overrepresentation of women in the informal sector, the sex segregation of the formal labor market, and the lack of data on women in both sectors. Although all workers in the informal economy share one thing in common, namely the lack of formal labor and social protection, even within countries, the informal economy is highly sex-segmented by location of work, sector of the economy, and status of the work undertaken. Hence conditions of work and the level of earnings differ markedly for men and for women. It is therefore important that the Committee formulates very specific recommendations directing States Parties to take specific steps to improve working conditions in the informal sector, with particular attention to those segments in which large numbers of women work as casual part-time, temporary, seasonal, home-based, contractual, and domestic workers. By addressing the different categories of women working in the informal sector in a more systematic manner, the Committee can contribute to a State Party's awareness of their precarious situation and consequently to better policies benefiting them.

Because the Convention is a dynamic document, the Committee has been flexible in applying the norms of nondiscrimination and equality to changing international as well as national circumstances and attitudes. Hence, the Committee should endeavor to ensure through its three monitoring procedures—scrutiny of reports, communication, and inquiry procedures—that women benefit from the era of globalization and that their increased participation in the informal labor market empower them. It is time for the Committee to take up the challenge of improving the lives of women in the informal sector so that they no longer remain invisible, unacknowledged, and excluded from the protection and benefits afforded to those male and female workers engaged in formal employment.

THE FEMALE FACE OF MIGRATION

ROSARIO G. MANALO, *PHILIPPINES*

It was while I was the Philippine Ambassador to Brussels in the mid-1980s that I had one of my earliest personal encounters with the "human face" of migration, and—as to be expected in hindsight—it was the face of a woman, a Filipina. Three people paid a call on me at the Embassy that day: the young Filipina, a Belgian man, and a Filipina Catholic nun. Apparently, the young Filipina was under threat of arrest by immigration authorities who had discovered that she had entered the country illegally and under false pretenses. But although it was essentially my young compatriot's problem, her companions were doing most of the talking, or rather, the haranguing—demanding that I, as the ambassador, "do something" to save her from being arrested. When the man, who had obviously had a hand in smuggling her into Belgium, began demanding that the Philippine Government produce the money needed for her airfare back to Manila, I lost my temper. "Shut up!" I told him firmly. Then, turning to the Filipina, I declared that I would talk to her and her alone.

It was only after the Belgian man and the nun left my office that the young woman visibly relaxed and stopped shaking. She admitted to me that, though she had come to Belgium on a tourist visa, she had had the intention all along of working illegally in the country. I assured her that, even though what she had done was illegal, I would do everything I could to prevent her from being arrested. But, I said, I could not accede to the man's demand that the Embassy pay for her airfare, since at that time the Philippine Government had no financial provisions for the repatriation of Filipinos who got into trouble abroad. Instead, with the help of the honorary consul in Antwerp, I managed to secure for her a passage on a ship bound for home. I don't know whatever happened to this young Filipina after that, but I often wonder what her fate would have been if she had not turned up at the Embassy that day.

In the decades since the woman and her companions paid a call on me, I have encountered, in both the diplomatic service as well as in my work with the CEDAW Committee, countless such cases, most of them involving women from poor countries who are either deceived and cheated by unscrupulous recruiters, apprehended by immigration or police officials for illegal entry into foreign countries, or who seek assistance after enduring abuse and exploitation at the hands of foreign employers or even foreign spouses. For many of them, migration is often impelled by economic necessity, a response to poverty and hopelessness, and the search for productive labor and a better life not just for themselves but also for their families. Other women find themselves traveling to foreign lands to join their families or spouses who have established themselves there. Some women migrants are also compelled to leave their countries of origin as refugees, fleeing armed conflict, natural disasters, or even sexual abuse, and placing themselves at the mercy of "receiving" States and international agencies.

Migration has emerged as a major concern of both sending and receiving governments around the globe. However, while the march of people across borders presents new and difficult challenges, receiving governments should see migrants also as a potential source of new energy and creativity. Often, they fuel entrepreneurial activity; sometimes they provide knowledge, skills, and talents that may be needed in the receiving countries; and in all cases, through associating with the nationals of their adopted country, they may expand the world view of these people. At the same time, remittances by overseas workers not only help lift their families back home out of the trap of poverty, but even keep afloat national economies of sending countries. Regardless of whether a country is mainly a "source" of or a "destination" for migrants, most governments have bound themselves to various international legal instruments that should help them to respect and protect the rights and the welfare of these "people on the move." Such instruments include the International Covenant for Civil and Political Rights (ICCPR) and the International Covenant for Social, Economic and Cultural Rights (ICESCR) of 1966, and various Conventions of the International Labour Organization (ILO).[1]

In more recent years this obligation to protect migrant workers was specifically captured in the UN International Convention on the Protection of the Rights of All Migrant Workers and Members of Their Families (ICMW) of 1990, which came into force on July 1, 2003. Unfortunately, the ICMW still has a fairly low number of ratifications, and it has not been ratified by the majority of the industrialized countries that are on the receiving end of migrant workers. In addition, its language is not gender-sensitive, and it does not differentiate between women and men or address human rights violations that may be specific to women migrants.[2] This is unfortunate, since women migrant workers may be discriminated against by employers and governments not only in the same way as men migrant workers, but also, and in addition, because they are women. While they thus may be suffering from multiple forms of discrimination, they are also subject to the lack of explicit recognition of these violations by international law. This is, therefore, where one would expect CEDAW to come in, but even this Convention does not explicitly refer to migrant women, though Article 1 does condemn discrimination in all its forms and in all fields of life, thus opening the way for a specific interpretation of the legal text in consideration of this group of women.

CEDAW AND MIGRANT WOMEN

Aware of the growing impact of migration on women around the world, the CEDAW Committee in 2003 decided to appoint a focal point for migrant women to study how specific provisions of the Convention could be applied to protect and promote their rights. At the time, I was the Committee's Vice-President for the Asia-Pacific region. Since the Philippines is a major "exporter" of migrant women workers, and I was raising questions about precisely this subject in the dialogue of the Committee with government delegations when discussing their States' reports, the post of "focal point" for migrant women fell on me.

When I talked with Lee Waldorf of the United Nations Development Fund for Women (UNIFEM), the Fund's liaison person to the CEDAW Committee, we decided, that though the Convention itself has no specific provision on migrant women, it was not only possible but necessary to work toward creating a general recommendation by the Committee about this group of women, in order to explain to States Parties how they are accountable under CEDAW to respect, protect, and fulfill the human rights of this group of women. According to international law opinion, a general recommendation approved by any of the human rights treaty bodies, including the CEDAW Committee, is to be considered "soft law." Thus, if it elaborates an article in the Convention including its implicit meaning, States Parties will be bound to implement the Convention according to that interpretation in good faith. Lee Waldorf and I therefore decided to undertake the initial step to draft a general recommendation on migrant women if the CEDAW Committee agreed that this work should be done.

In the following sections I will briefly describe the process of formulating and adopting such a general recommendation by the CEDAW Committee that will interpret the Convention as covering the issue of migrant women under various of its articles. I will emphasize the complexity of this process, show how exhaustive are the steps involved, and indicate the seriousness with which Committee experts commit themselves to this work. At the same time, and in order to identify some of the key elements of such a general recommendation while connecting them to the relevant articles of the Convention, I will describe the causes of migration—which often are already a result of discrimination against women forbidden under the Convention—and will outline many of the forms of discrimination migrant women may be subjected to in the migration process.

The Committee itself has laid down some rules in order to formalize the process of formulating general recommendations, which should include a general discussion in the Committee as well as input by UN specialized agencies and by nongovernmental organizations (NGOs). Given the complexity of a general recommendation on migrant women, additional steps had to be added. In August 2004, during the thirty-first session of the Committee in New York, various CEDAW experts decided informally to hold a workshop on the topic during the lunch break of the Committee. Invited to participate were CEDAW experts, non-CEDAW experts on migration, UNIFEM officials, the UN Special Rapporteur on migration,[3] representatives of the International Organization for Migration (IOM),[4] NGOs accredited to the United Nations, officials and staff from the Division for the Advancement of Women (DAW), and State Parties' diplomatic representatives based in New York, among others. The workshop, which produced a very informative and fruitful discussion, convinced the Committee to create a CEDAW Working Group of Experts on Migrant Women to formulate and propose elements for the draft general recommendation on migrant women.[5]

During 2005, this Working Group held three regional meetings—to determine the elements of a draft for a new General Recommendation No. 27 of the Committee in Bangkok in April, Manila in July, and São Paulo in December—all with the full collaboration and support of the regional offices of UNIFEM. The IOM sent non-CEDAW participants who were all experts in migration to the meetings in Bangkok and Manila. In all the regional meetings, NGOs in the countries of the region and from the developed world, academic researchers, and volunteers working for the improvement of the plight of migrants were present, enriching the discussions. Initially, at the meeting in Bangkok, the Working Group decided to include within the coverage of a draft document three categories of migrant women: women employees/workers, refugee women, and women joining their spouses. Eventually, however, this choice of categories was whittled down to two by removing refugee women from the draft, because we realized that the complexity of the situation of refugee women would require a general recommendation all of its own.

SCOPE AND FORMS OF WOMEN'S MIGRATION

Before the Working Group could sit down to craft the wording of the general recommendation, it needed to get as comprehensive and as general a view as possible of the scope and forms of women's migration around the world, and the challenges they faced as workers, family members, exiles, and expatriates. We also felt that we needed to understand the factors that serve to "push" women away from their homelands, even leaving their families behind, while risking their health, dignity, honor, and lives for often dangerous and demeaning work.

Migration—for contract employment, permanent residence and eventually foreign citizenship, family unification or, at its worst, as a result of trafficking—is said to be an offshoot of the globalization of production, the expansion of service sectors, a growing participation of women in the labor force, and aging populations (as well as growing affluence) in many receiving countries. The response to this demand for labor is overwhelming, largely because there is a virtually unlimited supply. Among the push-and-pull factors are: unemployment, large wage differentials between countries, and a web of social networks that encourages and facilitates recruitment and placement.

Unfortunately, many receiving countries have responded by implementing restrictive immigration and labor laws and policies instead of addressing the demand with favorable regulations. Consequently, countries of origin continue to be at a disadvantage, as a large proportion of their labor pool is not accorded appropriate and commensurate compensation by receiving States that could have been provided under the framework of a liberalized global economy. Also, the sending countries, in order to safeguard their women from being trafficked, may deny them the freedom to travel and to seek foreign employment, as was reported by government representatives from Nepal in their constructive dialogue with the Committee.

For the Philippines, the marketing and export of workers has grown from a temporary stopgap measure to address unemployment concerns in the country itself in the 1970s, to an economic strategy not only to provide jobs but also to raise essential revenue in the form of wages sent home. Migrant labor has also been increasingly feminized, with women comprising more that half of all newly-hired Filipino migrant workers since 1993. One need only visit various parks and shopping malls in Hong Kong, Singapore, or Kuala Lumpur on Sundays and mingle among the hundreds of Filipino domestic workers enjoying their day off to realize that women are now the face of Filipino migration.

The Philippines Department of Foreign Affairs continues to receive distressing reports of both female and male Filipinos overseas being severely maltreated in one way or another. Filipina migrant workers are forced into prostitution, cheated of their wages (including benefits), or made to work under subhuman conditions without opportunity or time to participate in recreational activities, which are all forms of discrimination forbidden under Articles 6, 11 and 13 of the Convention. Such situations happen mainly because many overseas Filipino workers remain unprotected by laws in both their home country and in their country of employment. In some countries, the Convention has not been incorporated into domestic law and thus does not have the power to protect women. Often, specific domestic laws do not even exist, or, if they exist, they are not effectively implemented. Many employers abroad have devised various schemes to abuse and exploit migrant workers in general, and women migrant workers in particular, all in violation of both the ICESCR, the ICMW, and CEDAW. In extreme cases, the victims return home physically and emotionally brutalized—or even dead. The sad reality is that these situations have become so commonplace that the world community seems to accept them as routine and unremarkable.

Just this year (2006), a Filipina domestic worker returned from Jordan paralyzed from the neck down after sustaining a severe spinal cord injury. Jennifer Perez, 24, had been working in the home of her Jordanian employer for just a day when she fell or was pushed from a second-floor balcony. Jennifer allegedly told friends and relatives that she had been pushed by her female employer, who in turn maintained her innocence and refused to pay for Jennifer's hospital bills. Jennifer's father was finally able to fly to Jordan to see his daughter, after the mayor in their hometown had sought help from the Government. But after eight months of treatment and seeing no signs of improvement, her father decided to bring Jennifer home. She died less than a month after her homecoming. Jennifer's fate is perhaps even more tragic than other cases where the migrant worker has come home traumatized, injured, or dead, since she had not earned even a dollar from her job, and had had to endure eight months of pain before dying from her injuries. Clearly, the problems confronting migrant women like her need solutions that go beyond laws or haphazard diplomacy to improve their situation.

Sex Trafficking

A particularly ugly feature of the feminine face of migration is sex trafficking, which is prohibited under many international laws including

Article 6 of CEDAW. Taking advantage of women desperately in search of jobs and better opportunities, illegal recruiters and international criminal syndicates prey upon their ignorance and innocence to lure, entrap, or deceive them into sex work, often under slavery-like conditions, as is also the case of children trafficked into forced labor. The global trafficking of women and children has become migration's ugly flip side, a cruel and inhuman practice that persists not only because the "supply" of victims is seemingly endless, but also because the "demand" is also apparently inexhaustible, earning for the perpetrators an estimated eight billion U.S. dollars a year.

What makes human trafficking so difficult to suppress is that it is a very difficult crime to track, hiding behind the face of increased migration and evading complex immigration rules, with traffickers cleverly taking advantage of their victims' personal vulnerabilities. Legitimately recruited workers are promised high-paying jobs, but find themselves working as prostitutes. Women traveling as tourists end up as domestic workers, dancers, or bar girls. Pilgrims who leave for religious shrines later surface as bonded laborers. Single women are enticed into exploitative marital arrangements contracted through mail-order clubs, agencies, alleged religious programs, or even through e-mail correspondence and Internet sites. Worst of all, trafficking in children (particularly the girl-child) has turned into a lucrative business, involving such devious schemes as outright abduction or the guise of adoption, which exploits the girl-child commercially through the use of her body for pornography and prostitution, or even through the sale and purchase of her organs for transplantation purposes. Obviously, such a lucrative "trade" in human beings would not flourish without the cooperation or connivance of law enforcers and regulators in both the countries of origin and destination.

In recent years, governments in "sending," "transit," and "receiving" countries have embarked on bilateral and even multilateral agreements that enable them to arrest and prosecute traffickers and sexual predators through regional or subregional arrangements. Legal and other efforts have been adopted and are being implemented to treat survivors of trafficking as victims in need of assistance, particularly for repatriation, rather than as accessories to the crime or as potentially illegal migrants.[6] Thus, the Working Group decided that a draft general recommendation on migrant women under CEDAW should address trafficking as an abuse of the process of migration, reaffirming that the Convention under Article 6 requires States Parties to prevent, investigate, and punish trafficking, and to provide women who have been trafficked with adequate remedies and services.

Spouses

Even when a migrant woman travels to her destination country to join her spouse who left earlier, or to marry a man she met through correspondence, she is still vulnerable to violence, abuse, and violations of her human rights, all of which are prohibited under CEDAW. Experts in the Working Group recognized that demographic imbalances skewed in favor of men—combined with cultural norms concerning marriage, family, and children that are condemned as discriminatory in Articles 5 and 16 of the Convention—lead to the demand for foreign wives from certain regions of the world. They also found that common stereotypes about women from certain regions of the world as good marriage partners (the "docile" Asian woman, for instance) increases the demand for migrant women as wives.

Aside from being forced into economic dependence, migrant wives often have to accept various forms of abuse, which are forbidden through General Recommendation No. 19 to the Convention, at the hands of their husbands for fear of losing their legal status (which in many cases is dependent on the marriage). In the event of desertion or divorce by a husband before a woman has attained citizenship in her own right, the Working Group noted that in many countries of destiny such a woman may be required to demonstrate that the marriage has lasted for a certain duration, that she has resided in the country for a specific period, that she is financially stable, and that she has a secure job. These immigration rules make it difficult, if not impossible, for a foreign spouse to leave the abusive partner and find employment in her new country. Even worse, women may forfeit custody of their children if they return to their home countries without attaining valid independent immigration status.

Women Migrants' Increased Personal and Social Costs

The Working Group also identified the increased personal and social costs of migration to women as compared to men. Women migrants suffer extreme stress because they worry that their children and extended families may suffer during their absence, largely because remaining male members of the family fail to take over the domestic duties of the migrating women. Research has shown that, while male migrants often come home to stable families, migrant women more often find marital instability and discord upon their return, including a husband's infidelity or alcoholism.

Flor Contemplacion, a Filipina domestic worker who was executed in Singapore in 1991, has come to represent to many Filipinos the tragedy of overseas work and what, in many of my compatriots' eyes, is the criminal neglect of overseas workers by our Government. Accused and convicted of the murder of another Filipina domestic and of her own young ward, Flor Contemplacion was hanged by Singaporean authorities, despite appeals from the Government of the Philippines based on new evidence that could have exonerated her. Her execution touched off a wave of protests in the Philippines and led to the resignation of two Cabinet members for their alleged inaction on the case.

But perhaps even more heartbreaking was the story that emerged after Flor Contemplacion's remains were repatriated. It turned out that even as she was working in Singapore and faithfully sending money to her family, her husband back in the Philippines had already abandoned their children and started a new family. Neither were her children enjoying the fruits of her labor, with one teenage daughter pregnant out of wedlock, and a teenage son who had not even been able to finish high school.

WORK PROCESS IN THE COMMITTEE

In January 2006, at its thirty-fourth session, the Committee started the process of "appropriating" the substance of the draft general recommendation proposed by the Working Group from its midst into a first draft text. The Committee agreed that the coverage and scope of the future General Recommendation No. 27 should be limited to the most vulnerable among migrant women: Those who voluntarily seek temporary employment abroad; and those who join their husbands who are also abroad working as temporary or "guest" workers. In the Committee's deliberations, it was also decided that specific provisions of the Convention would have to be spelled out in the final text as they apply to these women in their country of origin, the "transit" state, and their eventual destination. At the thirty-fifth session in May, this proposal was further refined. The Committee identified specific applicable provisions of the Convention to be interpreted as covering migrant women, such as Article 2 (obligation of a State Party to adopt nondiscriminatory immigration laws); Article 3 (obligation of a State Party to undertake general measures to advance the position of all women in its territory); Article 6 (obligation of a State Party to suppress trafficking of women and exploitation of prostitution); Article 11 (obligation of a State Party to nondiscrimination in the formal and informal employment sector); Article 12 (obligation of a State Party to nondiscrimination in the protection and promotion of women's health); Article 13 (obligation of a State Party to nondiscrimination in the area of economic and social benefits); Article 15 (obligation of a State Party to nondiscrimination before the law); and Article 16 (obligation of a State Party to nondiscrimination in marriage and family relations). In addition, several already existing general recommendations to the Convention were considered as relevant, in particular General Recommendation No. 19 on violence as a form of discrimination and No. 24 on nondiscrimination in health care.

Within the framework of Article 11 on formal and informal employment, the Committee recognized the prevalence of discrimination against women migrant workers on the grounds of sex and gender, in the form of either restrictions or bans by some countries on women's employment in certain sectors; or the reservation of inferior types of jobs for women and the lack of legal protections in sectors where women predominate. For instance, reports by States Parties have shown that gendered occupational segmentation results in women's concentration in low-end, tedious, and informal sector jobs in general, while migrant women workers will end up on the very lowest step of this scale. Occupations in which women predominate, especially domestic work or certain forms of entertainment, may even be excluded from legal definitions of work, so that women workers in general and migrant women workers in particular are deprived of a variety of legal protections.

In violation of Article 12, women migrant workers may also be subjected in some receiving countries to mandatory and sometimes concealed HIV/AIDS testing without their consent, with the test results transmitted to the employer and agent rather than the worker, and with the possibility that she would be fired or deported if the test results are positive. Even more repugnant in my opinion—and strictly prohibited by the Convention under Articles 4 (2) and 11 (2)—is the practice of penalizing women for getting pregnant while in foreign employment, forcing them to undergo mandatory pregnancy tests that lead to their deportation or forfeiture of their bonds by their employers if they are found to be with child. Even if the pregnant worker should manage to remain on the job, she is not entitled to maternity leave and benefits, which are available to most other women workers in many countries, and may even be dismissed when she reaches the advanced stages of pregnancy, which may result in her moving into an irregular immigration status and subsequently being arrested and deported.

One reason women feel compelled to conceal whatever abuse, exploitation, or discrimination they go through while working or living abroad is the stigmatization they know they will face when they reach home. The Committee will point to the fact in its general recommendation that women who return home early and without recovering debts, or traumatized by physical or sexual abuse, are often seen as morally loose, "corrupt," or "dishonored" rather than survivors of abuse in need of assistance. Such a stigma often prevents the victims from seeking redress or going public with their complaints, leaving exploitative recruiters, agents, or promoters to go scot-free and victimize even more young women. Moreover, police, prosecutors, and regulators in the "sending" countries also often fail to assist women who seek to file charges against their abusers, thereby discouraging reporting of illegal recruiters and traffickers.

CONCLUSION

It pains me to think that Flor Contemplacion—and many other Filipinas like her—may have, in the end, died in vain. My thoughts turn back to the young woman in the Embassy in Brussels decades ago, when my eyes were first opened to the ugly realities of migration. Women migrants suffer from multiple discrimination: on the grounds of being women and of being migrants. Often, violations of their rights do not only add up, but reinforce and compound each other. A new general recommendation by the CEDAW Committee on migrant women, putting them squarely under the Convention, will certainly assist States Parties to the Convention to address legal and other measures relating to this group of women in a more serious manner than up to now when implementing the Convention and when reporting on it. The CEDAW Committee is now in the process of moving toward the approval of the substance of such a recommendation. After this, it will address itself to the fine-tuning of the text in one of its future sessions.

Back in Brussels I did what I could at the time for the young Filipina. Hopefully, through our work in the CEDAW Committee, and through a new general recommendation, we can reach out to millions of woman migrants like her around the world, elucidate the protection of their human rights under the Convention, and remind States Parties of their obligations—in sending as well as receiving countries—to avoid violations of the rights of these women and thus mitigate the worst effects of migration on the world's women.

NOTES

1. While ILO Conventions No. 97 (Convention concerning Migration for Employment), No. 118 (Convention concerning Equality of Treatment of Nationals and Non-Nationals in Social Security), and No. 143 (Convention concerning Migrations in Abusive Conditions and the Promotion of Equality of Opportunity and Treatment of Migrant Workers) were drafted with the express intention of offering specific protection to migrant

workers, many other ILO Conventions are applicable to migrant workers, by virtue of being applicable to all workers. Of particular relevance are those ILO Conventions that offer protection to workers in industries or situations common to migrant workers, for example, No. 172 (Working Conditions [Hotels and Restaurants] Convention 1991), No. 171 (Night Work Convention 1990), No. 181 (Private Employment Agencies Convention 1997), and No. 110 (Convention concerning Conditions of Employment of Plantation Workers 1958). Also of note are the core ILO Conventions that seek to eliminate discrimination in the work place, namely No. 100 (Convention concerning Equal Remuneration for Men and Women Workers for Work of Equal Value) and No. 111 (Convention concerning Discrimination in Respect of Employment and Occupation).

2. The ICMW was not intended to create new rights for migrant workers but rather to restate migrant workers' existing rights in a way that addressed their particular situation and vulnerability. The Convention splits migrant workers into those with regular status and those with irregular status. Whilst granting all migrant workers core civil and political rights, it allows States to limit many core social and economic rights to those with regular status. Likewise, the Convention allows States to limit the rights of certain categories of temporary migrants, such as seasonal workers, project-tied workers, or specified employment workers. The Convention does not advance specific protection to women, nor does it give particular attention to the types of employment in which women dominate, for example, domestic work.

3. The mandate of the Special Rapporteur on the human rights of migrants was created in 1999 by the Commission on Human Rights, pursuant to resolution 1999/44. The mandate was extended for a further three years by the Commission in 2005 at its 62nd session (Res. 2005/47). It requested the Special Rapporteur to "examine ways and means to overcome the obstacles existing to the full and effective protection of the human rights of migrants, including obstacles and difficulties for the return of migrants who are undocumented or in an irregular situation." The Special Rapporteur carries out this mandate by (1) requesting and receiving information from all relevant sources, including migrants themselves; (2) formulating appropriate recommendations to prevent and remedy violations of the human rights of migrants, wherever they may occur; (3) promoting the effective application of relevant international norms and standards on the issue of migration; (4) recommending actions and measures applicable at the national, regional, and international levels to eliminate violations of the human rights of migrants; and (5) taking into account a gender perspective when requesting and analyzing information, as well as giving special attention to the occurrence of multiple discrimination and violence against migrant women.

4. The International Organization of Migration (IOM) was established in 1961 and is acknowledged to be the leading intergovernmental organization in the field of migration. It has 118 member States, a further 20 States holding observer status, and offices in over 100 countries. IOM's work is to help ensure the orderly and humane management of migration, to promote international cooperation on migration issues, to assist in the search for practical solutions to migration problems, and to provide humanitarian assistance to migrants in need, including refugees and internally displaced people.

5. The following CEDAW experts volunteered for the Working Group: Mary Shanthi Dairiam, Salma Kahn, Rosario G. Manalo, and Heisoo Shin from the Asia-Pacific region; Magalys Arocha and Silvia Pimentel from Latin America; and Krisztina Morvai from Eastern Europe. Meriem Belmihoub-Zerdani and Huguette Gnacadja from Africa also volunteered to join the Working Group, but could not attend the regional meetings. Sjamsiah Achmad, a former CEDAW expert, joined the Group in its first meeting in Bangkok.

6. For example, a bilateral agreement to combat trafficking between Belgium and the Philippines was signed on September 15, 1994. It was prompted by the acknowledgment of the massive sexual exploitation of women from developing countries into Europe. Most important of all is the UN Convention against Transnational Organized Crime, which entered into force on September 29, 2003, and its Protocols: the Protocol to Prevent, Suppress and Punish Trafficking in Persons, Especially Women and Children and the Protocol against the Smuggling of Migrants by Land, Air and Sea. These entered into force on December 25, 2003, and January 28, 2004, respectively and represent a major step forward in the fight against transnational organized crime, in particular trafficking of persons. The Protocol against the Smuggling of Migrants deals with the growing problem of organized criminal groups who smuggle migrants, often at high risk to the migrants and at great profit for the offenders. The Protocol against Trafficking in Persons provides a universally accepted definition of trafficking (Article 3) and aims to prevent and combat trafficking in persons, to protect and assist victims of it, and to promote cooperation between States to tackle the problem. The Protocols commit countries that ratify them to making the basic subject of the Protocol a criminal offense and to adopting other specific measures, such as controls on travel documents, to combat the problem.

WOMEN'S HEALTH: ACCOMMODATING
DIFFERENCE

CARMEL SHALEV, *ISRAEL*

My interest in the area of women's health started in the 1980s, when I was a graduate law student. At that time freedom of choice in abortion was a major constitutional issue, new frontiers were being reached through innovations in assisted medical reproduction, and feminist theory was just starting to develop. After completing my studies in the United States at Yale Law School, I returned to Israel and became involved as an academic and activist in women's rights and reproductive health. I was working in these areas at the Ministry of Justice when two major laws were passed in the Knesset (Israel's parliament) on patient rights and national health insurance, which expanded my interest to the general area of health rights. During that period, I was invited to join Israel's delegation to an international meeting in preparation for the Fourth UN World Conference on Women in Beijing and was subsequently nominated and elected to the CEDAW Committee.

One of the central areas of controversy at Beijing was women's health, a key factor in the overall status of women, and in the follow-up to that conference I was urged by NGO colleagues to lead the Committee in formulating a general recommendation on this matter. In the process, I focused on the reporting of governments on this sensitive subject and collaborated with fellow members and activists from international and local NGOs around the world to formulate a document that would reflect our common concerns and understandings and set standards of health and human rights in relation to women.

In this essay I attempt to paint a picture of the human rights issues that arise in the area of women's health, based on the understanding that I gained from serving on the Committee. There are myriad forms in which women's health rights have been violated in different parts of the world. I am well aware that more could have been said here on many matters, such as the rights of girl infants, children, and adolescents, or the rights of disabled and elderly women. The subjects I address within the limits of this short essay reflect my own interests, preferences, and views about which things matter most (Shalev 2000).

THE RIGHT TO HEALTH

Health is a human right; it is neither a commodity nor a privilege. Yet the right to health is a rather elusive concept, since our health is not entirely up to us but depends on multiple factors—including heredity and environment—that are not subject to our control. Article 25 of the Universal Declaration of Human Rights (UDHR) refers to health in the same breath as well-being, as part of a right to an "adequate" standard of living. Article 12 of the International Covenant on Economic, Social and Cultural Rights (ICESCR) is fraught with similar vagueness in recognizing the right to enjoy the "highest attainable" standard of physical and mental health.[1] Then comes Article 12 of the CEDAW Convention, which tells us that States have a duty to eliminate discrimination against women in the area of health. What does this mean?

A breakthrough in the discourse on the right to health occurred in the 1990s. At least three factors led to this. First, innovations in medical technology in the latter quarter of the twentieth century—organ transplants, imaging diagnostics, and infertility treatments, to mention just a few—had put the subject of health in the public eye all over the world. Second, the paternalistic model of doctor-patient relations, according to which the physician knew best regarding what was in the patient's interest, had made way for a new model of sharing in medical decision-making—one that was based on the notion of patient autonomy and choice and closely associated with the principle of liberty, a central pillar of the human rights regime. Third, by the end of the Cold War, the attention of international human rights scholars and activists was shifting from the classic realm of civil and political rights that characterized Western democracies, to embrace the more complex and challenging area of social, economic, and cultural rights, of which the right to health is a prime example.

The area of women's health underwent a similar process of change in the second half of the twentieth century. The invention of the contraceptive pill in the middle of the century was a technological innovation that made it possible for women to exercise personal control over their reproductive and sexual lives. The tyranny of biology over women's lives came to a symbolic end, making way for a new era of self-definition and freedom. The acknowledgment of women's right to choose whether and when to bear children, as a matter of privacy and personal autonomy, led many countries to decriminalize abortion under safe medical conditions. Then, the outbreak of the HIV/AIDS pandemic placed the subject of health and human rights on the international agenda, while exposing the vulnerability of women's sexual health. Around the same time, a profound change in attitudes toward women's social and political status occurred with the recognition that women's rights are human rights and that women's human rights include their reproductive and sexual capacities. In addition, by the end of the century, it had become clear that women's health could not be confined to issues of reproduction and sexuality but required a life-cycle approach, from infancy to old age.

The effect of these developments created a paradigm shift in the view of women's health in the international community. In 1994, the International Conference on Population and Development, held in Cairo, provided evidence of this radical change in attitude when it addressed women as the autonomous subjects of human rights in relation to their reproductive capacity, rather than as objects of population control. It stated accordingly, with reference to the language of Article 16 (1) (e) of the CEDAW Convention:

> Reproductive rights embrace certain human rights that are already recognized in national laws, international human rights documents and other consensus documents. These rights rest on the recognition of the basic right of all couples and individuals to decide freely and responsibly the number, spacing and timing of their children and to have the information and means to do so, and the right to attain the highest standard of sexual and reproductive health. It also includes their right to make decisions concerning reproduction free of discrimination, coercion and violence, as expressed in human rights documents. (United Nations 1994, para. 7.3)

One year later, at the Fourth UN World Conference on Women in Beijing, the issue of women's health was hotly debated. Certain governments with close connections to religious authorities challenged the gains that had been made in Cairo. Conservative diplomats in neckties talked openly about sexuality. As one of the activists later noted, it was very likely the first opportunity for them to do so without blushing. The negotiations continued until the early hours of the morning, but the international community of women stood its ground. The Beijing Platform for Action reiterated the Cairo text word for word, taking care not to reopen the sensitive consensus for new discussion (United Nations 1995a).[2]

Moreover, the Beijing Platform for Action acknowledged the importance of women's ability to control their fertility as the basis for the enjoyment of other rights, including the right to sexual health and to health in general. The new approach emphasized women's right to autonomy and at the same time looked beyond their reproductive and sexual functions to place their health in a broader social context. Individual freedom and autonomy were necessary but insufficient conditions for the realization of women's right to health. Social, economic, and cultural determinants, including gender discrimination and other conditions that affect vulnerable groups and minorities, were also to be taken into account.[3] Most notable of these was the issue of violence against women and its impact on health.

The life-cycle approach uncovers many health issues that are related to discrimination against women. A preference for sons leads to the abortion of female fetuses and to female infanticide and can manifest itself in discrimination in the care, nutrition, and feeding of infant girls. Harmful traditional practices, such as female genital mutilation (FGM) and early marriage and childbirth, may have lasting impacts on women's health. Sexual violence and abuse, not only in domestic circumstances but also in relation to prostitution and trafficking in women or to situations of armed conflict, incur high health costs from trauma, disease, and unwanted pregnancy. And the health of older women is also a matter of concern, since they live longer than men, often in poverty and isolation, and may have chronic conditions of physical and mental disability and discomfort.

HEALTH RIGHTS UNDER THE CEDAW CONVENTION

The intrinsic relation of gender equality to women's right to health finds expression throughout the CEDAW Convention but Article 12 is central: The first paragraph requires States Parties to take all appropriate measures to eliminate discrimination against women in the field of health care and to ensure equal access to health-care services. However, there are many more articles in the Convention that bear directly or indirectly on women's health. Several relate to family planning and the importance of education and information. Thus, Article 16 (1) (e) recognizes women's right to decide on the number of spacing of their children and to have access to the information, education, and means to enable the exercise of this right. Article 10 (h) mentions specifically the right to health education, including information and advice on family planning. Article 14 (2) (b) reiterates the obligation of States Parties to ensure access to family planning counseling and services for rural women, within the context of a special right to have access to adequate health-care facilities, while Article 14 (2) (h) mentions their right to enjoy certain living conditions, such as clean water and sanitation, that are prior conditions for health promotion and the prevention of disease. There are also provisions with regard to occupational health. Article 11 (1) (f) includes reproductive capacity in the right to protection of health and safety in the workplace, while Article 11 (2) (d) guarantees special protection from harmful types of work during pregnancy. As for provisions that may have an indirect impact on health, the most noteworthy are Articles 2 (f) and 5 (a), which set forth the undertaking to abolish and eliminate harmful customary practices. FGM is one example of traditional practices that violate women's right to physical integrity and to sexual health and may have consequences that impose a burden on health-care services.

Issues pertaining to women's health thus cut across the Convention, and indeed the CEDAW Committee has had occasion to address certain aspects of women's health in several general recommendations—on violence against women, FGM, HIV/AIDS, disabled women, and equality in family relations.[4] But the two world conferences in Cairo and Beijing had brought attention to bear on multiple issues related to women's health. In their wake, and based on an examination of the reports received from States Parties, the Committee began to work on what would become General Recommendation 24 on Article 12. These reports had revealed a dynamic reality in which women's right to health was implicated and violated, which had given rise to new insights on the meaning of Article 12 and resulted in a rich interpretation of its text.

SUBSTANTIVE EQUALITY: ACKNOWLEDGING DIFFERENCE

Article 1 of the Convention defines discrimination as any distinction, exclusion, or restriction made on the basis of sex that has the effect or purpose of impairing women's enjoyment and exercise of their human rights. The emphasis on the discriminatory effect of the distinction, regardless of the intention or purpose, indicates that the outcome of gaps in health status, characterized by gender, is what counts. General Recommendation No. 24 opens by acknowledging that biological differences between women and men may lead to differences in health status but notes at the same time that there are societal factors that are determinative of the health status of women.[5] This complex interplay between biological difference and social determinants of health calls for an approach of substantive rather than formal equality in addressing the obligations of States to eliminate discrimination against women in the field of health.

Under an approach of formal equality, it would be sufficient to provide for women's health needs to the extent that they are comparable with men's. But this would amount to gender blindness and exclude a broad range of health needs that are specific to women. For example, a formal approach to equality might lead one to conclude that a health insurance program that excluded childbirth-related expenses from its coverage was not discriminatory, since men would not be entitled to such benefits either.[6] An approach of substantive equality, on the other hand, requires more than merely guaranteeing women the same formal rights as men. This is of particular significance in the area of health, where many of women's health needs are different from men's because of biological and physiological differences. This is most understandable and clear when considering reproductive and sexual health, where we see different biological processes and different physiology of body organs. Women menstruate; men do not. Women have a womb and eggs; men have testicles and sperm. Likewise, because of physiological differences, women are more at risk than men of contracting a sexually transmitted disease from a partner. However, it has become increasingly evident that biological differences between women and men go beyond reproduction and sexuality. For example, women generally live longer than men, but at the same time they tend to suffer more than men from chronic illness and disability and from loneliness and neglect. There are also differences in the incidence of disease. For example, breast cancer and osteoporosis are diseases from which women typically suffer far more than men. And even where both women and men suffer more or less equally from common illnesses, such as heart disease, there are differences in the symptoms and in response to standard treatment.

To ensure equal or comparable outcomes in health status and well-being, it is therefore necessary to take into account sex and gender difference rather than require women to meet male standards. Health equality between women and men requires provision for women's special health needs, and failure to allocate the necessary resources to provide for those needs may be considered discrimination. Let us take, for example, the sensitive and contentious issue of women's right to abortion, to which I shall return below.[7] The word "abortion" is not expressly mentioned anywhere in the CEDAW Convention or in General Recommendation No. 24. Moreover, despite the fact that many consider freedom of choice in abortion to be key to women's autonomy over their lives and their social status, there has never been a consensus among the members of the Committee on the issue, except for the understanding that—if performed at all—abortion should take place under safe conditions. Nonetheless, General Recommendation No. 24 states clearly that it is discriminatory for a State Party to refuse legally to provide for the performance of "certain reproductive health services for women" (para. 11). In another reference to abortion (para. 14), it says that "laws that criminalize medical procedures only needed by women and that punish women who undergo those procedures" constitute a violation of the obligation of States Parties to respect the health rights of women, since they obstruct action taken by women in pursuit of their health goals. Both these statements reflect the CEDAW Convention's approach of substantive rather than formal equality.

SOCIAL DETERMINANTS

With the growing body of knowledge about the ways in which women and men differ in health, it has become clear that social factors also influence health-related discrimination and that cultural attitudes and prejudices compound the challenges of accommodating biological difference. Discriminatory practices in the area of health are closely associated with prejudice about women's reproductive and sexual functions. Patriarchal notions of women's roles as wives and mothers exact a heavy health toll. Women are often valued according to their ability to produce children, so that their health may suffer from early marriage and pregnancy, or from repeated pregnancies spaced too closely together, often as the result of efforts to produce male offspring because of the preference for sons. Should they fail to bear children, women tend to be blamed for infertility, and risk being cast out of a marriage and suffering dire social and economic loss as a result. Where women have access to medically assisted reproduction, it is their bodies that carry the health burdens of infertility treatment.

Stereotypes of women's sexuality are similarly related to practices that are harmful to women's health, including unnecessary medical interventions such as FGM, forced virginity examinations, and hymen repair. Prejudice about female sexuality may have more mundane implications, such as the obstruction of access to family planning services for teenage girls. For example, there were no legal restrictions in Zimbabwe on the provision of family planning services to minors, and the Government stated that it even subsidized the costs of contraceptives. However, it also reported candidly, "It is not unusual for health personnel to turn away sexually active schoolgirls requesting contraception on the grounds that the girls are still too young to indulge in sexual intercourse or that they are not married and therefore have no need for contraceptives" (Government of Zimbabwe 1996, 50).

Violence against women is also related to sexual stereotypes in ways that pervade gender power structures. Women, including girl-children and adolescents, are often subordinated to men and the satisfaction of male sexual needs, and because many do not have the social standing and personal resources to negotiate safe sex, they may be exposed to risks of sexually transmitted diseases, including HIV/AIDS. They are also vulnerable to different forms of nonsexual violence and abuse in the home that can affect their health. It is worth noting in this respect that General Recommendation No. 24 emphasizes that States are responsible not only for their own actions but also for preventing and imposing sanctions for violations of rights by private persons and organizations. This is of major importance in relation to gender-based violence. The General Recommendation mentions, among other things, the need to ensure that health-care protocols and hospital procedures are put into place to address violence against women and girls, along with gender-sensitive training aimed at enabling health-care providers to identify victims of violence (para. 15).[8]

Discrimination against women may find expression not only in private relations but also in health policy. For example, one of the major ongoing concerns in certain parts of the world is the high rate of maternal mortality and other complications related to childbirth and pregnancy. Illegal and unsafe abortion may be one cause, but in many cases it is related to lack of access to emergency obstetric care. Failure to provide such maternal health services often reflects the low priority attached to women's particular needs in the allocation of resources. The most obvious human right violated by avoidable death in pregnancy or childbirth is women's fundamental right to life itself. The gravity of this concern is reflected in Article 12 (2) of the CEDAW Convention, which actually requires States to grant free pre- and post-natal health services "where necessary." This is a remarkable requirement, since the general rule in regard to socioeconomic rights, including health rights, as stated by Article 2 of the ICESCR, is that the obligation of States to guarantee these rights is subject to the maximum of their available resources. The special mention of free services in the CEDAW Convention's Article 12 (2) provides grounds for arguing that the core minimum content of governmental obligations in relation to women's health rights is to provide access to free or affordable quality health services, including emergency obstetric care that could prevent this avoidable loss of maternal life.

Societal factors responsible for harm to women's health may vary among different groups of women, and the discourse on economic, social, and cultural rights is attentive to the most disadvantaged and vulnerable groups in society. These include, among others, ethnic minorities and rural and marginal urban groups, including migrant workers and women with disabilities, who may encounter barriers in accessing health facilities and services. But particular attention is due to two other groups: women in situations of armed conflict and women engaged in sex work. It is well known by now that rape is common in situations of armed conflict and that the impregnation of women can be part of a strategy of so-called ethnic cleansing. Victims often feel such violations to be shameful and are therefore reluctant to report them. However, this kind of violence may leave in its wake serious bodily injury and long-lasting emotional trauma, especially in the case of sexually transmitted diseases and unwanted pregnancy. In the case of the war in the former Yugoslavia, the Committee called for reports on an exceptional basis from the countries involved in the conflict.[9] I also remember in particular the oral report, requested by the Committee on the same basis, during the aftermath of the conflict in Rwanda, and the shocking statistics on the number of women who were raising children born of rape and on the demographic imbalance of women and men that resulted from the massacre of the males.

As for women engaged in sex work, the CEDAW Convention does not explicitly prohibit prostitution, but it enjoins States Parties to suppress the exploitation of prostitutes, as well as all forms of trafficking of women. In some countries, such as Germany and The Netherlands, prostitution is legal, and sex workers enjoy social and economic rights. But in most societies they are marginalized and at extremely high risk of suffering rape and other forms of violence, and the entailed health risks. At the same time, these women suffer additional discriminatory treatment by public health programs that target and blame them, rather than their clients, without adequately addressing their health needs. During the years in which I served as a CEDAW member, this became a problem of increasing concern as the current patterns of international trafficking in women and girls emerged. Trafficked women suffer a triple disadvantage: as women, as sex workers, and, most often, as illegal migrants.

AUTONOMY

Women may face different forms of coercion in relation to health that violate their rights to autonomy and bodily integrity. General Recommendation No. 24 mentions "nonconsensual sterilization, mandatory testing for sexually transmitted diseases, or mandatory pregnancy testing as a condition of employment" (para. 22). The right to autonomy in making health decisions in general derives from the fundamental principle of human rights: liberty. Autonomy is liberty in the positive sense. In the words of Isaiah Berlin, "It is not merely freedom 'from' but freedom 'to' . . . in the sense that one is entitled to recognition of one's capacity, as a human being, to exercise choice in the shaping of one's life" (Berlin 1969, 118). In medical law, the right to autonomy is the foundation of the right to choose whether or not to receive proposed treatment and can be understood as a right of self-governance.

Legal norms that stem from the right to autonomy include the right to informed consent, privacy, and medical confidentiality, all of which are instrumental to ensuring free decision-making. These rights impose correlative duties on health-care providers and deliverers of services. Providers are bound to disclose information on proposed treatments and their alternatives so as to obtain the informed consent of the person seeking care, and they must respect her right to refuse treatment. Likewise, they are bound to maintain confidentiality so as to allow her to make private decisions without the interference of others, such as male family relatives, whom she has not chosen to consult and who might not have her best interests at heart. The need for privacy and confidentiality is of particular importance when it comes to the rights of adolescents to sexual and reproductive health education, even though they are not necessarily considered of legal age for the purpose of informed consent to medical treatment.[10]

The right to autonomy also encompasses the right to be treated as a competent individual with full legal capacity to make decisions concerning one's own health. However, in some traditional societies women may not attend health clinics without a male escort as a matter of social convention, and in others male authorization to administer certain health-care procedures is even required by law. Such was the case in Indonesia, where the law required male authorization for sterilization, as well as the agreement of "the husband or the members of the family" for abortion, even though the only circumstances in which abortion could be performed lawfully were if the woman's life was in danger (Government of Indonesia 1997, 53). In Turkey, too, spousal consent was required for abortion, at which the Committee expressed concern, considering the requirement to be a violation of women's right to equality before the law under Article 15 of the Convention (CEDAW 1997, 28, para. 184).

REPRODUCTIVE CHOICE

Autonomy and choice are particularly important in regard to women's reproductive health. As already mentioned, abortion was decriminalized in many countries several decades ago, but in others it remains a crime, except in the extreme circumstance that continuation of the pregnancy poses a grave threat to the mother's life. For example, in Indonesia and Venezuela, even rape did not constitute grounds for legal abortion (Government of Indonesia 1997, 53; CEDAW 1997, 33, para. 236). In countries such as these, access to contraception and other family planning methods may also be limited. Nonetheless, women may actually be prosecuted, tried in court, and sentenced to terms of imprisonment for terminating a pregnancy. In the case of Mexico, where criminal law is in the jurisdiction of the various federal states and sentences may vary from state to state, abortion is a punishable crime with a sentence of between one and three years imprisonment—although the government report stated that the grounds on which abortion is not punishable in the criminal codes are many and various (Government of Mexico 2000, 13, paras. 61, 35–36, and 176).

Of course, the termination of an unplanned and unwanted pregnancy is an excruciating need for many women, so they continue to take the risks associated with illegal abortion—not just those of getting caught but also and mainly the health risks. These are so acute that it is often the woman's very right to life that is at stake—high rates of maternal mortality and morbidity may be a result of lack of access to family planning and safe abortion services. Thus, the Dominican Republic reported an increase in maternal deaths despite the prevalence of prenatal care and hospital births and noted that "clandestine" abortions were a leading cause of maternal death (Government of Dominican Republic 1997, 57, para. 289).

Reproductive choice means the right of women to choose whether or not to reproduce, including the right to decide whether to continue or terminate an unwanted pregnancy and the right to choose their preferred method of family planning and contraception. The right to family planning education, information, and services is central to reproductive choice and to women's sexual and reproductive health. Even in countries where abortion is legal, prevention of pregnancy is preferable to termination of pregnancy in terms of women's health, so it must be supported by adequate family planning services. However, these are particularly important where abortion is illegal. Arguably, where the State does not allow for safe legal abortion, it must at least provide those family planning services that guarantee women their right to exercise reproductive choice. General Recommendation No. 24 recommends accordingly that States prioritize "prevention of unwanted pregnancy through family planning and sex education" (para. 31 [c]).

In most cases, limitations on women' reproductive choice reflects the attitude that they should accept their biological roles as mothers. How-

ever, there are some instances where governments have adopted population policies to lower birth rates and have employed, to that end, coercive
measures that violate women's autonomy in other ways. The implementation of China's one-child policy provides the most notorious illustration.[12]
Coercive practices there took different forms, such as public menstrual
monitoring and round-ups of all the women in a village for forced medical interventions, including forced abortions and sterilizations. These violations of human rights occurred at the local level (mostly in rural areas of
ethnic minorities, such as Tibet) in order to overcome popular resistance
and meet target quotas set by central government. The main source of
information on these practices came from shadow reports submitted by
NGOs, while official statements deny their occurrence.

GLOBAL JUSTICE

It is fair to say that there are three major health issues today on the global
agenda: growing gaps in health status between rich and poor; the aging of
the population worldwide; and the rising costs of new health-care technologies.

The growing health gaps are associated, among other things, with the
impact of the private market on public health services. Private services
cater to those able to pay and operate in large urban centers, while poorer people's access to quality services is obstructed by economic and geographical barriers. An illustration of the detrimental effect of privatization
on health status was seen in the countries of the former Soviet Union
during the 1990s. The change in the political regime, and the budget cuts
associated with programs of structural adjustment in these "economies
in transition," led to the breakdown of what had been mostly adequate
health-care systems. Women's health needs were the first to be affected,
and this was seen clearly in maternal mortality rates. For example, Azerbaijan reported a five-fold increase in maternal mortality rates between
1990 and 1995 (Government of Azerbaijan 1996, 4, para. 12). Information from nongovernmental sources revealed that budget cuts had resulted in a decrease in the number of maternal health centers, and although
maternity care was officially provided at no charge, an informal fee-for-
service practice had developed that made hospital delivery unaffordable
to many women (Human Rights Center of Azerbaijan 1998; IWRAW
1997, 3 and 11).

In general, women suffer from poverty more than men and also
live longer. A bias in favor of high technology tends to obscure the fact,
for example, that elderly women who survive their partners may need

simple care and nutrition in their homes more than life-extending drugs and machines in hospitals. New technology captures the imagination, but it is often motivated by the private profit-making interests of multinational corporations rather than by public health considerations. Yet the pharmaceutical industry has a significant impact on public health systems.

The cost of technological innovation raises a multitude of concerns related to access to health care, distributive justice, and priorities in the allocation of resources for health. It is important to note that Article 27 of the UDHR recognizes a human right to share in the benefits of scientific advancement, while Article 15 of the ICESCR states in similar language that everyone has the right to "enjoy the benefits of scientific progress and its applications." However, prohibitive costs—due, among other things, to monopolies bestowed by patent law—make the universal enjoyment of the right a challenge. The conflict between corporate rights to intellectual property and the human right to health was highlighted when a consortium of pharmaceutical companies took the Government of South Africa to court after it enacted a law allowing local production of generic drugs for the treatment of HIV. The industry was essentially shamed into an out-of-court settlement, and the lawsuit led to significant price discounts and to a change in the international legal climate around the issue.[12] The organization of human rights activists around this lawsuit was also influential in the implementation of countrywide programs for the prevention and treatment of mother-to-child transmission of the disease.

RESEARCH AND DEVELOPMENT

The high costs of new drug development essentially leave the role of leading future research in the hands of private industry. Much stock is placed in the promises of genetics. Article 12 (a) of the Universal Declaration on the Human Genome and Human Rights, adopted by the United Nations Educational, Scientific and Cultural Organization (UNESCO) in 1997, reiterates that benefits from advances in biology, genetics, and medicine shall be made available to all and that the applications of research shall seek to offer relief from suffering and improve the health of individuals and humankind as a whole. Yet this area raises some particular concerns that are related to gender. An expert group convened by the UN High Commissioner for Human Rights noted that many of the biotechnology techniques touch on the process of human reproduction, in which women are involved and affected more than men, and considered the impact of biotechnological development on gender and sex to be a priority issue. Areas of concern include the use of genetic testing to avoid the birth of female babies and to select other sex-specific genetic traits in offspring, the need for appropriate support services for women to accompany the expansion of reproductive choice, and the underrepresentation of women in public debate and decision making (Office of the UN High Commissioner for Human Rights 2002, para. 34 [1]). The involvement of women in clinical trials of new biotechnological techniques is also a matter of concern.

Until fairly recently, women defined as "biologically capable of becoming pregnant" were excluded from clinical trials of new drugs, vaccines, and medical devices for various reasons, including a fear of affecting fetuses and a view that hormonal changes of the menstrual cycle would complicate interpretation of research data. As a consequence, drug dosages were established with male subjects, little being known about their safety and efficacy for women, whose bodily dimensions are typically smaller (Council for International Organizations of Medical Sciences 1993, paras. 33–34). But more generally, the result was that much less was known about women's than about men's normal physiological processes. A similar situation pertained to epidemiological data—that is, to data on patterns of health among the population at large. For this reason, CEDAW General Recommendation No. 24 stresses from the outset the importance of reliable statistical data disaggregated by sex on the incidence and severity of diseases and conditions of ill-health (para. 9).

But while women are now being included in clinical trials, they have also assumed a new function of providing eggs for research. Egg donation is one facet of the reproductive technology known as in vitro fertilization, which was developed in the early 1980s. Very different from sperm donation, it is an invasive procedure carried out after intensive hormonal treatment and usually performed under anesthesia. It can have serious side effects and even be life threatening in unusual circumstances. While previously a woman donated eggs to be used in the treatment of infertility for other women who suffer from ovulation disorders, in the past few years the new area of stem cell research has also begun creating a demand for eggs. Stem cell research (also sometimes referred to as "therapeutic cloning") is being heralded as a breakthrough in medical science that will produce replacement tissues and organs for transplantation. It is impossible to predict whether the optimistic forecasts will come true. The troublesome aspect, however, is that these future scenarios depend on a large supply of eggs. We are already seeing the early signs of an international trade in eggs, which exploits women from poor economies and is dangerously close to practices of trafficking in women for sexual services. And a scandal shocked the international scientific community when it became known that a research scientist from Korea, who announced in 2005 that his team had succeeded in cloning a human embryo, had fabricated some of the data—including the numbers of eggs used. An investigative panel at the university found that the laboratory had used 2,061 eggs from a total of 129 women (including two junior members of the research team), sixteen of whom were treated for symptoms of ovarian hyperstimulation. In addition, the procurement of the eggs was unethical, as the Korean National Bioethics Committee found that women were not properly informed of the health risks entailed in the egg extraction procedure (Center for Genetics and Society 2006).

CONCLUSION

In the two and a half decades that have passed since the adoption of the CEDAW Convention, there has been a major shift in political consciousness about women's social status and human rights and in attitudes about women's health: women's human right to autonomy regarding their sexual and reproductive rights has been recognized, a life-cycle approach has replaced the narrow obstetric-gynecological view, gender violence has gained recognition as a health issue, and attention is now given to the ways in which biological characteristics make a difference even in diseases common to women and men. Nonetheless, it seems that cultural attitudes resist the normative human rights and health discourse, that issues related to reproduction and sexuality are still outstanding, and that even the future portends new manifestations of the old forms of prejudice. A fair and equitable allocation of resources globally and locally, as stipulated by General Recommendation No. 24 for both state and private financing of health care, requires a sophisticated approach that takes into account all relevant factors of gender difference and also corrects failures where they occur.

NOTES

1. The vagueness of the right enshrined in Article 12 of the ICESCR is compounded by the vagueness of the general duty of the State set forth in Article 2 of the Covenant, to undertake steps "to the maximum of its available resources" so as to achieve "progressively" the full realization of the rights guaranteed under the Covenant.

2. Compare paragraphs 7.2 and 7.3 of the Programme of Action of the International Conference on Population and Development (United Nations 1994) with paragraphs 94 and 95 of the Platform for Action of the Fourth UN World Conference on Women (United Nations 1995a).

3. I use the term "gender" rather than "sex" because, in my understanding, sex is a biological characteristic whereas gender denotes and encompasses the social, cultural, and political constructions of biological sex.

4. General Recommendation No. 12 on violence against women; General Recommendation No. 14 on female circumcision; General Recommendation No. 15 on avoidance of discrimination against women in national strategies for the prevention and control of acquired immunodeficiency syndrome (AIDS); General Recommendation No. 18 on disabled women; General Recommendation No. 19 on violence against women; and General Recommendation No. 21 on equality in marriage and family relations.

5. CEDAW General Recommendation No. 24 on Article 12 (women and health). This was the first general comment on the subject to come out of the human rights treaty bodies. It was followed by General Comment No. 14 from the Committee on Economic, Social and Cultural Rights on the right to the highest attainable standard of health (CESCR 2000).

6. This was the ruling in *Geduldig v. Aiello* 1974 where the court reasoned that the policy did not exclude women as such but rather pregnant "persons."

7. I have addressed this issue at length elsewhere (Shalev 2004).

8. See General Recommendations No. 12 and No. 19 on violence against women, which were formulated earlier.

9. Article 18 (1) (b) of the CEDAW Convention allows the Committee to ask for reports to be submitted on an exceptional basis. The oral report submitted by Bosnia and Herzegovina and the report submitted by the Federal Republic of Yugoslavia (Serbia and Montenegro) (Government of Yugoslavia 1994) were examined and discussed by the Committee in its thirteenth session (CEDAW 1994, 128–33, paras. 732–57). Croatia's report (Government of Croatia 1994) was examined and discussed by the Committee during its fourteenth session (CEDAW 1995, 110–16, paras. 556–91).

10. Of course reproductive and sexual health care and education for adolescents is an extremely sensitive subject in many countries, including the United States (which has not ratified the CEDAW Convention).

11. For a summary and discussion of this subject in relation to the combined third and fourth periodic report of the People's Republic of China to the CEDAW Committee, which was discussed in January 1999, see Shalev 2001.

12. I have addressed this issue at length elsewhere (Shalev 2004).

RIGHTS OF RURAL WOMEN: EXAMPLES FROM LATIN AMERICA

AÍDA GONZÁLEZ MARTÍNEZ, *MEXICO*

As a diplomat for the Mexican Government, I have been associated with the CEDAW Convention from its very first beginning. Not only was I responsible for the organization of the First UN World Conference on Women (Mexico, 1975), which endorsed the preparation of the Convention, but also, as a representative of Mexico to the Commission on the Status of Women (CSW), I participated in the 1976 session of the CSW in which drafts of the Convention were discussed. I then had the privilege to be nominated and then elected to serve as a member of the CEDAW Committee from 1982 to 1992 and from 1996 to 2004.

When CEDAW was adopted by the General Assembly in December 1979, several States' representatives raised questions about the inclusion of a specific article that referred only to rural women. The reason for such an inclusion, however, dates back to discussions and conclusions of the First UN World Conference on Women, which had highlighted the multiple forms of discrimination suffered by rural women around the world. As early as 1975, the World Plan of Action, adopted by this Conference, emphasized the specific need of such women, who made up "just over half of the female population of the world," for access to health-care services, including adequate nutrition and other social services. Recommendations therefore underlined the need to guarantee adequate investments in public health and educational programs and facilities (United Nations 1976, paras. 139, 111, and 147). In addition, the Conference adopted a resolution whereby governments were urged to identify needs and to elaborate and apply, with greater financial and policy aid, programs of rural development, especially those that will benefit women and to ensure legal equality and the economic rights of women within rural families as an essential part of all rural development progress. The substance and language of Article 14, which was formulated with the assistance of many countries as well as the Food and Agriculture Organization (FAO), address many aspects of discrimination in rural women's lives, particularly in developing countries all over the world. Such discrimination may be more intense if these women dwell in poorer parts of rural areas or if they belong to indigenous groups. Article 14 guarantees to rural women the protection of their human rights under the entirety of the Convention's provisions thus reinforcing all other provisions for the benefit of rural women.

ACTIONS AND STRATEGIES ADOPTED IN SEVERAL STATES PARTIES

While examining the initial and subsequent periodic reports of States Parties from Latin America, the Committee noted the conditions of rural women's suffering in various countries. Customs, attitudes, beliefs, and traditions still persist in Latin America—as they do elsewhere—rooted in various social and cultural histories and practices, especially of both indigenous and imported religions. They discriminate against women in general, but women in rural or farming areas are specifically vulnerable regarding their limited access to health care, especially reproductive health services, education, employment, land ownership, and community decision-making processes. These women also are not recognized for their contribution to food production and, thus, to the family and community economy in general. Despite women's central work in sowing and harvesting, gathering firewood, and carrying water, such work is overshadowed by other responsibilities traditionally assigned to them, including child-rearing, care of ill or elderly family members, house-cleaning, food preparation, and other tasks. In dealing with Latin American States Parties' reports, the Committee also recognized the efforts of respective governments to raise standards of living for rural populations in general and to eliminate specific forms of discrimination that affect rural women. In several cases, the Committee found that the implementation of Article 14 was limited, to a large extent, by general economic factors—including scarce state resources—that made it almost impossible for the State Party concerned to provide health and sanitary services; expand electrical networks and access to water, transport, and communications; or create a road and irrigation infrastructure. In the following paragraphs, I will give a few examples of some measures adopted by States Parties to improve respect for as well as to protect and fulfill the human rights of rural women.

As indicated in its initial report, Bolivia's Office of Social Promotion for Women Farmers is directly responsible for the recognition of the rights of rural women and for development programs. Through this Office, strategies have been designed and programs have been developed, for instance, in education. Thus, a school system for women farmers was established in all rural communities, as well as technical vocational schools and rural normal schools. In some rural localities, bilingual education was provided up to the fifth basic year, with 75 percent in the students' native language and 25 percent in Spanish.

Other programs of the Office of Social Promotion for Women Farmers included activities aimed at eliminating discrimination against women in agricultural employment, in which women were paid less than men, in spite of the fact that the law determined that both sexes should receive equal daily wages (Government of Bolivia 1991).

In 1999, the Committee examined Chile's second periodic report and third periodic report, which indicated that, within the framework of the National Service of Women, the mainstreaming of a gender perspective had been explicitly promoted in the programs of several public sector entities related to agricultural development. Within the labor and health sectors, an Assistance Program for Seasonal Women Workers was carried out with the purpose of dealing with the precariousness of female work in agro-exportation and its relation to women's quality of life. Informational and educational workshops were also offered on the subject of labor rights and occupational health. Within the framework of this same program, a training pilot project for seasonal women workers of the agro-industry in modern production technologies was started in 1996 (Government of Chile 1995; 1999).

In 1987, the Committee observed that Colombia had not given detailed information with respect to the problems of rural women. During the dialogue with the Committee, however, the Government underlined that "Colombia was a country in which agriculture was so important that the economy and rural women could not be considered apart from one another" (United Nations 1990c, 414, para. 50). Thus, the Committee learned about the innovative integrated literacy programs for rural areas, to which were added training programs in agricultural techniques, with the aim of developing the skills of agricultural women workers in the production of coffee and flowers. Some of these programs were supported by the National Federation of Coffee Growers, which dedicated a significant part of its capital for community programs, a number of which were for women workers (461, para. 56).

In the fourth periodic report of Colombia, examined by the Committee in 1999, the Government emphasized the changes that it had initiated in the preceding decade. It highlighted in particular the decrease in the number of family workers without remuneration, which, in the case of women, had been reduced from 31.9 to 12.7 percent, indicating that participation of women in salaried work had increased. It further pointed out that, although men continued to use credit in greater numbers than women, the ability of women to obtain credit had increased significantly. Between 1991 and 1992, rural women received the benefit of a credit line created specifically for them by the Cashier for Agrarian Credit (Government of Colombia 1997).

The report also described the creation of an Office within the Ministry of Agriculture and Rural Development as a sort of national machinery for rural women. It had been set up to pay special attention to rural women's living conditions, as well as to their needs arising from these, in all the Ministry's programs. In addition, the Office developed specific training programs in leadership for rural women, in order to provide them with the necessary capabilities, knowledge, and tools for drawing up, implementing, and evaluating projects (Government of Colombia 1997). In the discussion that took place with the Government of Colombia, the Committee expressed concern at the delay in the provision of the infrastructure of basic services in rural areas, as such a lack could hinder the integration of women in development (CEDAW 1999, 38, para. 397).

The fourth and fifth combined report of Ecuador, examined by the Committee in 2003, indicated that the National Economic Development Plan placed a high priority on rural development and had mainstreamed gender into its programs between 1989 and 1992. Among the programs implemented were projects to support and train groups of women. This resulted in the formation of forty-nine micro-enterprises managed by women and the granting of land title deeds to 12,500 women in the period 1992–1996 (Government of Ecuador 2002).

A project entitled Integrated Development for *Campesina* Women was carried out, having as its objective the promotion and valuing of the work performed by peasant women in agricultural and livestock activity to increase their share in the benefits of development. This was being done by means of subprojects that included socio-organizational, technical-productive, and managerial-business topics as well as resource management. Workshops were being offered on the advantage of the benefits of development, self-management, political participation with emphasis on the ethnocultural particularities The same subprojects included the provision of community infrastructure, such as irrigation canals, home-workshops, water tanks, hangars and bulking centers. Likewise, the fact, that the National Division for Women, Youth, and the Family had been created within the Ministry of Agriculture and Livestock in 1996, pointed to the recognition that more needed to be done by the Government for rural women, including young rural women (Government of Ecuador 2002, 32–33, paras. 289 and 299).

El Salvador's initial report, examined by the Committee in 1986, made no reference to any actions carried out or to be developed in order to implement Article 14. Its combined third and fourth periodic report, examined by the Committee in 2003, stated that illiteracy affected the rural population—particularly rural women—more than the urban population. The report also recognized that women farmers had little access to land and that the agrarian policy, which had been in force between 1989 and 1994, had made no reference to rural women and thus had not taken their needs into account. In the same report some new steps were indicated as, for example, the creation of a program of education and literacy for adults with a specific focus on women, as well as a review of agrarian laws to identify discriminatory provisions toward women. Likewise, some programs were being promoted to train women leaders as multipliers of knowledge in animal production, organic agriculture, soil conservation, and agroforestry (Government of El Salvador 2001a).

In 2003, the Committee also examined El Salvador's fifth periodic report as well as its sixth periodic report. These provided more data on the situation of rural women, thus providing the Committee with a better understanding of their situation. The reports indicated that among rural women the overall fertility rate (i.e. the average number of children born to a woman over her lifetime) was 4.56, compared to 2.79 among women in urban areas. Rural areas lacked basic services, the most important of which was access to water, which prevented women from fulfilling their basic needs and having sufficient time for pursuing job-related training. In order to solve these problems, the reports indicated that measures to improve the infrastructure had been carried out in order to provide drinking water to rural communities, to train women in the adequate use of water, and to educate and create communal women leaders in preventive health care with a gender perspective (Government of El Salvador 2001b; 2002).

The Committee responded with recommendations in its concluding comments that put the emphasis on the necessity to fight poverty as well as illiteracy. The recommendations also stressed the need to give priority attention to rural and indigenous women through the allocation of budgetary resources, and to take appropriate measures to inform itself about their situation, with a view to formulating effective policies and programs to improve their socioeconomic condition and ensure that they received the services and support they needed (CEDAW 2003, 43, para. 262).

Guatemala ranks high among those countries of the region which, in their periodic reports, have given full details about the programs and actions they have carried out in order to implement Article 14. In its combined initial and second periodic report, examined by the Committee in 1994, Guatemala acknowledged a high rate of female illiteracy in general and in rural areas in particular, signaling that there was not only a low rate of school attendance by girls but also a high dropout rate. According to the Government, girls often dropped out because of the prevalence of social as well as sex-role stereotypes that permeated attitudes and actions in the country, a situation that was even worse in rural areas (Government of Guatemala 1991 and Amend.1 1993, 1–2). During the dialogue with the State Party, the Committee expressed concern over the unequal land distribution in rural areas and wondered if the prevailing gender attitudes would impair the girls' future, as they would choose only the professions defined as female (CEDAW 1994, 28, paras. 67–68).

The combined third and fourth report, and the fifth periodic report of Guatemala, examined by the Committee in 2002, contained important information on progress regarding rural women's lives. Thus, while the level of illiteracy continued to be very high, and school dropout rates were greater among girls of rural areas, it also pointed out that several programs had been adopted to improve the situation. For example, the national program of self-managed educational development was created in part to remedy the lack of teachers for rural areas. A school program for rural girls, which had been operating since 1995, involved lending parents money for their daughters' education through a community bank. A decentralized regional program of scholarships for indigenous rural girls had also been developed as an incentive to allow them to begin and continue to attend school. The State Party also informed the Committee that it had established a specific institution, the Women's National Council of Guatemala, which had among its objectives paying specific attention to the educational, cultural, social, and economic advancement of women in rural areas. In addition, the Program for the Advancement of Rural Women, supported by the United Nations Children's Fund (UNICEF), had been set up in 1996 to implement activities in the areas of health, education, basic services, and income generation, and to provide credit, training and technical support, and support for community organizing. The program functioned in eight of the country's provinces with a majority indigenous population, but there were plans to expand its coverage throughout the national territory.

In addition, a program of credit assistance to groups of women in rural areas was created in 1989. This program set up so-called community banks, made up of groups of women who normally had no access to conventional credit sources and who, in order to better themselves, organized to get training, technical assistance, and financing for productive activities to generate income. Many of the women were illiterate, and 95 percent of them were indigenous. The late payment rate on the credit granted was 0 percent (Government of Guatemala 2001). Regarding rural women, the Government also referenced two important Acts that were adopted to affirm women's participation in the formulation of development policies and strenghtening of the above mentioned programs: the Act and Policy on Social Development and the Act on Urban and Rural Development Councils.

Guatemala's sixth periodic report, examined by the Committee during its thirty-fifth session in May 2006, stated that the program of scholarships for rural and indigenous girls was still operating and had provided support to almost seventy-five thousand girls by the year 2003 (Government of Guatemala 2004, 48). While introducing the report, the representative of Guatemala stated, with reference to the implementation of Article 14, that in the previous two years, 11 percent of the women who had been granted land purchase loans through the program of access to land had been heads of households. She also mentioned the 2005 "Fight against Exclusions" Program, which contributed to social, economic, and political inclusion of rural and poor women.

Article 14 (2) (f), which protects rural women's right to participate in all community activities, can be interpreted as including their right to own farmland. In its initial report of 1982 (examined by the Committee in 1983), the Government of Mexico described its legal efforts at implementing this article by pointing out that Article 123 of the Agrarian Reform Federal Act stipulated the reservation in each parcel of public land of "an area equal to the endowment unit, located in the best lands contiguous to the urbanization zone, for the purpose of establishing farm and rural industries to be collectively exploited by the women of the agrarian nucleus, over sixteen years old, and not belonging to the *ejido* (Government of Mexico 1982).

In the second, the third and fourth combined, as well as the fifth periodic reports of Mexico, which were examined by the Committee in

1990, 1998, and 2002 respectively, the Mexican Government reported on the adoption of several programs and various plans designed to improve the implementation of the various provisions of Article 14. For instance, in its second periodic report of 1987, the Government indicated the creation in the early 1980s of the Integral Program for the Participation of *Campesinas* in the Attainment of Rural Development. Among the actions envisaged in this Program were:

- the establishment of law firms to provide rural women at no charge with counsel and legal advice related to family matters and to their economic activities and organizing;
- the creation of enterprises for and by women farmers through the allocation of credit, land, and/or skills training; and
- the promotion and endorsement of the creation and strengthening of women's organizations in the rural sector (Government of Mexico 1987).

The combined third and fourth periodic report described a New Agrarian Act (1992) in which the equality of women and men was duly recognized. Women were also recognized as eligible for credit and as having the right to be entitled to one or several public land parcels (Government of Mexico 1997). As a result of this Act, a Program of Certification of *Ejidos* was established, with the fundamental purpose of ensuring legal security in land ownership. The report indicated that by 1996 women held 20.9 percent of the total of certificates extended. Mexico's fifth periodic report of 2000 contained a detailed description of the programs that had been implemented in 1999 aiming specifically at rural women through the Alliance for Rural Development. Most of these programs were directed at the creation of jobs and income-generating opportunities, including the promotion of women's involvement in the productive activities of the country. For example, support was provided for almost fifteen hundred micro-enterprises, their main activities being embroidery and handicraft, livestock projects, baking, the processing of agricultural and livestock products, candy manufacture, shampoo and soap manufacture, tortilla and tortilla-corn manufacture, and stores. Women also received trade support, financial help toward land ownership, as well as training in managerial and commercial matters (Government of Mexico 2000). However, it must be observed that no reference was made in the fifth periodic report to any actions or programs established by the Government that paid attention to or provided services for the specific health needs of rural women, nor were any facts given regarding such needs.

On the other hand, the 2005 annual reports provided by the respective Mexican ministries for the health and agricultural sectors, which became part of the Annual Report presented to the nation by the President of Mexico, described several programs addressed specifically to problems of rural and indigenous populations and, in some cases, to women in particular. These included maternal and perinatal health, under the Start Out Equal in Life Program; sexual and reproductive health for indigenous communities; a program on cervical-uterine cancer; and a Program of Action on Woman and Health. Moreover, the Program of Social Development of the Rural Sector included the objective of developing a health policy oriented toward rural women. It tried to establish a strategy that would be culturally acceptable for reproductive health care (while still in accordance with Article 12 of the Convention and the Committee's General Recommendation No. 24 on health), as well as for the prevention of family and sexual violence and the care of its victims, who were mostly women and girls.

Experts in social development have pointed out in many analyses that one of the most serious problems facing Mexico at present is the so-called demographic dispersion: i.e. although the Mexican population is concentrated in urban areas, 25 percent of the population—approximately 25 million—lives in approximately 200,000 settlements or small towns, distributed in rural areas. This problem limits the Government's ability to address the needs of rural populations in general, and of those living in remote locations in particular, with appropriate and adequate health services (e.g. regular examinations that could lead to early detection of serious illnesses like cancer and their timely treatment). In an effort to tackle this problem, mobile units were put into place to provide immediate and free health services to a large number of rural and indigenous women, including the examination, diagnosis, detection, and treatment of cervical-uterine cancer.

Recently, on the occasion of the inauguration of the International Congress of Rural Women: Strategies for Their Development, which took place in Mexico City in October 2005, the President of the Women's National Institute of Mexico, admitted that rural women experienced living conditions inferior to those of the urban sector with regard to health, education, income, and access to basic goods and services. She pointed out that extreme poverty in the rural sector was ten times greater than in the urban sector.

In its sixth periodic report, discussed by the Committee in 2006, the Government of Mexico mentioned the Program of Women of the

Agrarian Sector, which gave financial support to productive projects, addressed organization and comprehensive training needs, and promoted the generation of productive employment. The Government also provided more details on the programs and activities mentioned above, including the amount of financial resources allocated to each of the programs and activities (Government of Mexico 2006).

Women in rural areas of Nicaragua, like others in the region, were the majority of the illiterate population. The number of illiterate women had increased because the countryside lacked secondary schools—only ten out of a hundred students in secondary education were from rural areas. In order to improve this situation, a training program for female and male municipal technical teachers had been established to enlarge the coverage and the quality of education in rural areas (Government of Nicaragua 1999).

The State report also recognized that women had minimum access to credit, as on very few occasions did they have fixed assets and resources to guarantee a loan. As a remedy, therefore, the national machinery for women, the Nicaraguan Institute for Women, and the Rural Credit Fund had drawn up an agreement to grant credit to women in rural areas, with a fund of a million cordobas (around $56,820.00 US). Also, women's land ownership rates remained much lower than men's at only 16.3 percent, in spite of the actions adopted by the Institute of Agrarian Reform and the Nicaraguan Women's Institute. However, some progress had been made: The Property Act 278, adopted in 1997, benefited rural women by making joint title deeds possible.

In addition, a new institution had been established within the governmental structure that was specifically directed to promote or improve rural women's condition: the Inter-Institutional Commission of Women and Rural Development, created by a decree of October 1997. This Commission was made up of the Nicaraguan Women's Institute, the Agriculture and Forestry Ministry, the Ministry of the Environment and Natural Resources, the Nicaraguan Institute of Agricultural Technology, the Office of Rural Title Deeds, the Institute of Rural Development, and the Research Center for Rural and Social Promotion and Development (Government of Nicaragua 1999).

Venezuela's initial report, examined by the Committee in 1986, did not include specific data regarding rural women's health, their standard of education, or the legal and actual status of their property rights. However, with regard to rural women's health, the report did mention the establishment of mobile diagnostic units, which operated in the most remote areas, and served also to implement family-planning programs. The report pointed out that the rate of illiteracy in rural areas was 11.5 percent; more than half were women. The Government of Venezuela was carrying out literacy campaigns at that time, and a number of rural schools had been established (Government of Venezuela 1984).

The third periodic report, examined in 1997, stated that the problems of rural women had increased over the previous twenty years, and that, while attempts had been made to direct the focus of programs toward women, these efforts had been inadequate. Women in rural areas continued to occupy a subordinate sociocultural position, reflected in low levels of participation in development projects (Government of Venezuela 1995).

FINAL COMMENTS

Due to space limitation, I have only mentioned some countries of the Latin American region. During twenty-five years of my participation on the CEDAW Committee, I have not seen notable specific measures taken in many countries, not only of Latin America but of several other regions, to implement each of the provisions of Article 14. In many cases, while governments said they granted priority to the conditions of rural women, no special programs were adopted to reform abuses and the lifelong problems faced by these women.

Nevertheless, all through those years I could also observe that, perhaps as a result of the comments and recommendations made during the dialogues between the Committee and the States Parties, some policies and particular activities were being undertaken that, although not designed to implement Article 14 as such, would essentially improve living conditions in rural areas in general. These have led to an improvement in women's access to health care, education, employment, credit, and land ownership under equal conditions to those of men. Such steps, though small, make a contribution.

Another problem I have observed results from changes in national power. When governments or political parties shift, then programs may be eliminated or, at best, changed or reoriented. Thus, when programs may not be fully implemented, their potential benefits are cut off.

In the end, I feel hopeful that the valuable dialogue between States Parties and the CEDAW Committee will continue to provide information about successful programs in the implementation of Article 14 and, therefore, about the elimination of discrimination against rural women and their actual enjoyment of human rights.

CEDAW AND VIOLENCE AGAINST WOMEN: PROVIDING THE "MISSING LINK"

HEISOO SHIN, *REPUBLIC OF KOREA*

I first heard about the CEDAW Convention in 1988 while I was studying as a Ph.D. student at Rutgers, The State University of New Jersey in the United States. Though I remember no substantial discussion about CEDAW, Charlotte Bunch taught a course called "Women, Violence and Human Rights," which I took with about thirty other women—graduate students, women's studies teachers, and activists. We studied various forms of violence experienced by women, the power structure as the root cause, and various means to protect women's rights. This course, together with my involvement in the establishment of the Center for Women's Global Leadership at Rutgers University, may have been why I began working directly on issues of violence against women soon after returning to South Korea and again later as a member of the CEDAW Committee.

SOUTH KOREAN WOMEN'S MOVEMENTS AGAINST GENDER VIOLENCE

Before I left Korea in 1982 to study in the United States, I had already worked for seven years in two women's organizations. My work at the Korean League of Women Voters and Korea Church Women United from the mid-1970s to the early 1980s related mostly to basic consciousness-raising activities for women in the context of patriarchal Korean society. Violence against women, whether wife battery, rape, or in any other form, remained hidden and invisible as a social issue. This was a time of dictatorship: Emergency decrees were issued frequently, and violence was rampant, especially by the military and the police.[1] As the whole state was under the control of the military, "democracy" or "freedom" became the most urgent issue for people involved in civic and social movements. Rape and domestic violence were not recognized as issues related to the "right to freedom" or the "right to life or personal security." Instead, an old saying that "a woman needs to be beaten every three days" in order to be "softened" and made amenable was commonplace throughout Korean society at the time.

When I went back to Korea in the summer of 1991 with a doctorate in sociology, Korea Women's Hot Line asked me to help them. The

Hot Line, established in 1983, played a pioneering role in challenging the deep-rooted Korean patriarchy by raising the issue of wife battery. After several months of involvement, I became one of the three vice-presidents of the Hot Line and was in charge of the national movement for legislation on gender violence. Because of the urgent need for legislation, the Korea Women's Associations United, with which the Hot Line was affiliated, formed a Special Committee for Legislation. We worked for several months on a draft bill on sexual violence.

It is worth noting that, until the Fourth UN World Conference on Women in 1995, few within the Korean women's movements knew of the CEDAW Convention and its General Recommendation No. 19 on violence against women. Korea had ratified the Convention rather early in 1984 under the military dictatorship government; it probably did so to improve its image internationally. But nobody in the country was aware of the ratification, except a handful of legislators who had participated in a discussion of the Convention in the National Assembly. The Korean Government's initial report and second periodic report were submitted and examined by the Committee in 1991 and 1993 respectively, but without the knowledge of Korean women's nongovernmental organizations (NGOs) or feminist scholars. It was not until 1998, when the third and the fourth periodic reports were examined together, that the first NGO report was submitted to the Committee.

From the mid-1980s through the mid-1990s, Korean society had witnessed an eruption of nation-shocking court cases of violence against women. I want to offer only a few examples here. In 1991, a thirty-year-old woman, raped at the age of nine, killed the rapist after twenty-one years of suffering from the trauma. Another case involved a university student who had been repeatedly raped for thirteen years, from age nine, by her stepfather, which only ended when she and her boyfriend killed the man. Her mother was also a victim of this man's violence. In 1993, a female research assistant of Seoul National University brought a civil lawsuit against her professor, which was recorded as the first sexual harassment case. There was also a case of domestic violence, which seemed to be more dramatic than a stage play—a woman was charged with killing her live-in male partner, but it turned out that her seventy-year-old mother had killed him to save her daughter from the violent man.

Acting on various cases of violence against women, feminist organizations working against violence in Korea provided legal, financial, and psychological assistance to the victims, organizing lawyers and collecting funds, as well as fighting against the unfair blame put on the victims, such as "She was beaten because she deserved it" or "She invited rape with her sexy dress." I led the legislation movement in 1992 as the Chairperson of the Special Committee for Legislation on Sexual Violence within Korea Women's Associations United and, after 1993, continued my activities while working as an assistant professor at a university in another city. The law on sexual violence was passed at the end of 1993, but its contents were far from the draft we had originally prepared.

When I again led the movement for legislation on domestic violence, we were much wiser in lobbying the Government and major political parties. We sent questionnaires on the domestic violence bill to all candidates for the 1996 general election and released their answers to the press. At the time of the presidential election in 1997, we also visited the leaders of each political party, requesting their unconditional support for the legislation beyond any specific party interest. Thus, the political parties became competitive with each other and copied our draft bill, with only slight modifications. We also mobilized wider social support by going beyond the previous coalition of women's organizations to create a Citizen's Coalition for Domestic Violence Legislation. Finally, two laws on domestic violence were passed in December 1997, one detailing the range of punishment for perpetrators of domestic violence and another with provisions for "prevention of domestic violence and for the protection of its victims." Both laws came very close to our original draft.

Soon after I had began work on Korea Women's Hot Line, I was also asked to join a movement to bring justice to the "comfort women," a euphemistic term for female sex slaves who were forced to service Japanese soldiers from 1931 until the end of the Second World War. During this period, Japan used deceit or force to draft an estimated two hundred thousand young women and girls from Korea, China, Taiwan, the Philippines, Malaysia, Indonesia and Timor-Leste, as well as Dutch women living in Indonesia. These young women and girls were trafficked to the war fronts and kept in sexual slavery in "comfort stations." About 80 percent of the women were from the colonized Korean peninsula, and only a small number survived the atrocities during captivity; the end-of-the war massacre; and the desertions, starvations, shipwrecks, or other hardships encountered during their journeys home.[2]

The issue of Japanese military sexual slavery was publicly raised in Korea at an international conference organized by Korea Church Women United in 1988. Faced with the denial of these crimes by the Japanese Government, a coalition of thirty-seven organizations, including Korea Women's Hot Line, was formed in 1990 under the name of Korean

Council for the Women Drafted for Military Sexual Slavery by Japan. I willingly accepted the request from the Korean Council to join and in 1992 became the Chairperson of its International Relations Committee.

We made seven demands of the Japanese Government: to acknowledge the crime of military sexual slavery; to provide the full facts; to make an official apology; to provide legal reparations; to punish those responsible; to record the truth in history textbooks; and to create a memorial or a museum. When the Japanese Government failed to agree to our demands,[3] we decided to bring the issue to the UN Commission on Human Rights in Geneva. In August 1992, four of us, including a survivor of the slavery, participated in the UN Sub-Commission on the Promotion and Protection of Human Rights, a subsidiary body of the Commission on Human Rights. That was my first direct encounter with a UN human rights mechanism, before I became familiar with the treaty body system.

With the help of several international human rights organizations based in Geneva—including the World Council of Churches, the International Commission of Jurists, and the World Alliance of Reformed Churches—I lobbied through the Commission on Human Rights, its Sub-Commission, and the Working Group on Contemporary Forms of Slavery under the Sub-Commission. We also raised the issue of military sexual slavery by Japan at the Women's Human Rights Tribunal in Vienna in 1993 and at the NGO Forum in Huairou at the time of the 1995 Fourth UN World Conference on Women in Beijing. We fiercely lobbied as many governments' delegations as possible and succeeded in having the issue of sexual slavery during wartime recognized as a serious violation of women's human rights.

In the early 1990s, another example of women's brutal treatment had shocked the world. The systematic raping of Croatian, Muslim, and Serbian women, but in particular of Muslim women in massive numbers in Bosnia and Herzegovina, was an eye-opening realization of the fact that rape could be used as a weapon of war. Many organizations as well as the Commission on Human Rights sent missions to investigate the atrocities, and special sessions of the Commission were held in 1992 to deal with these terrible violations of human rights.[4] At its twelfth session in 1993, the CEDAW Committee requested each of the three new States in the territory of the former Yugoslavia to submit reports on an exceptional basis with respect to the situation of women under their jurisdiction, which it discussed in the following sessions of 1994 and 1995.

After Bosnia, therefore, the human rights community could under-

stand immediately the gravity and magnitude of the issues we were raising. Moreover, in comparison to the relatively short period of captivity and
forced impregnation of women within the framework of ethnic cleansing
in the territories of the former Yugoslavia, the "comfort women," enslaved
by the Japanese army half a century ago, often suffered several years of
enslavement. The forms of violence they had to endure were also different. Contrary to the European women's suffering in the form of forced
pregnancy, the Asian "comfort women" had to endure forced sterilization
or abortion conducted by the Japanese army doctors. In addition, repeated
rapes and venereal diseases permanently damaged the reproductive functions of most of the victims.

With the world's renewed understanding of what women have suffered through war and armed conflicts, the Korean Council for the
Women Drafted for Military Sexual Slavery by Japan, together with the
help of other NGOs, succeeded in getting the support of the UN human
rights system. In 1993 the Sub-Commission appointed one of its experts,
Linda Chavez, as the Special Rapporteur on systematic rape, sexual slavery, and slavery-like practices during wartime. The Special Rapporteur on
violence against women, Radhika Coomaraswamy, whose mandate was
created in 1994 in response to the urgent call from the women's movements at the 1993 Vienna UN World Conference on Human Rights,
also agreed to my request to take up the issue of "comfort women" as her
first field mission in 1995. As a result, two missions were carried out, and
two excellent reports were published, one written by Radhika Coomaraswamy (United Nations 1996c) and the other by Gay McDougall (United Nations 1998), who replaced Linda Chavez in 1997.[5] These reports
recognized the various forms of violence—including rape, sexual slavery,
forced pregnancy, and forced sterilization—that women have had to suffer for thousands of years during wars and armed conflicts, as violations
of women's human rights. The reports no longer accepted these crimes as
natural or inevitable wartime events. Instead, they concluded that the perpetrators of war crimes and crimes against humanity such as the Japanese
military sexual slavery should be punished, and that the victims should
receive reparations. Gaining strength through the Vienna and Beijing
world conferences, and because of intensive lobbying by the global wom-
en's movement, a new international standard was set in 1998, defining
rape and other forms of violence against women during war as war crimes
and crimes against humanity. Hence violence against women during wartime was explicitly codified as a punishable crime in the Rome Statute of
the International Criminal Court (ICC).

CEDAW

At a number of international conferences I was introduced to other forms of violence against women within the Asian region such as acid attacks in Bangladesh, infanticide in China, bride burning in India, sexual exploitation in Japan, and "honor" killings in Pakistan, to name only a few. Training provided by the International Women's Rights Action Watch (IWRAW Asia Pacific) taught me to monitor the implementation of the CEDAW Convention. I first directly encountered the Committee in 1998 as an activist, presenting the "shadow" report of the Korea Women's Associations United. Then, in August 2000 I was elected to serve a four-year term on the Committee as an independent expert and in 2004, I was reelected to serve another term (2005–2008).

Considering the importance and gravity of the issue of violence against women, it might at first seem strange that there is no specific article on it or even an explicit reference to this human rights violation in the CEDAW Convention. The Convention only speaks, in its Article 6, of the suppression of "all forms of traffic in women and exploitation of prostitution of women," phenomena that are only two of many different forms of violence against women. Throughout the preamble and the substantive articles of the Convention, there is not a single word on rape, battery, sexual harassment, or female genital mutilation (FGM), which negatively affect millions of women in their everyday lives in the enjoyment of their human rights.

But now I understand, through a study of history and my own activism, that rights enjoyed by women today are the results of hard struggles by individual women and by national and international women's movements, over several hundred years. Although women have always tried to fight back against sexual, domestic, or other forms of violence, it took the new women's movement of the late 1960s to bring such issues to public attention. But still, in the mid-1970s, when CEDAW was being drafted, violence against women was not yet on the global agenda. The human rights community failed to recognize violence against women as a serious social or human rights issue until the mid-1980s. In domestic violence cases, for example, wives might be locked up, stripped naked, and burned with cigarette butts, but these acts of violence were not recognized as torture, enslavement, or a threat to one's life (Bunch 1991). Only through years of women's movements' activism and their criticism of male-biased interpretations of human rights did this recognition emerge.

In 1989 the CEDAW Committee began to take a leading role in defining violence against women as a human rights violation in several general recommendations. These activities culminated in General Rec-ommendation No. 19, which was not only the Committee's contribu-tion to the Vienna UN World Conference on Human Rights but also finally provided the "missing link" in the chain of human rights (Pietilä 2002, 27). Most important, here the Committee defined violence against women, also referred to as gender-based violence, as "a form of discrimi-nation that seriously inhibits women's ability to enjoy rights and freedoms on a basis of equality with men" (para. 1). It is violence "directed against a woman because she is a woman or that affects women disproportionately" (para. 6). It includes not only acts that inflict physical harm or suffering but also harm of a mental or sexual nature. Threats of such acts, coercion, and other deprivations of liberty are also included. This definition of vio-lence against women was reconfirmed in the Declaration on the Elimina-tion of Violence against Women, which was adopted by the UN General Assembly in 1993.

Defined as such, violence against women impairs or nullifies the enjoyment by women of human rights and fundamental freedoms. Speak-ing in traditional human rights terms, these rights and freedoms include the right to life; the right not to be subject to torture or to cruel, inhu-man, or degrading treatment or punishment; the right to equal protection according to humanitarian norms in times of armed conflict; the right to liberty and security of person; the right to equal protection under the law; the right to equality in the family; the right to the highest standard attainable of physical and mental health; and the right to just and favor-able conditions of work. Thus, within the meaning of Article 1 of the Convention, gender-based violence may breach specific provisions of the Convention, whether or not those provisions explicitly mention violence. Violence against women *is* discrimination against women.

Today, more than a decade after the adoption of this important gen-eral recommendation, and with the additional support of the Platform for Action agreed to at the Fourth UN World Conference on Women in Bei-jing (United Nations 1995a), it has become normative that governments should take measures to combat all forms of violence against women and include information about such efforts in their reports to the Committee. However, there are still some States Parties whose reports on the imple-mentation of the Convention lack such information—as, for example, Bhutan and Kuwait most recently.

STATE OBLIGATION: PUNISHMENT, PROTECTION, PREVENTION

It is important to realize that, under the CEDAW Convention, women are entitled to protection from acts of violence, whether committed by public officials or by nonstate individuals such as one's husband, a colleague at the workplace, or a stranger on the subway. Article 2 (e) of the Convention calls on States Parties to "take all appropriate measures to eliminate discrimination against women by any person, organization or enterprise." As the Committee's General Recommendation No. 19 reminds us, States, under general international law and specific human rights covenants, "may also be responsible for private acts if they fail to act with due diligence to prevent violations of rights or to investigate and punish acts of violence, and for providing compensation." Appropriate measures by governments to eliminate violence against women should include the punishment of the perpetrators, the protection of the victims, and the prevention of acts of violence.

Sending a signal to society that violence against women is a punishable crime is an essential step in combating gender-based violence. Specific legislation or legal provisions in the criminal law should define specific acts of violence, including killings in the name of "honor," FGM, rape inside or outside of marriage, sexual assault, wife battery, and sexual harassment as punishable criminal behavior. The legal measures should of course include the obligation of the actual prosecution and punishment of the violent aggressor.

In some countries, there is even today no recognition that perpetrators of certain forms of violence against women should be charged with a criminal offense. In the Lao People's Democratic Republic, for example, domestic violence is still considered to be fairly normal by young people, and the criminal law grants exemption from penal liabilities in cases of physical violence without serious injury. In December 2005, I was invited by United Nations Development Fund for Women (UNIFEM) to attend a training program in that country for government officials on the implementation of the evaluative concluding comments of the Committee with respect to the Lao People's Democratic Republic's report. When I was explaining the nature of sexual harassment, one of the male officials asked me in a somewhat protesting tone, "But then, how do you let a woman know that you like her?" Clearly, he had no understanding of the concept of harassment, and it is very likely that he had never heard of the term "stalking."

In some societies, violence will be excused in the name of custom, tradition, or religious performance. Thus in Kyrgyzstan, despite the legal prohibition of bride abduction, the continuing existence of this practice has been condoned as a "centuries-long custom, which had become merely play-acting, a ritual that involved mutual consent of both parties" (CEDAW 2004b, 8, para. 43). And in some other countries, the rapist may not be punished if he marries his victim.

While many countries now have legislation prohibiting violence against women, these laws might not work in actual situations. Proper implementation of the law—i.e. active investigations, indictments, and convictions—requires training on gender sensitivity for law enforcement officials and the judiciary. Committee experts frequently pose questions to a government delegation about whether human rights education and relevant training are provided to the police, prosecutors, and judges on how to deal with incidents of violence against women. A manual or clear guidelines for the police are recommended to guarantee proper investigation and prosecution procedures, as well as the provision of awareness-raising regarding women's human rights and the CEDAW Convention for prosecutors and judges. In some countries with a socialist tradition—as, for example, in Cambodia and China—a village committee or village council functions like a court at the community level, dealing with important issues including violence against women. However, it is usually composed of mostly male members and lacks a women's human rights perspective in its judgments. Thus, it often tries to mediate rather than punish the perpetrator and provide redress for the victim.

The government is required to take measures to protect the victims of violence. Hotlines and shelters should be available for women and children, so that immediate help can be provided to women (and any children who accompany them). More long-term psychological and rehabilitation assistance should also be available to victims who suffer from trauma. A shelter should not be known to the general public. Otherwise, women may be endangered to experience social stigma or even renewed attacks by the original perpetrator. In a small community, whether a rural village or an island, where most people know each other, a shelter would probably not be useful and other solutions must be found. Women with disabilities or migrant women speaking only their native languages need special support to be able to use a hotline or be accommodated in a shelter.

When a victimized woman is seeking legal redress, effective complaint procedures and remedies, including compensation, as well as other kinds of assistance and support should be available as needed. At the same time, protective measures such as restraint orders for the perpetrator, witness protection, or (temporarily) canceling fathers' custody rights over their children might also be necessary.

In combating violence against women, prevention should be the ultimate goal. This requires changing the various social and cultural factors that contribute to violence. Stereotyped views of women and discriminatory attitudes or prejudices against women perpetuate widespread practices of violence or coercion. Poverty, unemployment, and armed conflict are underlying and contributing factors to women's vulnerability to violence, and in particular to trafficking and prostitution.

The subordinate position of women and the worldwide prevalence and persistence of gender inequality create or contribute to violence against women, and this violence in turn keeps women in a disadvantaged position in the family and society. Violence is thus the cause as well as the consequence of discrimination against women. Traditional practices and stereotyped views of women, which must be modified or eliminated according to the Convention, contribute to violence against them. In this regard, education of men and boys on gender equality and respect for women's human rights become a prerequisite, as well as rehabilitation programs for violent men to correct their behaviors.

In East Asia, the traditional, stereotyped view of a woman was a "wise mother and good wife," her life confined to managing the family. Today, women are understood to hold up "half the sky," and a "professional woman" may be presented as an ideal. In Korea, there was an old saying that "If a hen cries, the whole family goes into bankruptcy," meaning that a woman should be quiet and obedient. The women's movement changed this saying to "If a hen cries, she lays an egg," thus creating a positive and productive interpretation of women. The media can significantly influence either maintaining or changing stereotyped views of women.

As societies have changed, forms of gender-based violence have also changed. Scientific advances now enable amniocenteses and sex selection, for example, leading to the killing of female fetuses to support a preference for male children. The abnormal sex ratio in China, Korea, and India is the result of violence against female fetuses. In today's world of information and communication technology, cyberspace and mobile phones can become new sites of violence. At the same time, with deepened and expanded understanding, a society might recognize a phenomenon as a form of violence that was not formerly seen as such. Thus, intentional economic deprivation by a husband—not giving his wife money for household subsistence and thus controlling her existence—is now recognized as economic violence.

To combat various forms of violence against women, efforts to eliminate discrimination against women and promote gender equality are

essential. Equality in education, employment, and political representation are the shortcuts toward a violence-free society. The ongoing work
of the CEDAW Committee, UN intergovernmental entities and the UN
Secretariat (United Nations 2006a), together with women's continuing
activism around the world, as well as the heightened level of global and
national commitment to fight against violence against women, will hopefully bring about a world without gender-based violence. Can we shorten
the number of days for this goal to be reached?

NOTES

1. The military dictatorship in Korea began with a coup in 1961 by General Park Chung
Hee, who became President in 1963 and ruled until his assassination in 1979. During his
eighteen years of power, emergency decrees were issued nine times, and thousands were
arrested, tortured, and imprisoned. He was succeeded by two other generals, and it was only
in 1993 that Korea was able to celebrate a democratic civilian government again.

2. A survivor, Kim Hak-Soon, first came forward in 1991, and the total number of
former "comfort women" who have officially registered in South Korea as victims of the
Japanese sexual slavery system are less than 250, half of whom have passed away during
the last fifteen years. Survivors in their old age are still continuing their weekly Wednes-
day demonstrations demanding official apology and state accountability from the Japanese
government, which have been going on for fifteen years in front of the Japanese Embassy
in Seoul. See the website of the Korean Council, http://www.womenandwar.net.

3. In 1990, in response to a question regarding the "comfort women" raised by a member of the Japanese Diet, an official from the Ministry of Labor answered that private
entrepreneurs recruited the "comfort women," denying the involvement of the Japanese
Government or the acts of forcible drafting. Later, due to international pressure, the Japanese Government had to publish reports in which it acknowledged that there was a partial
involvement of the Japanese military, and that force was also partially involved.

4. The Commission on Human Rights also designated the former Polish Foreign Minister Tadeusz Mazowiecki as Special Rapporteur to investigate the human rights violations
in the former Yugoslavia. In its twelfth session on January 22, 1993, the CEDAW Committee addressed a letter to him "to investigate all allegations concerning sexual and other
violations" of women, to which the Special Rapporteur replied positively on February 1,
1993 (CEDAW 1993, Annex 1, 115 and Annex II, 116).

5. Linda Chavez made a field trip to the Philippines, Korea, and Japan in May 1995.
She submitted a working paper on the situation of systematic rape, sexual slavery and slav-
ery-like practices during wartime (United Nations 1995e) and a preliminary report (United
Nations 1996b).

WOMEN IN WAR AND ITS AFTERMATH: LIBERIA

CHARLOTTE ABAKA, *GHANA*

Liberia is a small country on the northwest coast of Africa with a population of more than 3.4 million. Originally inhabited only by indigenous Africans, it became the home for liberated American slaves in the nineteenth century, and thus the name "Liberia" was adopted, meaning "Land of the Free." The country is rich in natural resources, such as diamonds, gold, and timber, and it holds vast rubber plantations. However, over the last two decades it has suffered from fourteen years of devastating civil conflicts. The first period of conflict, which began when Charles Taylor launched a rebellion to unseat then President Samuel K. Doe lasted from 1989 to 1996. This ended with an internationally brokered peace accord that included a general amnesty. However, the 1997 election—which Taylor won—was conducted in an atmosphere of threats and intimidation, and there was a return to civil war from 1999 to 2003.

In August 2003, Liberia's warring factions signed an internationally brokered peace agreement in Accra, Ghana, called the Accra Comprehensive Peace Agreement (ACPA). The accord installed a broad-based interim Government—the National Transitional Government of Liberia (NTGL)—which took on the task of guiding Liberia toward elections in 2005. Since August 2003, several positive factors have contributed to a marked decrease in political instability and human rights abuses—particularly killings, disappearances, and arbitrary arrests—thus helping to establish the enabling environment for the election in October 2005 and the run-off election a month later. These factors include the departure of Taylor into exile, the establishment of the United Nations Mission in Liberia (UNMIL) in September 2003, and the subsequent deployment in the country of about fifteen thousand peacekeepers and one thousand civilian police.[1] It is important to mention that the Economic Community of West African States (ECOWAS), which actually sent the initial peacekeeping force to Liberia before UNMIL took over, was instrumental both in facilitating the ceasefire agreement and the ACPA and in the follow up of its implementation.[2]

The positive developments in the area of human rights notwithstanding, there are very serious violations of almost all of the sixteen substantive articles of CEDAW as well as noncompliance with the Convention's procedural Article 18, which obligates the country to report to the CEDAW Committee on a regular basis. Liberia has been a State Party to the Convention since July 17, 1984. Laudably, it acceded to it without reservations, and on September 22, 2004, it also signed the Optional Protocol to the Convention. However, the Government of Liberia has so far not submitted a single report.

Despite these shortcomings of the past twenty-two years with respect to all aspects of the implementation of the Convention due to a lack of political will and resources and the civil conflicts, the Convention can and should be utilized as an important tool to guarantee Liberian women the exercise and enjoyment of their human rights, and on this basis to transform Liberian society so that peace can be sustained and development can progress. When I was appointed as UN Independent Expert on the Situation of Human Rights in Liberia in 2003, I was determined to apply my knowledge of the Convention—gained as a member (1991–2002) and former Chairperson (2001–2002) of the Committee as well as a member and Chairperson of the Ghana National Council on Women and Development (1990–1993, 2000–2002)—to contribute to achieving the guarantee of Liberian women's human rights in law and their realization in practice.[3] The following will be a short description of the human rights violations Liberian women have been and still are subjected to. I will point to recent efforts by the Liberian Government to conform with the obligations it carries under the Convention and will identify additional efforts needed in order to fully guarantee Liberian women's enjoyment of their human rights in all areas of their lives.

ELECTIONS

The most recent electioneering process in Liberia has been a remarkable success story. The ACPA mandated the National Electoral Commission (NEC) to hold parliamentary and presidential elections in October 2005. Fortunately, a well-qualified woman, Frances Johnson-Morris, was appointed Chairperson of the NEC. Her leadership, together with the committed team of commissioners, who worked under very difficult conditions, led to the success story. Over 1.35 million Liberians braved rainy weather and almost impassable roads to register. Of the registered voters, over 50 percent were women. Two of the more than twenty presidential candidates were also women. The Ministry of Gender and Development, which functions as the Government's national machinery for women, supported by the Gender Section of UNMIL and many women's groups, including rural women's groups, spearheaded a campaign to encourage women to register, offer themselves as candidates, and, very important, to cast their votes in the October 2005 parliamentary and presidential elections and the run-off presidential election in November of that year. Liberia then democratically elected the first female president in Africa, which is certainly a victory for the women of the country and of Africa at large. It is also a victory for the Convention, which was referred to and used extensively during the campaign. It is my hope that in the future there will be parity in terms of female and male representation in the Cabinet and high echelons of the government administration, which would certainly speed up the full implementation of the Convention in all its aspects.

HUMAN RIGHTS OF WOMEN

The second civil conflict in Liberia impacted on every aspect of women's lives. The transitional period, which ended on January 16, 2006, with the inauguration of the new democratically elected president, Ellen Johnson-Sirleaf, has only partly addressed women's disproportionate disadvantages. Incidents of domestic violence and harmful traditional practices such as female genital mutilation (FGM) are reportedly increasing. Sexual and gender-based violence, notably rape, is prevalent throughout the country. In 2004, 1,204 cases of sexual exploitation and abuse were reported, with rape accounting for 1,060 of the cases. The girl-child is particularly at risk, and cases are most often mediated outside the law as the victims accept material compensation in lieu of a lawful trial. Perpetrators of sexual offenses against children very often go unpunished, and the community frequently appears to accept such acts as hazards of life rather than serious crimes, let alone as serious violations of their rights.

The access of women to justice is limited by multiple factors, such as the post-war weakness of the judicial system itself; judges' and magistrates' lack of knowledge and understanding of the Convention; a reluctance to investigate and prosecute cases of domestic violence or property disputes; the absence of a legal aid service; and the lack of awareness among most women of their right to freedom from abuse. The association of Liberian female lawyers is currently the only organization that provides free legal advice and representation for women and children, and its services are available mainly in Monrovia.

The legal system is highly discriminatory against women. Unwritten customary laws based on tribal practices in the rural areas of the "hinterland,"[4] which are part of the local government laws, as well as statutory legislation based on Anglo American common law, are embedded in patriarchal norms or often interpreted in a manner resulting in the deprivation of women's rights as proscribed under the Convention. Many of these laws and policies violate some of the provisions of Liberia's Constitution as well as international human rights instruments, including the African Charter on Human and Peoples' Rights.[5] In addition, traditional rulers retain and exercise a great amount of power, including adjudicating at traditional courts. Thus, rural women are even more at risk than urban women with respect to various aspects of the guarantee and enjoyment of their human rights. Added to this complex legal situation in general and for women in particular is the fact that the society maintains a number of discriminatory and harmful traditional practices that violate the rights of women. These include, in addition to FGM, forced marriages, early marriages with concomitant early pregnancies, payment of dowries, and the persecution of women, who are suspected to be witches. The laws of the hinterland still permit trial by ordeal for people suspected of witchcraft.

The enjoyment of women's rights is also very much linked to how well the Convention on the Rights of the Child (CRC) is implemented.[6] In Liberia, domestic legal provisions vary greatly in their definition of a child and thus formal recognition of the special needs of the girl-child is limited in many areas. The absence of national birth registration records and other forms of identification have significant consequences for girls' and young women's enjoyment of many of the rights and provisions under the CRC as well as under CEDAW. In addition to early marriage and subsequent teenage pregnancies, some of the rights violations are child labor, unequal resource allocation, and lack of separation of juvenile suspects from adults.

WOMEN'S RIGHT TO PHYSICAL AND MENTAL HEALTH

Today, the population's human rights pertaining to physical and mental health in Liberia are negatively affected by a number of factors, and women and girls suffer additional disadvantages due to their biological and social circumstances. During the conflict, virtually all health facilities in the country were destroyed. There were and still remain profound public health challenges, such as the lack of potable water, the prevalence of HIV/AIDS, the continued scourge of malaria, and reported cases of cholera outbreaks in the southeast of the country. Maternal and infant mortality rates are very high, and teenage pregnancies are common, particularly among girls living in the camps for internally displaced persons (IDPs).

Mental health issues, especially post-conflict trauma due to experiences of violence, are serious concerns. Such illnesses may also arise among the many widows or mothers who have lost their children. Some of these children, both girls and boys, were actually killed; others were displaced; a number survive as former child soldiers. Specific problems arise in many cases of former child soldiers when communities are not prepared to accept them back, even after the difficulties associated with locating their parents have been solved. Such children, both girls and boys, end up living on the street, while a few lucky ones are taken in by institutions such as "Don Bosco," again mainly in Monrovia.[7] Sadly, there are some people who are exploiting this situation by establishing so-called "orphanages," which have not been sufficiently monitored by governmental institutions and in which there have been incidents of inhuman and degrading treatment of these children.

WOMEN'S RIGHT TO EDUCATION

After the war and during the transitional period, an appreciable number of schools were rehabilitated in Monrovia and thus many girls and boys are back in school. Outside the capital, however, the situation is very critical. Even where schools have somehow been rehabilitated, there are no teachers. The Ministry of Education has designed a crash program to train more teachers. The United Nations Educational, Scientific and Cultural Organization (UNESCO) is helping with the publishing of books and also reviewing school curricula to include human rights education starting in primary school. A local nongovernmental organization (NGO) has also initiated the formation of Human Rights Clubs in schools. This is a commendable initiative, as it will help overcome the notion held by some citizens of Liberia that human rights are a foreign ideology. In addition, the Ministry of Education is pursuing nonformal education and has already begun to offer distance-learning programs. Both are being used by women. Liberia is thus making laudable efforts in this aspect of the implementation of the Convention. School dropout rates for girls, however, due to the fact that teenage pregnancy rates are very high, remain a serious concern.

TRAFFICKING

The devastating situation in Liberia, with the collapse of the family and social bonds, breakdown of law and order, displacement and extreme poverty, creates opportunities for crimes such as trafficking in women, girls, and boys. The war has orphaned many children and adolescents, and mothers, often also widows, may be too poor to provide for their children. These children are taken away under the pretext of adoption or the promise of a better life with educational or economic opportunities for them; most likely, they find themselves forced into prostitution or slavery. There have been reports and allegations of abuse in adoption processes. For example, a foreigner who solicited children from the hinterland in Monrovia turned out to be a possible conduit for the trafficking of children for illegal adoption purposes. The Office of the UN High Commissioner for Human Rights (OHCHR) in Geneva has taken these warning signs seriously and has issued guidelines that offer wide-ranging multidisciplinary recommendations on counteracting trafficking for all relevant professionals in the field. UNMIL has established a Trafficking in Persons Unit within its Civil Police also to address this serious violation of human rights. While these are small steps to counter a severe and probably widespread human rights violation, I hope to be able to bring to the attention of all concerned Article 6 of the Convention, which obliges States Parties "to suppress all forms of traffic in women and exploitation of prostitution of women," in the hope that these crimes will be more speedily and widely detected and punished. At the same time, however, major efforts of the Government and the international community are needed to eliminate the root causes underlying both phenomena.

WOMEN IN ARMED CONFLICT

The Convention does not explicitly refer to violence or discrimination against women in armed conflict. However, in its General Recommendation No. 19 the Committee has stated that gender-based violence, including violence in armed conflict, is a form of discrimination. In addition, the final document of the Fourth UN World Conference on Women (1995), the Beijing Declaration and Platform for Action, raises the issue of "women and armed conflict" as one of its twelve areas of concern. It contains an analysis of the various ways in which women and children, and in particular the girl-child, can be victims of discrimination in armed conflicts. It also contains a number of recommendations, including the involvement of women in conflict-resolution processes at decision-making levels; the promotion of nonviolent forms of conflict resolution; the provision of protection, assistance, and training for refugee women and internally or internationally displaced women; and the promotion of women's contributions to fostering a culture of peace (United Nations 1995a, paras. 131–49). Based on these recommendations for action, which the Platform addressed not only to governments but also to the UN system itself, the UN Security Council on October 31, 2000, passed Resolution 1325 on Women, Peace, and Security to stimulate both the UN system and its member States to protect women and girl-children from all forms of violence in conflict situations; to give women prominent positions in conflict prevention, conflict management, and resolution, and in post-conflict peace and reconstruction processes; and to include a gender dimension in all post-conflict reconstruction programs (United Nations Security Council 2000).[8]

Many factors create opportunities for females and males, as well as children and adolescents, to get involved in armed conflicts. The first derives simply from the facts of war. The long duration of an armed conflict means that young people of both sexes are born into the conflict environment, and experience war as the normal everyday situation in their lives. Living in a violent situation means that they need to protect themselves, and since violence may be all they knew, this is used for self-protection. Liberia's wars also totally destroyed the educational infrastructure. This situation brought children and adolescents onto the streets, making them more vulnerable to being forced into the conflict, many times without the knowledge of their parents. Their engagement then exacerbated social tensions, such as family breakups, and increased poverty, which in many cases also led to their involvement in the conflict.

For females, including adolescents, there were specific additional aspects to the general violence. When combatants entered communities, they raped women and girls and forced them into service, and those who put up any resistance were either beaten or killed. To avoid losing their lives, many women and girls had no choice but to join the combatants in the conflict and begin performing varied duties as demanded by them. Some of these women and girls carried arms; others were unarmed. Many served as "wives" to the combatants, including boy combatants, and became pregnant. Women and girls are also raped in the IDP centers. Again, because of the nature of the conflict, with all the health facilities totally destroyed, those who became pregnant had no medical care during pregnancy. This situation led to very high maternal and infant mortality rates, compounded by the fact that, in some cases, it was young girls who were actually delivering the babies of other girls and women. Although a few health facilities have been rehabilitated, most of them are in Monrovia and in the IDP camps. The very high rate of HIV/AIDS is another effect of the rampant rapes.

DISARMAMENT, DEMOBILIZATION, REINTEGRATION, AND REHABILITATION

The ACPA, signed by all stakeholders in the conflict, included a program to disarm, demobilize, reintegrate, and rehabilitate the former combatants as a priority action within the two-year transitional period. When the program was started in December 2003, and then restarted in April 2004, it met with many general problems of administration, logistics, and security. Additionally, there arose particular problems with respect to women and girls, which underline once more the importance of including a gender dimension in the application of such a program, as stipulated by Security Council Resolution 1325.

Many women and girls, based on their own decisions and because of cultural and social stereotypes, did not go through the disarmament and demobilization (DD) process at all. Those who were reluctant to participate did not want to identify themselves as having been involved with the conflict because of the negative repercussions in terms of reintegration and possible prospects, including marriage. This meant that those women and girls were not able to enjoy the package of financial and material benefits due to them as part of the process. On the other hand, those women and girls who presented themselves for the DD process were initially turned away by the then UNMIL leadership, since the policy at that time was that every former combatant had to hand over a gun in order to be eligible. But since many of the women and girls were involved in the conflict as wives, servants, cooks, and in other servicing functions for the male combatants, they had no guns to hand over. Even those who had carried guns had them taken away by former male combatants. This discriminatory policy created tension and unrest. After days of protests by female former combatants, the United Nations Children's Fund (UNICEF), and civil society groups, including many women's groups, this policy was changed.

However, additional challenges arose. By this time, many of the women affected by this policy had become mothers—single mothers, of course. Although those women finally went through the DD process, making them eligible for the reintegration and rehabilitation program and its benefits, it was almost impossible for single mothers to have access to education, vocational training, and regular employment in practice, because they had to take care of their babies. The problems of these single mothers were compounded by the fact that these babies called attention to the stigma of the women's sexual activity during wartime. In the absence of rehabilitation programs for the specific needs of female ex-combatants, some with babies, women's and girls' involvement in conflict will hurt their opportunities to realize their human rights. They may have to live with these consequences for the rest of their lives. While both girls and boys, young women and men are keen to receive education and skills training in the reintegration process in order to be able to engage in viable economic activities, many opportunities for girls are obstructed by societal attitudes. Measures will have to be designed by the Government, in conformity with the relevant articles of the Convention and supported by a proper understanding of the necessity to apply temporary special measures, in order to give preference to such girls in all educational programs so that the elimination of their multiple disadvantages can be accelerated.

CHALLENGES IN THE IMPLEMENTATION OF THE CONVENTION IN POST-CONFLICT LIBERIA

Liberia, reborn after fourteen years of devastating conflict, must be encouraged and assisted to utilize the Convention in the transformation of its society, in particular with respect to the status of women and the guarantee of their human rights. The armed conflict had severe adverse effects on the enjoyment of these rights. Preliminary information from an ongoing survey on war-related sexual and gender-based violence indicates that 69 percent of the women who responded had been victims of various forms of abuse. But, even as security progressively improves and the situation gradually normalizes, women continue to be at great risk of suffering such human rights abuses as increased sexual exploitation, including sexual favors in exchange for goods and services, rape, and domestic violence. Various harmful traditional and cultural practices also continue to violate women's rights and impede their enjoyment of equal opportunities with men in education, health, employment, and in the family. These must be addressed.

Until recently, the definition of rape in Liberian law was limited to forced penetration with a penis. This was revised in a new law that was guided by UN human rights instruments, including CEDAW and some of its general recommendations.[9] The problem still remaining is the inclusion of a prohibition of marital rape, which was opposed by many with the argument that this would break with tradition and lead to the breakdown of marriages. The establishment of a Women and Juvenile Unit of the National Liberian Police (NLP), headed by a high-level female senior officer and strongly supported by UNICEF, is highly commendable. It has led to increased reporting of offenses and has resulted in the fact that courts will not unduly delay acting on cases. Here again attitudes will need to change, so that victims will have the confidence to report incidents of gender-based violence. Judges, law enforcement agencies, and health-care providers need to be trained to understand that domestic violence and rape constitute violations of women's rights.

Inheritance rights of spouses under the common-law-based statutory law and under customary laws also negated women's human rights. Recently, another positive aspect in the implementation of the Convention, particularly of its Article 15 (equality before the law), was the adoption in October 2003 of the Act to Govern the Devolution of Estates and Establish Rights of Inheritance for Spouses of both Statutory and Customary Marriages. By widening the scope of applicable existing law, this Act aims at the streamlining of inheritance rights to benefit spouses under the current dual legal system. The challenge now is the implementation of the Act, including making Liberians, particularly women, aware of it.

A review of the national legislation in conformity with Liberia's international human rights obligations is a priority action that must be planned and implemented. While the National Transitional Government of Liberia (NTGL) signed or acceded to all the principal international human rights treaties in 2003 and 2004, thereby providing a comprehensive legal framework for the protection of human rights, including women's rights, nevertheless, these instruments have yet to be incorporated into national laws and implemented through legal reform. Based on my experience with CEDAW in Ghana, where studies had been done to analyze whether the laws of the country comply with the Convention and where Ghana's Labour Law had been amended with reference to Article 11 of the Convention (women's right to nondiscrimination in employment),[10] I recommended the establishment of a Law Reform Commission to ensure that the laws of Liberia conform to all international instruments to which the country is a State Party. This recommendation has been adopted by President Johnson-Sirleaf and all other arms of the Government. A law establishing the Law Reform Commission is before the Legislature.

Beyond legal reform, however, the country needs to build the legal and human rights capacity of men and women in all functions and professions, including men and women in the executive branch of government, the legislature, judiciary, and all law enforcement agencies. Health-care providers, teachers, and the entire civil society, including national NGOs and women's groups, including rural women's groups, must also be targeted and educated. Traditional rulers are also a very important target group, because they deliver the rule of law and the dispensation of justice in the hinterland at the paramount courts.[11] These courts are part of the local government structure and are widely patronized by women because of their easy accessibility and straightforward procedures, handling also cases related to traditional and customary practices. Women's access to justice, particularly rural women's access, is essential so that the violations of their rights under the Convention can be addressed and remedies offered. In post-conflict Liberia, there are rural areas where it can take between three to ten hours or even longer on foot to reach the nearest police station. This situation is doubly disadvantageous for women in a society where domestic violence and rape occur disturbingly often. Thus, all deficiencies in the administration of justice must be vigorously addressed and general campaigns for public awareness of human rights must be carried out. Fundamental human rights cannot be guaranteed in Liberia without the establishment of the rule of law based on democratic principles and practices. CEDAW can be an important tool in the process of transforming Liberian society. The application of temporary special measures to accelerate efforts toward closing the gap between women and men on the one hand and between urban and rural women on the other is necessary. By bringing about equality between men and women sustainable peace and development will be achieved in the country.

NOTES

1. The mandate of UNMIL included: to support the effective and timely implementation of the ACPA; to offer assistance, training, and advice to the Liberian law enforcement authorities and other criminal justice institutions; and to monitor the implementation of various programs, such as the disarmament, demobilization, and reintegration program. In addition to an HIV/AIDS policy adviser, a senior gender adviser with staff, was situated in the Office of the UN Special Representative of the Secretary-General to undertake and support gender mainstreaming within the various pillars of the Office with civil society and other external partners.

2. ECOWAS is a regional group founded on May 28, 1975, when sixteen West African countries signed the Treaty of Lagos (it currently has fifteen members). Its mission is to promote economic integration. It was founded to achieve "collective self-sufficiency" for the member States by means of an economic and monetary union creating a single large trading block.

3. The former UN Commission on Human Rights, superseded since 2006 by the UN Human Rights Council, established several mechanisms, also referred to as "special procedures," to address human rights issues either by analyzing specific country situations or by pursuing thematic issues related to human rights in all parts of the world. The UN Independent Expert on the Situation of Human Rights in Liberia, established in 2003, is such a special procedure. Mandate holders serve in their personal capacity, and their independent status is crucial so that they are able to fulfill their functions in all impartiality.

4. Liberia has a decentralized form of government with a president. The country is

divided into counties, and each county has both towns and large rural areas. The rural areas are referred to as "hinterland" in the law books. Although there are official government representatives in these areas, traditional rulers have much authority.

5. The African Charter on Human and Peoples' Rights entered into force on October 21, 1986, and is a regional human rights instrument specifically designed to reflect the history, values, traditions, and development of Africa. The Charter aims to combine typical African values with international norms by not only promoting internationally recognized individual rights, but also proclaiming collective rights and individual duties.

6. The Convention on the Rights of the Child (CRC) came into force on September 2, 1990, and, as of September 2006, every member State of the United Nations has become a party to it, except for Somalia and the United States of America, though both have signed it. Though written in gender-sensitive language, it does not refer to the gender-specific situations of the girl-child. Liberia submitted its first report, which had been due on July 3, 1995, to the Committee on the Rights of the Child on May 7, 2003. On September 22, 2004, Liberia also signed the Optional Protocols to the CRC on the Rights of the Child on the Sale of Children, Child Prostitution and Child Pornography and on the Involvement of Children in Armed Conflicts.

7. "Don Bosco" institutions are homes and educational institutions for poor, disadvantaged, or orphaned children and adolescents, both boys and girls, established in many countries of the world.

8. UN Security Council Resolution 1325 was passed unanimously on October 31, 2000. It can be found on various UN and NGO websites, including the website of Peace-Women, which gives a detailed history and analysis of the text; a history of its implementation by UN member States and of follow-up activities in the Security Council since 2000; a description of the advocacy activities of "1325 Peacewomen;" and references to other resources (http://www.peacewomen.org).

9. The new rape law came into force on January 17, 2006.

10. Between 1991 and 2000, the National Council on Women and Development of Ghana, in collaboration with the Federation of Female Lawyers in Ghana, commissioned a study to analyze how the laws of the country complied with CEDAW. The results of the study showed that, although much legal reform had been achieved by using the Convention, much more needed to be done, particularly in the area of property rights. One successful example of utilizing the Convention was in the area of labor law. A provision did not allow women to work underground in the mining industry, thus cutting many qualified female mining engineers off from work with high pay. Article 11 of CEDAW (elimination of discrimination in formal and informal employment) was used to amend that provision through a parliamentary act.

11. A paramount chief is the highest-level traditional (usually tribal) chief or political leader in a regional or local polity or country that typically is administered politically with a chief-based system. A paramount chief also has judicial powers and presides, when sitting in court, over a paramount court.

THE WORK OF THE COMMITTEE

THE NATURE AND MANDATE OF THE COMMITTEE

HANNA BEATE SCHÖPP-SCHILLING, *GERMANY*

The CEDAW Convention established the creation of a body of independent experts—the Committee on the Elimination of Discrimination against Women—to monitor its implementation through a review of States Parties' reports. The procedural articles of the Convention describe the nature of this Committee, the characteristics of its members, their election through States Parties, and the modalities of the election process (Article 17); States Parties' obligations to submit reports on a regular basis to the Committee for review (Article 18); the rights of the Committee to adopt its own Rules of Procedure and elect its own officers (Article 19); the Committee's working time (Article 20); the Committee's reporting obligations within the UN system as well as its right to make suggestions and general recommendations (Article 21); and the role of the UN specialized agencies in the review process (Article 22). The Optional Protocol to the Convention of 1999 allows the Committee to carry out two additional monitoring functions in addition to the reviews of the States Parties' reports: the communication and inquiry procedures, which put the Convention on an equal footing with some of the other human rights treaty bodies.

MEMBERS OF THE COMMITTEE

The Committee started out in 1982 with the full twenty-three members allotted to it according to the Convention. Committee members are nominated by their respective countries, each a State Party to the Convention. Members must be "of high moral standing and competence in the field covered by the Convention" (Article 17 [1]). Every two years, States Parties elect new or reelect previous experts for a four-year term by secret ballot from a list of candidates.[1] The Convention encourages States Parties, in selecting Committee members, to consider "equitable geographical distribution" and "representation of the different forms of civilization as well as the principal legal systems" (Article 17 [1]). In the practice of the UN system, this means distribution according to "regional groups." These were originally characterized not only by geographical but also by political factors as a result of the Cold War. Thus, while the "Eastern European States" are no longer part of a "socialist bloc," this region still exists for election and other purposes in the UN system, and experts are nominated by States Parties from this regional group as well as from the other regional groups comprising African States, Asian States, Latin American and Caribbean States, as well as Western European and Other States (with Kiribati not being a member of any regional group).

Different "forms of civilization" and "principal legal systems" refer to different stages of economic development, different political and legal systems, and different cultures. All these factors contribute to the formal and practical realization of women's human rights. In some countries, several legal systems exist side by side and affect the implementation of the Convention. Acceptance of such political, legal, cultural, or developmental differences does not, however, allow for a relativistic view of experts in evaluating the achievements of a given State Party. Nor do experts "judge" any of these systems. The work of the Committee over the past twenty-five years has benefited decisively from members' detailed knowledge of these differences, in particular the legal ones and their interaction. Only on this basis can the Committee do justice to the variety of States Parties, their reports, and the actual human rights situation of women under their jurisdictions.

Tensions between experts from different regional groups and political, economic, and legal systems characterized work in the early years of the Committee. This situation changed with the end of the Cold War, but depending on individual experts and their life experiences, other tensions may also flare up, including those among experts from the so-called "North," or developed, highly industrialized countries, and from the "South," or developing and often formerly colonized countries. While there was a strong preponderance of experts from socialist States from Eastern Europe and elsewhere in the early years, due to the fact that these countries rapidly ratified the CEDAW Convention because they believed that women had already achieved equality with men in their jurisdictions, the Committee did not have any experts from the Eastern European region from 1995 until the end of 2002. While Latin American, Caribbean, and African States consistently had members on the Committee, the numbers of these members fluctuated. Some countries, however, were successful in always or almost always having a national as an expert on the Committee once they became a State Party and nominated one for election.[2]

Since 1982, women have dominated as members of the Committee— as men have dominated as members of the other human rights treaty bodies.[3] CEDAW experts have come from all walks of life and represented all professional disciplines, including law, history, literature, psychology, international studies, political science, sociology, and medicine.[4] Thus, the Committee has been able to draw on the professional expertise and experience of its members with respect to a variety of life situations, and experts have been able to discern and evaluate the full potential of discriminatory actions against women under all articles of the Convention. Some members, in their professional lives, work as government officials in the so-called national machinery for women, for example, the Ministry for Women/Gender or National Commission on Women. Others serve as diplomats in the Foreign Offices of their country. Members also work as independent professionals, teach at universities, or hold high positions in nongovernmental organizations (NGOs). Sometimes, they combine several of these functions.

Once elected, experts "shall serve in their personal capacity" (Article 17 [1]). Thus, their governments cannot and should not tell them what to say or do. Experts, in fact, swear their impartiality in a solemn oath at the beginning of the first session they attend. Nevertheless, there have been instances when pronouncements on States Parties' reports by some experts sounded remarkably like their governments' official policies, although of course these statements may also have been completely in accordance with their own beliefs. Fairly soon after its inception the Committee consistently applied a rule that an expert may not speak in the Committee's dialogue with her or his country's delegation or be involved in any assessment of her or his country's report. The principle of regional group representation also governs the composition of the Committee's bureau—consisting of a Chairperson, three Vice-Chairpersons, and the rapporteur—who are elected by the Committee on a rotational two-year basis. The chair, and sometimes the vice-chairs, facilitate the meetings, and the bureau prepares the Committee's agenda—apart from the task of considering States Parties' reports— for a session. They also represent the Committee in seminars or UN entities when invited, but closely adhere to the Committee's decisions in their pronouncements when in these roles.

The CEDAW Committee, like the UN itself, is an experiment in intercultural learning. Apart from broadening individual members' understanding of cultures and legal and political systems that differ from their own, interaction among Committee members also requires cultural sensitivity and consensus-finding skills within a framework of the six official languages that rely on the accuracy of the translators. All members of the Committee would agree that the experience of serving on the Committee has been an enriching one on the personal and professional level.

MANDATE OF THE CEDAW COMMITTEE

The Convention gives the Committee the following mandate: first, to review States Parties' reports at regular intervals; and second, to formulate "suggestions and general recommendations based on the examination of reports and information received" from States Parties. The Platform for Action of the Fourth UN World Conference on Women in Beijing (1995) added the additional task of monitoring the implementation of the Platform's goals and detailed strategies for achieving women's equality with men in the equal exercise and enjoyment of their human rights (United Nations 1995a, paras. 322–23). The fact that in 1979, when the Convention was adopted, UN member States did not allow for more than one procedure for its monitoring body was in stark contrast to what they had allowed for the International Convention on the Elimination of All Forms of Racial Discrimination (ICERD) in 1965, which, through its Article 14, allows its treaty body to receive communications from individuals or groups of individuals. While that procedure became effective only in the 1980s, thus revealing a general reluctance by UN member States to seeing it practiced, it is still remarkable that fourteen years after they had included such a procedure into the text of the ICERD they did not do the same for the CEDAW Convention. In 1999 the adoption of an Optional Protocol to the Convention did finally grant the Committee its two additional monitoring procedures—a special triumph of the global women's human rights movement.

Monitoring Through the Reporting Procedure

According to Article 18 (1) of the Convention, States Parties have to submit reports to the UN Secretary-General for consideration by the Committee "one year after the entry into force for the State concerned" and then "at least every four years and further whenever the Committee so requests." The reports should cover the "legislative, judicial, administrative or other measures" that States Parties have adopted in order to implement the Convention and indicate the "progress made in this respect." States Parties "may indicate factors and difficulties" that may affect the implementation of the Convention (Article 18 [2]).

In its first session in October 1982, the Committee developed Rules of Procedures and in its second session in August 1983 it adopted Guidelines to assist States Parties in writing their reports. Over the years, both have been amended and expanded several times. Also in its second session, the CEDAW Committee reviewed the first seven initial reports in the following order—the German Democratic Republic, Mexico, the Union of Soviet Socialist Republics, the Byelorussian Soviet Socialist Republic, the Ukrainian Soviet Socialist Republic, Sweden, and Cuba—which had been written even before any guidelines existed (United Nations 1989b, 26–54).

Of importance is the mandate of the Committee to request the submission of reports outside of the usual time frame on an exceptional basis (Article 18 [1] [b]). The Committee has used this power five times so far.[5] To act in a consistent manner with respect to requesting such reports , the Committee formulated a number of criteria, including that it must have reliable information on grave or systematic violations of women's human rights that are gender-based or directed at women because of their sex (CEDAW 1999, 47).

In the early years the Committee encountered many obstacles of a technical and organizational nature, including the restriction of its meeting time to "normally . . . not more than two weeks annually," according to Article 20 (1) of the Convention, as well as a lack of support by the secretariat servicing the Committee, the Division for the Advancement of Women (DAW), due to the fact that it took UN member States some time to grant adequate resources.[6] The restriction in meeting time proved to be a severe handicap for the Committee's work, since a rapid increase in the number of States Parties to the Convention caused a severe backlog of reports. While the purpose of this provision was not to discriminate against the Committee, it certainly did have that effect.[7] Legal acceptance by States Parties of an amendment to Article 20 (1) in 1995, lifting the restriction, has proven to be a slow process. Apart from the amendment, however, the UN General Assembly has been granting the Committee increasingly more meeting time over the years. In 2006, the Committee met, very adequately supported by the DAW, in three sessions for three weeks each, working in two chambers in two of those sessions. It was thus able to discuss in one year the reports of thirty-eight States Parties, rather than sixteen as it had done in the previous years when it had met in only two sessions of three weeks.

Many changes in the working methods of the Committee over the past twenty-five years have been initiated by the Committee's Chairpersons as well as by committee members. Meetings of members of treaty bodies, as the by now annual Meeting of Chairpersons and the Inter-Committee Meeting convened at the Office of the High Commissioner for Human Rights (OHCHR) have also contributed to the improvement as well as the harmonizing of working methods among the currently seven treaty bodies since 1994, though full harmonization is still a goal. Today, the CEDAW Committee treats initial reports and subsequent periodic reports in the same manner and devotes the same amount of time to the discussion of each. To prepare for discussion of reports the Committee selects a small group of experts from its midst, again attempting to follow the principle of regional group representation and including those Committee members who have been assigned the task of country rapporteurs for specific States Parties. This group meets as a "pre-session group" several months in advance of the session in which the reports are going to be discussed. With the assistance of the secretariat, it draws up a list of questions on the basis of the information given in each report—as well as of previous reports in the case of periodic reports—and of additional oral or written information it receives from UN specialized agencies and from international and national NGOs. These questions are sent to States Parties with the request to receive answers in writing well before the next session.

Both the report and the written answers to the list of questions are then discussed orally with the delegation of the respective State Party for about five hours in the following session. By allotting the same amount of time to each report, the Committee adheres to the UN principle and the practice of all other human rights treaty bodies to treat each UN member State or State Party to a Convention equally in the formal sense. It has to be acknowledged, though, that such a rule does not necessarily do justice to the principle of substantive equality in dealing with States Parties. The dialogue with the delegation, which is often headed by the Minister for Women's Affairs of that country, is "constructive," e.g. to be "classified as 'carrot' rather than 'stick'" (Evatt 2002, 530). While experts point to what they consider a lack of implementation, they do not act as a court and do not pass "verdicts" on a State Party. Rather, the Committee develops specific guidance for each State Party, suggesting the adoption of a variety of measures, legal and otherwise, including temporary special measures to accelerate the achievement of substantive equality. Such recommendations may include suggestions by UN specialized agencies and NGOs, if the Committee finds them to be applicable. The respective country rapporteur then formulates a draft of the so-called concluding comments to the State Party, which contain the Committee's acknowledgment of the achievements of a State Party in the implementation of the Convention, its concerns about the partial or nonimplementation of the obligations under specific articles, and its recommendations concerning further action. The actual application of this format, which the Committee has been following since its thirteenth session in 1994, has been improved on in almost each session. Thus, the Committee has dropped the category of comments in which it had listed those factors and difficulties, such as natural disasters or political and economic transformations, to which a State Party might have pointed as impeding the implementation of the Convention. The Committee feared being misunderstood as condoning the nonimplementation of the Convention under extraordinary circumstances, since disadvantageous contexts do not allow for discrimination against women. Further improvement of the concluding comments is still warranted. The Committee's biggest—and so far unresolved— challenge has been to achieve a balance between acknowledging a specific country's situation on the one hand and the consistency of its formulations in all concluding comments on the other. The Committee finalizes and adopts its concluding comments in closed meetings at the end of each session.[8] Due to its lack of working time, the Committee has not yet developed a follow-up procedure on its concluding comments, one that might discern, at interim intervals, to what extent these comments have been disseminated and implemented by a State Party before its next report is due.

Because not all States Parties report on time and because some have not been reporting at all, the Committee allows the submission of a combination of reports so that a State Party may catch up on its reporting schedule. While this practice helps States Parties to meet their overdue reporting obligations and helps the Committee to reduce its backlog of reports, the Committee also has noticed with concern that some States Parties utilize this informal rule to "normalize" their reporting schedule into an eight-year reporting cycle. Non- or late reporting of States Parties still remains a problem.

Monitoring the Beijing Platform for Action

The Platform for Action of the Fourth UN World Conference on Women in Beijing (1995), to which almost all UN member States committed themselves, gave the Committee the additional task of taking into account the implementation of the Platform's recommendations when considering States Parties' reports. It is important to point out, though, that the Platform is not a legally binding document for UN member States. In addition, they are only "invited" to include information on "measures taken to implement the Platform for Action" (United Nations 1995a, para. 323). However, the CEDAW Committee adopted an innovative approach by linking the Beijing Platform's twelve areas of concern to the articles of the CEDAW Convention. Thus, in the view of the Committee, the contents of the Platform recommend *programmatic* details to States Parties for implementing *rights* articulated in the Convention. The Committee subsequently changed its reporting guidelines accordingly, and it regularly reviews States Parties' efforts in this respect, including the commitments deriving from the conclusions of the Beijing follow-up conferences. More recently, it has also taken note of the Millennium Development Goals (MDGs) adopted by the UN General Assembly in its fifty-fifth session in 2000, and it requests this additional relevant information in States Parties' reports.[9]

Suggestions and General Recommendations

Article 21 (1) gives the CEDAW Committee the right to formulate suggestions and general recommendations. The Committee normally directs such suggestions to UN organs or to UN conferences. The most important ones were Suggestion No. 4 (1993), which focused on reservations to the Convention, and Nos. 5 (1994) and 7 (1995) on the feasibility of preparing an Optional Protocol to the Convention and on the elements of such a treaty. The Committee has been concerned about reservations since an early session when it first encountered their effects in the discussion of the initial report of Egypt in 1984 (United Nations 1989c, 255–56, paras. 185, 190). The Committee has since questioned respective States Parties about the specific impact of such reservations on the women living under their jurisdictions and has urged such States Parties in its constructive dialogue and concluding comments and more generally in several suggestions, general recommendations and statements to review, amend, and withdraw such reservations. Of specific concern to the Committee are reservations and declarations which it sees as being incompatible with the Convention.[10]

The Committee addresses its general recommendations, through which it interprets the meaning of the Convention's articles, to States Parties. Such interpretations proved contentious in the early years due to political and legal differences among experts. Committee members disagreed about whether the Committee had a mandate to interpret the Convention, as for example with regard to the context of reservations, and the attempt to standardize statements on implementation addressed to States Parties that were at different stages of development, had different cultures, and different legal systems (Evatt 2002, 536). The issue was resolved on the basis of legal advice from the UN Secretariat as to the meaning of Article 21 (1) of the Convention. The Committee began to formulate general recommendations in 1986, and at a later point decided on a formalized process for drafting and adopting them.[11]

Monitoring Through the Communication and Inquiry Procedures

The CEDAW Committee's work under the Optional Protocol officially began in 2001 with the establishment of a standing Working Group from its members to deal with communications coming from individual women or groups of women who see themselves as victims of discrimination that violates their rights under the Convention. It dealt with its first case starting in 2003. The working group prepares a decision for the Committee on the admissibility and merit of a communication, and—if these criteria are met—formulates draft recommendations to the State Party for remedies, which the Committee will then adopt as its "view" with or without modifications or minority opinions. To deal with potential inquiries to be conducted under the Optional Protocol, the Committee appoints one or several rapporteurs from its midst, who examine and evaluate the "reliability" of the information received and then pursue an inquiry if the Committee so decides. An inquiry of an alleged grave or systematic human rights violation against women will result in a report that also will contain recommendations addressed to the respective State Party.

ROLE OF UNITED NATIONS SPECIALIZED AGENCIES, PROGRAMS, AND FUNDS

Article 22 allows certain UN specialized agencies not only to be present at the "constructive dialogue" with a State Party, but also to "submit reports on the implementation of the Convention in areas falling within the scope of their activities" to the CEDAW Committee. The interpretation of this provision also created some contention among members in the early years, although today, the Committee has established contact with all such entities, regularly receives their reports in written form, and devotes a certain part of its meetings at each session to receiving further oral input and discussing it with the representatives of such agencies as the Food and Agriculture Organization (FAO), UN Development Fund for Women (UNIFEM), UN Development Programme (UNDP), UN Educational, Scientific and Cultural Organization (UNESCO), the International Labour Organization (ILO), and the World Health Organization (WHO) and the UN High Commissioner for Refugees (UNHCR).

In a more recent development, field offices of the OHCHR in specific countries have started to connect confidentially with field offices of UN agencies in order to collate their information on the respective country for the Committee. In addition, such collaboration has allowed these offices to assist a State Party in its implementation of the Convention and to integrate aspects of the Committee's concluding comments into their fieldwork. Most important, UNIFEM has decided to put the dissemination and implementation of the Convention at the core of its worldwide activities.

INTERNATIONAL AND NATIONAL NGOS

In contrast to the UN specialized agencies, NGOs—whether they are international or national—are not referred to in the CEDAW Convention, although their role is recognized and described in detail under the communication and inquiry procedures of its Optional Protocol. However, NGOs—which may offer and promote advocacy, litigation, or a variety of services, ranging from dissemination of information, to training, to provision of social services—do assist in the implementation of the Convention both at the national and at the grassroots levels of States Parties through empowering women to claim their rights under the Convention.

This process was initiated and has been increasingly supported over the years through the work of international NGOs, which have been helpful by providing additional information in alternative or "shadow" reports to the Committee and under the Optional Protocol, and by creating a relationship between the CEDAW Committee and national women's groups. Of decisive importance in this respect in the early years was the work of the International Women's Rights Action Watch (IWRAW), created in 1985 and based in the U.S. IWRAW also convened CEDAW experts in weekend seminars on specific topics related to articles of the Convention and produced the first guide for States Parties, NGOs, and Committee experts alike for the assessment of the implementation of the Convention.[12] In the early 1990s, IWRAW and women from the South began to see the need for a regionalization of activities in order to do more effective on-the-ground work with women. In 1993, the International Women's Rights Action Watch Asia Pacific (IWRAW Asia Pacific) emerged as an autonomous organization in Malaysia, connecting national women's NGOs, in particular from developing countries and from countries in political and economic transition, to the review process of States Parties' reports at the international level of the Committee, by training them to provide alternative reports to the Committee and bringing them to the Committee's sessions. It thus crucially aided women's empowerment as rights holders at the grassroots levels. Other international NGOs at various points during the past twenty-five years have also seen the potential of raising their own specific concerns to the level of international visibility by addressing the Committee and by connecting the Committee to their national entities.[13]

Today, the CEDAW Committee has formalized the recognition of

NGOs by accepting short oral presentations of their concerns in some parts of its meeting time, including a few minutes of dialogue on them; by making reference to the various functions of such NGOs in its concluding comments, including their need for nondiscriminatory access to organizing, funding, and expression at the national level; and by valuing their practical defense of women victims as defined in the Optional Protocol. States Parties themselves have been pursuing different strategies toward the inclusion of NGOs in the review process. These range from a total disregard of NGOs or a clear separation of NGOs' and a State's roles to integrating NGOs' critical comments into the a State's reports, or adding these in separate sections. Sometimes NGOs are even included in the government delegation.

LINKS BETWEEN THE COMMITTEE AND OTHER UN ENTITIES

The Committee sends its final report of each session—which is comprised of its concluding comments, suggestions, statements, decisions, general recommendations, views and specific reports under the Optional Protocol, as well as lists of the number of States Parties and of submission—or lack of submission—of their reports through the UN Economic and Social Council (ECOSOC) to the UN General Assembly. As mentioned before, the Committee cannot sanction any State Party that does not comply with its reporting or implementation obligations. Having a public UN document that lists States Parties' action or lack thereof is thus one way of "shaming" those who evade accountability. The Secretary-General also transmits the Committee's report to the Commission on the Status of Women (CSW), and the Committee's chair usually speaks at the CSW's annual session. More recently, the CSW formally asked the Committee to provide input into the topics it discusses. Since the mid-1990s, DAW has posted both the States Parties' reports and the Committee's concluding comments on its specific website for CEDAW (http://www.un.org/womenwatch/daw/cedaw).

IMPACT OF THE COMMITTEE'S WORK, CHALLENGES AND OUTLOOK

Dutch feminists developed a valuable analysis for assessing a State Party's accountability for results in the implementation of the Convention. According to this framework, governments have an obligation first, to achieve full equality of women with men before the law and in public administration; second, to improve the material position of women to one of substantive equality with men through programs and resource allocation; and third, to fight the dominant gender ideology and thus effect cultural change through which women's equality with men will become acceptable (Groenman et al. 1997). The Committee has seen such positive developments in many countries, although much remains to be done and new challenges to the realization of women's human rights emerge. While there is no doubt that the Committee's work has contributed to a worldwide awareness of women's human rights and an increase in their factual enjoyment of these, it is sometimes difficult to identify the Committee as the decisive influence. Many other factors—such as UN world conferences or national developments apart from the CEDAW review process, and, more lately the communication and inquiry procedures— also have been significant. Committee members themselves have converted their experiences in the Committee into legal and other action to benefit women within their own countries. Sometimes, direct impact can be acknowledged, in part from statements by governments themselves or from Committee members, from court verdicts referring to the Convention, and also from pronouncements by NGOs about their own advocacy or litigation. The current discussion on treaty body reform, including such issues as a *unified* treaty body comprised of all human rights treaty bodies and consolidated reporting formats, poses a threat to the specificity of the Committee's work and to the benefits women derive from it. Given the nature of discrimination against women based on their sex and gender, which, in the Committee's view, quantitatively and qualitatively differs from discrimination against them or other groups on other grounds, this specificity must not be lost whatever organizational changes may take place. The past twenty-five years of the Committee's work have proven the need for a separate monitoring body and for reports that focus on States Parties' efforts to achieve women's human rights.

The Committee supports reform of UN treaty bodies, since current discussions also open new opportunities for emphasizing the norm of women's equality with men in the enjoyment of their human rights as a guiding as well as cross-cutting principle in the activities of all treaty bodies. The Committee's move to Geneva where it will be serviced—together with other human rights treaty bodies—by the OHCHR will facilitate this process. Currently, the Committee is an active participant in the reform debate where it argues for close collaboration and coordination of all treaty bodies in a harmonized and integrated *system* but insists on keeping the distinct specificity of each of them (Schöpp-Schilling 2007).

Twenty-five years from now, when the Committee hopefully will celebrate the fiftieth anniversary of its work, there will be universal ratification of the Convention and its Optional Protocol; withdrawal of all declarations and reservations; a worldwide acceptance of nondiscrimination based on sex and gender as international customary law; the achievement of substantive equality of women and men in law, all life circumstances and in all cultures. The Committee will be part of an integrated, sophisticated and effective UN human rights monitoring system composed of independent experts on the one hand and intergovernmental bodies on the other, including an International Court for Human Rights. At the same time, there will exist similar independent and effective monitoring bodies and instruments at all regional and national levels, including national human rights institutes. A vibrant civil society will support the respect for and the protection and fulfillment of women's human rights in all countries. In short, there will hopefully be a world based on "the inherent dignity and [on] the equal and inalienable rights of all members of the human family [as] the foundation of freedom, justice and peace in the world" (UDHR, Preamble).

NOTES

I thank Cees Flinterman for making valuable suggestions of a substantive and an editorial nature.

1. Eleven of the experts of the first election originally could serve only for two years, to accommodate the rule calling for an election every two years. As indicated by the Convention, they were chosen by lot by the first Chairperson, Luvsandanzangyn Ider. Some of them were then renominated and reelected and served for additional terms on the Committee (United Nations 1989a, 6).

2. Countries with elected independent experts on the Committee for three or more election periods are: China, Cuba, Egypt, Germany, Ethiopia, Japan, Mexico, Nigeria, the Philippines, Portugal, and the Scandinavian countries (Denmark, Finland, Norway, Sweden), which established a practice of rotating nominations among themselves. In contrast to the early years and due to the high number of States Parties and the enhanced visibility and status of the Committee, to be elected requires extensive campaign efforts by States Parties as well as by nominees themselves.

3. Three men have served on the Committee in the past twenty-five years: Johan Nordenfelt from Sweden (1982–1984), Göran Melander from Sweden (2000–2004), and Cees Flinterman from The Netherlands (2003–2010).

4. The adoption of the Optional Protocol to the Convention in 1999 was followed by an increase in experts with legal training.

5. In 1994 it discussed such reports from Bosnia and Herzegovina, the Federal Republic of Yugoslavia (Serbia and Montenegro) and in 1995 from Croatia to assess the extent of gender-based violence against women in the wars and conflicts in the territories of the former Yugoslavia, including the mass rapes of women for ethnic purposes. It also requested such a report from Rwanda in 1995, after having received information on violence directed specifically against women during the acts of genocide; and it did so again to deal with the

disproportionately disadvantageous impact of the economic crisis on women in Argentina in 2002.

6. These obstacles have also been documented by many other commentators (e.g. Byrnes 1999; Bustelo 2000; Bayesfky 2001).

7. The clause, which cannot be found in any of the other human rights treaties, exists because UN member States had discussed two different monitoring bodies during the drafting process, namely either an intergovernmental ad hoc group to the CSW or a committee of independent experts. The ad hoc group was to meet before the session of the CSW for not more than two weeks. In the final deliberations on this provision in the Third Committee, a decision for a committee of independent experts was made, but an alteration of the time limitation was "forgotten" (Rehof 1993, 206-207; personal communication by CEDAW Committee member Aída González Martínez).

8. The concluding comments can be found in the annual reports of the Committee and, more recently, also on the CEDAW website under the respective session and country, http://www.un.org/womenwatch/daw/cedaw.

9. In 2005 the Committee added a paragraph to its concluding comments pointing out that the achievement of the MDGs depends above all on the complete and effective implementation of the Convention, including the integration of a gender perspective into all governmental efforts based on an explicit consideration of the Convention's provisions.

10. The Committee addressed the issue of reservations directly and indirectly in at least eight Decisions, Suggestions, General Recommendations and Statements from 1987–1998 and also included requests for information in its reporting guidelines since 1995 (Schöpp-Schilling 2004, 13–28). The Committee's views on reservations are mirrored in respective sections of the outcome documents of both the Vienna and Beijing UN Conferences, in Resolutions of UN organs and in the new harmonized reporting guidelines for all treaty bodies.

11. First, the Committee makes a decision to develop a general recommendation and identifies members who will be responsible for producing drafts. Second, these members write a background paper containing the main elements of a future general recommendation, which is discussed in an open meeting of the Committee at which NGOs and scholars are also invited to present papers. Third, the first draft is produced and is discussed in substance. Fourth, an editorial committee may polish the draft general recommendation and present it for final adoption. On several occasions, international NGOs such as IWRAW and IWRAW Asia Pacific or scholars attached to universities have also convened conferences, to which some members of the Committee were invited, to assist the process.

12. IWRAW developed its first guide in 1988. It has since been updated several times, and its latest version was published together with DAW and the Commonwealth Secretariat. It is also available in other languages than English (United Nations 2000e).

13. Such organizations include Amnesty International, Human Rights Watch, Minority Rights Group International, the World Organization against Torture, and the Center for Reproductive Rights.

PERSONAL REFLECTIONS:

SUPPORT BY THE UN DIVISION FOR THE ADVANCEMENT OF WOMEN

INGEBORG CREYDT, GERMANY

My work for the CEDAW Committee began in 1980 as a consequence of the many early ratifications of the Convention, which caused it to enter into force in 1981 less than two years after its adoption by the UN General Assembly. Nobody had anticipated such speedy and widespread recognition of the Convention in the first years of its existence, as the ratification process of other human rights treaties had proceeded far more slowly. The successful start of the Convention, however, made the work of the Secretariat—i.e. the UN Division for the Advancement of Women (DAW)—very difficult.

DAW was originally established in 1946 under a different name —the Section on the Status of Women, Human Rights Division, Department of Social Affairs—and with a lower status. It subsequently underwent several name changes and upgrades. It also moved from New York to the UN Office in Vienna in 1972, and then moved back to New York in August 1993. The program budget for the Committee, which had been adopted together with the Convention, did not match the workload resulting from the early adoption. Moreover, the Committee comprised twenty-three expert members from the beginning, while other human rights treaty bodies had only ten to eighteen. The Committee's sessions were also open to nongovernmental organizations (NGOs) and the general public, while other treaty bodies held closed meetings. As a member of the Human Rights Committee once informally said to me: The Human Rights Committee meets in working groups, but the CEDAW Committee convenes in conferences. Since only half of the Division's staff had moved from New York to Vienna, new staff had to be recruited. However, the work of the Committee started on time and proceeded without delay, thanks also to its highly motivated elected members.

DAW is responsible for the substantive and administrative preparation, servicing, and follow-up of the annual sessions of the Committee and the biannual meetings of the States Parties. The Secretariat has to secure the work of the Committee, but it is not permitted to influence the content of its work. The Committee is, after all, an organ of the States Parties, not of the United Nations. In support of the implementation of the Convention and the monitoring process by the

Committee, DAW has undertaken various educational and informational activities and provided technical assistance to States Parties. Thus, it has convened a number of interregional seminars in various countries and participated in and supported related conferences, such as the Mediterranean Conference on Human Rights in March 1993 in Taormina, Italy. The Secretariat has also helped individual countries (e.g. Namibia) to bring national laws in line with international instruments concerning the status of women.

THE EARLY YEARS

LUVSANDANZANGYN IDER, MONGOLIA

On this twenty-fifth anniversary of the CEDAW Committee, I want to say that it was a great honor for me to serve as its first Chairperson during its first two years. I also chaired the Working Group of the Third Committee, which thoroughly considered the draft CEDAW Convention during the UN General Assembly session in 1977. The UN's Third Committee deals with social, humanitarian and cultural issues.

The adoption of CEDAW was a landmark in the quest by the United Nations for equality and justice for women. It has become one of the most widely ratified human rights treaties, and as such it serves as an effective tool which women and organizations can use to redress women's inferior, unjust status.

The first CEDAW Committee included twenty-three experts— twenty-two women and one man—representing four continents. Since the Committee had to be composed of experts from those countries that had ratified the Convention, it had at that time wide representation from Europe (West and East) and Latin America but only one expert from Africa. The members were very different. Some had a wealth of firsthand experience of women's problems while working in women's organizations; some had a legal background; some held high posts in central and regional governments in their respective countries.

During its first two years the Committee spent much of its time considering and adopting its Rules of Procedure as well as Guidelines for Reporting, in order to help States prepare reports. In general, the spirit of understanding and cooperation among members prevailed during the deliberations. The members of the Committee came from different cultures,

*and spoke different languages, yet had a very similar attitude
to the problems faced by women and ways to solve them. At times,
however, a heated debate arose over wording, in some cases due to
ideological differences. At such moments, when it was difficult to find
common ground, Johan Nordenfelt from Sweden, the only male expert
on our Committee whose term ended in 1984, used to come to the rescue
to suggest some neutral formulation that could satisfy the arguing parties
and bring them to an agreement. He was very respected, and perhaps even
somewhat privileged as the single male member, yet he never abused his
position, and stepped in only when he considered that his help was required
and would be useful.*

*During the twenty-five years that have passed since the creation of
the Committee, the world has changed beyond recognition. The communist
system has collapsed, some big States have broken up, and many new
sovereign States have appeared on the world map. Mongolia was one of
those States in which fundamental political and socioeconomic changes
took place, beginning from the early 1990s, that ended up transforming a
one-party political system with its centrally planned economy into a multi-
party system with a market-oriented economy. How did that affect the
status of our women? In my view, it had both positive and negative effects.
Mongolian women, like Mongolian men, have acquired the cherished right
of choice, a very important right for human beings. Now we may choose
whether to be a member of a political party or not, to work or stay at home,
to choose the place of our residence, and to go to any part of the country—or
to any place in the world, once a visa is issued to us and if we can afford the
cost of travel. We have freedom of expression, freedom of press and so on. At
the same time many new problems, mainly of a socioeconomic nature, have
arisen, such as the rapid impoverishment of a large part of the population,
widespread unemployment, street children, and a decline in the quality of
education and health services. Women continue to be underrepresented in
the Parliament, and their number is even steadily decreasing. There is only
one woman in the Cabinet. This is taking place in a country where women
have attained a higher level of education than men.*

*With respect to the issues that need to be considered more widely and
actively at the international level, I believe that more attention should be
given to the eradication of discrimination against women in the family, in
marriage relations, and in inheritance and property laws, which women
continue to suffer from so persistently in many countries. Another issue that
deserves more attention is to involve the courts and judicial procedures more
widely in the implementation of CEDAW provisions and to help women*

use such procedures in their claims for their rights under the Convention. This would be very helpful in many countries, particularly in post-communist countries.

CHALLENGING GOVERNMENTS

MARIE CARON, CANADA

In 1967 a Royal Commission was created in Ottawa, the capital of Canada, to inquire into the status of women in the country in order to give women equal rights with men in all spheres of society. Canada was a participant from the beginning in the elaboration of a Convention to eliminate discrimination against women, advising the UN Secretary-General as early as 1973 that it would be in order to draft an international instrument to guarantee women rights equal to those of men. After the adoption of the CEDAW Convention by the UN General Assembly, Canada was one of the first countries to ratify it.

I was elected from Canada to the CEDAW Committee in 1982 and sat on the Committee for six years. It is interesting to note that different States Parties, when presenting their reports to the Committee, were convinced—according to the general statements given by them—that the goal of the Convention had been achieved, since the principle of equality between women and men was embodied in their constitution. Surely, there could be no discrimination in their country! Some States Parties claimed that the ratification of the Convention by their country was a standard procedure, reflecting the fact that women already enjoyed broad rights. Others went even further by insisting that not only did their constitution and laws reflect the spirit and the letter of the Convention, but also that their country went over and above the obligations of the Convention. For example, some claimed that everything was so great in their country in general and for women in particular that there was absolutely no prostitution! Luckily, thanks to the experts' questions, the Committee always brought government delegates back to earth so they might see the difference between fantasy and reality.

Often I disagreed especially with Committee members from the communist countries. It was impossible for me to believe Aleksandra Biryukova's claim that everything was wonderful in her country. I asked more and more questions, which made her impatient, even angry, with me. And of course I felt equally angry and so we battled verbally. Yet when I

went to Moscow to attend a meeting, in a reception at the Kremlin I met
Aleksandra and we fell into each other's arms and were really happy to see
each other again. Clearly, I knew also that we always respected each other,
regardless of our different political views.

There remain today many areas of life where women have yet to reach
equality and where there is still discrimination. Many women continue to
bear a double burden in that they work outside the home and at the same
time they have to take care of housekeeping and child rearing. Women are
underrepresented at the higher echelons of society. Even equal pay for work
of equal value has not been achieved. Much is being done, but it is a long
and hard climb left before us.

I truly enjoyed my experience on the Committee. It made me realize
that women cannot abdicate control of international human rights
to patriarchal governments. We must take an active interest in the
Convention to see that it is not only implemented, but also interpreted
in such a way that it promotes the equality of women and men for the
betterment of our societies. We must stand up for our own rights, because
nobody will do it for us.

THE FIRST TWELVE YEARS

DÉSIRÉE PATRICIA BERNARD, GUYANA

In 1982 I became part of the elected group of experts who comprised the
first members of the CEDAW Committee, when I was asked at very short
notice to replace the elected expert from Guyana who had died a few months
earlier. At this meeting I was appointed the Committee's first Rapporteur
from 1982 to 1984, and thereafter had the honor of serving as the
Committee's Chairperson for two terms (1985–1988).

I look back with a great degree of nostalgia at that very first meeting
held in October 1982, when twenty-three experts drawn from the world's
geographical regions—and comprising twenty-two females and one male—
met in Vienna, Austria. For me, it was an unparalleled experience as it
was my first exposure to the international scene. The time allocated for that
first meeting was just one week, during which we succeeded in adopting
the Rules of Procedure after long hours of deliberation and a great deal of
compromise. The next meeting was held in New York in August 1983, and
there we formulated Guidelines to assist States Parties in the preparation of

their reports. We also began the examination of initial reports of States that had ratified the Convention. In those early days, not much time or resources (whether human or financial) were allocated to the Committee, which was not taken seriously and was treated as the adopted orphan of the UN treaty bodies. Time allotted for the consideration of reports and discussion of the business of the Committee was never enough.

Membership of the Committee changed over the years from being initially comprised mainly of lawyers to later including other professional expertise. A very significant change occurred with the break-up of the Soviet Union, and the consequential shift in its political philosophy and that of its allies. When the Committee was inaugurated, many of the experts were from socialist countries—Cuba, Bulgaria, China, German Democratic Republic, Hungary, Mongolia, Poland, USSR, Vietnam, and Yugoslavia— with many belonging to the Soviet bloc. Most of these experts invariably presented a united position on important aspects of the Committee's work, and experts from the Soviet bloc looked to the USSR expert for guidance in deciding how they should approach any issue that came up for discussion. After 1989 the composition of the Committee changed. There were fewer members from the Soviet bloc, and only one Russian expert from the former USSR. This resulted in a shift in the types of questions that experts posed to representatives of States Parties in dialogue with them. Hitherto, the criteria used by the Soviet bloc experts tended to reflect women's responsibilities as wife and mother, and the protection and glorification afforded them by the State. The reports of these States also reflected only positive aspects of women's lives and denied the existence of any negative situations found in Western countries such as prostitution. In later years, the reports received from the majority of the former Soviet bloc States Parties were more open and frank, with admissions of negative situations as well as discussions of positive progress made in implementing the Convention.

Over time, the Committee expanded its mandate to undertake analyses and interpretations of individual articles of the Convention. This included identifying serious issues that greatly affect women, but that were not addressed specifically in any article. One such issue was the all-pervasive problem of violence against women, which resulted in 1992 in the formulation of General Recommendation No. 19.

Having the honor to serve as a member of the CEDAW Committee was an enriching experience that I cherish deeply. I formed friendships that have endured over the years, and that, as we worked together, united us to ensure the elimination of all forms of discrimination against women throughout the world.

THE MIDDLE YEARS

SALMA KHAN, BANGLADESH

After I came home from the United States in the mid–1960s with an advanced degree in development economics from the University of Chicago, I had a simple goal in life: to be a teacher of economics at my alma mater in Bangladesh. However, as I was developing my lectures on development economics in the national context, I soon recognized that women's issues were routinely bypassed in all economic policy formulations. Women were treated as passive recipients of development. With my instinctive urge to establish the fact that women were as much active agents of development as their male counterparts, I also soon realized that my work at the university did not put me in a position to take a stand and make a difference.

This led to an inevitable change in my career path, and I took up a job in the Planning Commission (Economic Planning Ministry), where I joined a team of young economists. Within a few years I came nearer to my immediate goal by persuading the Ministry to set up a separate Women's Wing in the Commission, with myself as its head. This position offered me my first opportunity to attend an important women's conference, and I accompanied the Minister for Women's Affairs to the Second UN World Conference on Women, held in Copenhagen in 1980. This conference also featured the official opening for signature and ratification of the CEDAW Convention by UN member States. Bangladesh was one of the sixty-four countries who then signed the Convention. That was my first introduction to CEDAW, and I felt as if I had found the magic instrument that spoke to the sense of gender inequality agitating within me for so long.

In 1992 I was nominated by my Government as a candidate for the CEDAW Committee. I joined the Committee as a member in 1993 for a first term of four years and was reelected for a second term until the end of 2000. I came back for a third term in 2003. In 1997 Committee members also elected me as Chairperson of the Committee for 1997 and 1998.

During my tenure as Chairperson from the Committee's sixteenth through nineteenth sessions, some important developments were instrumental in transforming the working methods of the Committee and improved the implementation of the Convention. During the sixteenth session in January 1997, one of the most significant of these took place: lengthening the allowed meeting time, which helped reduce the undesirable backlog of States Parties' reports waiting to be considered. In addition, the Committee, as a temporary measure, invited States Parties to combine a maximum of two reports to encourage them to report in a timely fashion and to meet compliance obligations. Two annual sessions increased the Committee's working time and its visibility.

Another important development during my Chairpersonship, and one that would have a long-term impact on the Committee's work, was the decision to meet informally with NGOs outside regular working time. This enabled NGOs to offer additional country-specific information on the States Parties to be reviewed by the Committee. While the Committee had received so-called "shadow" reports from international and national NGOs for many years, the reports by local NGOs began to increase in number at that time. Since then they have proven to be an important source of information regarding all areas of the implementation of the Convention that require further investigation by the Committee and additional efforts by States Parties. The Committee also recommended to States Parties that they consult national NGOs in the preparation of their reports.

Another noteworthy development from the sixteenth session was that the Committee decided to move the meeting of its presession working group to the end of the session prior to the one in which the respective reports would be considered. This decision, which was implemented somewhat later, significantly improved the collaboration of the Committee and States Parties since the latter now had more time, i.e. more than a month, to respond to the list of issues and questions in written form to the Committee prior to the oral discussion of their reports.

At the seventeenth session (July 1997), steps were taken to review and revise the existing Rules of Procedure of the Committee. The Committee also developed and agreed on a three-stage process for the preparation of general recommendations. For the first time, this process also created opportunities for the Committee to exchange views on the proposed subject of a general recommendation with NGOs and academics—a practice that still continues and involves broad-based participation. In considering reports, the Committee began to adhere to a more analytical approach and evaluated progress between the previous and the current report. This encourages a State Party to establish measurable indicators with respect to any advancement in women's enjoyment of their human rights within the context of the implementation of the Convention, and helps to identify areas in which further efforts by a State Party are required.

At its nineteenth session (June/July1998), the Committee also decided to revise its procedures for the elaboration of concluding comments, including their format, with a view to being consistent in the language it used while retaining flexibility with respect to a State Party's specificity.

This topic is one on which the Committee is still making improvements in 2006.

In 2004 the Committee held a round table to commemorate the twenty-fifth anniversary of the adoption of the Convention. The event was organized by DAW to celebrate the progress made in the implementation of the Convention at the national, regional, and international levels. It was indeed a memorable and unique occasion, moderated by the then Chairperson of the Committee Feride Acar. Written and oral statements of four past Chairpersons (Ivanka Corti, Aída González Martínez, Charlotte Abaka, and myself) highlighted major accomplishments during their respective terms of office. This was also an occasion for the Committee to recognize the remaining challenges faced and the need for better elaboration of the articles of the Convention in the constructive dialogue with States Parties and through its general recommendations.

The Convention and the Committee have come a long way. I was in the Committee during the 1990s and in the early years of the twenty-first century. To me, these years were the most exciting period, as the Committee was continuously going through the process of reexamining its working methods to strengthen the monitoring process and to develop strong collaborative partnerships with all major stakeholders. I also credit my time as a Committee member with broadening my own perspective on women's human rights issues and drawing out my innate feminist consciousness.

OUTREACH AND IMPACT

NORMA MONICA FORDE, BARBADOS

It was at the 1986 meeting of the States Parties that I was elected a member of the CEDAW Committee. My own country, Barbados, had established a National Commission on the Status of Women in 1976, with wide-ranging terms of reference relating to the family in general and the status of women in particular. A background of chairing that Commission, as well as prior involvement in regional and international human rights activity, heightened my desire for wider knowledge of the legal and social systems of the several States that then were parties to the Convention. My first meeting of the Committee was at its Sixth Session in 1987.

A rudimentary categorization of the eight sessions that I attended between 1987–1994 could be classified under two broad heads: vigorous outreach and determined monitoring of reports. Members of the Committee were encouraged and on occasion facilitated by the Division for the Advancement of Women (DAW) to promote the Convention and to emphasize the benefits that could flow from ratification and implementation of its provisions. Representatives of countries were brought together for detailed examination of their implementation of the Convention from regions as far apart as Antigua in the Caribbean and the Cook Islands in the South Pacific. I recall traveling with individual Committee members to Brazil, Sweden, and Russia. Governmental, quasi-governmental, and nongovernmental organizations and bodies that we met with included the Commonwealth Secretariat and the International Women's Rights Action Watch (IWRAW).

This vigorous outreach sought not only to advocate ratification and implementation of the Convention, but also to underscore the importance and, what is more, the value of reporting to it. As ratification increased, so did the number of submitted reports. The Committee sought to devise methods to deal, expeditiously, with presentation and consideration of these reports. Two of many suggestions were easily approved. It seemed practical to request from the General Assembly an extension of the time allocated for each session or that additional sessions be convened. An equally realistic idea, particularly for consideration of periodic reports, was the setting up of a presession working group consisting of members of the Committee, whose brief included detailed examination and study of the reports selected for review at the session. The group was expected to provide documents—lists of issues and questions based on the States Parties' reports—that could assist country representatives in the presentation of relevant information to the Committee.

By the Sixth Session the Committee had settled the much-discussed issue of its authority to make general recommendations. During my term several substantive general recommendations were adopted. The importance and real value of these cannot be disputed, particularly General Recommendation No. 19, which addresses violence against women. Steeped as I was in common law traditions, it was reassuring to discover that, despite the differences in legal and social systems existing in several States, reform measures to effect beneficial change in the status of women were not entirely dissimilar. The independent countries in the Commonwealth Caribbean have all ratified or acceded to the Convention. Barbados, Dominica, and Guyana were among the first countries to ratify, in 1980, and without reservations. With knowledge of the changes in law and policy that resulted from such total acceptance of the Convention, it was gratifying to be among Committee members when the initial reports of Caribbean States were presented. Additionally, personal knowledge of the legal, social, economic, and religious systems and of cultural processes of twenty-two countries was irreplaceable. We may have held individualistic views in the plenary committee and the working group meetings at each session, but memories of the social interaction, camaraderie, and friendship are indelible.

DUAL PERSPECTIVES

MERVAT TALLAWY, EGYPT

I joined the CEDAW Committee at its inception, receiving the highest number of votes from member States. The first years of its work were very challenging in terms of both time and resources. The limited time allocated to the Committee and the long periods that elapsed between meetings meant that we always had a backlog of reports for review with governments. We had little administrative and financial support, and we had to struggle to be given equal importance with other human rights supervisory bodies.

Some of the other challenges I recall were setting the agenda of the Committee, deciding on the articles to be addressed first, drawing up recommendations to governments in order to ensure implementation of the articles of the Convention, and drafting guidelines for the reporting system. The Committee had to devise a proper working relationship between its members and the representatives of the States Parties to the Convention for discussing their reports. The process involved building confidence to assure the government representatives that the purpose of the Committee was to guide them in implementing the articles of the Convention, to ultimately achieve equality between men and women, and to ensure the protection of women's rights.

Maintaining a constructive dialogue with government representatives in order to the Convention and their relation to Islamic law was a primary concern of mine. Islamic law does not contradict the principle of equality between the sexes, and therefore reservations to the Convention were often a point for discussion. According to international treaty law, reservations are acceptable only with regard to articles that are incompatible with national law, provided that they do not negate the main objective of the Convention.

I later switched roles when I became my country's Minister of

Insurance and Social Affairs and had to defend the report of the Egyptian Government in front of the Committee. My experience as a Committee member facilitated this new task, since I had learned the importance of being frank and discussing the weaknesses and obstacles facing women in my country. I had also learned that drafting the report requires the involvement of nongovernmental organizations (NGOs) and other social participants in the country. So I formed a delegation of NGOs and legal experts to present the report to the Committee.

The future program of the Committee would benefit from focusing on and strengthening the interaction with Ministry personnel at the national level to ensure that all those concerned with women's issues are aware of the results of the discussions of the national report, of the recommendations of the Committee, and of the issues to be addressed in a subsequent report. The gap between the debate in New York and the situation at the national level can be bridged by publicizing the work of the Committee and making it known throughout the country that is being discussed. When I was responsible for presenting my country's report, the Ministry received over sixty written questions on the report submitted from the Committee's presession group before we actually appeared in front of the Committee. Approximately forty additional questions were asked in the oral constructive dialogue with the Committee. Over twenty Committee members inquired about all aspects of a woman's life in Egypt. The distribution of these questions, which relate to all facets of a State Party's implementation of the Convention, the State Party's answers to them as well as the Committee's concluding comments will be helpful for governmental and nongovernmental groups working in the respective country to improve women's enjoyment of their human rights. Finally, I would like to mention that the experts who have worked on the CEDAW Committee over its twenty-five years of service have gained valuable experience in the social legislation of States Parties to the Convention. This expertise should be utilized at the national and regional levels. To preserve this knowledge and expertise, an association of CEDAW Committee members could be created.

WORKING FOR EQUALITY

MERIEM BELMIHOUB-ZERDANI, *ALGERIA*

The United Nations have always fascinated me during my life as an activist for issues such as peoples' rights, women's human rights, as well as the right to free oneself of the colonial yoke. My candidature for membership in the Committee was presented by my country, Algeria, and I was elected in August 2002 to serve as an expert for a four-year term, starting on January 1, 2003. During the second part of my first term, I was given the privilege of serving as one of the three vice-presidents of the Committee. I was reelected in 2006 to serve a second term, starting on January 1, 2007. I feel greatly honored to be part of this Committee, which works for the achievement for equality between women and men without any discrimination.

As a confirmation of the essential rights of women in the world, the Convention marks a historical turning point. It has been supported by various international women's conferences. The Beijing Declaration and Platform for Action, which emanated from the Fourth UN World Conference on Women, have become important instruments to ensure the promotion and protection of the rights of women. At that same event, the industrialized States Parties to the Convention solemnly pledged to assist poor countries by paying the equivalent of 0.7 percent of their Gross Domestic Product (GDP) in Official Development Assistance (ODA), while keeping in mind the ever-increasing need for human and financial resources for programs that advance the status of women and create the material basis for the enjoyment of their human rights. It is regrettable that so far very few industrialized nations have actually fulfilled this pledge.

The way in which the activities of the CEDAW Committee are organized and embedded in the United Nations as a whole adds transparency and publicity to the work of the Committee. Being mandated to defend the interests and rights of half of the world's population, namely women, it also serves humanity as a whole, because some would consider that any progress for women constitutes progress for men as well.

Currently, a reform process is taking place in the UN human rights system. Our Committee needs to remain vigilant in order not to be marginalized or to be integrated into the system as a whole in a way that would trivialize its importance. Women need a Convention and a monitoring Committee that looks after the specificity of the various forms of discrimination they unfortunately still are suffering. The CEDAW

Committee should not become invisible in its task of promoting and protecting the fundamental rights of women as laid down and defended in the Convention. The "rebirth" of women's rights at the date of the Convention's coming into force in 1981 must be defended, further strengthened, and not be lost.

ACHIEVEMENTS AND OBSTACLES

VICTORIA POPESCU, ROMANIA

I was an expert on the CEDAW Committee for one term, from 2003 until 2006. I had the honor to be invested as one of the vice-chairs of the Committee for two years. It was a short and yet particularly intense and enriching experience that helped me to understand the complex situation of women worldwide, and most of all, the major work of the CEDAW Convention in addressing gender inequalities and various forms of discrimination against women.

Throughout the period of my term, the Committee constantly refined its working methods in order to fulfill its responsibilities in a timely and effective manner. The Committee's framework for conducting a dialogue with national and international nongovernmental organizations (NGOs) and UN entities also improved. The Committee devoted special attention to the critical issue of reservations and to the slow pace of implementation of the Convention at national level in some countries. A landmark in the strengthening of women-related monitoring procedures was the adoption and coming into force of the Optional Protocol to the Convention. In 1999, I participated in the successful completion of the negotiations concerning this important tool. In my diplomatic function and as the Romanian delegate to the Commission on the Status of Women (CSW), I had supported Aloisia Wörgetter, the Austrian Chairperson of the CSW's open-ended working group on the elaboration of the Optional Protocol, as facilitator. I had been entrusted with the task of enabling the final revision of some difficult paragraphs of the text of the new treaty. Later on, as a CEDAW Committee expert, I joined the collective efforts to develop the Committee's practice under this new instrument. And I witnessed how it became operational with the Committee's first decisions in response to individual complaints and to its first inquiry under Article 8.

Coming from Romania and being most familiar with Eastern Europe,

I have followed with particular attention the reports from the countries of this region. The profound democratic reforms they have undergone, in the aftermath of the Cold War, have created new opportunities for the achievement of women's equality with men. But transition costs have also brought new challenges affecting women to a greater extent than men. For example, the region has been confronted with a substantial increase in the illegal trafficking in women and children. At the same time, the reports highlight the greater capacity of women to adjust to change and to become successful entrepreneurs. Women have also become visibly active in the civil society of those countries, influencing the transformation of their societies.

From the examination of the reports of the States Parties I have learned that no country, be it poor or developed, can achieve genuine democracy and sustainable development without the legal and material conditions guaranteeing real equality of opportunities to women and without an equitable division of resources and power between the sexes. And yet, nowhere in the world, not even in the most advanced countries, can women claim to have the same opportunities or enjoy the same rights as men. Effective promotion and protection of women's human rights require strong political will by States Parties as well as ongoing joint efforts by the main stakeholders: governments, civil society, and the international community.

CHALLENGES AND IMPACTS

KONGIT SINEGIORGIS, *ETHIOPIA*

Colleagues who were members of the Committee during the early years will agree with me that at times the work of the Committee was somewhat politicized because of the particular focus that different groups wished to give to different issues. Some chose to emphasize peace, others equality, and still others development. Though Zagorka Ilic, who encouraged me to join the Committee, came from a socialist country, she did not blindly support the position of the Eastern group. On the contrary, her ability to find compromise and to refocus issues was crucial to the function of the Committee. I would like to pay homage to her indefatigable efforts.

I came onto the Committee in 1985 and served for four terms until the end of 2000. As a multilateral officer who had been attending a large number of meetings for quite some time, I went to my first meeting of

*the Committee about 10–15 minutes late, thinking that I would be just
about on time. But most of the members were already there, heads bent
over their documents, and the Chairperson was about to call the meeting
to order. Since members are elected in their personal capacity, the seating
arrangement was by alphabetical order of names, and I must say it was
quite something to look for my seat in that serious and somber atmosphere.*

*The members of the Committee had interesting backgrounds. They
were highly qualified and experienced judges, lawyers, medical doctors,
social scientists, diplomats, politicians—in short, professionals in many
different fields. With such varied professional backgrounds and the personal
commitment of the experts, the dialogue with States Parties was not
only of high caliber but also utterly serious. It must be mentioned that
the Committee during my membership was composed entirely of women
experts. I believe, therefore, that the experts must have felt that being a
member of the Committee was a mission; at the risk of being accused of
exaggeration, one could say that the full implementation of all the rights
and obligations enumerated in the Convention was intimately intertwined
with the personal lives of members. Members felt a great responsibility and
carried out the task at hand with utmost care and impartiality.*

*In my view, the election of experts from a wide variety of professional
backgrounds has contributed considerably to the enrichment of the
Committee's work, particularly during the early stages of its existence. The
experts had to study and consider the voluminous States Parties' initial and
periodic reports; they were further obliged to look very closely at the working
methods of the Committee. The most crucial challenge was the disparity
between the Committee's limited meeting time of only two weeks annually
and the number of reports submitted to it as compared to the rest of the
treaty bodies. As a result, it had—and I believe still has—a huge backlog of
initial and periodic reports, which demanded the consideration of numerous
reports at each session. In this regard, the decision to allow the Committee
to hold three meetings a year—albeit for only two years so far (in 2006 and
2007)—must be welcomed. I would like to note that the decision to have
the Committee meet in two chambers to consider States Parties' reports is
also a very practical move and no doubt will help in reducing the backlog.
However, I am wondering whether this practice should be encouraged. I
must emphasize that, more often than not, each report is examined from a
different angle by each expert, which has made the consideration of reports
rich and detailed. To take away the practice of plenary consideration of
reports because of time constraints would not be advisable, particularly
since periodic reports are submitted only every four years. Therefore, I would*

argue that three sessions per year on a permanent basis would be a better solution, since discrimination against women still exists and persists in every society—and is highly unlikely to disappear for a long time to come.

Another critical challenge faced by the Committee is the fairly large number of reservations entered by States Parties on some important articles in the Convention. As in other treaties the Convention permits reservations, but it has also made it clear that a reservation "incompatible with the object and purpose of the present Convention shall not be permitted" (Article 28 [2]). Reservations vary in substance, some referring to Article 29, which is a dispute settlement provision, but others to Article 16 on equality in family law, thereby denying women equality in an important area of their lives; some relate to military service, legal capacity, citizenship, and a few are so general and vague that it is difficult to know what the reservation is all about.

The reservations to Article 2, which elaborates the obligations of States Parties and constitutes without any doubt the foundation of the Convention, are the most difficult ones for the Committee to accept. Such substantive reservations considerably limit the obligations entered into by the reserving States and definitely undermine the aim and purpose of the Convention. There are members who hold the view that such reservations should not be allowed. Others are of the opinion that—given the abysmal condition of the majority of women—a ratification even with such reservations is better than no ratification. From this point of view the Committee is in a catch–22 situation. Since it does not have the power to decide whether a reservation is incompatible with the aim and purpose of the Convention, it will continue to encourage States Parties to review and withdraw their reservations.

Another problem faced by the Committee in its consideration of States Parties' reports had to do with a certain misconception of the Committee's role. The Committee is mandated to monitor and follow the progress made by States Parties in the implementation of the provisions of the Convention. This is done primarily through considering the initial and periodic reports submitted by States Parties. The oral presentation of States Parties' reports is supposed to lead to a constructive dialogue between the States Parties concerned and the experts of the Committee. Unfortunately, some representatives of reporting States, oblivious of this fact, consider the dialogue as an adversarial procedure, or joke about the role of women and indeed about the work of the Committee. Rare as it has been, this kind of behavior was admonished and sternly criticized. Many efforts have been undertaken to develop a constructive dialogue and to change the atmosphere of the discussion to a free exchange of views. I think that after a number of years, confidence between the States Parties and the Committee was slowly established, and due deference was given to the Committee's work.

Thus, one can point to the Convention as an inspiration and driving force for women around the world. It has had a positive impact on legal and policy development at the national level and it has instilled greater awareness of gender issues in governments.

DEVELOPMENTS IN AFRICA

From February 2000 to May 2006 I have served as my country's Permanent Representative to the African Union (AU), which in its Constitutive Act states that "[t]he Union shall function in accordance with the following principles . . . promotion of gender equality." Moreover, at the inaugural session of the AU the leaders of Africa adopted a decision to uphold the principle of gender parity. This was implemented a year later (2003) by the election of an equal number (5+5) of female and male top management posts (e.g. Chairperson, Deputy Chairperson, and eight commissioners). At its third session the Assembly of Heads of State and Government adopted a Solemn Declaration on Gender Equality in Africa. In its first preamble paragraph the Declaration reaffirmed the principles, goals, and action plans set out inter alia in the CEDAW Convention. To monitor the implementation of the provisions of the Declaration, the African Union Women's Committee was included in the mechanisms of the AU soon after the adoption of the Declaration. The AU Commission also has a Directorate for Women, Gender and Development and the framework for all their activities is the CEDAW Convention.

The Declaration in its operative paragraph 5 agrees to expand and promote the gender parity principle adopted apropos the Commission of the AU to all the other organs of the AU and at national and local levels. Moreover, the policy of the Union is to recruit staff based on fifty percent division between women and men. This is an example that should be emulated by all organizations and governments as much as possible. The AU is seriously trying to implement the policy in its recruitment of staff. Furthermore, the Protocol to the African Charter on Human and Peoples' Rights on the Rights of Women in Africa—in other words, a Protocol on the Rights of Women in Africa—was prepared and adopted. Having received the necessary ratifications, the Protocol entered into force in November 2005. In April 2006 a consultant was engaged to develop an AU five-year gender mainstreaming strategic plan and budget. Once completed, the study will be distributed to member States so that they can develop a strategic plan to integrate gender into their programs. This step will facilitate the implementation of the human rights of their female citizens according to the regional and international treaties. Without doubt the Convention has been an inspiration and a driving force for all the activities in prompting gender equality.

PROGRESS AND OBSTACLES

PHILOMENA KINTU, UNITED REPUBLIC OF TANZANIA

I joined what is now called the Division for the Advancement of Women (DAW) in March 1982 as Associate Social Affairs Officer. From that time on, I worked with the CEDAW Committee, and in 1994 I was appointed its Secretary, a post I still hold. Moving from Vienna to New York was a most difficult time, especially for organizing the documents and the sessions. John Mathiason was then Deputy Director of the Division and took responsibility for organizing the sessions after the departure of Ingeborg Creydt, the first Secretary of the Committee. He did so together with his responsibilities for helping with preparations for the Fourth UN World Conference on Women, and he succeeded in involving the Committee as a whole in the Conference.

When I became Secretary of the Committee, only 121 States were party to the Convention. Moreover, the Committee met only for one session a year. We received reports from UN specialized agencies on the States being considered by the Committee, in accordance with Article 22 of the Convention, but UN Funds and Programs had only begun to provide information. Although some NGOs followed the Committee's work, they had no formal forum in which to share their views. At the time of the adoption of the Convention, no specified human resources were provided to the Committee. There was a significant delay in the submission of reports by States Parties, a fact often pointed out by the Division in its reports to the General Assembly. At the same time, the Committee's limited meeting time also resulted in a large backlog of reports awaiting review.

During my time as Secretary, I have seen the Convention gain recognition as one of the key instruments to promote women's rights. I have been privileged to work with nine remarkable Chairpersons. I have witnessed the changes in the implementation of the Convention as well as in the Committee's approach to women's discrimination, especially since the

1993 UN World Conference on Human Rights in Vienna and the 1995 Fourth UN World Conference on Women in Beijing, which integrated women's rights into the general human rights system. These changes occurred particularly after the Division was relocated to New York. With the adoption of General Assembly resolution 51/68 in 1996, which allowed the Committee to meet twice annually for three weeks, preceded by a presession working group, the Committee entered an exciting period of development. With new resources provided after the Beijing Conference, the Division was restructured and a Women's Rights Unit was created. Jane Connors, an experienced human rights lawyer and women's rights activist who had followed the Committee's work from its inception, was recruited to head the Unit. She encouraged the Committee to introduce working methods consistent with other human rights treaty bodies, such as in relation to NGO participation and concluding comments, so that it could take its place as a central body for women's rights in the human rights machinery.

Looking back over my more than twenty-four years of service with the Convention and at the Committee, I can see enormous progress achieved. Many countries have used CEDAW to remove barriers to substantive equality by taking measures to introduce legislative reforms to repeal discriminatory laws. Some countries have taken initiatives to amend their constitution to incorporate the provisions of the Convention. Several States Parties have created the post of Secretary of State for Women to coordinate policy. Others have set up ministries for women's affairs; some have created an independent government advisory service on the gender dimensions of legislation, policies, and programs of equality. In some States Parties, international treaties, including CEDAW, take precedence over domestic legislation, while in others legislation has been adopted to implement the Convention. Many States Parties have repealed discriminatory provisions in civil, penal, and personal status codes to bring them into conformity with the Convention. Equal Opportunity Acts aim at improving women's legal and material position. New laws have been adopted on violence against women, especially domestic violence, in order to create protection and remedies for women.

The Committee has also identified challenges to implementation of the Convention. These include new and emerging issues, such as the adverse economic consequences for women of transitions to a market economy. There is persistent and deepening poverty among women, particularly heads of households, sometimes as the result of the withdrawal of social assistance. Armed conflict has resulted in a flow of refugees and internally displaced women, who frequently experience violence each day in the camps. Trafficking in women and children and the exploitation of prostitution have emerged as serious challenges to the implementation of the Convention. Prostitutes continue to suffer as a result of the application of laws discriminating against them. In addition, the feminization of migration in the absence of methods to respond to abuses experienced by migrant women has resulted in the violation of these women's rights.

The Committee has also identified the persistence of stereotypical attitudes as a critical challenge to the implementation of the Convention. These attitudes perpetuate traditional practices and customs prejudicial to women, such as violence against women, polygamy, forced marriage, the preference for sons, and "honor" killings. These attitudes also create a pervasive climate of discrimination. Discriminatory laws, especially those governing marriage, marital property, divorce, and custody also persist. Many States continue to have laws discriminating against women in relation to nationality and penal laws, particularly with regard to family rape or penalties for "honor" killings.

I am honored and privileged to have a professional career that has allowed me to support the work of the Committee. Its members have been, and remain, remarkable women's rights activists with vast experience and commitment. I pledge to continue to do as much as I can in my capacity as a Secretary of the Committee to support its members and strengthen its work.

ON TWENTY YEARS OF INVOLVEMENT

JANE CONNORS, *AUSTRALIA*

As an academic working at the School of Oriental and African Studies (SOAS) in the University of London, I was asked to participate in the Commonwealth Secretariat delegation to the Third UN World Conference on Women in Nairobi in 1985. As part of its contribution to the Conference and the parallel nongovernmental forum, the Secretariat had prepared an accession kit to encourage ratification of the CEDAW Convention. The Convention had entered into force on September 3, 1981, but had attracted only limited attention from governments, international and national nongovernmental organizations (NGOs), and the academic community.

Thus began my more than twenty-year association with the Convention and its Committee, first as a scholar and university teacher, a women's rights and feminist activist, and, then as the first person to occupy the post of Chief of the Women's Rights Unit, with direct responsibility within the United Nations for supporting the Committee. This more-than-twenty-year period has seen acceptance of the Convention by 185 States Parties, making it second only to the Convention on the Rights of the Child as the most broadly ratified human rights treaty. This period has also seen the Committee develop its jurisprudence, adopt innovative working methods, and gain recognition as a central part of the international machinery to promote and protect human rights. Perhaps the most dramatic advance, however, has been the strengthening of the Convention and the Committee by the adoption of an Optional Protocol, now accepted by 83 States, which provides individuals with an opportunity to submit complaints of alleged violations of CEDAW to the Committee, and entitles the Committee, on its own initiative, to inquire into grave or systematic violations of the Convention's terms.

At the time of the Nairobi Conference, the emphasis of the international women's movement was on issues relating to women and development, with little attention being paid to human rights. The elaboration and adoption of the Convention after the First UN World Conference on Women in 1975—and its opening for signature, ratification, and accession just prior to the Second UN World Conference on Women in Copenhagen in 1980—had highlighted the linkages of equality and nondiscrimination with development and peace. As a result, some NGOs shifted their attention to questions of equality and the influence of law and custom on women's status. At Nairobi itself, during the NGO Forum, workshops were held on the Convention, with over five hundred women and men from over fifty countries attending a week-long series co-sponsored by the Commonwealth Secretariat's Women and Development Programme, the Women, Public Policy and Development Project at the University of Minnesota's Humphrey Institute of Public Affairs, and the Development, Law and Policy Program of Columbia University's Center for Population and Family Health. Members of the CEDAW Committee attended this workshop, as did several individuals who were elected to the Committee subsequently.

The International Women's Rights Action Watch (IWRAW), a global network to monitor, analyze, and encourage law and policy reform in accordance with the principles of the Convention, emerged out of this workshop series, and was officially launched in February 1986 just prior to the Committee's fifth session, which met at UN Headquarters. In 1993, IWRAW Asia Pacific was established as an autonomous organization to monitor and encourage the implementation of the Convention in the

Asia Pacific region, and to lobby for its strengthening at the international level—as well as for further acceptance of the concept of the human rights of women. During this period, as well as being part of the IWRAW network and working with other NGOs focused on CEDAW such as the International League for Human Rights (which provided support to the development of the Committee's General Recommendation No. 19 on violence against women), I encouraged the inclusion of the Convention and the work of the Committee into undergraduate and graduate courses on human rights in the SOAS, which introduced a course on the Human Rights of Women into its Master of Laws program of London University in 1995. I also participated in training activities for government officials tasked with preparing reports for the Committee, as well as for others, such as the judiciary and law enforcement personnel on how to use the Convention in their work.

At the beginning of September 1996 I joined the Division for the Advancement of Women (DAW). As part of the selection process, candidates for the post had been requested to prepare a paper delineating their vision for the strengthening of human rights. The driving elements of my vision were the Convention and the Committee. During my six years in the Division, many of the proposals in my paper have been realized. The Optional Protocol was negotiated and concluded by 1999, and entered into force a little over one year later, and the groundwork was laid for the consideration of complaints and the conduct of inquiries. CEDAW adopted a formal procedure, similar to that of other treaty bodies, to receive NGO information. The Committee was granted more meeting time, and was also granted an exceptional session to address reports awaiting review. Innovative working methods, building on those of other treaty bodies, were introduced. These included the transmission of lists of issues to reporting States well before their reports were considered so as to encourage written answers to improve the quality of the dialogue, and to refine concluding comments, and structured procedures for the formulation of general recommendations. Importantly, the Committee, although isolated geographically from the other human rights treaty bodies, moved closer to those bodies in terms of approach, with members considering the Convention as a human rights treaty and part of the human rights framework. In late 2002, when I left DAW to take up a post in the Office of the High Commissioner for Human Right (OHCHR), I left a Committee that had been transformed from a body that met for two weeks annually, and had weak implementation procedures and limited exposure, to a body that would soon be granted three sessions a year, had enhanced implementation procedures, and was highly visible as part of the human rights framework.

Since its first meeting in 1982, the Committee has proved itself to be a remarkable force for change. With the recent decision of the Secretary-General to transfer the responsibility for supporting the Committee's work to the OHCHR, the Committee has the opportunity to place itself at the center of UN human rights machinery and to be an even more effective vehicle to achieve the objectives of the Convention.

STRENGTHENING WOMEN'S HUMAN RIGHTS THROUGH INDIVIDUAL COMPLAINTS

CEES FLINTERMAN, *THE NETHERLANDS*

Human rights are inclusive: they include both women and men, they include any individual without distinction as to race, sex, language, or religion (UN Charter, 1945). It is that fundamental message of human rights that has always motivated me. For that reason I was more than pleased when The Netherlands government asked me to chair The Netherlands delegation to the UN World Conference on Human Rights (Vienna, 1993) and later to represent The Netherlands in the negotiations on the Optional Protocol to the CEDAW Convention (New York, 1996-1999). It is an even greater pleasure and responsibility that presently, as a member of the CEDAW Committee, I am in a position to help implement the Convention and its Protocol, thereby contributing to strengthening the principle of equality of women and men around the world.

With hindsight the year 1993 can be regarded as a catalyst in the development of human rights of women. In that year the member States of the UN through the Vienna World Conference on Human Rights rec-ommended:

> New procedures should also be adopted to strengthen implementation of the commitment to women's equality and the human rights of women. The Commission on the Status of Women and the Committee on the Elimination of Discrimination against Women should quickly examine the possibility of introducing the right to petition through the preparation of an optional protocol to the Convention on the Elimination of All Forms of Discrimination against Women. (United Nations 1993b, para. 40)

It took some time before the Commission on the Status of Women (hereinafter CSW) heeded the call of the Vienna World Conference on Human Rights; this was inter alia due to the important role of the CSW in the preparation of the Beijing World Conference on Women (1995); this World Conference also called on all UN member States to support the elaboration of the Optional Protocol (United Nations 1995a, para. 230k). In 1996 an open-ended Working Group was established by the CSW which was mandated to draft an Optional Protocol and which met parallel to the sessions of the CSW in the years 1996–1999. This Working Group made use of Suggestion No. 7 by the CEDAW Committee, setting out the desirable elements of an Optional Protocol (CEDAW 1995, 8–11, paras. 1–29); the Working Group also had access to a draft of an Optional Protocol, which was prepared by members of the CEDAW Committee, members of the Committee on the Elimination of Racial Discrimination, and by experts in the field of international human rights law and the human rights of women at a meeting in 1994 at Maastricht University in The Netherlands, where at the time I was teaching public international law and international human rights law.[1] One of the members of the CEDAW Committee, Sylvia Cartwright, who had also participated in the Maastricht meeting, attended the sessions on the Working Group as a resource person.

The Working Group has been remarkably successful. At its fourth session in 1999 it reached consensus on a draft Optional Protocol which provides for two additional procedures in the CEDAW Convention: the individual communication procedure and the inquiry procedure. The draft Optional Protocol was unanimously agreed upon by the CSW, ECOSOC and eventually adopted by consensus by the General Assembly, at its fifty-fourth session, on October 6, 1999, twenty years after the adoption of the CEDAW Convention. The CEDAW Optional Protocol entered into force on December 22, 2000 and has been ratified as of December 2006 by 85 States out of the 185 States Parties to the CEDAW Convention.

The main question to be discussed in this essay is whether the individual communication procedure will help "the full and equal enjoyment by women of all human rights and fundamental freedoms."[2] I will try to answer this question by first addressing some innovative features of the Optional Protocol. Then I will have a look at the emerging, although still limited, quasi-jurisprudence of the CEDAW Committee under the Optional Protocol. In the final section I will address a number of the challenges which the Committee will be facing in the future in the implementation of its mandate under the Optional Protocol.

INNOVATIVE MAIN FEATURES

The individual communication procedure under the Optional Protocol is modeled after similar existing procedures under other binding international human rights instruments, such as the Optional Protocol to the

International Covenant on Civil and Political Rights (1966). Individual communication procedures at the United Nations are only available after the exhaustion of all local remedies. They are written in nature and they lead to nonbinding views containing specific and general recommendations for the State Party, if that State is found to have violated the right(s) of the claimant.

The Optional Protocol to the CEDAW Convention is based on these characteristics, but it further contains some innovative elements. In its Article 2 on standing (*locus standi*), it provides that not only women but also groups of women, claiming to be victim of a violation of any of the rights set forth in the Convention, may submit a communication. A proposal to include the possibility of the submission of a complaint by someone or an organization having a "sufficient interest in the matter," (*actio popularis*) was rejected during the negotiations (Flinterman 1995, 85–93). On the other hand it was agreed that a complaint can be submitted on behalf of an individual or group of individuals, albeit with their consent unless the author can justify acting on their behalf without such consent (Article 2). One can conclude, therefore, that the Optional Protocol provides for a broad standing, through which individuals can seek effective redress.[3]

Another element important in the negotiations was that communications may be submitted on the violation of *any* of the rights set forth in the CEDAW Convention. Attempts to restrict the right to submit a complaint to so-called "justiciable" rights (in particular, civil and political rights, such as the rights to vote and to be eligible for election to all publicly elected bodies) were not successful. It was feared at the time of the negotiations on the Optional Protocol that States Parties would be tempted to restrict the scope of the Optional Protocol by following a "pick-and-choose" policy on the substantive provisions of the CEDAW Convention for which it would accept an individual communication procedure. In order to avoid this, the Protocol explicitly prohibits the making of reservations by States Parties. The inclusion of a prohibition of reservations implicitly underlines the basic principle of the indivisibility of all human rights, both civil and political and economic, social and cultural rights; both categories of rights can be found in the CEDAW Convention.

The wide substantive scope of the individual communication procedure is certainly of great significance. The aforementioned acceptance of a non-reservation clause at the final steps of the negotiations was part of a package deal that further included that States Parties to the Optional Protocol may, at the time of ratification or accession, declare that they do not accept the inquiry procedure, the so-called "opt-out" clause (Article 10 [1]). So far only a few of the States Parties to the Optional Protocol CEDAW have availed themselves of this opportunity.[4] A declaration to opt out may at any later time be withdrawn by the State Party concerned (Article 10 [2]).

A third important, innovative element of the Optional Protocol relates to the power of the CEDAW Committee to take "such interim measures as may be necessary to avoid possible irreparable damage to the victim or victims of the alleged violation" (Article 5 [1]). Such interim measures may be requested at any time after the receipt of a communication by the Committee and before a determination on the merits has been reached. The power to take interim measures is, of course, of a far-reaching, sensitive nature. The CEDAW Committee has established a Working Group on Communications to assist it in its work under the Optional Protocol; this Working Group has also been entrusted with the mandate to take interim measures, which, depending on the urgency of a matter, can also be taken intersessionally after consultations among the members of the Working Group. So far, the Working Group has used this power twice in appropriate cases. It is clear that the imposition of interim measures does not imply a determination on the admissibility, let alone the substance, of a communication. The inclusion of the power to take interim measures in the Optional Protocol itself, instead of in the Rules of Procedure as is the case with other treaty bodies, creates an extra stimulus for States Parties to comply with such measures. This power can certainly be regarded as one of the strong elements of the Optional Protocol to CEDAW.

Other innovative elements of the Optional Protocol to CEDAW are of a less far-reaching character, but they are nevertheless relevant. The Optional Protocol contains, for example, a provision on follow-up by the CEDAW Committee after it has decided a communication on its merits by the adoption of views. These views are not binding, but a State Party is nevertheless required to give due consideration to these views and to submit to the Committee, within six months, information on any action it has taken in light of the views and recommendations of the Committee. Thereafter, the CEDAW Committee may request the State Party concerned to submit further information on its compliance with the views and recommendations in the context of its periodic reports (Article 7 [4], [5]).

It is further of interest to note that the Optional Protocol explicitly provides that individuals making use of the procedures under the Protocol may not be intimidated or subjected to ill-treatment (Article 11). Moreover States Parties oblige themselves to make widely known and give publicity to the Convention and Optional Protocol and to facilitate access to information about the views and recommendations of the Committee

(Article 13). Both latter provisions relate to the individual communication procedure as well as the inquiry procedure.

It is clear that the Optional Protocol creates a strong framework for the strengthening of the enforcement of the human rights of women. With the Protocol women have a potentially effective instrument in their hands to fight discrimination (Bijnsdorp 2000, 355). In the next section I will look into the question of whether the still limited practice of the CEDAW Committee in using its powers under the individual communication procedure confirms this high expectation.

CASE LAW

The individual communication procedure under the Optional Protocol can be divided into two stages: the admissibility stage and the merits stage. Given the size of the membership of the Committee (twenty-three members), the Committee has, as mentioned earlier, established a five-member Working Group on Communications to assist it in the implementation of its mandate. One of the first important achievements of this Working Group has been the preparation of a number of rules of procedure which, after adoption by the Committee, have been included in the Rules of Procedure of the CEDAW Committee (CEDAW 2001, 86–115, Rules 56–75).

After registration by the Working Group of a communication of an individual woman or group of women, the Working Group submits it to the State Party concerned for its explanations and statements on admissibility and merits. By December 2006 the CEDAW Committee had registered fourteen communications, out of which eight are still pending. While this may seem to be a small number six years after the entry into force of the Optional Protocol, one must remember that communications may only be submitted after all local remedies have been exhausted, a primary admissibility requirement in all international and regional individual complaint mechanisms (Article 4 [1]). The basic rationale of this admissibility rule is that a State should be given the opportunity to put its house in order before it can be held accountable in individual cases at the international level. It is well-known that the exhaustion of local remedies, including in most cases an appeal to the highest competent court in the State Party concerned, may take a long time; it is for that reason that the Optional Protocol further provides that, if the application of local remedies is unreasonably prolonged or unlikely to bring effective relief, the CEDAW Committee may nevertheless declare the communication admissible (Article 4 [1]). It should, further, be noted that communications may only be submitted concerning alleged violations which have occurred after the entry into force of the Optional Protocol to CEDAW for the respective State, the *ratione temporis* rule, another basic admissibility criterion. Even though this rule is not of an absolute nature (Article 4 [2] [e]), it makes clear that this latter requirement, together with the exhaustion of the local remedies rule, has restricted the inflow of communications at least in the early years after the entry into force of the Optional Protocol.

ADMISSIBILITY

Three communications have so far been declared inadmissible by the CEDAW Committee at the advice of its Working Group on Communications. This happened to the very first communication (*B.-J. v. Germany* 2004), which was submitted to the Committee on August 20, 2002 and declared inadmissible on July 14, 2004. The issue raised by the author of the communication concerned the negative financial consequences of an unwanted divorce, in particular for older women who are divorced after long marriages and are left in situations of "discrimination, disadvantage and humiliation." The Committee decided that the communication was inadmissible on two grounds: the claimant had failed to exhaust all local remedies (some aspects of the complaint were still pending in the domestic courts) and because the facts presented by the author had occurred prior to the entry into force of the Optional Protocol and the claimant had failed to make convincing arguments that they had continued after that date. Two members of the Committee wrote a dissenting opinion, suggesting that the claim should have been declared partially admissible. In any case, it is to be hoped that the CEDAW Committee will have another opportunity to address the situation faced by older, divorced women.

In another case (*Rahime Kayan v. Turkey* 2006), a Turkish woman complained about her dismissal as a schoolteacher and the termination of her status as a civil servant for wearing for religious reasons a headscarf, a piece of clothing that is unique to women. She stated that the termination of her civil servant status violated her right to work and her right therefore to equal employment opportunities and equal treatment. The State Party contended that a similar case had been submitted earlier to the European Court of Human Rights (*Leyla Sahin v. Turkey* 2005), and that, for that reason, the communication should be declared inadmissible (Article 4 [2] [a]). The Committee did not accept this argument, however, since the matter before the European Court of Human Rights had been raised by another individual. The Committee nevertheless considered the communication inadmissible because Rahime Kayan had based her claim before the Turkish domestic courts on various grounds but not on sex-based discrimination. The domestic courts had, thus, not had the opportunity to express themselves on sex discrimination. For that reason the Committee concluded that Kayan had not exhausted all local remedies. The substance of the communication before the Committee should also have been submitted to domestic courts in order to fulfill the requirement of exhaustion of local remedies.

The third case concerned a British woman married to a Colombian citizen complaining about a violation of her right to transfer her British nationality to her child born in Colombia in 1954, long before the entry into force of both the CEDAW Convention and the Optional Protocol for the UK (*Salgado v. United Kingdom* 2007). In 1954 the then-relevant British nationality legislation made it impossible for British women married to foreigners to transfer their nationality to their children. This nationality legislation was later changed in conformity with the CEDAW Convention after the United Kingdom's ratification in 1981,[5] but the new Nationality Act had only been made retroactive to 1962. Salgado argued that that was an arbitrary measure and that in any case the facts of the alleged discrimination in 1954 still existed for her in 2006. The Committee concluded that the communication was not admissible because the author had ceased to be a victim at the time that her son had come of age in 1972; from that year onward the son had a right of his own to nationality. Moreover the author had never availed herself of available domestic legal remedies; she had never challenged the refusal of the British authorities to grant her son the British nationality in the High Court. Also for that reason the Committee declared the communication inadmissible.

It appears that the Committee has been applying the admissibility requirements to the communications submitted to it rather cautiously so far. Potential claimants of violations of women's human rights are advised to give careful attention to admissibility issues before submitting their case to the CEDAW Committee.

MERITS

On three occasions so far the CEDAW Committee has addressed the merits of a communication. One of the difficulties in this respect is that the CEDAW Convention is not so much formulated in terms of rights of women but rather in terms of obligations of States Parties. The Preamble to the Optional Protocol fortunately provides, however, that States Parties reaffirm "their determination to ensure the full and equal enjoyment by women of all human rights and fundamental freedoms and to take effective action to prevent violations of these rights and freedoms," thus making it clear that the obligations of States Parties under the CEDAW Convention correspond with (a nonexhaustive list of) human rights and fundamental freedoms of women.

Another difficulty is that the CEDAW Convention does not explicitly cover some important issues relating to the protection of human rights of women, such as the elimination of violence against women. It was only through General Recommendation No. 19 that the CEDAW Committee brought the issue of violence against women within the scope of the Convention by stating that the definition of discrimination against women in Article 1 of the CEDAW Convention includes gender-based violence. This General Recommendation also conveys the idea that States Parties can be held accountable if "they fail to act with due diligence to prevent violations of rights or to investigate and punish acts of violence."

Domestic violence was the main issue in the first communication decided by the CEDAW Committee on its merits. In this case the author complained of a violation of her rights following a failure of Hungary to protect her from serious risk to her person (*A.T. v. Hungary* 2005); A.T. had claimed that, for four years, she had suffered severe and regular domestic violence and serious threats to her life by her husband. No remedies, such as a restraining order and even not a shelter, were available to her under Hungarian law. The Hungarian courts had moreover decided that the husband was entitled to the continuous use of the common flat and that the author could have been expected to try to settle the dispute by lawful means, instead of the arbitrary conduct she had resorted to in the eyes of the court. Criminal procedures had also been initiated against the violent husband, but the sanctions imposed were minimal.

The Committee found in favor of the author under Article 2, as follows:

> [T]he Committee notes that the State party has admitted that the remedies pursued by the author, were not capable of providing immediate protection to her against ill-treatment by her former partner and, furthermore, that legal and institutional arrangements in the State party are not yet ready to ensure the internationally expected, coordinated, comprehensive and effective protection and support for the victims of domestic violence. . . . The Committee further notes the State party's general assessment that domestic violence cases as such do not enjoy high priority in court proceedings. The Committee is of the opinion that the description

provided of the proceedings resorted to in the present case, both the civil and criminal proceedings, coincides with this general assessment. Women's human rights to life and to physical and mental integrity cannot be superseded by other rights, including the right to property and the right to privacy. . . . In this connection, the Committee recalls its concluding comments from August 2002 on the State party's combined fourth and fifth periodic report, which states . . . '[T]he Committee is concerned about the prevalence of violence against women and girls, including domestic violence. It is particularly concerned that no specific legislation has been enacted to combat domestic violence and sexual harassment and that no protection or exclusion orders or shelters exist for the immediate protection of women victims of domestic violence.' Bearing this in mind, the Committee concludes that the obligations of the State party set out in Article 2 (a), (b) and (e) of the Convention extend to the prevention of and protection from violence against women, which obligations in the present case, remain unfilled and constitute a violation of the author's human rights and fundamental freedoms, particularly her right to security of person. (CEDAW 2005b, 80–92, para. 9.3)

Having determined a violation of the CEDAW Convention, the Committee made recommendations to the State Party regarding A.T., as well as recommendations of a more general character. The CEDAW Committee urged the State Party with regard to A.T. to take "immediate and effective measures to guarantee the physical and mental integrity of A.T. and her family" and secondly to ensure "that A.T. is given a safe home in which to live with her children, receives appropriate child support and legal assistance and that she receives reparation proportionate to the physical and mental harm undergone and to the gravity of the violations of her rights." The recommendations of a general character called upon Hungary to take action on a number of issues, such as to investigate "promptly, thoroughly, impartially and seriously all allegations of domestic violence and bring the offender to justice in accordance with international standards" (para. 9.6).

It should further be highlighted that the CEDAW Committee in the case of *A.T. v. Hungary* had also made use of its power to take interim measures. Ten days after the submission of the communication, the Working Group had requested Hungary to give adequate protection to A.T.

It is fair to say that the first CEDAW Committee's decision on the merits of a communication can be seen as very positive. The Committee acted on the issue of domestic violence with appropriate rigor, "supporting a worldwide movement to highlight the practice (of domestic violence against women) as being a violation of the human rights of women in particular" (Sakhi-Bulley 2006, 10).

The CEDAW Committee used this case also as a basis for further developing the follow-up procedure provided for in the Optional Protocol. Two members of the Committee were designated to discuss with a representative of the Hungarian mission in New York the responses that the Hungarian government had given to the specific and general recommendations that the Committee had adopted. Such a follow-up procedure is designed to stimulate the State Party concerned to comply with the non-binding recommendations of the CEDAW Committee on individual cases.

The second case decided on its merits by the CEDAW Committee also related to Hungary (*A.S. v. Hungary* 2006). In this case Hungary was again found in violation of the rights of a (Roma) woman who had been sterilized in the course of an emergency operation to remove her still-born fetus; on admission to the hospital she had been given a partially handwritten note: by signing this note she had approved of both operations; fifteen minutes later the operations had taken place. The CEDAW Committee found, in the light of its General Recommendation No. 24 on Women and Health (para. 20), that Article 12 of the CEDAW Convention implicitly prohibits nonconsensual sterilization; the procedure provided for in the present case did not comply with the requirement of informed consent which is necessary in cases of sterilization. The Committee further found that A.S.'s rights under Articles 10 (h) and 16 (l) (e) of the CEDAW Convention were violated, since the hospital personnel had failed to provide appropriate advice and information on family planning and because the sterilization had deprived her of her natural reproductive capacity. In light of its findings the CEDAW Committee recommended that Hungary provide compensation to A.S. which should be commensurable with the gravity of the violations of her rights. This formula allows the State Party certain discretion to decide on suitable compensation which fits within its overall domestic legal framework. The CEDAW Committee also adopted a number of more general recommendations for Hungary, including a request that Hungary review its domestic legislation on the principle of informed consent in cases of sterilization in order to ensure its conformity with international human rights and medical standards.

In a third case decided on the merits, the Committee concluded that

The Netherlands had not violated Article 11 (a), (b) of the CEDAW Convention by not guaranteeing self-employed women full pay during their maternity leave (*Dung Thi Thuy Nguyen v. The Netherlands* 2006). The Committee held that States Parties have a certain margin of discretion to devise a system of maternity leave benefits to fulfill the requirements of the Convention; such a system should cover all employed women but could have separate rules for self-employed women that take into account fluctuating income and related contributions. States Parties also may apply those rules in combination to women who are partly self-employed and partly salaried workers. The Netherlands legislation on maternity leave which put a ceiling to the maternity benefits of women who are both employee and self-employed (in this case a co-working spouse) fell within the discretion of The Netherlands and, thus, did not constitute a violation.

Three CEDAW Committee members wrote a joint dissenting opinion in which they argued that The Netherlands legislation may constitute a form of indirect discrimination. Their view was based on the assumption that the situation in which the complainant found herself is typical for women: in general, mainly women work part-time as salaried workers in addition to working in (small) family enterprises. This assumption could, however, not be substantiated, since The Netherlands had not been requested to provide relevant information on the combination of salaried work and self-employed work disaggregated by sex in The Netherlands.

FUTURE CHALLENGES

Since the adoption of the Optional Protocol by the UN General Assembly, less than half of the States Parties to the CEDAW Convention have ratified it. A first important task is, thus, to stimulate the further increase in the number of States Parties to the Optional Protocol. The CEDAW Committee raises this issue at the time of the examination of all initial or periodic State reports.

Even in States which have ratified the Optional Protocol, however, the procedure may not be well known. In all States Parties there is an urgent need to circulate information on the Optional Protocol and, of course, the CEDAW Convention itself, among women, women's and human rights organizations, and in particular the legal profession. The legal profession should also be urged to raise the substantive provisions of the CEDAW Convention in domestic court proceedings and to urge the judiciary to take those provisions into account while applying and interpreting relevant domestic laws.

There is no doubt that the use of the individual communication procedure under the Optional Protocol is most demanding for the individual complaining woman or group of women. It is only after the exhaustion of local remedies, which may take years, that such a complaint can be submitted to the CEDAW Committee. The procedure requires that a written document be presented to the Committee. The Committee's proceedings may take two years or more. For these reasons, women who wish to use the Protocol need the support of lawyers or NGOs who should observe the same standards that apply in filing cases before national courts. They need to provide the information necessary for informed consent to file the case; to assess the risk of retaliation and economic or social pressures on the victims; and determine whether measures in accordance with Article 11 Optional Protocol for protecting them against retaliation exist or can be put in place; and maintain the confidentiality of all information unless the victim has given informed consent to disclosure.

Another problem is that in many countries individual women or groups of women have a relatively wide choice of international communication procedures, both at the regional level and at the international level. Some of these procedures offer legally binding results (such as the European Court of Human Rights and the Inter-American Court of Human Rights) or they offer a strong basis in existing case law for predicting success. Not only the quality of the case law of the CEDAW Committee, but also its willingness to approach its responsibilities under the individual communication procedure in a creative and assertive manner will be important criteria for potential complainants to find their way to the CEDAW Committee.

Whether or not the results under the Optional Protocol will contribute to broad-based changes in women's lives only time will tell. But there is no doubt that the Optional Protocol has enlarged the toolbox of the CEDAW Committee and its capacity to contribute to such changes and to strengthen the enjoyment by women around the world of their human rights and fundamental freedoms.

NOTES

1. The Maastricht meeting took place on the basis of a working paper prepared by Andrew Byrnes and Jane Connors, entitled "Complaint Procedures" (1996, 682–797).

2. See Preamble of the Optional Protocol to the CEDAW Convention, para. 5.

3. See Bijnsdorp "The Strength of the Optional Protocol to the United Nations Women's Convention" (2000, 329–55).

4. These States are: Bangladesh, Belize and Colombia.

5. Article 9 (2) CEDAW Convention obliges States Parties to grant women equal rights with men with respect to the nationality of their children.

THE JUÁREZ MURDERS AND THE INQUIRY PROCEDURE

MARIA REGINA TAVARES DA SILVA, *PORTUGAL*
YOLANDA FERRER GÓMEZ, *CUBA*

As members of the CEDAW Committee—Yolanda Gómez on her second mandate and Regina da Silva on her first—we were directly involved in the first inquiry by the Committee under the Optional Protocol to CEDAW. Both us have been deeply engaged in the struggle for sex and gender equality in our countries and at the regional and international levels. This has provided us with many challenging, joyful or depressing experiences, but we can truly say that this particular experience was a powerful and disturbing one that we cannot forget.

The Ciudad Juárez inquiry involved the abduction, rape, and murder of women occurring in a systematic manner for about a decade in Ciudad Juárez, in the state of Chihuahua, northern Mexico (close to the border with the United States, facing El Paso, Texas, on the other side of the frontier).[1] Ciudad Juárez is an open door to immigration, both legal and illegal, as well as both internal, from other regions of Mexico, and external, from other countries. This has created a dangerous environment for vulnerable young women arriving to work in the *maquilas* established in the area. *Maquilas* or *maquiladoras* are assembly factories usually established in industrial parks on the outskirts of a city that produce for export, primarily to the United States. These assembly plants, also known as export processing zones (EPZs), are mainly owned by multinational companies and deal with various products, including electronics, television and stereo equipments, computer components, etc.

THE INQUIRY PROCEDURE—MAIN FEATURES

The Optional Protocol not only provides a communication procedure for individuals and groups to submit individual complaints, but also establishes an inquiry procedure. Both procedures aim to make the rights guaranteed under the Convention effective by denouncing and combating violations of those rights and by putting pressure on States Parties toward this end. The inquiry procedure is a mechanism through which the CEDAW Committee can look into a specific situation of "grave or systematic violations" of rights covered under the Convention. Being a State Party to the Optional Protocol, however, does not automatically allow for an inquiry procedure, since an opt-out clause allows for non-recognition of it by the State Party at the time of signature or ratification. Compared to the communication procedure it has the advantage of not requiring the exhaustion of domestic remedies and its less formal process makes a timely response possible. The Committee can conduct an inquiry and transmit its findings, including comments and recommendations, to the State Party concerned to stop the violations and to prevent them from happening again. Because the issues are of a more general nature than the ones addressed by the individual communication procedure, the recommendations can also be of a more general nature, pointing to remedies in the way of policies and measures to address the underlying causes of such situations. The State Party commits to responding to the Committee with its observations within six months

REQUIREMENTS TO INITIATE AN INVESTIGATION

The process starts when the Committee receives "reliable information indicating grave or systematic violations by a State Party of rights set forth in the Convention" and invites the State Party to "submit observations with regard to the information concerned" (Article 8). This is thus the first step.

The reliability of the information is evaluated by the Committee on the basis of its consistency, corroborating evidence, the credibility of its sources, as well as information from other sources, national or international, official or nonofficial. Although there are no specific guidelines the information must be as complete and illustrative as possible. It must include a clear description of the alleged violations, their gravity or systematic nature, their impact and consequences, and the specific provisions of CEDAW being violated. Information should also be provided on the alleged perpetrators; on complaints filed; on investigation(s) undertaken; on involvement of the police or other authorities; on support of civil society organizations, women's nongovernmental organizations (NGOs), or human rights NGOs; as well as on measures taken, or not taken, within the jurisdiction of the State Party, to respond to the situation. Information can be supplied by a person, a group, or an organization, national of the State Party or not; it can be in writing, on videotape or other electronic means, or oral; and it can present different types of evidence, according to each specific situation.

The violations are not required to be both grave *and* systematic; they can be either one or the other. A *grave* violation means that a severe abuse of fundamental rights under the Convention has taken place or is taking place.[2] *Systematic* violation means that the violation is not an isolated case, but rather a prevalent pattern in a specific situation; one that has occurred again and again, either deliberately with the intent of committing those acts, or as the result of customs and traditions, or even as the result of discriminatory laws or policies, with or without such purpose.[3]

THE CIUDAD JUÁREZ INQUIRY

With regard to the first inquiry under the Optional Protocol—the Ciudad Juárez disappearances and murders of young women—we can say that all the requirements were fully met. The situation presented to the Committee was an emblematic case of grave violations of women's fundamental human rights on a large and systematic scale, and therefore ideally suited to the type of inquiry foreseen under the Optional Protocol.

In October 2002, the Committee received information from two international and national NGOs—namely Equality Now and Casa Amiga. The murders of women in Ciudad Juárez had already been noted by the Committee, as a matter of serious concern, in the concluding comments addressed to the Government of Mexico following the discussion of Mexico's fifth periodic report in the special session of the Committee that took place in August 2002. The Committee had been particularly alerted to the situation by information provided by the Mexican Commission for the Defense and Promotion of Human Rights, and had raised questions on the issue during the dialogue with the Government representatives (CEDAW 2002, 210, paras. 439–40).

At its twenty-eighth session, in January 2003, the Committee considered the request presented by the two NGOs and appointed the two of us to undertake a detailed evaluation of the information provided, together with data from other sources, including bodies of the UN system and regional bodies. This included information contained in reports by the UN Special Rapporteur on extrajudicial, summary, or arbitrary executions and by the UN Special Rapporteur on the independence of judges and lawyers, who had visited Mexico in 1999 and in 2001 respectively. Of particular interest also was the report by the Special Rapporteur on the Rights of Women of the Inter-American Commission on Human Rights, who had conducted a comprehensive investigation into the situation of women in Ciudad Juárez in 2002 (United Nations 2000c; United Nations 2002a; Inter-American Commission on Human Rights 2003).

Taking into account all the elements before it, including our assessment, the Committee decided that the information was reliable and invited the Government of Mexico to cooperate and submit its observations.

THE PROCESS OF AN INQUIRY

The second step of the Protocol calls for the State Party's responses to the Committee. Then the Committee may take the third step and designate one or more of its members to conduct an inquiry into the alleged violation and to report to the Committee. The Rules of Procedure, as developed by the Committee, indicate that the modalities of the inquiry are determined by the Committee, and that the designated members determine their own methods of work. Not surprisingly, the inquiry may include a visit to its territory, for which the consent of the State Party is clearly important for the inquiry's effectiveness. The Protocol and the rules wisely suggest, "the cooperation of the State Party shall be sought at all stages of the proceedings" (Article 8 [5]), even to "nominate a representative to meet with the member or members designated by the Committee" (Rule 85).

The fourth step is the inquiry itself. While it may include a visit, more important are the analysis and evaluation of the situation by all possible and available means. The inquiry involves contacts with authorities at different levels, with witnesses, victims and/or victims' relatives, and with civil society organizations; attending hearings and listening to testimonies, conducting interviews, and visiting specific institutions and places linked to the facts under investigation; and the study of reports and analysis of documents and other pieces of information.

At the twenty-ninth session of the Committee, in July 2003, the information provided by the Government of Mexico was carefully analyzed. It showed recognition of the gravity of the situation and willingness to cooperate; it also elaborated on some of the measures already being taken to address the problem. However, additional information provided by the two NGOs that had originally provided information to the Committee, as well as by the Mexican Commission for the Defense and Promotion of Human Rights, indicated that the murders continued to occur and that no solutions were in sight.

In view of these facts, the Committee decided to initiate a confidential inquiry to be conducted by two of its members. It entrusted the task to us. We would visit the territory in October 2003, for discussions with authorities in institutions at the federal level in Mexico City, in the city of Chihuahua (capital of the state of the same name), and in Ciudad Juárez itself. We would also interview individual members of NGOs, including those that have led a persistent campaign to denounce the crimes, as well as human rights defenders and victims' families.

Finally, in the fifth step of the process, we would have to prepare a report, to which we would append our comments and proposals for recommendations all of which to be adopted by the Committee. The Committee's report would be sent to the State Party, aiming to put an end to the violations and preventing such situations from occurring in the future. Within a period of six months, the State Party would then be obligated to submit its observations to the Committee with regard to the findings, comments, and recommendations of this report.

THE CIUDAD JUÁREZ INQUIRY—THE REPORT AND ITS RECOMMENDATIONS

At the thirtieth session of the Committee, in January 2004, our proposals for a Report and the Recommendations were discussed, adopted, and sent to the Government of Mexico. It has to be noted that the Committee does not act as a court and cannot give binding decisions, but only recommendations. However, it can expect their implementation, because the State Party by ratifying the Optional Protocol has accepted the authority of the Committee to conduct inquiries. In accordance with the provisions of the Protocol, a period of no more than six months was given to the Government to submit information on measures taken in response to these Recommendations (Article 8 [4]). At the end of the thirty-first session, in July 2004, and again at the thirty-second session, in January 2005, the Government responded to the Committee, thus concluding the confidential part of process. According to the Optional Protocol, the whole process must be conducted confidentially until the submission of information on measures taken by the State Party brings the inquiry formally to a close. Of course, such confidentiality must be strictly respected by the Committee, even if it does not apply to the other participants, namely the NGOs or people involved who may, legitimately, want to make public the fact that an inquiry is taking place.

As the process ends, such confidentiality ends and publicity must be given to the situation and to the inquiry, including the Committee's Report and Recommendations and the State Party's Response. Such publicity makes visible a grave situation that must be urgently addressed and solved; publicity is one more way to put pressure on those responsible for finding solutions. The Committee, therefore, made public its Report and the Recommendations, together with the Government's Response, in a press conference at UN headquarters in January 2005. A significant number of media representatives, both national and international, attended. Committee members answered many questions and also agreed to be interviewed.

When a formal inquiry ends, the need of a lasting solution may still remain. For this reason the Protocol includes a system of follow-up actions, to be undertaken by the Committee as a sixth step. Two possibilities are envisaged under the Optional Protocol: Either an invitation that the State Party include, in its regular reporting on the implementation of the Convention, details of any measures adopted in response to the inquiry (Article 9 [1]); or a formal request *after* the end of the first six months given for a response by the State Party, that the State Party provide further information on the same matter (Article 9 [2]).

In our view, this possibility of follow-up is particularly relevant in instances in which questions are broader than individual problems, and not likely to be solved by individual answers, legal or administrative. Solutions to grave or systematic violations of women's human rights dealt with by the inquiry procedure may be even of a deep structural and long-lasting nature. As such, they may require time to be fully addressed and implemented, not only with respect to the ongoing violations, but also with respect to their root causes and their social consequences.

THE MEXICAN CASE: A MORE DETAILED LOOK AT THE FACTS

In the eyes of the Committee the facts of the case fully justified the requirements for an inquiry. They concerned grave violations of fundamental rights expressed in the murders and disappearances of women, occurring in a specific region, and seeming to follow a specific pattern, particularly after 1993. The murders occurred in very large numbers, even though these numbers varied according to different sources, national and international, governmental and nongovernmental. While these crimes had been consistently denounced by civil society organizations, particularly women's organizations, they had initially been ignored or minimized by authorities. Different motivations have been suggested for the crimes, including trafficking in women for sexual exploitation or for the production of violent videos, drug trafficking, or trafficking in organs. About one third of the victims had suffered some form of sexual abuse, rape, or mutilation, thus indicating sexual violence as a significant component. The suggested motivations seemed to be based on the profile of the victims— all similarly young and pretty, mostly poor, working in shops or *maquilas*, or still students. The women themselves had sometimes been blamed, and victims' families had complained of harassment by some authorities. On the whole, a general climate of impunity seemed to be the rule.

Following investigations by some international organizations, a progressively clearer perception of the situation began to emerge, which then led to some recognition of its gravity by the Mexican authorities. Nevertheless, not until 2004 did Mexican authorities take several specific steps to address the problem. Our main concern as investigators was to look at the situation as a whole—not only at specific criminal cases, but within a context of enormous complexity, in a society where socioeconomic changes were occurring very rapidly, and where economic development had not been accompanied by structural and human development, or by basic infrastructures and community building. The context was also one of widespread sex discrimination and gender-based violence, which seemed to be taken as natural and unquestioned realities. The establishment of *maquilas* employing mainly women, located in isolated areas on the outskirts of the town without secure transportation, together with a lack of economic alternatives for men, had produced specific tensions, particularly against young women. On the whole, we were looking at a violent society, with social and familial tensions, within a culture of misogyny and discrimination, where women were easily devalued and discarded.

Particularly in our meetings with victims' families and with NGOs involved in efforts to denounce the crimes, we became fully aware of the intensity of danger and suffering beneath the surface of life. Such meetings, sad and painful as they were, were also very important sources of information for the inquiry.

THE RECOMMENDATIONS OF THE COMMITTEE TO THE GOVERNMENT OF MEXICO AND THE GOVERNMENT'S RESPONSE

The Committee's sixteen Recommendations focused both on aspects related to the investigation and subsequent punishment of the crimes, and on the need to intervene in a wider social context and to address the issue of discrimination and violence against women in its various forms and its social and human consequences (CEDAW Report 2005a, paras. 258–86). The Recommendations fell into three categories and responded to the overriding concern of looking at the situation in a holistic and structural way.

Four recommendations were of a general nature. They focused on the compliance by the Mexican State with its CEDAW obligations and on the full responsibility of all the authorities at different levels of power to prevent violence against women and to protect their human rights; on the need to incorporate a gender perspective into various social policies, particularly regarding gender-based violence; and on the need to adopt an effective dialogue and close relationship with NGOs and civil society in general. These seemed to us to be the overriding dimensions constituting the essential framework of all responses to the situation, whether criminal, social, cultural, or any other.

Eight recommendations addressed the specific matter of the investigation of the crimes, dealing both with the punishment of the perpetrators and with support to the victims' families. Among other things, they required better coordination of the different levels of authority—federal, state, and municipality—and the possibility of transferring the investigation of the unsolved crimes to the federal level, as they constitute serious human rights violations; the investigation and punishment of negligence, complicity, and tolerance by some authorities, both with regard to the disappearances and to the investigation of the murders; the establishment of early warning and emergency search mechanisms in cases of disappearance; and the autonomy and independence of the investigations and the capacity building of investigators (not merely technical training for the criminal investigation, but also capacity building with regard to gender-based violence as a human rights violation). Recommendations were also made regarding measures to guarantee the respectful and compassionate treatment of mothers and relatives of victims and to ensure the protection of victims' relatives and human rights defenders who had suffered threats and harassment. Finally, a recommendation was made on the possibility of establishing an agreement with the United States, taking into account the border situation and aiming at systematic cooperation with regard to prevention and solution of the crimes.

Four recommendations addressed the broader matter of preventing violence, guaranteeing security, and promoting and protecting the human rights of women. The most important of these emphasized women's human rights through awareness-raising campaigns and the training of public officials and judicial personnel, and sensitizing the media to view violence against women as a human rights violation. Recommendations on measures for the intensification of policies and programs to prevent violence, to guarantee security, and to restore the social fabric were also put forward. The provision of legal support to all victims of violence and their families in their search for justice and of medical and psychological treatment and economic assistance where needed were also strongly recommended. Finally, it was recommended to provide the necessary resources, both human and financial, to combat violence in Ciudad Juárez, along with a Special Commissioner.[4]

While other investigatory bodies had particularly emphasized certain aspects—like the persistence of impunity, the lack of effective judicial response, the inefficient and incompetent investigations, or the inaction on the part of authorities—the CEDAW Committee pursued a holistic approach within a framework of respect for women's human rights. It thus also stressed the need to address the root causes of violence against women, making links not only to poverty and social conditions, but also to a prevailing culture of misogyny and of stereotypical and negative views of women's worth and dignity.

The Government's responses included a general description of the actions taken and of the programs adopted to address the situation, in relation to each one of the Recommendations made by the Committee. Two main lines of action were described, the first aiming at "social development and promotion of human rights"; the second aiming at "criminal investigation and administration of justice." Measures taken at the federal level, as well as at the level of the state and of the municipality, to promote social development and protect and promote the human rights of women, among others, included: awareness-raising and media campaigns to prevent domestic violence; assistance programs addressed to victims' close relatives, including medical and psychological care and legal counseling; emergency telephone lines; an improvement of housing conditions; the creation of shelters; the development of social and educational projects; a review of urbanization and transport policies; the creation of early warning systems and surveillance operations in high-risk areas; and the creation of a trust fund to support relatives of murdered women.

Measures taken with regard to the investigation of the crimes included: the establishment of the Office of the Special Prosecutor for the investigation of the murders; the systematization of information on the number and types of crimes; a review of all case files and of the status of each investigation; the creation of a database of missing women and immediate action in cases of disappearances; the creation of a national register of crime victims; the establishment of responsibilities, both administrative and/or criminal, of public officials; the establishment of protective measures for individuals or associations involved in the cases; the establishment of cooperation with the FBI in regard to capacity building for criminal investigation; and the establishment of cooperation with the border police of El Paso.

While few indicators were offered of results achieved, certainly the Optional Protocol had increased awareness of the issues at stake in Ciudad Juárez (and in Chihuahua, because the crimes were extending beyond that city to other parts of the state) and in the nature, social meaning, and terrible consequences of the pattern of these murders. One may briefly assess the Government's response as an attempt to provide some integrated investigation of the crimes, as well as attending to underlying social issues, of poverty, the environment, and education. The Government identified measures aimed at going forward with investigations of the crimes, bringing those guilty to justice, and assisting the victims, and adequate resources seemed to be allocated for the investigations and social programs. The response made constant reference to the political will of the Government to address the situation, both in the short term (the pursuit of justice) and in the long run (the eradication of violence). And yet, there are still no specific results demonstrating the real efficacy of the measures taken and of the structures established. The crimes are still continuing, and NGOs complain that not enough progress has been achieved, that investigations are slow, that many of those found responsible are left free, that there is not enough political will. It was for these reasons, and also acknowledging that this process requires a social and cultural change over time which must be regularly monitored and evaluated, that the Committee has requested further information on developments in the situation in connection with Mexico's periodic reporting on the Convention.[5]

FINAL REMARKS

Today, the questions of abduction, rape, and murder of women in Ciudad Juárez are fully recognized as serious problems and responsibilities of the State as a whole and at all its levels: federal, state, and local powers. The CEDAW inquiry was only one more step in this process, but it was certainly helpful.[6] However, beyond an inquiry, it was also a process of dialogue that must continue, both with the Government and with the NGOs that have been involved in this process. They know the real situation on the ground, and their views help the Committee to keep a balanced view of the issue. Such a dialogue must place its emphasis on the issue of violence against women, both on the crimes and on the environment surrounding them, and, above all, on the need to change an underlying culture of violence, misogyny, and discrimination.

This culture goes beyond the borders of the state of Chihuahua into other regions of Mexico, where the murder figures in some states even surpass the ones of Ciudad Juárez. It also exists in other countries of Latin America. For example, at its thirty-fifth session, which took place in May 2006, the Committee reviewed the sixth periodic report of Guatemala and was confronted, also through information provided by NGOs, with a distressing situation of disappearances and murders of women in appalling numbers. These situations have been given less visibility than the one of Ciudad Juárez, but are equally horrible and have to be equally denounced and combated.

What is the final assessment of the first process of inquiry conducted by the Committee? From our point of view, and in spite of the problems that still persist and must still be vigorously addressed, it is a positive one. The inquiry procedure under the Optional Protocol is, certainly, a valid procedure for women and women's organizations to be aware of, and utilized when rights under the Convention are violated in a grave *or* systematic manner. We have an important instrument in our hands that must be well known, valued, and used!

NOTES

1. Mexico is a federal State comprising thirty-one states and a Federal District that includes Mexico City and the neighboring areas. Each state has its own constitution shaped on the national charter. Following federal organization at the national level, states have executive, legislative, and judicial branches. While Mexico is one of the most industrialized countries in Latin America, there is great economic polarization between rich and poor, and poverty drives many Mexicans to cross the border into the United States in search of a job and a better future. High crime rates are persistent. Investigation of the crimes addressed by the inquiry falls under state jurisdiction, although during the inquiry proposals for transfer of such crimes to federal jurisdiction were being put forward.

2. This includes discrimination against women expressed in the abuse of their right to life and security, to their integrity, both physical and mental, or to any other fundamental right protected by the Convention. Severe violence or torture, disappearances or kidnappings, trafficking or killings could certainly be motives for an inquiry under the Optional Protocol.

3. Systematic denial of equal rights for women regarding, for example, nationality or inheritance; laws that permit polygamy or are sex-specific in regard to adultery; tolerance of sex tourism, or recruitment of labor under false promises leading to forced prostitution; systematic acceptances of forced marriages; tolerance of violence against women, including the practice of female genital mutilation (FGM) or other traditional harmful practices—all of these could be potential themes for investigation and could well be challenged on the basis of the inquiry procedure.

4. A Special Commissioner for the Prevention and Punishment of Violence against Women in Ciudad Juárez was appointed on October 17, 2003. The mandate included making an analysis of the various areas of work and the respective tasks of the federal and state authorities and agencies in Ciudad Juárez, an assessment of the compliance of the Government with the plan of action adopted—the so-called 40-point plan—and the establishment of a calendar for the completion of the agreed actions.

5. In August 2006 the Committee reviewed the sixth periodic report of Mexico (Government of Mexico 2006), which provided new information on actions taken, some successes achieved, and on remaining problems. Two Mexican officials involved in dealing with the issue took part in the constructive dialogue. The Committee reiterated its recommendations from the final report of the inquiry in its concluding comments and urged Mexico to establish concrete monitoring mechanisms for them, since the crimes continue (CEDAW 2006, 266, paras. 595–96).

6. In addition to ones mentioned many other investigations were conducted and visits took place in the late 1990s and the first years of the present decade, the most recent one by the Special Rapporteur on violence against women, Yakin Ertürk (United Nations 2006b).

PERSONAL REFLECTION:

THE CIRCLE OF EMPOWERMENT

AURORA JAVATE DE DIOS, *PHILIPPINES*

As one of the CEDAW experts from 1994–1998, I had the rare opportunity of "engaging the State" in a critical dialogue about the Convention. Until then, I had always thought of UN processes as too remote to be appreciated by NGOs and much less by ordinary women. As an activist, who had worked for many years in social movements and in the "parliament of the streets" in the Philippines, I found the Committee's work and processes too tedious and bureaucratic at first. Over time, however, I realized how valuable it was to learn from the experiences and insights of my colleagues as well as from representatives of countries reporting to the Committee.

I began to appreciate that although sustained monitoring by Committee members of compliance with and implementation of the Convention can be tedious, it is an urgent and necessary task requiring full dedication and commitment of the experts. The interdisciplinary expertise of CEDAW Committee members, coming from different regions and cultures, enriched my own understanding of the complex tapestry of issues and problems affecting women in various parts of the world in the context of differing cultures, as well as legal and political systems. Indeed, working in the Committee gave me the feeling of being part of a long and historical process as well as of the chain of women and men who have fought for women's voices to be heard and respected at the international level.

During my four years in the CEDAW Committee, I was fortunate enough to participate in some of the highpoints in its history. These were the participation of the Committee in the Fourth UN World Conference on Women in Beijing and the discussion and debate on the Optional Protocol to the Convention. The massive and global mobilization of women for the Beijing Conference infused it with the dynamism of tens of thousands of women who had participated at every stage of the preparatory processes (Friedman 2003). Interest in the Beijing Conference and the discussions on the draft Beijing Platform for Action brought renewed attention and interest in the Convention, as evidenced by most intense discussions and new documents produced by international organizations, governments, and NGOs focusing on the work of the CEDAW Committee.

It became obvious that the transnational women's movement that had emerged in the 1990s had effectively utilized opportunities for participation in the United Nations and had developed expanded structures for mobilization through networking and evolving similar or shared frameworks. The parallel NGO conferences alongside official UN Conferences in the 1990s provided NGOs with a much needed opportunity to consolidate their agendas and lobbying efforts to influence the final official Conference outcomes (Friedman 2003). At the NGO Forum in 1995 in Huairou, which lasted for ten days, almost four thousand workshops and panels were held, many of which referred to the Convention and its Committee. In addition sixty thousand e-mail messages were recorded and over one hundred thousand visits to the NGO website were noted (Anand et al. 1998, 25–26), reflecting the massive engagement of women in the Beijing processes.

Participating in the Philippine delegation to the UN World Conference in Beijing as well as in the parallel NGO Forum, I witnessed the excitement and the tensions resulting from intense divisions both between and among governments as well as among women's groups. Such divisions centered mostly on issues of reproductive rights and sexual orientation. Anti-abortion and antireproductive health and rights groups conducted an aggressive campaign throughout both the NGO Forum and the official Conference in Beijing, sometimes disrupting proceedings with their unauthorized presence in closed-door meetings of the official Conference. The challenges and difficulties posed by conservative countries and groups during the negotiations in Beijing crystallized the strategic importance of the CEDAW Convention as the only legally binding human rights instrument for women that a majority of UN member States have committed to implementing. Although the Convention has been in force since 1981, many feminists and women's groups began to view it in a new light after 1995, and saw the programmatic Beijing Platform for Action as a powerful instrument to complement it. Fortunately, despite the intense debates and the strong opposition of conservative groups, the legitimacy of women's rights as human rights was firmly established in the Beijing Platform for Action.

While working in the CEDAW Committee, I was constantly faced with the challenge of communicating the value of the Committee's work to NGOs back home in a way that was easily understood by leaders as well as by ordinary women at the grassroots level. Many women NGOs often inquired about the nature of my work and the relevance of spending time and energy on reviewing reports of States Parties. In general, they perceived any UN work to have very little effect on the immediate and urgent realities, problems, and issues faced by Filipino women on a daily basis. I have to acknowledge that decades of women's alienation from male-dominated institutions like the United Nations, with its bureaucratic processes and its unique UN language, have had a disempowering effect on most women, especially those from grassroots. As a result, women generally have difficulty in appreciating the work of the United Nations and locating themselves in its processes.

In my orientation sessions and lectures on the Convention and its Committee, especially in the Philippine provinces, I realized that I had to present a framework that would allow all women to understand how they fit into the picture of human rights. This framework, which I called the "circle of empowerment," presents the work of the Committee in the light of the continuing, dynamic process of women's struggles to claim their rights. Women have been part of these struggles from the very beginning of formulating international law and throughout the process of knowing, claiming, and asserting rights from the local level, moving up to the international level, and then back to the local level. I still use this framework in my training sessions on the CEDAW Convention and its Committee.

The emergence of women's voices and rights was not accidental, but the result of a dynamic collective and historical process through which individual groups claimed spaces and rights for themselves. At the center of this process are grassroots women, their advocates, and women's movements, in different countries. Over time, they exerted pressure on governments to enact laws and adopt policies and programs that improved women's political, economic, and social conditions to enjoy their human rights; and change discriminatory social attitudes toward them. Initiatives for legal and policy reforms guaranteeing women their rights at national levels later found expression at the international level. This cumulative process of empowering women—as they negotiated, struggled for, and claimed their political, economic, and cultural rights through the suffrage and other women's movements—has been uneven in many countries, but is the basis on which the international women's movement was built. Through global networking, furthered by advances in information technology and the increased mobility of people to come together, women's voices and perspectives have been strengthened globally.

Codification of the rights of women at the international level was important in establishing a universally valid set of standards for the treatment of women. While many of these gains have been achieved in the past twenty-five years through the CEDAW Convention and its Committee, these rights are by no means secure. As evidenced by the intense struggles among States over the nature and interpretation of women's rights during the Beijing Conference, as well as the debates on the Optional Protocol to the Convention, these gains may be challenged, undermined, and eventually eroded (Butegwa 2001).

International law often needs to be translated into laws at the domestic level to make it operational. In the final analysis, the relevance and efficacy of human rights for women lies in the extent to which women actually claim and reclaim, as well as assert and reassert, these rights by pursuing a number of strategies, such as monitoring States Parties' compliance with respect to their obligations in protecting, respecting, and fulfilling human rights; sharpening and specifying the general human rights discourse by integrating a gender perspective; documenting violations of women's human rights; and sustaining public awareness of women's human rights. Without this proactive process, international law such as the CEDAW Convention would be a dead instrument. In the last analysis, women's activism infuses the Convention and the work of its Committee with meaning and relevance. Women can only achieve the goal of enjoying their human rights if they themselves are empowered and continually engaged in further empowering themselves and other women as part of a movement for social change.

NOTE

With the permission of the author, the title of this essay was chosen for the title of this book.

FROM GLOBAL TO LOCAL: THE INVOLVEMENT OF NGOS

SHANTHI DAIRIAM, *MALAYSIA*

My engagement with the CEDAW Convention started in 1989, when I read about it and subsequently attended a meeting held in Vienna to discuss this treaty in the context of reproductive rights. At that time, I was working with a regional program on women, law, and development that was based in Malaysia. Previously, however, I had worked for more than twelve years as a volunteer and then staff member with the national voluntary family planning program in Malaysia, and I was still involved with advocacy relating to women's reproductive rights. It is in dealing with these rights that I had become keenly sensitive to issues of women's equality, I felt that gaining insights into using international human rights standards to address the intransigent nature of the resistance to women's reproductive rights would be useful. Gradually, on getting to know the potential of the Convention, I realized that the elimination of discrimination and the fulfillment of women's right to equality were key to the exercising of rights by women in every context and in all spheres.

The meeting in 1989 was one of a series organized by Arvonne Fraser as the founding director of the International Women's Rights Action Watch (IWRAW), based at the Humphrey Institute of Public Affairs, University of Minnesota, Minneapolis. IWRAW had been formed to publicize and monitor the Convention and its implementation. Recognizing the significance of the relationship between the CEDAW Committee and women's groups, it had organized an international network of women activists, motivating them to take an interest in the monitoring process of the Convention. IWRAW also submitted "alternative" or "shadow" reports to the Committee which it compiled on the basis of its own research and of independent information collected from academics or NGOs in the respective country, and which enhanced the Committee's work of reviewing the implementation of CEDAW by States Parties.

In the early 1990s, inspired by Arvonne Fraser's work, and with permission from the IWRAW Minnesota program in Minneapolis to use the same name, I founded an independent and autonomous program in the Asia Pacific region, the International Women's Rights Action Watch Asia

Pacific (IWRAW Asia Pacific 2007a). I believed that links needed to be built between the international advocacy of women's rights and national advocacy. IWRAW Asia Pacific was built on the premise that, without a politically aware and active constituency of women at the national level, the normative gains made in relation to women's human rights at the international level could not be sustained. Its program focused on creating constituencies of women at the national level who could use the processes of the Convention at the international level to invoke their rights and generate the necessary political will for action by their governments. The contribution that IWRAW Asia Pacific has made is as a bridge: By creating a synergy between national and international activism, it supports the application of international human rights norms and standards at the national level.

At an operational level, IWRAW Asia Pacific focuses on building capacity for the implementation of CEDAW through collaboration with national women's groups, governments, intergovernmental bodies, and other institutions. At the regional level, it has been working in twelve countries. It coordinates a global program related to the reporting and review processes under the Convention. To date, it has facilitated the presence of women from more than one hundred countries during these processes at the United Nations. It also implements a global campaign on the ratification and use of the Optional Protocol to the Convention.

In 2004, I was elected to the CEDAW Committee for a four-year term, 2005–2008, becoming the first Malaysian to hold this position. It was for me a natural step to go from being an advocate for the implementation of the Convention to taking a formal role of engaging in constructive dialogue with governments. As I see it, the progression in my professional life is in itself an example of the effectiveness and dynamism of NGOs. The need for national NGO involvement in the monitoring treaties of UN bodies, and in particular of the implementation of the CEDAW Convention, is the topic of my essay.

THE VITAL RESPONSIBILITY OF NGOS

Although there is a certain amount of cynicism about the Convention, especially in those countries where its principles have not been incorporated into domestic legislation, one can point to other examples of the impact of the Convention through NGO advocacy and activism. Constitutions and domestic laws have been reformed to comply with its principles; discriminatory laws have been challenged; it has been used to interpret ambivalent provisions of the law or—when the law has been silent—to confer rights on women; and development policies have been formulated using its framework. NGOs have worked for many of these gains in a number of ways.

First, a synergy between the national and international processes relating to the implementation of the Convention needs to be created, and this can be done by NGOs. In some countries, NGOs have advocated that States Parties submit their reports to the United Nations on time. Second, the Committee requires accurate information on women's de jure and de facto situation of their enjoyment of their human rights to make useful recommendations to the State. Toward this end, women's groups can provide relevant information to the Committee—and they have done so.

At the same time, women's groups advocating for equality at the national level have a powerful tool in the Convention if they can learn to harness it for domestic application. The Committee's concluding comments are useful in setting priorities for advocacy through its identification of areas of concern and recommendations for action. Concluding comments provide the basis for a national collaborative process to be set up between governments and NGOs for the implementation of the Convention, thus indicating conscious efforts by governments to pursue the Committee's recommendations as well as to build collaborative relationships with NGOs.

LEGITIMIZING THE PARTICIPATION OF WOMEN IN THE CONVENTION REPORTING AND REVIEW PROCESSES

In view of the above, in 1997, IWRAW Asia Pacific initiated a program called "From Global to Local," funded initially by the Ford Foundation and with the United Nations Development Fund for Women (UNIFEM) as a funding and collaborating partner. As of 2004, agencies such as the United Nations Population Fund (UNFPA) have supported this effort. This program aims to build the capacity of women's groups from reporting countries. It facilitates their presence during the review process in the Committee, thereby allowing NGOs to observe the presentations, responses, and commitments of their governments; it enables NGOs to provide alternative information to the Committee and raise pertinent issues not contained in the States Parties' reports; and it allows NGOs to make plans for monitoring State Party compliance with the recommendations of the Committee's concluding comments. Thus, the program has helped systematize the crucial relationships between the Committee and women's NGOs. To support these activities, IWRAW Asia Pacific set up two electronic discussion lists to generate information flow among

NGOs. One, called "cedaw4change," was open globally for anyone to impart and receive information on the use of the Convention and the practices and challenges in making it an effective instrument to promote women's rights. The other, called "global2local," was private and reached out only to former "From Global to Local" program participants.

While there had been informal relationships between the Committee and NGOs since 1988, and "alternative" reports had been submitted by some groups, a clear mandate for a formal role for NGOs in the CEDAW review process was absent from the Convention. The IWRAW Asia Pacific program created a legitimate space for national NGOs to interact with the Committee. In this context it is important to note that the first "From Global to Local" project was organized just at the time when the Committee and other human rights treaty bodies were starting to explore how they could establish a more clearly defined relationship with NGOs. The need for such a relationship had been reiterated at the sixth Meeting of Chairpersons of Human Rights Treaty Bodies in 1995, at which the Chairpersons stressed the central function of NGOs to provide reliable information necessary for the conduct of the activities of the treaty bodies. The Chairpersons recommended that the UN Secretariat facilitate the exchange of information between treaty bodies and NGOs (United Nations 1995c, para. 23). As a result of these developments, a report on this matter prepared by the UN Division for the Advancement of Women (DAW) was discussed by the Committee during its sixteenth session, resulting in a decision "to invite the United Nations Secretariat to facilitate an informal meeting with nongovernmental organizations outside the regular meeting time of the Committee" (Decision 16/II in CEDAW Report 1997, 1). This decision was made in the same session for which the first "From Global to Local" project training was conducted. Later, the Committee included specific mention of the role of NGOs in its revised Rules of Procedure adopted in January 2001, thus giving more legitimacy to the presence of NGOs at the review of States Parties' reports (CEDAW 2001, 100, Rule 47). Although there were many other factors behind the creation of stronger NGO-treaty body relationships— such as recommendations from the UN World Conferences on strengthening the role of NGOs in human rights implementation—the "From Global to Local" program contributed to creating a momentum for such a change in the relationship with the Committee (UNIFEM 2004, 14).

THE WORK OF NGOS IN THE REVIEW OF STATES PARTIES' REPORTS AND ITS BENEFITS

With regard to the entire treaty process, NGOs have prepared written and oral "alternative" reports and used them for advocacy during the review process; they have raised awareness on and advocated for the implementation of the concluding comments of the Committee on law reform and other issues; they have developed skills and capacity for implementing the Convention nationally; and they have engaged in litigation and the provision of services for the claiming of rights. Over the past few years, the practice of the Committee has been to provide a small amount of time for NGOs in its agenda on the first days of the first and second week of a particular session. During this time NGOs have approximately five to seven minutes each for an oral presentation. A short dialogue between the Committee and the NGOs follows. NGOs are also present at and observe the formal review process, but they may not participate in it. However, they have many opportunities to speak informally to the members of the Committee, and they may provide clarifications and information as necessary throughout the review.

NGO interventions and advocacy have had good results. Since the NGOs may often be aware of why the effects of good policies, laws, or programs do not reach all the women concerned and of gaps that may exist between law, policy, and practice, they are best placed to present information to the Committee on the situation of women's lives at the grassroots level. Furthermore, they are able to report on the consequences of legislation that may seem neutral on the surface but may be discriminatory in effect. NGOs' "alternative" reports can therefore reveal why commitments to women's rights often do not translate into practical realization.

The review process itself has benefited from the participation of NGOs in a number of ways. For example, it has made for sharper and more specific recommendations by the Committee in its concluding comments. These, in turn, have facilitated better advocacy by NGOs at the national level and better guidance to other UN or bilateral agencies and donors who are in a position to offer technical and financial assistance to governments to implement the Convention.

At times NGOs have come together to discuss important aspects of state action; to collaborate in expanding ideas and activism around rights; to create greater media awareness; to provide a basis for dialogue and for communication with a government; and to ensure that state interventions are being monitored and assessed for effectiveness. NGOs have helped to publicize States Parties' reports and the Committee's concluding comments to a wider national audience, when governments themselves may have avoided doing so. As a consequence, discussions around concepts and practice of women's rights have taken place at the local level, providing a very sound basis for influencing policy. NGOs have been able to identify areas for effective interventions and to provide support services to create enabling conditions for women's rights to be achieved (IWRAW Asia Pacific 2007b).

NGO advocacy at the national level can benefit tremendously from the observation of the Committee's review process at the United Nations. NGOs gain knowledge of commitments their governments have made during the dialogue with the Committee. They are also able to assess gaps in the knowledge or the capacity of their governments. This allows them to identify areas for future collaboration. They also learn how to act more strategically at the national level. For example, at the eighteenth session of the Committee, the Government of Zimbabwe was praised for the Legal Age of Majority Act (1982), which gives women above the age of eighteen the legal capacity to marry or enter into commercial contracts. On the Government's return home, however, it announced that it was going to repeal the Act. Drawing on their experiences from the review process in New York, four women from Zimbabwe, who had participated in IWRAW Asia Pacific's "From Global to Local" program in January 1998, were able to publicize the contradictory action effectively. The Government subsequently withdrew its intention to repeal the Act (IWRAW Asia Pacific 1998, 4).

The observance of the review by NGOs has also helped them in some cases to establish better relationships with their governments and has at times contributed to better government transparency. Governments seem to have greater respect for the women of their countries present at the review processes when they realize that these women were not there as individuals but as part of an international group, i.e. facilitated by IWRAW Asia Pacific. It would appear that the visibility of NGOs at the review process has raised their standing in some countries, resulting in some governments being more willing to acknowledge them and even consult them on follow-up processes.

Thus, NGOs from Azerbaijan reported that their presence at the review of Azerbaijan's initial report enhanced their status with their Government, and that the Government acknowledged for the first time the presence of women's human rights organizations in the country. Subsequently, channels opened for communication between women's NGOs and the Government in the country (IWRAW Asia Pacific 1998, 3).

Another example comes from Turkey. The Turkish NGOs present during the Committee's review of Turkey's combined fourth and fifth periodic report had the opportunity to speak informally with the Turkish Minister. One of the items they were lobbying for at that time was their inclusion in the Turkish Government's delegation to the forthcoming UN meeting on the assessment of progress in implementing the Beijing Platform for Action (Beijing +10). Later, they were of the view that the fact that their "alternative" reports had been welcomed by the Committee at the review had influenced the Minister to accept their demand. As a result, two NGO members were part of the Turkish Government's delegation to the Beijing +10 meeting, where they felt that their presence made a difference. Creating a better relationship between the Turkish Government and these women's NGOs was a critical achievement and essential for the sustainability of advocacy on the Convention after the review (global2local listserv April 2005). A third example comes from Sri Lanka. After the CEDAW review of Sri Lanka's combined third and fourth periodic report, the Sri Lankan Government and the national NGOs held a consultation on every paragraph of the Committee's concluding comments, including a discussion of plans for their implementation. NGOs offered their expertise and resources in pursuing the subsequent plan of action (IWRAW Asia Pacific 2002, 25).

EXAMPLES OF NGO ACTIVISM AND ADVOCACY FOR CHANGE IN THEIR COUNTRIES

Good examples of NGO advocacy with regard to the rights of women may be seen in the publicity given to the concluding comments by NGOs; and in laws as well as in litigation as means of initiating reform. The following examples are selective, and but one of many other factors in the success of reform processes in States Parties. Thus an NGO representative from Moldova stated that, after the CEDAW Committee had made its recommendations, it became easier for the NGO to plan its work since now it had specific directions (cedaw4change listserv October 2003). At the same time, the review process functions as an accountability mechanism since the State Party has to submit to periodic scrutiny at the international level. The obligation to appear again and again before the Committee has the potential for motivating a State Party to show progress. The political activism of NGOs in engaging with the review process and in the follow-up to the review is one key to these efforts.

In some cases important concluding comments by the Committee have remained unimplemented. Publicity given to these by NGOs has had the effect of mobilizing public opinion on the obligations of the State Party, thus facilitating accountability. In Morocco, for example, after the review of the Government's initial report in 1997 and second periodic report in 2003, the *Association Démocratique des Femmes du Maroc* (ADFM), the NGO that had coordinated the preparation of the "alternative" report, organized debriefing meetings and shared the Government's responses to the questions posed by the CEDAW Committee and the Committee's concluding comments with women activists. ADFM also organized a press conference to inform the media of what had taken place in the CEDAW session. NGOs from Argentina, Brazil, India, and Nepal, who had attended CEDAW sessions, organized similar initiatives. UNIFEM assisted the NGOs from Kyrgyzstan who had been present at the review to organize a roundtable with high-level Government representatives and other NGOs on their return home. This process led to an action plan for the implementation of the concluding comments as well as an NGO plan to monitor the Government's action plan. UNIFEM facilitated a similar process in the case of Kazakhstan (UNIFEM 2004, 13, 18).

At the review of Turkey's combined fourth and fifth periodic report, the Committee raised a number of questions with the Government based on information provided by Turkish women's groups present at the session. Subsequently, through the advocacy of the NGOs when back in Turkey, a woman member of Parliament (MP) posed approximately a dozen questions in the Parliament to the Minister in charge of Women's Affairs, trying to get a commitment from the Government to implement the Committee's concluding comments. The questions raised were related to the issues that had been the subject of the dialogue between the Government's delegation and the Committee, i.e. discriminatory articles of the Turkish Penal Code on "honor" killings and virginity testing; the lack of an explicit provision for temporary special measures on gender equality in the Constitution; and the lack of government action to improve women's labor force participation and apply the domestic violence law. The NGOs also managed to get wide newspaper coverage of their experience at the Committee's review. The NGOs concerned believe that these actions definitely built a bridge between the international monitoring process of the Convention and the national context (global2local listserv April 2005).

At the review of States Parties' reports, NGOs have advocated for law and policy reform as a means of developing new standards for women's rights at the national level that would be in compliance with the international standards set by the Convention. Their recommendations in this regard have been reflected in relevant concluding comments. In some instances there has been a positive impact at the national level, in that subsequent to the review process such law and policy reform took place. In 2002, the Eleventh Amendment Bill to the Country Code of Nepal eliminated more than twenty discriminatory provisions in the law. Particularly significant were those in inheritance laws, adoption, divorce, and criminal laws, including laws on abortion. The need for such reform had been identified by NGOs at the Committee's review of Nepal's initial report in 1999 and had been included in the Committee's concluding comments (CEDAW 1999, 61, para. 139).

The concluding comments addressed to India after its initial report in the Committee's twenty-second session referred to several areas of discrimination against women in the law. They also touched on the need for compulsory marriage registration and sufficient and targeted resource allocation for the advancement of Indian women (CEDAW 2000, 10, paras. 57–60). These issues had been brought to the attention of the Committee by Indian NGOs in their "alternative" report. Since then, the Government has amended some of the personal laws such as the Indian Divorce Act in 2001, which covers women and men of Christian faith. Provisions in this Act that were discriminatory to women have been eliminated and uniform provisions for women and men with regard to grounds for divorce have been added (Government of India 2005, 4). In addition, the 1956 Hindu Succession Act was amended by the central Government in 2005 in order to establish equality in property rights. By virtue of this amendment, females—including widows of *co-parceners* who have remarried—can inherit ancestral property with the same rights as their male counterparts.[1] The provisions of the Act also cover agricultural holdings. Some states had already amended the provisions in the Hindu Succession Act for their areas. In addition, the recommendation of the Indian National Commission on Women to make registration of marriage compulsory has also been accepted by Parliament. In its National Policy on Empowerment of Women of 2001, the central Government committed itself to ensure that all marriages were registered by the year 2010.

In 2002, when the Government of Zambia reported to the Committee in its twenty-seventh session, women's groups who were present expressed their concerns about clauses in the Zambian Constitution that allowed for discrimination against women on the basis of culture-based personal and customary laws. They advocated that the Bill of Rights should include provisions of CEDAW and the Convention on the Rights of the Child (CRC). The Committee's concluding comments reflected these concerns (CEDAW 2002, 110, paras. 230 and 231). Following the session, these women's groups worked with women MPs to generate a private members' motion to remove laws that discriminate against women, which was successfully passed.[2] The Committee also urged Zambia to assign high priority to the issue of violence against women (111, para. 239). An affiliate of the regional network on Women in Law and Development in Africa (WiLDAF Zambia) has drafted a Bill on Gender-based Violence and Violence against Children and is preparing to have this presented in Parliament as a private members' bill. In the meantime, the same women's groups are carrying out sensitization campaigns on violence, including identification of weaknesses in the current laws. They are also preparing for a parliamentary motion to have a minimum of 30 percent women in Parliament and in government positions by 2006 (global2local listserv March 2004).

In 2004, Moroccan women's groups successfully lobbied for amendments to Morocco's Personal Status Code, involving the removal of discriminatory provisions. Again, such a recommendation had been made by the CEDAW Committee (CEDAW 1997, 13-14, paras. 64 and 71 and CEDAW 2003, 105–6, para. 163). As a result of the advocacy of these groups, Muslim women in Morocco now enjoy formal equality on the basis of their country's family laws. The new Family Code raises the minimum age of marriage for girls to eighteen, makes polygamy almost impossible, improves inheritance rights, makes divorce provisions more equal for women and men, and no longer contains humiliating expressions with regard to women. Speaking on the role of Moroccan women in the reform of the Family Code at an international seminar on "Trends in Family Law Reform in Muslim Countries," held in Kuala Lumpur in March 2006, Amina Lemrini of the ADFM said that a coalition of 200 women's associations had organized an unprecedented campaign to promote their cause between 1999 and 2004.

In 2004 the Committee requested the Government of Kyrgyzstan to undertake a study on women's legal and practical enjoyment of ownership and inheritance of land to be followed by appropriate action where necessary (CEDAW 2004a, 33, para. 172). Recent amendments to the laws in Kyrgyzstan on land rights to guarantee women's equality with men can also be attributed to the advocacy of NGOs (UNIFEM 2004, 19). In 2005 the CEDAW Committee discussed the revision of the new Turkish Penal Code with the Government and urged for additional amendments regarding the physical and sexual rights of women (CEDAW 2005b, 61, para. 363). The Government postponed the entry into effect of the new Penal Code to conduct a final review with a possibility for further amendments, which provided another opportunity for women's groups to have their demands included (global2locallistserv April 2005).

An important lesson for advocacy to be drawn from these and other examples is that, while good laws may have been passed through NGO lobbying, these laws may remain unimplemented if efforts stop there and no further advocacy is done. The Committee's review of Georgia's initial report in its twenty-first session in 1999 resulted in concluding comments that had utilized information presented in the "alternative " reports by NGOs (CEDAW 1999, 57, paras. 97 and 98). The Committee recommended that the Georgian Government increase women's participation in employment—and especially in the political arena—through the use of temporary special measures, including quotas. As a response to this, and because of NGO advocacy, the Georgian President issued a decree on "Measures on Strengthening the Protection of Human Rights of Women in Georgia" in August 1999. On the basis of this Decree, the Georgian Parliament was asked to discuss quotas for the improvement of women's positions in the sphere of political representation. Certain ministries were asked to gather information on the situation of women as well as to elaborate and implement special programs for the improvement of their conditions. Women's groups in Georgia report, however, that this has only been a formal reaction on the part of the Government and that no implementation of the Decree has taken place (cedaw4change listserv October 2003).

Similarly, women's advocates in Guatemala report that three years of sustained advocacy contributed to the adoption of the Law for the Promotion of Women's Status, which contains several provisions set forth in the CEDAW Convention. However, the groups note that this law is hardly known or applied in the country (cedaw4change listserv December 2002). Hence the advocacy needs to continue.

One method that some NGOs have engaged in is the use of litigation as an important means of giving effect to the law as well as to inspire new laws. By claiming rights and thus by activating existing laws through litigation, NGOs contribute to the realization of the material consequences of law. Sometimes a recommendation from the Committee's concluding comments may have enough persuasive effect in domestic courts to bring about positive effects for women. The point I wish to make is that wherever and whenever possible, women must make use of the law and bring cases to court based on the recommendations of the Committee in its respective concluding comments. Concluding comments by the Committee or any other treaty body are not legally binding, but if women can persuade courts to take note of the comments, the positive ruling of the court can help create new standards or interpret existing standards.

This may be illustrated by an example from Japan where, in 2004, the Osaka Appeals Court ruled that the appellants (all women) and the respondent in a labor case reach an amicable settlement, based on the principles of equality and nondiscrimination, and gave specific recommendations with regard to the same. The Court in its statement pointed out that national action must concur with international efforts toward the elimination of discrimination based on sex. The appellants had made specific reference to the Committee's concluding comments on Japan's fourth and fifth periodic report in 2003 (CEDAW 2003, 136, paras. 369–70), which pointed to "the lack of understanding regarding the practice and the effects of indirect discrimination as expressed in the Government Guidelines to the Equal Employment Opportunity Law" (Koedo 2004).

As seen from the above examples, women around the world have helped to reshape the legal framework for women's rights within international standards. However, in addition to laws, a series of programs and services also need to be in place. The lack of services to provide support for women to claim and thus exercise their rights is one reason why laws may have little effect. For example, in the context of gender-based violence, NGOs have provided shelters in numerous countries to ensure short-term personal security for women and an environment that enables them to make choices for the next steps to be taken. NGOs have also provided services for legal literacy and legal aid for women. In almost every set of concluding comments, the CEDAW Committee recommends that the government recognize and support NGOs providing such services.

One other aspect of NGO work that needs to be mentioned is awareness-raising, training, and capacity building not only for women themselves and women's NGOs, but also for officials, the judiciary, and social and medical workers who are to implement the Convention. Women's NGOs have worked tirelessly on such training, including IWRAW Asia Pacific, which created a program called "Facilitating the Fulfillment of State Obligation to Women's Equality." This research-based program was intended to help women in Asia move from understanding a set of treaty standards to applying a certain "methodology" for their implementation at the national level. IWRAW Asia Pacific identified strategies to be applied at the national level in twelve Asian countries in order to facilitate an ongoing monitoring process of States Parties' effective progress in compliance with their obligations under the Convention.

CONTINUING CHALLENGES

Problems still remain. First, a lack of understanding of and a resistance to the principles of gender equality persists at many levels. Second, custom and culture often override considerations of state obligations under the Convention. As the Appeals Court of Japan in the case cited above stated, "It must be borne in mind, that to tolerate the vestiges of discrimination based on past social understandings would result in turning one's back to the progress in the society" (Koedo 2004). This is a point of view that needs to gain more currency. Third, in many countries the Convention remains unincorporated into domestic law so that the full potential of its application at the national level is not attained. Fourth, global economic trends such as privatization often pose threats for the fulfillment of government obligations in the areas of economic and social rights of women. Fifth, by and large there does not always seem to be a concerted effort by States Parties to put into place a coherent plan for the implementation of the Convention. In such cases, many reforms occur in piecemeal fashion so that discrimination against women continues to exist. The indivisibility and interrelatedness of all women's rights are therefore not appreciated. Furthermore, even where good laws are in place, policies, strategies, or even human and financial resources for implementing them may not exist. An increase in the demands of civil society, in particular of women's NGOs, through advocacy for greater state accountability, is essential to create the political will necessary for full implementation of the Convention.

NOTES

1. Traditionally, *co-parceners* were male inheritors of undivided immovable Hindu ancestral property that has been in the family for several generations.

2. In some parliamentary systems an individual MP can present a new draft law for the consideration of the parliament. This is called a private member's bill.

PERSONAL REFLECTIONS:

ACHIEVING FRUITFUL RESULTS

FENG CUI, CHINA

When I sat on the CEDAW Committee, I felt very much honored and duty-bound. We faced representatives from highly industrialized and rich countries and from comparatively poor countries, all with a unique history and all with different social systems and traditional cultures. The ambassadors and representatives of ministries from those countries reported in detail on the progress being made in eliminating discrimination against women, and waited for questions and evaluations from the Committee.

As a diplomat for decades and in women's work over a long time, I have witnessed how the States Parties have applied CEDAW. The examination of States Parties reports by the Committee has been based both on adhering to the principle of universality and on understanding the different particularities of various countries. The reviews thus have led to good results throughout the world, and the Convention has become a cornerstone of the development of women's cause—one of its key objectives.

During my term in the Committee, I examined reports from nearly seventy countries, which had been implementing provisions of the Convention in great honesty and in accordance with their respective situations: New laws were passed, and existing legal instruments with contents discriminatory of women were either revised or eliminated. In the spirit of the Convention, a number of preferential policies and measures for women have been adopted. In many countries, women's status in politics, economy, culture, society and families has been elevated, and their rights and interests have been protected, enabling them to further benefit the society.

China, my home country, has been doing a significant amount of work in implementing the Convention and has achieved fruitful results. The latest and very important legal progress is the newly revised Law of the People's Republic of China on the Protection of Rights and Interests of Women in 2005, in which a new provision on the elimination of all forms of discrimination against women was included, which used the exact wording of Article 1 of the Convention.

In this respect, I would like to highlight the obligation of States Parties to adopt nondiscriminatory legislation and secure the equal rights of rural women with rural men as required by Article 14. As in other developing countries, the majority of the Chinese population lives in the countryside; many rural women stay in the villages and only sometimes leave for seasonal work elsewhere. Thus, these provisions in the Convention are very important for China in order to accelerate equality between women and men and, in particular, to raise the status of rural women.

The day-in and day-out work in the Committee is tense, busy, and serious. I will never forget one terribly cold evening after a long and intense day; it had been snowing heavily. On my way back to the hotel, it was freezing. However, thinking of the significance of the Convention, I could only conclude that the occasional difficulties in the meetings and this bad weather amounted to nothing! Behind the birth of the Convention, a global legal landmark and an accomplishment of the international women's movement, are the countless women who had suffered from discrimination and paid high prices, many with their lives, as well as numerous scholars, experts, and devoted people who had struggled, many for a lifetime. Committee members are doing their jobs, monitoring and promoting the global implementation of the Convention.

The Convention has been in force for more than twenty-five years, and today, the general environment has become more favorable to the development of women. However, deeply rooted discrimination against women still exists in all parts of the world, regardless of a country's developmental stage, history, cultural heritage, or political system. China is no exception. With my increased knowledge gained through my work in the Committee I will continue to play an active role for women in my country. To realize the Convention's objectives, which aim at eliminating all forms of discrimination against women, and to say "no" to inequality between women and men, we still have to accomplish arduous tasks and walk a long road. Yet, this is a journey we, as humankind, must embrace. It is a duty to realize equality between women and men in order to build a harmonious society and a peaceful world. We should all shoulder that responsibility. That day of equality will certainly come; let us make it happen as early as possible!

A LAWYER'S PERSPECTIVE

MIRIAM ESTRADA-CASTILLO, ECUADOR

When I was a little girl in Ecuador, we used to jump rope and sing a song. The words were in Spanish, but the song went something like this:

To become a woman of honor
Look after your husband, look after your sons
Go to the church, don't talk too much
And suffer, suffer, suffer a lot.

As a child, I did not have any reason for suffering and neither did my friends, but still we found ourselves kneeling on corn kernels in the corner of our school's church, fasting every other day, and not talking for hours as a sacrifice to Jesus! We really wanted to be honorable! However, to the complete horror of my parents, I did not become a "woman of honor." When I was fourteen years old I married, and by my twenty-fifth birthday I had three children ages ten, seven, and two. The first two were boys (general approval); the third was a girl (that's OK—anyone can make mistakes). On that front, I succeeded totally. The dishonor came when I decided to finish school, attend university, and—even worse—work as a lawyer. I was officially declared insane and my husband a complete pervert for allowing me to do this. At that time, being a pervert and being a woman working as a lawyer were synonymous. Therefore, what good could a respectable society expect from such people? It was then that I learned the meaning of "suffer, suffer, suffer a lot."

The 1960s in my country was a time when no decent woman would ever dare to go anywhere by herself, do any exercise other than ballet, or wear red nail polish or red lipstick. Smoking, driving, and drinking were out of the question. Only prostitutes did those things! Decent women kept silent, waiting for their husbands, with warm meals and a big smile despite any bad, unfaithful, violent, or mean conduct on the part of those husbands. I remember my mother instructing me loudly and clearly, "Marriage was a cross that we have to carry until our death," and that a decent woman would accept any behavior from her husband. After all, "He was a man and men can do whatever they want; that is why they are men."

"Remember," she used to say, "it is much better to be mistreated than to be divorced. After all, you will always be his legitimate wife, the lady of his house, his queen, and the mother of his legitimate children."

I was one of five young women out of a class of thirty attending the first year of law studies in 1967. In our first class on the Philosophy of Law, the teacher, a very well-respected Ecuadorian lawyer, said to the whole class: "Aha, five women! We will have the opportunity to prove that women's brains are quite similar to those of pigs." We were shocked, but nobody actually thought that "our rights" had been affected. We did not *know that we had rights. After all, we had to ask for permission from our fathers or husbands in order to study, visit friends or family, work, or even spend the money of our own, very small salaries. Actually, we had to ask for permission for doing anything but "going to the church, looking after our husbands, and taking care of our sons."*

On March 1975, almost eight years later, I was passing by the Conference Room of the Ecuadorian Supreme Court one fine afternoon when my attention was attracted by a group of very poor women, looking like members of some sort of union, who had gathered around a placard that read "United Nations World Conference for International Women's Year, July 1975, Mexico" "Is this a tour?" I asked, quite ignorant despite my law degree.

"No, comrade," was their response. "This is the preparation for a meeting in Mexico City where we have to go to ask the United Nations to adopt a resolution establishing a Decade for Women."

They handed me copies of the Inter-American Convention on the Granting of Civil Rights to Women, the UN Convention on the Nationality of Married Women, and several studies on the draft of a new UN convention on the elimination of all forms of discrimination against women.

"We need to start organizing ourselves, comrade," they said.

It was like a revelation. I understood in a flash everything that had happened in my life up to that day. In that moment I received an explanation for the pain that I had always seen in the eyes of women who supposedly were happy "because they had it all"—except, as I could see now, rights. *At this moment, again as in a revelation, I found my path and the purpose of my life both at the personal and professional levels. I understood from the core of my soul that "suffer, suffer, suffer a lot" was just another way to say:* discrimination. *I was reborn, and in this new life, I closely linked myself with the issue of women rights, only to discover later that this was a match made in heaven!*

Twenty years later, I was elected to be an expert member of the CEDAW Committee. In the meantime, the group of women lawyers with "pigs' brains" had organized a group of lawyers (including men) who fought and succeeded in amending the Ecuadorian Civil Code in order to allow women to exercise their legitimate rights in accordance with the provisions in CEDAW. Next, we wanted a law that would end violence against women (in Ecuador, nine out of every ten women are victims of violence); the organization of Special Legal Tribunals for Women Victims of Violence; and the provision of shelters. In these efforts, we were also successful. Later, we succeeded in passing the Law on the Protection of Labor, Equality of Opportunities, and Political Quota for Women. My last battle in Ecuador was to amend the National Constitution (1998), but I should say that by this time there was not only one group of women and men who fought this battle, but a very important national sociopolitical movement. Still, if we talk about implementation, change of stereotypes, eradication of discrimination and violence, or access to real equality, there is still a long path that needs to be followed. We know that the law alone cannot necessarily change society, but we also know that it is a powerful weapon.

Throughout all these years, and as a result of my discovery of CEDAW, I have also "conquered several mountains" in my personal and professional life. I got divorced—no decent man would allow his wife to go out in the world, like a "madwoman," proclaiming that all women have the right to be equal. I jumped into the political arena; I was elected Minister of Social Welfare, and as a parliamentarian I traveled the world by myself. I was President of the Supreme Court for Juvenile Justice, wrote the first Family Code for the country (rejected as too revolutionary). I fought about women's rights with Presidents of the Republic, Presidents of the Supreme Court, Presidents of the Parliament, Prosecutors, and Attorneys General in my country. Sometimes I lost pitifully; other times I won marvelously.

I am confident when saying that I have fought a good fight in this life so far and that, when I have to leave this planet, I will be able to go saying "good bye and well done." I will be smiling, not because of what I achieved, thanks to CEDAW, in my professional life, but because, thanks to CEDAW, I was able to contribute in making an important difference in Ecuador's social conscience and as a result, in the life of so many Ecuadorian women. This difference has been reflected in my brave and courageous daughter. She has never hesitated to pursue her dreams, because her mother taught her loudly and clearly that she is a human being with the same rights as anyone on earth, and that the only limits in the world are the ones she sets herself.

THE FINNISH ACT ON EQUALITY

PIRKKO MÄKINEN, FINLAND

The adoption of CEDAW in 1979 gave new momentum to demands in Finland for legislation prohibiting gender-based discrimination. The Council for Gender Equality, together with women's and other nongovernmental organizations (NGOs), had been making active attempts to influence the Government in this matter ever since the early 1970s, but their demands had not been taken seriously. It was claimed that there was no gender-based discrimination in Finland—Finnish women had been given full political rights as early as 1907; they were highly educated and worked outside the home almost as frequently as men. Other Nordic countries—such as Denmark, Norway, and Sweden—ratified the Convention quickly. However, although Finland signed the Convention on July 17, 1980, it did not ratify it until September 4, 1986.

In Finland, international human rights conventions have to be transformed into law in order to become a binding part of national legislation. Before ratification, it has to be ascertained that the rest of the country's legislation is not in contradiction with the respective convention. This was the procedure with the CEDAW Convention, too. The biggest defect in the then-existing Finnish legislation was considered to be that, while gender-based discrimination was prohibited in labor legislation, there was no similar legislation for the other sectors of society. This is why it was necessary to have an act on gender equality. In the preparatory stages for this new act, it was found that the existing Names Act also had to be amended, so that women could keep their own surnames on marriage. Provisions on custodianship of children and visiting rights also had to be revised. It is noteworthy that, around the same time, another important reform was under way—one geared toward opening up the priesthood to women in the Evangelical-Lutheran Church, which has the status of a state Church in Finland.

The drafting of the Act on Equality between Women and Men took exceptionally long. It was not submitted to the Finnish Parliament until 1986, and entered into force only at the beginning of 1987. With the CEDAW Convention as its model, the Act prohibited discrimination in all areas of life, and it regulated gender equality in working life particularly strictly. In comparison, the Swedish Gender Equality Act was restricted to working life only. The Finnish Act also included an obligation to promote gender equality in the policies and activities of public authorities, in education and training, and at the workplace.

An Ombudsman for Gender Equality was created as the special authority focusing on the enforcement of the Act. The Ombudsman is appointed for a fixed period of five years and is an independent law enforcement authority. At the same time, an Equality Board was set up to handle issues and questions submitted to it by the Ombudsman. Courts of law could also request an opinion from the Board in cases of gender discrimination handled by them.

The Finnish Government submitted its first national report to the

CEDAW Committee in 1988. A new method was adopted in preparing the report: An open hearing was arranged with various public authorities and NGOs at which the content of the report was discussed. From the very beginning, it was also considered important that the report should include statistics on key areas as an appendix. In later years, women's organizations prepared "shadow reports" with the purpose of providing the Committee with critical information on the status of women in Finland.

The Finnish Ombudsman for Gender Equality and other gender equality authorities have always urged that the Finnish Government report is presented to the CEDAW Committee by the Minister for Gender Equality in order to ensure that the Government is informed of the evaluation and, later, of the concluding comments of the Committee directly and without delay.

When the first report was discussed in the Committee's Eighth Session in 1989, the Committee surprised those of us present by asking how common violence against women was in Finland. The then Minister for Gender Equality, Tarja Halonen, who is currently the President of the country, had to answer that no surveys had been undertaken on the issue. As soon as the delegation returned to Finland, the Council for Equality set up an organ to survey the situation concerning violence against women. Since then, there has been a research study on violence and the costs of violence against women, and cooperation between various public authorities has been developed. Legislation has also been amended with a Restraining Orders Act and by making it possible for a woman who has been a victim of violence to have a support person with her during court proceedings.

I was a member of the CEDAW Committee from 1993–1996, which also gave me the opportunity to attend the Fourth UN World Conference on Women in Beijing (1995) as a Committee member. The most memorable experience was preparing for the Beijing World Conference. I had the opportunity to participate in the formulation in Paris of a joint UNESCO-CEDAW document on education, which was officially presented during the Conference. Both the High Commissioner for Human Rights and the Director General of UNESCO were present, as well as all the members of the CEDAW Committee. The presentation attracted numerous women from all parts of the world, who actively joined in the discussion of education as one of the inalienable rights of a human being.

I myself have been working with gender equality and human rights issues since 1987, when I became head of the Office of the Ombudsman for Gender Equality and deputy for the Ombudsman. I was Ombudsman for Gender Equality in 1995–2002, and the experience I gained from the

CEDAW Committee was a significant advantage in this work. Discussing and analyzing government reports from many countries gave me valuable background information for handling gender equality issues.

In 1995, Finland joined the European Union. Again, it was time to review national legislation on gender equality in order to see if the Act on Equality between Women and Men met the criteria of European Union gender equality regulations. It was instructive to find that, once again, we found justification for further developing our own Act and making it more precise.

A SOURCE OF INSPIRATION

SJAMSIAH ACHMAD, INDONESIA

During my four-year membership from 2001–2004, the Committee reviewed the reports of about eighty States Parties. In those reports, two distinct features emerged. One relates to the similarities among the major obstacles and challenges encountered by most countries, such as a lack of understanding of the basic aspects of nondiscrimination and substantive equality, of state obligations, and of temporary special measures. The other relates to country-specific obstacles and challenges, such as those arising from a country's legal, political, and economic system, including its level of development and its sociocultural values. A concern that arose for me was that most States Parties' reports, both initial and subsequent ones, did not clearly demonstrate an acknowledgment by governments of the importance of ensuring concerted, complementary, and mutually supporting actions by all state governing bodies, including the legislative, executive, and judiciary. In addition, most reports did not adequately reflect the need for continuous and constructive dialogues and for joint actions among state governing bodies, civil society, and nongovernmental organizations (NGOs), in particular women's rights advocacy groups.

Given the broad range of academic background, expertise, and personal experiences of the twenty-three members of the Committee, the challenges for the members were enormous. A great deal of understanding and appreciation of each other's views was required, not only about progress achieved and obstacles encountered, but also about the commitment and ability of States Parties to achieve further progress in the implementation of the Convention. Some members seemed to forget, at times, that the

Committee is not a court. The Committee, therefore, needs to enhance its ability to establish a truly "constructive dialogue" with States Parties to explain the meaning of certain provisions, including the application of temporary special measures and to facilitate the identification of ways and means to overcome the often multidimensional obstacles and challenges that States Parties encounter, particularly those related to "state neglect" or "non-performance" at the country level.

Regarding the impact of the Committee's work on Indonesia, it is fair to say that this was much greater after the reform movement began in 1998. While the Convention had been signed in 1980 and ratified in 1984 during the New Order Regime (the Government of former President Suharto from 1966–1998), its provisions were not being used as principal standards for the advancement of women. The authoritarian regime's main vision of the role of women in society was as good mothers to their children, obedient wives to their husbands, and pillars of family welfare. Furthermore, national development policies and strategies, which focused on economic growth and political stability, viewed citizens—including women—in terms of their instrumentality to the achievement of these goals. It is commendable to note, however, that advocates of women's equality, both in the Government and in women's organizations, had already succeeded in 1978 in including a paragraph about the advancement of women in the State Policy Guidelines for the Second Five-Year National Development Plan and also in the Guidelines of 1983. This effort led to the ratification of the Convention in 1984, and also contributed—in terms of accommodation to the Convention's norms—to a gradual improvement in the 1988, 1993 and 1998 State Policy Guidelines and the consecutive five-year development plans. The approach remained, however, heavily focused on welfare rather than on empowerment for equality. A national machinery for the advancement of women was developed in the sectoral ministries and provincial and district government structures. A legal awareness program for women was also launched soon after ratification in the mid-1980s.

The end of the New Order Regime in 1998 after more than three decades marked the beginning of a period of substantial growth of democratic freedom. Political activism by all segments of society, including women's equality advocates, began to rise and flourish more publicly. Democracy in and of itself does not, however, guarantee justice and human rights. In this period of challenges and counterchallenges to power, opposing views of nationhood were constantly exchanged—from the dinner table, street stalls, and meeting rooms to the halls of parliament. In such confusing times, people, including women's rights advocates, seek and hold on to standards that reflect their core values as human beings. In this chaotic post-authoritarian period, Law No. 7 of 1984, which ratified the Convention, became a standard for women and gender justice advocates. Many arguments have been and continue to be based on this Law, in public debates, courtrooms, and also in parliament. Both the historic Election Law of 2003, guaranteeing at least 30 percent of women on the list of political parties' candidates for parliament, and the Law on Domestic Violence, which was successfully passed in 2004, used the Convention as one of their legal foundations.

New bills on women's rights continue to refer to the Convention. Arguments of women's rights advocates against discriminatory bills are based on the conviction that the Convention's standards should have been an integral part of Indonesian national law for more than two decades. The significance of the Convention for the achievement of full equality of women with men in Indonesia can certainly not be underestimated and my commitment to make its standards come alive in the daily experiences of Indonesian women will continue.

AN IMPORTANT PART OF HISTORY

RYOKO AKAMATSU, JAPAN

I served as an expert for the CEDAW Committee for two terms, from 1987 to 1994. In March 1987, I attended the Committee for the first time in Vienna. Since I was living in Uruguay as an ambassador at that time, I flew to Vienna from Montevideo via Rio de Janeiro and Amsterdam. I remember feeling a thrill of joy in the airplane flying up to the North over the Atlantic Ocean. I also remember the time the Convention was adopted, when it came into force, and the morning that the Committee was first organized. I was then Minister of the Permanent Mission of Japan to the United Nations, and I reported on the Committee's developments with much pleasure.

However, Japan was not able to nominate a candidate for the Committee when it was first set up. In the spring of 1982, my country had not yet ratified the Convention. Although Japan had signed it in Copenhagen in 1980 at the Second UN World Conference on Women, some obstacles still needed to be cleared in Japanese law before ratification could take place. The Government then decided to try to revise the relevant laws and regulations by 1985 so that it would be able to ratify the Convention before the end of the UN Decade for Women. Thus, for three years after Copenhagen, the drafting of a bill for accommodating requirements of the Convention became a top priority of my work as the Director General of the Women's Bureau in the Japanese Ministry of Labor.

In May 1985 the Japanese Government enacted the Law on Securing Equal Opportunity and Treatment between Men and Women in Employment, and in June 1985 finally ratified the Convention. Next, Japan started searching for a candidate to nominate for the elections to the CEDAW Committee. The Government eventually decided to nominate me because of my long experience in the Women's Bureau, and because I had been designated to be appointed Ambassador of Japan to Uruguay. I was elected at the Third Meeting of the States Parties, held in New York in March 1986, the very same month I arrived in the Republic of Uruguay to take up my new position. In the second part of 1986, documents began to arrive from the CEDAW Committee's secretariat, the Division for the Advancement of Women. I devoted myself to reading the initial reports of eight countries in the study of my residence, spreading papers all over the room. I had promised myself to become a very good expert, because I felt this was going to be the most precious work I could do in my long career of fighting discrimination and prejudice against women.

Thanks to my good preparation, I was able to pose appropriate questions to the government delegates in the Committee's meetings of this session. And I tried to live up to my own resolve to be a good expert throughout my two terms—with the exception of my last session in 1994. At that time, I was the Minister of Education in Japan and I could not leave Tokyo due to the rule that all Ministers had to be present at the Budgetary Committee of the National Diet. I had already prepared my farewell speech to my dear colleagues with a "thank you" in eight different languages. Missing this session was my biggest regret during my career in the CEDAW Committee.

I have kept a close interest in the Convention even after I resigned from the Committee. There is a nongovernmental organization (NGO) called the Japanese Association of International Women's Rights (JAIWR), of which I am the president. This NGO aims to study and disseminate the CEDAW Convention. Members of JAIWR often go to observe the sessions of the Committee, and the organization's annual journal carries reports on the Committee's activities and its general recommendations. JAIWR has also published a commentary on the Convention in both Japanese and English (JAIWR 1995). The book was presented to the experts of the Committee, and I believe it has been helpful to them. Furthermore, JAIWR honors individuals and organizations that have made valuable contributions to the promotion of the Convention and presents them with the Ryoko Akamatsu Award. Award recipients have included Luvsandanzangyn Ider, who was the first Chairperson of the CEDAW Committee, and Ivanka Corti, who served on the Committee for sixteen years and held the Chairpersonship for two terms.

JAIWR is actively involved in submitting alternative information to the Committee when it examines the government reports of Japan. When the Japanese Government's fourth and fifth reports were considered by the Committee in 2003, JAIWR organized a network called the Japan NGO Network for CEDAW (JNNC). JNNC's efforts to convey voices of NGOs to the Committee were very successful; and the concluding comments by the Committee on Japan have been commended, because they exerted a large impact on government policies for women.

In conclusion, I would like to say that the CEDAW Convention holds an important position in the history of my country. At the same time, my relationship with the Committee has also been of great value to my life.

SPREADING THE CONVENTION'S NORMS THROUGH EDUCATION

HADJA ASSA DIALLO SOUMARÉ, MALI

I was elected as a member of the CEDAW Committee thanks to the support of the States Parties to the Convention of the African, Latin American, and European regions. Along with my practice in the public health area in Mali, working with the Committee from 1987 to 1990 was a fantastic experience. The Committee impressed me with its sympathetic spirit. I can say that it forms a true school of kindness, whose experts are committed to one ideal: the advancement of the human rights of women worldwide. That is why I dedicated myself to spreading the CEDAW spirit and aims through education, in particular after I left the Committee.

Together with the Committee of Action for the Rights of the Child and of Women (Comité d'action pour les droits de l'enfant et de la femme, CADEF), founded in 1990, and with the support of media campaigns financed by the United Nations Children's Fund (UNICEF), the United Nations Development Programme (UNDP), and the Embassies of Canada and the United States—I worked for the dissemination of CEDAW norms at most levels of education in Mali: among young people, health professionals, members of political parties, and labor union movements. This undertaking successfully resulted in setting the ground for the enforcement of the CEDAW Convention in Mali in 1990, and at the same time raising the interest in the CEDAW Committee's goals of many other organizations in Mali working in the field of women's rights. In 1991, I challenged the Mali Government to look closely into the provisions of the country's Constitution and other legislation and institutions through which certain violations of women's and children's rights were still existent. By the time of the National Democratic Conference of July 3, 1991, the standards of the two UN Conventions relating to women's and children's rights— CEDAW and the Convention on the Rights of the Child (CRC)—were taken into account in the country's new democratic Constitution. This was a true triumph of the CEDAW and CRC Conventions in West Africa, particularly Mali.

My commitment to the CEDAW Committee at the international level consisted of participating in 1989 in drafting guidelines and questions to support States Parties in preparing their reports. I also paid special attention to the organization of national and regional seminars in Africa and the Middle East dedicated to women and their rights under the CEDAW Convention, as well as to training activities. As an expert consultant for the Office of the High Commissioner for Human Rights (2002) in Geneva, I assisted with training in administrative management and the drafting of national reports for representatives from nongovernmental organizations (NGOs) and also for five hundred senior African executives.

Is the worldwide advancement of women's rights a possibility under CEDAW? At the time of the democratic election in Mali, the CEDAW commitments to women's rights were highlighted in two million posters in five languages within eight territorial areas. At the 1994 African Regional Preparatory Conference in Dakar for the Fourth UN World Conference on Women in Beijing, fifty thousand French booklets and numerous other materials on the CEDAW Convention were distributed to the participants. Considering the activities of the CEDAW Committee so far, I would say that the dissemination of the Convention's aims has been successful, providing the necessary impetus for its implementation in most of the UN member States.

REMAINING CHALLENGES AND THE WAY FORWARD

PERSONAL REFLECTIONS:

THOUGHTS ON THE COMMITTEE'S PAST, HOPES FOR ITS FUTURE

FERIDE ACAR, *TURKEY*

By the time I took office as Chairperson of the CEDAW Committee (2003–2004), its accumulated experience and the remarkable work it had been doing since it was established had come to be quite well recognized both at the international level and in many national contexts. This recognition and relevance became even more widespread in the ensuing years. The speed of ratifications picked up pace, and the number of States Parties to the Convention rose steadily from 164 in 2000 to 179 by 2004. Also, significantly sharpened competition was observed in the CEDAW Committee elections in 2000, 2002, and 2004, with more States nominating candidates to this body than ever before. At this time, the appearance of high-level delegations from States Parties reporting to the Committee, mostly led by Ministers or state secretaries, became a routine occurrence. Most noticeably, however, the participation of women's nongovernmental organizations (NGOs) in the CEDAW process rose to unprecedented levels.

During those years, the Committee was also very well supported by a competent and devoted professional cadre at the Division for the Advancement of Women (DAW), and it had come to enjoy considerable visibility and respect in the United Nations and throughout the international arena. With the Optional Protocol becoming a real operating tool, and both the individual communication and inquiry mechanisms being used for the first time, both the Convention and the Committee finally had the "teeth" they had been missing for years. In its treatment of the first individual complaint and the first inquiry, the Committee demonstrated its capacity to use these mechanisms effectively and responsibly.

While all of these developments could be read as positive and as indicating a significantly elevated status and more active role for the Committee in the international arena, they also perhaps marked a time well-suited to evaluate anew the past achievements and future potential of the Committee. On October 13, 2004, at the 25th Anniversary Celebration of the adoption of the CEDAW Convention, as the then Chairperson of the Committee, I summarized the most significant developments of my tenure by referring to these facts. I also described such age-old challenges as the large number of reservations and the slow and hesitant record of national implementation, particularly with respect to discriminatory cultural practices and stereotypes, as roadblocks in efforts to universalize the Convention's principles.

On that occasion, I also underlined, as an "emerging" concern, the need to consolidate and reinforce the Committee—as the main monitoring tool of women's human rights protection—in all efforts to mainstream women's rights into the core of the human rights framework in the United Nations. Reiterating my concluding remarks there, I would argue that on the basis of the ground covered in the twenty-five years since the adoption of the Convention, there are now far greater expectations of the CEDAW process than ever before. There is also every reason to expect the Committee to be key to the realization of such expectations in the future.

It is not possible to say how much or what aspects of the overall improvement in the area of gender equality and women's human rights in the world can be attributed specifically to the implementation of CEDAW. It is, nonetheless, a fact that many substantive and political advances recorded in the past have been initiated, facilitated, or supported by the CEDAW process. Clearly, the drafters of the Convention provided the international community with a very sensitive and potentially powerful legal instrument, but one whose effectiveness depended on its use. I believe that the way the CEDAW Committee has gone about fulfilling its mandate of monitoring women's human rights in the last twenty-five years has been an important catalyst in the translation of a legal instrument into a living document.

In this sense, I would argue that the real achievement of the CEDAW process lies in the consistent, sensitive, and creative handiwork of the Committee. The Committee's success lies in having been able to maintain a reputation of expertise and professionalism, as well as genuine commitment, in the rather contentious area of women's human rights. It is remarkable that, particularly in the aftermath of the 1995 Fourth UN World Conference on Women in Beijing, when the international arena witnessed retrogressive pressures and resulting polarization of views on women's rights, all indicators pointed to the improved status of the Committee in the eyes of many governments and women's groups. Through building bridges with States, governments, and their various agents; opening up new spaces for women's human rights in the international system; and, most remarkably, establishing and reinforcing alliances with civil society and women's movements all over the world, the Committee has ensured that the principles of the Convention have become relevant for women's real lives all around the world. While there are those who still do not agree with the essential premises of universal human rights of women, and thus challenge the authority of the Committee when it promotes these rights, today most recognize it as the legitimate and internationally respected voice for women's human rights.

The Committee has achieved this reputation because of its members' exemplary dedication, competence, and integrity. It is, therefore, very important that in the next phase of its work, the Committee members' independence from political, regional, or ideological affiliations is carefully protected. Now that the Committee is more relevant and influential than ever before, States Parties to the Convention, as well as women's movements around the world, should demonstrate their genuine support for the cause of nondiscrimination of women by ensuring this body's continued success through the work of independent and competent experts.

While over the years the Committee has relentlessly defended its ground by holding States accountable for their commitments to nondiscrimination of women, in the last decade it has been increasingly concerned about the implementation of the Convention's provisions in de facto terms. Examination of State reports and the "constructive dialogues" have addressed routinely such matters as women's actual access to justice, education, health services, and employment. In earlier years, dialogues were confined to the existence of legislation guaranteeing these rights to women.

The Committee is famous for integrating progressive standards into its interpretation of the Convention and for using them when carrying out its mandate. This attitude has, in turn, helped legitimize such standards, particularly in the eyes of government officials and civil society members, thereby ensuring the validity and currency of the CEDAW process. The gist of the Committee's quasi-jurisprudence as well as the positions taken and views expressed by most Committee members in the constructive dialogues with States Parties, bear testimony to a remarkably bold interpretation of the Convention. The CEDAW Committee has long forced the limits of its mandate to allow an ever-expanding range of women's human rights to find their way into the Convention and the Committee's purview. In doing so, it has ensured that the CEDAW process has remained viable and relevant for the "emerging" concerns of the world's women. Thus, over time, violence against women in all its forms has become part of the Committee's monitoring of the Convention. Similarly, such issues as "multiple" and "compounded" discriminations against women, on account of their religion, ethnicity, age, or disability, or violations of women's human rights in armed conflict areas or natural disasters, are nowadays routinely taken up by the Committee in its examination of State Party reports. The fact that no State Party has ever objected to being questioned on these and other "new" issues, despite the fact that they are not part of the letter of the Convention, no doubt points to the increased legitimacy of the CEDAW process in the international context. Today in many countries, not only is the Convention cited as a piece of binding international law in judicial and legal proceedings, but also the Committee's concluding comments constitute powerful legitimate references to prod governments, initiate reforms, and to remind agents of civil societies to hold governments accountable.

The Committee has been consistent in its criticism of the cultural and traditional forces that have a negative impact on the universal rights of women, and it has not refrained from identifying a seemingly infinite variety of women's human rights violations in the reporting States. These range from unequal pay for work of equal value to female genital mutilation (FGM); from denying girls access to education to forced marriage; from unequal inheritance rights to limited access to public office. While many of these practices are justified in the places where they exist by reference to some cultural, tradition and/or religion, they have come to be legally labeled by the CEDAW Committee as "discrimination against women" in international contexts.

It is noteworthy that the Committee's position has long been rather uncompromising regardless of the perceived source of discrimination. While it is a fact that in its efforts to reach diverse audiences, the Committee has often thought long and hard on how best to word its comments, particularly when those on discriminatory practices associated with religion or sacred beliefs, it has not refrained from being forthright. In this context, I have found it very interesting that in the unspoken division of labor among Committee members, directing questions on personal status matters to representatives of Muslim countries, or voicing criticism of such discriminatory practices as polygamy or unequal inheritance assumed to stem from religious dictates, often fell on the shoulders of Muslim members.

In recent years, while the Committee has made strong calls to some States to eliminate the pervasive discriminatory norms and practices in their traditions and cultures, in numerous cases it has also asked other States not to overlook or tolerate, in the name of "cultural relativism" or "religious freedom," any violations of women's human rights in and among minority or immigrant communities. The CEDAW Committee has refused to treat religion, tradition, or culture as untouchable walls behind which violations of women's human rights can be allowed to take cover from international scrutiny.

The Committee's creative reading and liberal elaboration of such matters as violence against women (General Recommendation No. 19) and temporary special measures (General Recommendation No. 25) have provided very strong foundations for women's rights activists around the world. In fact, I believe such attitudes have formed the basis of the Committee's increasing rapprochement, over the years, with local and national women's movements.

The Committee's overwhelmingly female, professionally varied composition has also allowed for the relatively easy access of women's NGOs to this treaty body. Its culture of fostering close association with NGOs, of welcoming their increasing participation in the process, has been a particular source of its strength and is often seen as a "good practice" example in human rights circles.

During the period I was a member of the Committee (1998–2005), the increase in the participation and impact of local women's groups in the meetings of the Committee was striking. At the time I first joined the Committee, a national or local civil society group which had traveled from home to New York to follow its government's presentation of its report was a rare occurrence, and almost always such individuals or groups saw their responsibility as "learning from the CEDAW process" rather than contributing to it. By the time I left the Committee in 2005, the participation of local and national NGOs in every session of the Committee had become commonplace. The Committee members routinely received first hand oral and written information from and engaged in discussions with NGO representatives as part of their preparation for the examination of the State reports. In July 2003, when more than 160 women from women's organizations in Japan were present at the presentation of that country's report, the session was clearly a high point and a memorable occasion for all.

Despite the debilitating reality of the continuing reservations, the Convention now has a crucial impact around the world in defining and legitimizing standards of "right" and "wrong" for women's rights. Even States Parties that have entered many reservations (some of which are clearly against the "object and purpose" of the Convention), rarely, if ever, have been known to cite these as reasons for not implementing at least parts of the Convention. I believe the Convention's principles have acquired an implicit legitimacy even in cases where they do not have explicit legality.

The CEDAW Committee has benefited greatly from being made up of successful women with different world views and life experiences. Thus, despite the presence of a few very effective male members in recent years, it has been the "Women's Committee." The biographies of the women who have constituted the Committee reflect their outstanding achievements at national and international levels. Many come to the Committee as accomplished professionals with distinguished careers in different fields. While some members are civil society activists, interestingly only very few of these women could ever be described as "card-carrying" feminists. Many CEDAW members I have worked with have moved on to higher public offices at the end of their tenures in the Committee including ministerial portfolios in their countries, Chief Justices or even Head of State or high-level international positions. Others have gone back to their careers, communities, and families. I have always found a special assurance in the knowledge that wherever they are and whatever they are doing, CEDAW members carry the legacy of having been responsible for reducing discrimination against the world's women.

Over the years, the Committee has been remarkably successful in keeping in touch with the realities of women around the world, following a progressive and constructive course of action with States while simultaneously maintaining an unyielding women's rights perspective in carrying out its mandate. The dedication, integrity, and expertise that so many of the members have demonstrated over a quarter century define the CEDAW Committee's collective identity. It is a legacy that should well guide its future.

IMPORTANT CHANGES AND FURTHER REFORMS NEEDED

GÖRAN MELANDER, *SWEDEN*

I was a member of the CEDAW Committee between 2001 and 2004, the only male among the twenty-three members during the first two of those years. In fact, from 1985 to 2000 only women had been members of the Committee. It must have been slightly surprising to the Secretariat that the States Parties had elected a male member, because documents were addressed to Melander. I was also listed as Melander on the website of the UN High Commissioner for Human Rights (UNHCHR). When I sent an e-mail to the UNHCHR webmaster, pointing out the erroneous listing, I got an immediate response with an apology, beginning, "Dear Madam." I have framed that letter.

I was made most welcome by the other experts, many of whom believed that the progress of the Committee could be strengthened if, out of the twenty-three members, four to five were male. But the States Parties normally nominate women.

Nongovernmental organizations (NGOs) have frequently expressed the view that States should consider a balance between women and men when nominating treaty body members. They stress, for example, the imbalance on other treaty bodies, on all of which there are far more men than women. But no reference is ever made to the CEDAW Committee, where the imbalance is even greater. Do NGOs consider that women's human rights should only be dealt with by women?

According to Article 17 (8) of the Convention the members of the Committee shall receive emoluments from UN resources on such terms and conditions as the General Assembly may decide having regard to the importance of the Committee's responsibilities. Initially CEDAW experts received $3,000 US per year. But from 2003 the emoluments were limited to $1 (one) US per year. The same was done for other treaty bodies. Is that the way the United Nations evaluate human rights in general and women's human rights in particular?

The time allotted for the examination of a country report, the so-called "constructive dialogue," is limited to five hours. Any examination starts with an introductory statement by the State Party's head of delegation, and during my first year in the Committee this could go on for hours. It was a wise decision by the Committee to limit the introductory statement to thirty minutes. Experts' remarks during the constructive dialogue could also be quite long and detailed, sometimes a shorter or longer lecture that eventually ended with a question. The Committee has now established a time limit for asking questions to the State Party's delegation: Each expert is entitled to speak for not more than three minutes at each intervention. The procedure has certainly made the examination more effective and is not to the detriment of the carefulness of the review.

An additional reform, not yet realized, is to limit the time for an answer by the State Party's delegation. It frequently happened, in particular if an expert asked an uncomfortable question, that the answer by the State Party was far too long and detailed. Time passed and other uncomfortable questions were thus avoided. A time limit should also be set for the State Party's replies.

The Committee has issued guidelines for submitting reports, and a State Party is expected to submit the report in conformity with these. However, it seems as if the guidelines are too detailed and as a consequence reports are sometimes voluminous (one that had to be examined during five hours was about 300 pages). It was a wise decision by the Committee to limit the number of pages to one hundred pages for an initial report and seventy-five pages for a subsequent periodic report. It would also be a wise decision if the Committee were to to simplify the guidelines.

The five hour time frame applies equally to a country like Sweden and a Federal State like Canada, Brazil, or Russia. It is true that the UN Charter is based on the principle of the sovereign equality of all its members. However, there is a difference between unified States and Federal States, as in the latter case the various states may have legislative power. It is not unlikely that cultural varieties exist to a greater extent in a country like Russia than in San Marino. It is virtually impossible to examine on an equal basis the situation of women's rights in States of very different sizes during the five hours allotted for the examination.

The reporting obligation imposes certain problems to the Committee as some States do not report, while other States report every four years as required by the Convention! The nonreporting is certainly a phenomenon that applies to all UN treaty bodies, and several methods have been adopted to persuade States Parties to submit their report, though with varying success.

Another side of the problem is, however, that a State Party submits a report that is not examined before the next report is due and submitted. For example, when Germany submitted its combined second and third report in the early 1990s (late due to the unification process the country had undergone), the Committee had a backlog of reports and could not discuss it. Germany then submitted its fourth periodic report in 1998 in accordance with the periodicity requirements of the Convention. When the Committee finally examined Germany at its twenty-second session in early 2000, all reports were discussed, but the previous combined second and third report was, of course, outdated and of less interest. This meant that the Government had spent resources to write a report that was ultimately of little importance. To address this issue the Committee will have three sessions annually in 2006 and 2007, and also has the possibility to examine reports in two chambers. It is hoped that this will lead to submitted reports being examined within an acceptable time frame.

The Committee has so far not expressed a clear policy regarding the nature and extent to which NGOs should be involved in drafting reports and in the examination procedure. Some experts argue that NGOs should participate in the writing of the report, others that the government's report should be given to NGOs before it is submitted to the United Nations. However, an NGO should not be a member of the State Party's delegation, in particular if the very same NGO has submitted a shadow report.

After the oral examination of a State Party's report, it is expected that the Committee will adopt concluding comments that evaluate the situation in the State under review and express its views on how to interpret the various articles of the Convention. The concluding comments are thus of extreme importance and ought to be seen as an important source of international law. Yet, hardly any scholar is willing to accept a treaty body's evaluative and interpretative comments as an important source, equal with a judgment from a Court of Human Rights. It must be admitted that the concluding comments lack consistency and conformity. For instance, the Committee has no clear standing on issues like prostitution, right to education, right to health and so on. Sometimes it is a mere coincidence what kinds of issues will lead to a concluding comment and a checklist for formulating such comments does not exist.

Moreover, the Committee limits its concluding comments to situations that clearly fall under the Convention and is not willing to support other treaty bodies. If torture is an issue in a particular country, it will not adopt a concluding comment condemning this practice if discrimination is not at stake. Likewise, the Committee is in principle not willing to make any recommendations mentioning other treaties in the field of human rights. It will not advocate that the State being examined should become a party to other treaties. Occasionally it may happen, that the Committee reminds a State Party of the 2001 Palermo Protocol to Prevent, Suppress and Punish Trafficking in Persons, Especially Women and Children, but seldom other UN human rights treaties and certainly not regional human rights treaties.

I have always been surprised at how little the concluding comments are used within the various States. Perhaps it is asking too much of a government to translate and disseminate the criticism expressed by the Committee. However, there are fewer excuses for national NGOs not to make use of the concluding comments on the domestic scene, by disseminating them and using them when arguing with the government.

The Optional Protocol to the CEDAW Convention entered into force in December 2000. I had expected that the Committee would immediately be overwhelmed with individual petitions, because discrimination against women takes place in virtually all States. However, the first case was submitted only in 2003, and since then there have been only a handful of cases. The reason for the underutilization of the Protocol remains an open question. It is not that the Protocol and the possibility to submit petitions under it are unknown, as might be the case under the ICCPR, for example. Women's NGOs were instrumental in lobbying for the adoption of the Protocol, they are aware if its existence, and they can easily spread the message. An explanation for the lack of petitions so far could be the provision of the Protocol in its Article 4 that "all available domestic remedies" must be exhausted. However, such remedies do not exist in many cases. I am afraid that the real reason is that women do not see nondiscrimination as a legal issue. For many of them, it has more to do with social behavior, which should not be decided upon by an international treaty body. It remains to be seen what will happen in the future.

REFLECTIONS ON THE FUTURE

DUBRAVKA ŠIMONOVIĆ, CROATIA

In 2006 I completed my first term as a member of the CEDAW Committee. I continue my second term through 2010. In reflecting on the current and future work of the Committee, I will follow the format of its concluding comments to States Parties: a paragraph of introduction followed by paragraphs of concerns and corresponding recommendations.

Introduction: My observations here on the Committee's work are based on my experience while examining some fifty States Parties' reports on the implementation of the CEDAW Convention. Treaty bodies are currently being discussed as in need of reform based on the following concerns. These, from my perspective, should be addressed through the recommendations as outlined, though I am aware they still warrant a lot of discussion and not every member of the Committee may agree.

Concern: The system of periodic reporting under the Convention is still in a developing stage. Many States Parties are late in reporting or fail to report altogether, while the Committee itself has built up a backlog of reports awaiting review. To address this problem, the UN General Assembly approved the Committee's holding three annual sessions of three weeks each, effective from January 2006, but only as a temporary measure for two years. The Committee was also allowed to work in two chambers during this period in order to cope with the backlog of State reports.

Recommendation: This temporary measure should be extended for the next few years for the benefit of all concerned, especially women. After that, if the CEDAW Committee will require more meeting time to fulfill its demanding role, it should be transformed into a permanent body. This would enable it to allocate appropriate time to a thorough preparation of the examination of State reports, the examination of the State report itself, the consideration of individual communications, the initiation of independent inquiries, the discussion on and drafting of general recommendations, and many other matters on its agenda.

Concern: The work of CEDAW under its Optional Protocol on specific cases is quasi-judicial in nature and requires the expertise of lawyers; the Committee members are, however, professionals with varying disciplinary backgrounds.

Recommendation: Since the work of the Committee under the Optional Protocol is predominantly of a legal nature, I am in favor of the establishment of either a specific body (permanent, if need requires) to deal with complaints under all UN human rights treaties, or the establishment of a UN Human Rights Court. Both could be established with chambers that would follow treaty bodies' lines and competencies and be composed of members of a respective treaty body.

Concern: The main tool of the Committee consists of the concluding comments to the States Parties, based on their reports and on the constructive dialogue, to guide them on the application of the Convention. The open sessions of the Committee are attended by some governmental and NGO representatives, but the meeting room is never full, which is a clear sign of limited public interest in its work. The media are almost never present.

Recommendation: More transparency and publicity of the Committee's work are the keys for stronger accountability of States Parties to eliminate discrimination against women, in particular on issues that have been indicated as matters of concern by the Committee. The media should be more utilized in that respect.

Concern: The heads and members of government delegations who engage in the constructive dialogue with the Committee are often strong personalities who are willing to respond honestly to the numerous questions raised by the Committee members. From my experience this dialogue is often an enriching experience for such delegations, who, supported by NGOs are the agents of change at home.

Recommendation: Government authorities and NGOs should be supported by the various UN agencies working in the respective countries in the implementation of the Convention and the Committee's concluding comments.

Concern: The "shadow" reports of NGOs are very useful tools for the Committee in assessing progress achieved. The current practice, however, is that mainly women's rights NGOs from developing countries and countries in transition are supported by the UN system to submit such reports and be present at the discussion of their country's report in the Committee. Submission and presentation of separate reports by independent national human rights institutions (NHRIs) is also a useful practice that has recently started and is supported by the Committee.

Recommendation: Women's rights NGOs from all States Parties should be strongly encouraged to submit "shadow" reports in order to enable the Committee to objectively assess progress achieved in the implementation of the Convention. Separate reports from independent national human rights institutions should be also encouraged. and further developed as a tool for progress assessment.

The past, present, and future Committee members, including myself, are small contributors to this great international monitoring system that aims at giving a real meaning to the universally accepted norm of equal rights for women and men. It is also an enriching learning experience, though at the same time a sad one. It is discouraging to see that the Convention and the Committee are not yet able to contain violence against women and to prevent murder of and discrimination against women occurring all too often around the globe. Many more appropriate measures are needed to move the gender equality agenda forward, and to translate the rights contained in the Convention into truly universal rights of all women. The Committee should be transformed into a more efficient body along the lines described above.

WORKS CITED

LITERATURE

Ali, Shaheen Sadr. 2004. *Study on CRC and Islamic Jurisdictions.* New York: UNICEF, unpublished.

Alston, Philip (ed.). 1994. *The Best Interests of the Child.* Oxford: Clarendon Press.

Anand, Anita, and Gouri Salvi. 1998. *Beijing! UN Fourth World Conference on Women.* New Delhi: Women's Feature Service.

An-Na'im, Abdullahi A. 1990. "Human Rights in the Muslim World: Socio-Political Conditions and Scriptural Imperatives." *Harvard Human Rights Journal* 3:13–52.

Arieli, Yehoshua. 1999. "The Theory of Human Rights, Its Origin and Its Impact on Modern Society." In *Mishpat ve-Historyah* [Law and History], eds. Daniel Gutwein and Menachem Mautner. *Merkaz Zalman Shazar le-toldot Yisra'el* (in Hebrew), 25–72.

AWID. 2002. "The World Bank and Women's Rights in Development." Women's Rights and Economic Change, No. 5, October. Association for Women's Rights in Development. http://www.awid.org/publications/primers/factsissues5.pdf, 1–8.

Banda, Fareda. 2004. "The Protection of Women's Rights in Africa." *Interights Bulletin*, 14:147–50.

Bayefsky, Anne F. 2001. *The United Nations Human Rights Treaty System: Universality at the Crossroads.* Ardsley, NY: Transnational.

Berger, Michael S., and Deborah E. Lipstadt. 1996. "Women in Judaism from the Perspective of Human Rights." In *Religious Human Rights in Global Perspective: Legal Perspectives*, eds. Johan D. van der Vyver and John Witte. The Hague: Martinus Nijhoff Publishers, 295–322.

Berlin, Isaiah. 1969. "Two Concepts of Liberty." In *Four Essays on Liberty.* Oxford: Oxford University Press, 118–72.

Bisnath, Savitri. 2001. "Globalization, Poverty and Women's Empowerment." Paper prepared for UNDAW Expert Group Meeting on "Empowerment of Women throughout the Life Cycle as a Transformative Strategy for Poverty Eradication," November 26–29, New Delhi, India. EGM/POV/2001/EP.3. http://www.un.org/womenwatch/daw/csw/empower/documents/Bisnath-EP3.pdf.

Bijnsdorp, Mireille G.E. 2000. "The Strength of the Optional Protocol to the United Nations Women's Convention" in *Netherlands Quarterly of Human Right* 18: 329–55.

Bora Laskin Law Library. 2004. Women's Human Rights Resources Programme. http://www.law-lib.utoronto.ca/diana/cedaw/articles.htm.

Borresen, Kari E. 1995. *The Image of God: Gender Models in Judeo-Christian Tradition.* Minneapolis, MN: Fortress.

Brodnig, Gernot. 2001. "The World Bank and Human Rights: Mission Impossible." Working Paper T-01-05. Cambridge, MA: Carr Center for Human Rights Policy.

Bullock, Susan. 1994. *Women and Work.* London and Atlantic Highlands, NJ: Zed Books Ltd.

Bunch, Charlotte. 1991. "Women's Rights as Human Rights: Toward a Re-Vision of Human Rights." In *Gender Violence: A Development and Human Rights Issue*, eds. Charlotte Bunch and Roxana Carrillo. New Brunswick, NJ: Center for Women's Global Leadership, 7–22.

Burkert, Walter. 1996. *Creation of the Sacred: Tracks of Biology in Early Religions.* Cambridge, MA: Harvard University Press.

Bustelo, Mara R. 2000. "The Committee on the Elimination of Discrimination against Women at the Crossroads." In *The Future of Human Rights Treaty Monitoring*, ed. Philip Alston and James Crawford. Cambridge: Cambridge University Press, 79–111.

Butegwa, Florence. 2001. "The Achievements and Challenges of the Women's Human Rights Movement." In *Holding on to the Promise: Women's Human Rights and the Beijing + 5 Review*, ed. Cynthia Meillon in collaboration with Charlotte Bunch. New Brunswick, NJ: Center for Women's Global Leadership.

Byrnes, Andrew. 1999. "The Committee on the Elimination of Discrimination against Women." In *The United Nations and Human Rights. A Critical Appraisal*, ed. Philip Alston, 2nd edition. Oxford: Clarendon Press.

Byrnes, Andrew, and Jane Connors. 1996. "Enforcing the Human Rights of Women: A Complaints Procedure for the Women's Convention?" in *Brooklyn Journal of International Law* XXI (3): 682.

Canadian Feminist Alliance for International Action (FAFIA). 1999. "Women and Globalisation: Focus on the World Trade Organization." http://www.fafia-afai.org/en/node/169.

CEDAW. 1993. *Report of the Committee on the Elimination of Discrimination against Women (Twelfth Session)*. UN General Assembly, Official Documents, Forty-Eighth Session, No. 38, A/48/38.

———. 1994. *Report of the Committee on the Elimination of Discrimination against Women (Thirteenth Session)*. UN General Assembly, Official Documents, Forty-Ninth Session, No. 38, A/49/38.

———. 1995. *Report of the Committee on the Elimination of Discrimination against Women (Fourteenth Session)*. UN General Assembly, Official Documents, Fiftieth Session, No. 38, A/50/38.

———. 1997. *Report of the Committee on the Elimination of Discrimination against Women (Sixteenth and Seventeenth Sessions)*. UN General Assembly, Official Documents, Fifty-Second Session, No. 38, A/52/38/Rev.1.

———. 1998. *Report of the Committee on the Elimination of Discrimination against Women (Eighteenth and Nineteenth Sessions)*. UN General Assembly, Official Documents, Fifty-Third Session, No.38, A/53/38/Rev.1.

———. 1999. *Report of the Committee on the Elimination of Discrimination against Women (Twentieth and Twenty-First Sessions)*. UN General Assembly, Official Documents, Fifty-Fourth Session, No.38, A/54/38/Rev.1.

———. 2000. *Report of the Committee on the Elimination of Discrimination against Women (Twenty-Second and Twenty-Third Sessions)*. UN General Assembly, Official Documents, Fifty-Fifth Session, No. 38 A/55/38.

———. 2001. *Report of the Committee on the Elimination of Discrimination against Women (Twenty-Fourth and Twenty-Fifth Sessions)*. UN General Assembly, Official Documents, Fifty-Sixth Session, No.38, A/56/38.

———. 2002. *Report of the Committee on the Elimination of Discrimination against Women (Twenty-Sixth, Twenty-Seventh, and Exceptional Sessions)*. UN General Assembly, Official Documents, Fifty-Seventh Session, No.38, A/57/38.

———. 2003. *Report of the Committee on the Elimination of Discrimination against Women (Twenty-Eighth and Twenty-Ninth Sessions)*. UN General Assembly, Official Documents, Fifty-Eighth Session, No.38, A/58/38.

———. 2004a. *Report of the Committee on the Elimination of Discrimination against Women (Thirtieth and Thirty-First Sessions)*. UN General Assembly, Official Documents, Fifty-Ninth Session, No.38, A/59/38.

————. 2004b. *Summary Record of the 632nd Meeting* (Thirtieth Session). United Nations. CEDAW/C/SR.632.

————. 2005a. *Report on Mexico Produced by the Committee on the Elimination of Discrimination against Women under Article 8 of the Optional Protocol to the Convention, and Reply from the Government of Mexico* (Thirty-Second Session). CEDAW/C/2005/OP.8/MEXICO.

————. 2005b. *Report of the Committee on the Elimination of Discrimination against Women (Thirty-Second and Thirty-Third Sessions).* UN General Assembly, Official Documents, Sixtieth Session, No. 38, A/60/38.

————. 2006. *Report of the Committee on the Elimination of Discrimination against Women (Thirty-Fourth, Thirty-Fifth, and Thirty-Sixth Sessions).* UN General Assembly, Official Documents, Sixty-First Session, No. 38, A/61/38.

CEDAW: Treaty for the Rights of Women. n.d. http://www.womenstreaty.org.

cedaw4change listserv. n.d. http://list.iwraw-ap.org/lists/info/cedaw4change.

Center for Genetics and Society. 2006. "The Korean Stem Cell Scandal." Center for Genetics and Society Newsletter, January. http://www.genetics-and-society.org/newsletter/archive/20060127.html.

Center for Women's Global Leadership. 2007. http://www.cwgl.rutgers.edu. New Brunswick, NJ: Center for Women's Global Leadership.

Cerna, Christina M., and Jennifer C. Wallace. 1999. "Women and Culture." In *Women and International Human Rights Law, Vol. I,* eds. Kelly D. Askin and Dorean M. Koenig. Ardsley, NY: Transnational, 623–50.

Committee on Economic, Social and Cultural Rights. 2000. *General Comment No. 14 of the Committee on Economic, Social and Cultural Rights: The Right to the Highest Attainable Standard of Health.* Twenty-Second Session. E/C.12/2000/4.

Churchill, Randolph S. 1966. *The Young Churchill.* New York: Lancer Books.

Cohn, Haim. 1997–1998. "Religious Human Rights." *Dine Israel* 19:101–26.

————. 2000. "The Law of Religious Dissidents: A Comparative Historical Survey." *Israel Law Review* 34:100–39.

Comaroff, Jean, and John L. Comaroff. 1991. *Of Revelation and Revolution, Vol. 1: Christianity, Colonialism, and Consciousness in South Africa.* Chicago, IL: University of Chicago Press.

————. 1997. *Of Revelation and Revolution, Vol. 2: The Dialectics of Modernity on a South African Frontier.* Chicago, IL: University of Chicago Press.

Connors, Jane. 2005. "United Nations Approaches to 'Crimes of Honour.'" In *'Honour': Crimes, Paradigms, and Violence against Women,* ed. Lynn Welchman and Sara Hossain. London/New York: Zed Books Ltd; Victoria: Spinifex Press, 22–41.

Cook, Rebecca. 1994. "State Accountability Under the Convention on the Elimination of All Forms of Discrimination against Women." In *Human Rights of Women. National and International Perspectives,* ed. Rebecca Cook. Philadelphia: University of Pennsylvania Press, 228–56.

Cotran, Eugene. 1968. "The Changing Nature of African Marriage." In *Family Law in Asia and Africa,* ed. James N.D. Anderson. London: G. Allen and Unwin.

Council for International Organizations of Medical Sciences. 1993. *International Ethical Guidelines for Biomedical Research Involving Human Subjects.* Geneva: Council for International Organizations of Medical Sciences.

Council of Europe International Seminar. 2005. "Prevention and Combating Human Trafficking." Collection of Materials. Moscow.

Cover, Robert. 1987. "Obligation: A Jewish Jurisprudence of the Social Order." *Journal of Law and Religion* 5:65–74.

Dahlström, Edmund (ed.). 1971. *The Changing Roles of Men and Women*. Boston: Beacon Press.

de Beauvoir, Simone. 1952. *The Second Sex*. Trans. and ed. Howard M. Parshley. 1989. New York: Alfred A. Knopf.

Donohoe, Sam. 1999. "Intellectual Property Rights (TRIPS) Agreement of the WTO." Seattle, WA: University of Washington. http://www.washington.edu/wto/issues/trips.html

Edwards, Maud. 1995. "Participation Politique des Femmes et Changement Politique: Le Cas de la Suède." In *La Place des Femmes, les Enjeux de L'identité et de L'égalité, au Regard des Sciences Sociales*, ed. Ephésia. Paris: La Découverte, 504–08.

Eide, Asbjørn. 1989. *Right to Adequate Food as a Human Right*. New York: United Nations.

Emerton, Robyn, Kristine Adams, Andrew Byrnes, and Jane Connors (eds.). 2005. *International Women's Rights Cases*. London: Cavendish Publishing Ltd.

Evatt, Elizabeth. 2002. "Finding a Voice for Women's Rights: The Early Days of the Committee." *The George Washington International Law Review* 34(3):515–53.

Fagan, Patrick F. 2001. "How U.N. Conventions on Women's and Children's Rights Undermine Family, Religion, and Sovereignty." The Heritage Foundation, February 5. http://www.heritage.org/Research/InternationalOrganizations/BG1407es.cfm.

Fenn, Richard. 1978. *Toward a Theory of Secularization*. Storrs, CN: Society for the Scientific Study of Religion.

Flinterman, Cees. 1995. "The Maastricht Draft Optional Protocol" in *Netherlands Quarterly of Human Rights* 13: 85–93.

Fraser, Arvonne S., and Irene Tinker (eds.). 2004. *Developing Power: How Women Transformed International Development*. New York: The Feminist Press.

Freire, Paulo. 2001. *Pedagogy of Freedom*. Lanham, MD: Rowman & Littlefield Publishers, Inc.

Friedman, Elizabeth Jay. 2003. "Gendering the Agenda: Impact of Transnational Women's Rights Movement at the UN Conferences of the 1990s." *Women's Studies International Forum* 26(4):313–31.

Global Policy Forum. 2002. "The World Bank Defends Its Record on Human Rights." http://www.globalpolicy.org/socecon/bwi-wto/wbank/2002/1101rights.htm.

Global Survival Network. 1999. *Crime and Slavery: An Exposé of the Traffic in Women from the Newly-Independent States*. Moscow.

global2local listserv. n.d. (not publicly accessible).

Goonesekere, Savitri. 1990. "Colonial Legislation and Sri Lankan Family Law: The Legacy of History." In *Asian Panorama*, ed. K. de Silva. New Delhi, India: Vikas Publications.

———. 1997. "Nationality and Women's Human Rights in the Asia Pacific Region." In *Advancing the Human Rights of Women*, ed. Andrew Byrnes, Jane Connors, and Lum Bik. London: Commonwealth Secretariat, 86–100.

———. (ed.). 2004. *Violence Law and Women's Rights in South Asia*. New Delhi: Sage Publications.

Government of Azerbaijan. 1996. *Initial Report under the CEDAW Convention*. United Nations. CEDAW/C/AZE/1.

Government of Bolivia. 1991. *Initial Report under the CEDAW Convention*. United Nations. CEDAW/C/BOL/1 and Add.1.

Government of Chile. 1995. *Second Periodic Report under the CEDAW Convention*. United Nations. CEDAW/C/CHI/2.

Government of Chile. 1999. *Third Periodic Report under the CEDAW Convention*. United Nations. CEDAW/C/CHI/3.

Government of Colombia. 1997. *Fourth Periodic Report under the CEDAW Convention.* United Nations. CEDAW/C/COL/4.

Government of Croatia. 1994. *Report Submitted on Exceptional Basis under the CEDAW Convention.* United Nations. CEDAW/C/CRO/SP.1.

Government of Dominican Republic. 1997. *Fourth Periodic Report under the CEDAW Convention.* United Nations. CEDAW/C/DOM/4.

Government of Ecuador. 2002. *Fourth and Fifth Periodic Report under the CEDAW Convention.* United Nations. CEDAW/C/ECU/4-5.

Government of El Salvador. 2001a. *Combined Third and Fourth Periodic Report under the CEDAW Convention.* United Nations. CEDAW/C/SLV/3-4.

———. 2001b. *Fifth Periodic Report under the CEDAW Convention.* United Nations. CEDAW/C/SLV/5.

———. 2002. *Sixth Periodic Report under the CEDAW Convention.* United Nations. CEDAW/C/SLV/6.

Government of Guatemala. 1991. *Combined Initial and Second Periodic Report under the CEDAW Convention.* United Nations. CEDAW/C/GUA/1- 2. and Corr. 1 and Amend.1.

———. 2001. *Combined Third and Fourth Periodic Report under the CEDAW Convention.* United Nations. CEDAW/C/GUA/3-4.

———. 2004. *Sixth Periodic Report under the CEDAW Convention.* United Nations. CEDAW/C/GUA/6.

Government of India. 2005. *Combined Second and Third Periodic Report under the CEDAW Convention.* United Nations. CEDAW/C/IND/2–3.

Government of Indonesia. 1997. *Second and Third Periodic Report under the CEDAW Convention.* United Nations. CEDAW/C/IDN/2-3.

Government of Mexico. 1982. *Initial Report under the CEDAW Convention.* United Nations. CEDAW/C/5/Add.2.

———. 1987. *Second Peridodic Report under the CEDAW Convention.* United Nations. CEDAW/C/MEX/131/Add.10 and Amend.1.

———. 1997. *Combined Third and Fourth Periodic Report under the CEDAW Convention.* United Nations. CEDAW/C/MEX/3-4.

———. 2000. *Fifth Periodic Report under the CEDAW Convention.* United Nations. CEDAW/C/MEX/5.

———. 2006. *Sixth Periodic Report under the CEDAW Convention.* United Nations. CEDAW/C/MEX/6.

Government of Nicaragua. 1999. *Fifth Periodic Report under the CEDAW Convention.* United Nations. CEDAW/C/NIC/5.

Government of Venezuela. 1984. *Initial Report under the CEDAW Convention.* United Nations. CEDAW/C/VEN/5/Add.24 and Amend.1.

———. 1995. *Third Periodic Report under the CEDAW Convention.* United Nations. CEDAW/C/VEN/3.

Government of Yugoslavia. 1994. *Report Submitted on Exceptional Basis under the CEDAW Convention by Federal Republic of Yugoslavia (Serbia and Montenegro).* United Nations. CEDAW/C/YUG/SP.1.

Government of Zimbabwe. 1996. *Initial Report under the CEDAW Convention.* United Nations. CEDAW/C/ZWE/1.

Groenman, L.S., et al. 1997. *Het Vrouwenverdrag in Nederland anno 1997.* Den Haag: Ministerie van SZW.

Habbard, Anne C. 2001. "Statement on the Integration of Human Rights in Corporate Principles." Presentation by the General Secretary of the International Federation for Human Rights (FIDH) at the Meeting on the OECD Guidelines for Multinational Enterprises and Other Global Instruments for Corporate Responsibility, Paris, June 19. http://www.oecd.org/dataoecd/37/10/2348834.pdf.

Halberstam, Malvina. 1997. "United States Ratification of the Convention on the Elimination of All Forms of Discrimination against Women." *George Washington Journal of International Law & Economics* 31:49–96.

Hatch, Elvin. 1988. *Culture and Morality: The Relativity of Values in Anthropology.* New York: Columbia University Press.

Heritage Foundation. 2001. http://www.heritage.org/Research/InternationalOrganizations/BG1407.cfm.

———. 2002. http://www.heritage.org/Press/Commentary/ed082802.cfm.

Hevener, Natalie K. 1986. "An Analysis of Gender Based Treaty Law: Contemporary Developments in Historical Perspective." *Human Rights Quarterly* 8:10–88.

Holtmaat, Rikki. 2004. *Towards Different Law and Public Policy: The Significance of Article 5a CEDAW for the Elimination of Structural Gender Discrimination.* The Hague: Ministry of Social Affairs and Employment.

Human Rights Center of Azerbaijan. 1998. Comments on Government Report. Translated by International League for Human Rights. http://www.ilhr.org/reports/azerbaijan/azerbaijan_b.html.

Human Rights Committee. 1993. *General Comment 22.* July 30, CCPR/C/21/Rev.1/Add.4.

———. 1996. *Concluding Observations: Nigeria.* Seventy-Ninth Session, July 24, CCPR/C/79/Add.65.

———. 2000. *General Comment 28.* March 23, CCPR/C/21/Rev.1/Add.10.

———. 2005. *Concluding Observations: Yemen.* Eighty-Fourth Session, August 9, CCPR/CO/84/YEM.

Ibhawoh, Bonny. 2001. "Cultural Tradition and Human Rights Standards in Conflict." In *Legal Cultures and Human Rights: The Challenge of Diversity,* ed. Kirsten Hastrup. The Hague: Kluwer Law International, 85–102.

Inter-American Court of Human Rights. 2000. *Annual Report.* OEA/Ser.L/V/II.111, Doc. 20 rev.

Inter-American Commission on Human Rights. 2003. *The Situation of the Rights of Women in Ciudad Juárez, Mexico: The Right to Be Free from Violence and Discrimination.* Report of the Special Rapporteur on the Rights of Women, Marta Altolaguirre, OEA/Ser.L/V/II.117.

International Institute for Democracy and Electoral Assistance. 1995. http://www.idea.int/gender/quotas.cfm.

International Labour Organization. 1977. "Tripartite Declaration of Principles Concerning Multinational Enterprises and Social Policy." Geneva: ILO. http://www.ilo.org/public/english/employment/multi/download/english.pdf.

———. 1999. *New Challenges for Employment Policy.* Geneva: ILO.

———. 2002. *Women and Men in the Informal Economy—A Statistical Picture.* Geneva: ILO.

———. 2005. *A Global Alliance against Forced Labour: Global Report under the Follow-Up to the ILO Declaration on Fundamental Principles and Rights at Work.* Report of the Director General, International Labour Conference, Ninety-Third Session. Geneva: ILO. http://www.ilo.org/declaration.

Inter-Parliamentary Union. 1995. *"Les Femmes et le Pouvoir Politique: Enquête Menée au Sein des 150 Parlements Nationaux Existant au 31 Décembre 1991."* Series "Reports and Documents," No. 23, Geneva: IPU. http://www.ipu.org/parline-f/parlinesearch.asp

Inter-Parliamentary Union. 2006. http://www.ipu.org/parline-f/parlinesearch.asp.

Isaacs, Dan. 2002. "Nigerian Woman Fights Stoning." BBC News, July 8, http://news.bbc. co.uk/1/low/world/africa/2116540.stm.

IWRAW. 1997. *Independent Report on Azerbaijan, Submitted to the Committee on Economic, Social, and Cultural Rights.* IWRAW. Minneapolis: Hubert Humphrey Institute of Public Affairs, University of Minnesota.

———. 2006. http://www.igc.org/iwraw. Hubert H. Humphrey Institute of Public Affairs, University of Minnesota: USA.

IWRAW Asia Pacific. 1998. *Report of "From Global to Local—A Convention Implementation and Monitoring Project."* Kuala Lumpur, Malaysia.

———. 2002. *Annual Report.* Kuala Lumpur, Malaysia.

———. 2004. *Lack of Access, Lack of Care: A Reference Guide to Women's Right to Health in the International Trading System.* IWRAW Asia Pacific Occasional Paper Series, No. 3. http://www.iwraw-ap.org/aboutus/pdf/OPSIII.pdf. 2006.

IWRAW. 2007a. http://www.iwraw-ap.org.

———. 2007b. *Building Capacity for Change: A Training Manual on the Convention on the Elimination of All Forms of Discrimination against Women.* Updated version.

Jabre, Kareen, and Ségolène Samouiller. 2006. "Les Enjeux du suffrage et de la participation politique des femmes." In *Le Livre noir de la condition des femmes*, ed. Christine Ockrent, Sandrine Treiner, and Françoise Gaspard. Paris: XO éditions, 793–824.

Jalal, Patricia. 2005. *Dossier 27: The Campaign For Gender Equality in Family Law.* London: Women Living Under Muslim Laws. http://www.wluml.org/english/pubsfulltxt. shtml?cmd%5B87%5D=i-87-531764.

JAIWR (Japanese Association of International Women's Rights) (ed.). 1995. *Convention on the Elimination of All Forms of Discrimination against Women: A Commentary.* Tokyo: Shogakusha. (Original Japanese version: 1992. *Joshi sabetsu teppai joyaku chukai.* Tokyo: Shogakusha.)

Kafka, Franz. 1925. *The Trial (Der Prozess).* Trans. by Willa and Edwin Muir. 1968. New York: Alfred A. Knopf, Inc.

Koedo, Shizuko. 2004. "The Sumitomo Electric Wage Discrimination Case." http://www. iwraw-ap.org/resources/case_japan.htm.

Korean Council for the Women Drafted for Military Sexual Slavery by Japan. 2001. http:// www.womenandwar.net.

Kuper, Adam. 1999. *Culture: The Anthropologists' Account.* Cambridge, MA: Harvard University Press.

Lerner, Natan. 1996. "Religious Human Rights under the United Nations." In *Religious Human Rights in Global Perspective: Legal Perspectives*, eds. Johan D. van der Vyuer and John Witte. Leiden: Martinus Nijhoff Publishers, 79–134.

———. 2000. *Religion, Beliefs and International Human Rights.* Maryknoll, NY: Orbis Books.

Levy, Jacob T. 1997. "Classifying Cultural Rights." In *Ethnicity and Group Rights*, eds. Ian Shapiro and Will Kymlicka. New York: New York University Press, 22–68.

Mayer, Anne 1995. "Reform of Personal Status Laws in North Africa: A Problem of Islamic or Mediterranean Laws." *Middle East Journal* 49(3):432–46. http://www.wluml.org/ english/pubs/pdf/occpaper/OCP-08.pdf.

———. 1996. "Reflections on the Proposed United States Reservations to CEDAW: Should the Constitution Be an Obstacle to Human Rights?" *Hastings Constitutional Law Quarterly* 23: 728–823.

————. 2001. "Religious Reservations to the Convention on the Elimination of All Forms of Discrimination against Women: What Do They Really Mean?" In *Religious Fundamentalism and the Human Rights of Women*, ed. Courtney W. Howland. New York: Palgrave, 105–16.

Mbote, Patricia. 2002. *Gender Dimensions of Law, Colonialism and Inheritance in East Africa: Kenyan Women's Experiences*. Geneva: International Environment Law Research Centre. http://www.ielrc.org/content/a0205.pdf.

Merry, Sally E. 2003. "Constructing a Global Law? Violence against Women and the Human Rights System." *Law and Social Inquiry* 28(4):941–79.

Ministry for Social Development. 2005. *Women and Development: Realities and Prospects. Proceedings of the Seminar*. Moscow: Variant.

Muthu, Rajendran. 2001. "Gender in Malaysian Society: Issues, Responses and Challenges." *Journal of South Asian Women's Studies* 10:44–62.

Mydans, Seth. 2002. "Raped Woman Is Sentenced to Death in Pakistan." *International Herald Tribune/New York Times*, May 18.

Nolan, Justin. 2005. "With Power Comes Responsibility: Human Rights and Corporate Accountability." *UNSW Law Journal* 28 (Part 3):581.

Nussbaum, Martha. 1999. *Sex and Social Justice*. Oxford: Oxford University Press.

Office of the UN High Commissioner for Human Rights. 2002. *Expert Group on Human Rights and Biotechnology—Conclusions*. Geneva: OHCHR. http://www.unhchr.ch/biotech/conclusions.htm.

Organisation for Economic Co-operation and Development. 1976. *Guidelines for Multinational Enterprises*. (Revised in 2000.) http://www.oecd.org/dataoecd/56/ 36/1922428.pdf.

Pachi, Pierella. 2003. *Gender Problems in Transition Countries*. Moscow: Ves' Mir Publishing House.

Pannikar, Raimundo. 1982. "Is the Notion of Human Rights a Western Concept?" *Diogenes* 120:75.

Parsons, Talcott. 1963. "On the Concept of Influence." *Public Opinion Quarterly* 27:232–62.

Pietilä, Hilkka. 2002. *Engendering the Global Agenda: The Story of Women and the United Nations*. Geneva and New York: UN Nongovernmental Liaison Service.

Pintat, Christine. 1997. "Les Femmes dans les Parlements et les Partis Politiques en Europe et en Amérique du Nord." In *Encyclopédie Politique et Historique des Femmes*, ed. Christine Faure. Paris: PUF, 793–824.

Polenina, Svetlana V. 2005. *Gender Equality: Equal Rights and Equal Opportunities for Men and Women*. Moscow: Aspect-Press.

Pope John Paul II. 1995. "Letter to Women." June 29. http://www.vatican.va/holy_father/john_paul_ii/letters/documents/hf_jp-ii_let_29061995_women_en.html.

Population Review: A Quarterly Scientific Journal. 2002. 4. http://www.populationreview.com.

Promotoras Legais Populares. 2007. São Paulo, Brazil. http://www.promotoraslegaispopulares.org.br.

Raday, Frances. 1992. "Israel: Incorporation of Religious Patriarchy in a Modern State." *International Review of Comparative Public Policy* 4:209–25.

————. 2003. "Culture, Religion and Gender." *International Journal of Constitutional Law* 1(4):663–715.

Rehof, Lars A. 1993. *Guide to the Travaux Préparatoires of the United Nations Convention on the Elimination of All Forms of Discrimination against Women*. Leiden: Martinus Nijhoff Publishers.

Robinson, Fiona. 1998. "The Limits of a Rights Based Approach to International Ethics." In *Human Rights Fifty Years On: A Reappraisal*, ed. Tony Evans. Manchester: Manchester University Press, 58–76.

Robinson, Mary. 2000. *Statement at the Beijing +5 Review Conference*, June 9. http://www. unhchr.ch/huricane/huricane.nsf/view01/DB6643258A4CC97F802568FD005B10BA ?opendocument.

———. 2001. *Humanising Globalization: A Role for Human Rights*. Remarks by the High Commissioner for Human Rights at the International Conference on Globalization, Ghent, October 30. http://www.unhchr.ch/huricane/huricane.nsf/0/ 6D617C0A4DA48882C1256AF6005CAD12?opendocument.

Romany, Celina. 1994. "State Responsibility Goes Private: A Feminist Critique of the Public/ Private Distinction in International Human Rights Law." In *Human Rights of Women. National and International Perspectives*, ed. Rebecca Cook. Philadelphia: University of Pennsylvania Press, 85–115.

Rome Statute of International Criminal Court. 1998. http://www.un.org/law/icc. Codification Division, Office of Legal Affairs: United Nations.

ROSSPEN. 2002. *Women of New Russia: What Are They Like? How Do They Live? What Do They Strive For?* Moscow: ROSSPEN.

Rosstat. 2000. *Statistical Reports. Women and Men in Russia*. Moscow: State Statistical Service (Rosstat).

———. 2004. *Statistical Reports. Women and Men in Russia*. Moscow: State Statistical Service (Rosstat).

Ruggie, John. 2006. *Interim Report of the Special Representative of the Secretary-General on the Issue of Human Rights and Transnational Corporations and Other Business Enterprises*. United Nations, February 22. E/CN.4/2006/97.

———. 2007. *Business and Human Rights: Mapping International Standards of Responsibility and Accountability for Corporate Acts*. United Nations, February 9. A/HRC/4/035.

Russian Academy of Sciences, Institute for Studies of Population. 2002. *Russia: 10 Years of Reform. Socio-Demographic Situation. Collection of Materials*. Moscow.

Rzhanytsyna L.S. 2002. *Gender Budget. First Experience in Russia*. Moscow: Helios ARV.

Sakhi-Bulley, Bal. 2006. "The Optional Protocol to CEDAW, First Steps" in *Human Rights Law Review* 1–17.

Schöpp-Schilling, Hanna Beate. 1995. "The Impact of German Unification on Women: Losses and Gains" In *A Rising Public Voice: Women in Politics Worldwide*, ed. Alida Brill. New York City: The Feminist Press, 27–40.

———. 2003. "Reflections on a General Recommendation on Article 4 (1) of the Convention on the Elimination of All Forms of Discrimination against Women," In *Temporary Special Measures. Accelerating de facto Equality of Women under Article 4 (1) of the Convention on the Elimination of All Forms of Discrimination against Women*, eds. Ineke Boerefijn et al. Antwerp, Oxford, New York: Intersentia, 15–33.

———. 2004. "Reservations to CEDAW: An Unresolved Issue or, (No) New Developments?" In *Reservations to Human Rights Treaties*, ed. Ineta Ziemele. Leiden: Martinus Nijhoff Publishers, 3–39.

———. 2007. "Treaty Body Reform: The Case of the Committee on the Elimination of Discrimination against Women." *Human Rights Law Review* 7(1): 201–24.

Shalev, Carmel. 2000. "Rights to Sexual and Reproductive Health: The ICPD and the Convention on the Elimination of All Forms of Discrimination against Women." *Health and Human Rights* 4(2):39–66.

———. 2001. "China to CEDAW: An Update on Population Policy." *Human Rights Quarterly* 23(1):119–47.

———. 2004. "Access to Essential Drugs, Human Rights and Global Justice." *Monash Bioethics Review* 23(1):56–74.

Sjørslev, Inger. 2001. "Copywriting Culture: Indigenous Peoples and Intellectual Rights." In *Legal Cultures and Human Rights: The Challenge of Diversity*, ed. Kirsten Hastrup. The Hague: Kluwer Law International.

Skjeie, Hege. 1991. "The Uneven Advance of Norwegian Women." *New Left Review* 187:79–102.

Steiner, Henry, and Philip Alston. 2000. *International Human Rights in Context*. Oxford: Oxford University Press.

Subirats, Marina. 1998. "La Educación de las Mujeres: de la Marginalidad a la Coeducación. Propuestas para una Metodología de Cambio Educativo." *Serie Mujer y Desarrollo 22*. Santiago de Chile: CEPAL, Unidad Mujer y Desarrollo.

Sullivan, Donna. 1988. "Advancing the Freedom of Religion or Belief through the UN Declaration on the Elimination of Religions Tolerance and Discrimination." *American Journal of International Law* 82:487–520.

Timothy, Kristen, and Marsha Freeman. 2000. *The CEDAW Convention and the Beijing Platform for Action: Reinforcing the Promise of the Rights Framework*. Minneapolis: IWRAW.

Tyuryukanova Elena V. 2004. *Forced Labour in Modern Russia: Irregular Migration and Trafficking in Human Beings*. Moscow: International Labour Office. (English edition: 2005. Geneva: ILO).

Tyuryukanova, Elena V., and Marina M. Malysheva. 2001. *Women. Migration. State*. Moscow: Academia.

UNDAW. 2001. "Empowerment of Women throughout the Life Cycle as a Transformative Strategy for Poverty Eradication." Final Report of the United Nations Division for the Advancement of Women (UNDAW) Expert Group Meeting, November 26–29, New Delhi, India. http://www.un.org/womenwatch/daw/csw/empower/reports/Final_report.pdf.

UNDP. 2000. *Human Development Report 2000: Human Rights and Human Development*. New York: Oxford University Press.

UNESCO. 1995. *UNESCO Education*. http://portal.unesco.org/education/en/ev.php-URL_ID=46881&URL_DO=DO_TOPIC&URL_SECTION=201.html.

———. 2000. *The Dakar Framework for Action. Education for All: Meeting Our Collective Commitments*. World Education Forum. Paris: UNESCO.

———. 2002. *Proyecto Regional de Educación para América Latina y el Caribe (PRELAC)*. Primera Reunión Intergubernamental PRELAC. Santiago de Chile: OREALC/UNESCO Santiago.

———. 2003a. *EFA Global Monitoring Report 2003/4: Gender and Education for All: The Leap to Equality. Summary*. Paris: UNESCO.

———. 2003b. *EFA Global Monitoring Report 2003/4: Gender and Education for All: The Leap to Equality. Regional Overview: Latin America and the Caribbean*. Paris: UNESCO.

———. 2006. *EFA Global Monitoring Report 2006: Education for All: Literacy of Life*. Paris: UNESCO.

UNHCHR. 2005. *Report of the United Nations High Commissioner for Human Rights on the Responsibilities of Transnational Corporations and Related Business Enterprises with Regard to Human Rights*. February 15. E/CN.4/2005/91, Paras. 47–48 (home country regulation). http://www.ohchr.org/english/issues/globalization/business/index.htm.

UNICEF Innocenti Research Centre. 1999. *Women in Transition*. MONEE Project, Central and Eastern Europe/ CIS/ the Baltic.

UNIFEM. 2004. *Assessment of From Global to Local: A Convention Monitoring and Implementation Project*. New York: UNIFEM.

UNIFEM and Institute of Social Studies Trust. 2005. *Progress of South Asian Women*. New Delhi, India: UNIFEM.

UNIFEM South Asia Regional Office. 2002. *South Asia Regional Consultation: CEDAW*. New Delhi, India: UNIFEM.

UNIFEM, German Federal Ministry for Economic Cooperation and Development, and Deutsche Gesellschaft für Technische Zusammenarbeit (GTZ). 2005. *Pathway to Gender Equality: CEDAW, Beijing and the MDGs*. New York: UNIFEM. http:/www.unifem.org. jo/pages/articledetails.aspx?aid=505–15k.

United Nations. 1976. "Declaration of Mexico. Plans of Action." In *Report on the First UN World Conference on Women, June 19–July 2, 1975, Mexico City*. E/CONF.66/34. http:// documents.un.org/simple.asp.

———. 1981. *Declaration on the Elimination of All Forms of Intolerance and of Discrimination Based on Religion or Belief*. UNGA Res. 36/55 of November 25, A/36/684.

———. 1985. *Report of the Committee on the Elimination of Discrimination against Women on the Achievements of and Obstacles Encountered by States Parties in the Implementation of the Convention on the Elimination of All Forms of Discrimination against Women, July 15–26, Nairobi*. Third World Conference on Women. A/CONF.116/13.

———. 1988a. *Summary Record of the 125th Meeting*, CEDAW/C/SR.125.

———. 1988b. *Summary Record of the 127th Meeting*, CEDAW/C/SR.127.

———. 1989a. "CEDAW Committee Report 1982." In *The Work of CEDAW. Reports of the Committee on the Elimination of Discrimination against Women (CEDAW), 1982–1985, vol. I*. New York: United Nations, 1–15.

———. 1989b. "CEDAW Committee Report 1983." In *The Work of CEDAW. Reports of the Committee on the Elimination of Discrimination against Women (CEDAW), 1982–1985, vol. I*. New York: United Nations, 19–228.

———. 1989c. "CEDAW Committee Report 1984." In *The Work of CEDAW. Reports of the Committee on the Elimination of Discrimination against Women (CEDAW), 1982–1985, vol. I*. New York: United Nations, 231–466.

———. 1989d. *Summary Record of the 144th meeting*, CEDAW/C/SR. 144.

———. 1990a. *Summary Record of the 152nd Meeting*, CEDAW/C/SR.152.

———. 1990b. *Summary Record of the 157th Meeting*, CEDAW/C/SR.157.

———. 1990c. *The Work of CEDAW. Reports of the Committee on the Elimination of Discrimination against Women (CEDAW)*. Vol. II: 1986–1987. New York: United Nations.

———.1993a. *Declaration on the Elimination of Violence against Women*, UNGA A/ RES/48/104 of December 20, A/RES/48/104.

———. 1993b. "Vienna Declaration and Programme of Action." *In Report on the World Conference on Human Rights*, June 14-25, Vienna. A/CONF.157/23. http://www.unhchr. ch/huridocda/huridoca.nsf/(Symbol)/A.CONF.157.23.EN.

———. 1994. "Programme of Action of the International Conference on Population and Development" In *Report of the International Conference on Population and Development (ICPD)*. A/CONF.171/13/Rev.1. http://www.unfpa.org/upload/lib_pub_file/570_file name_finalreport_icpd_eng.pdf.

———. 1995a. "The Beijing Declaration and Platform for Action." In *Report of the Fourth World Conference on Women*, September 4–15, Beijing. A/CONF.177/20 & A/ CONF.177/20/Add.1. http://www.un.org/documents/ga/conf177/aconf177-20en.htm.

———. 1995b. *Report by the Committee on the Elimination of Discrimination against Women on Progress Achieved in the Implementation of the Convention on the Elimination of All Forms of Discrimination against Women*. Fourth World Conference on Women, September 4–15, Beijing. A/CONF. 177/7.

———. 1995c. *Report of the Sixth Meeting of Persons Chairing the Human Rights Treaty Bodies.* General Assembly, Fiftieth Session, A/50/505.

———. 1995d. *The United Nations and the Advancement of Women 1945–1995.* United Nations: New York.

———. 1995e. *Working Paper on the Situation of Systematic Rape, Sexual Slavery and Slavery-Like Practices during Wartime, Including Internal Armed Conflict Submitted by Ms. Linda Chavez in Accordance with Subcommission Decision 1994/109.* UN Commission on Human Rights, Sub-Commission on Prevention of Discrimination and Protection of Minorities, Forty-Seventh Session, E/CN.4/Sub.2/1995/38.

———. 1996a. *Amendment to Article 20, Paragraph 1, of the Convention on the Elimination of All Forms of Discrimination against Women.* General Assembly, Fiftieth Session. A/RES/50/202.

———. 1996b. *Preliminary Report of the Special Rapporteur on the Situation of Systematic Rape, Sexual Slavery and Slavery-Like Practices during Periods of Armed Conflict, Ms. Linda Chavez.* UN Commission on Human Rights, Sub-Commission on Prevention of Discrimination and Protection of Minorities, Forty-Eighth Session, E/CN.4/Sub.2/1996/26.

———. 1996c. *Report of the Special Rapporteur on Violence against Women, Its Causes and Consequences, Ms. Radhika Coomaraswamy, in Accordance with Commission on Human Rights Resolution 1994/45: Report on the Mission to the Democratic People's Republic of Korea, the Republic of Korea and Japan on the Issue of Military Sexual Slavery in Wartime.* UN Commission on Human Rights, Fifty-Second Session, E/CN.4/1996/53, Add.1.

———. 1997. *Report of Special Representative of the Commission on Human Rights on the Situation of Human Rights in the Islamic Republic of Iran, 15 October 1997.* Economic and Social Council, Commission on Human Rights, Fifty-Fourth Session, A/52/472.

———. 1998. *Final Report Submitted by Ms. Gay J. McDougall, Special Rapporteur: Systematic Rape, Sexual Slavery and Slavery-like Practices during Armed Conflict.* UN Commission on Human Rights, Sub-Commission on Prevention of Discrimination and Protection of Minorities, Fiftieth Session, E/CN.4/Sub.2/1998/13.

———. 1999. *1999 World Survey on the Role of Women in Development.* United Nations: New York

———. 2000a. *Millennium Development Goals and Targets.* http://www.undp.org/mdg/basics.shtml.

———. 2000b. *Report of the Ad Hoc Committee of the Whole of the Twenty-Third Special Session of the General Assembly (Beijing +5).* Supplement No. 3 (A/S-23/10/Rev.1). http://www.uneca.org/acgd/gender/en_ungass.pdf.

———. 2000c. *Report of the UN Special Rapporteur on Extrajudicial, Summary or Arbitrary Executions, Ms. Asma Jahangir, Submitted Pursuant to Commission on Human Rights Resolution 1999/35—Addendum: Visit to Mexico.* UN Commission on Human Rights, Fifty-Sixth Session, E/CN.4/2000/3/Add.3.

———. 2000d. *United Nations Millennium Declaration.* Adopted by UNGA Resolution 55/2 of September 18. A/RES/55/2. http://www.ohchr.org/english/law/millennium.htm.

———. 2000e. *Assessing the Status of Women: A Guide to Reporting Using the Convention on the Elimination of All Forms of Discrimination against Women.* New York: United Nations.

———. 2001a. *Report of the Committee on the Elimination of Discrimination against Women (Twenty-Fourth and Twenty-Fifth Sessions),* Annex I, Rules of Procedure. UN General Assembly, Official Documents, Fifty-Sixth Session, No. 38, A/56/38.

———. 2001b. *Report by the Secretary General: Traditional or Customary Practices Affecting the Health of Women and Girls, 22 August 2001.* General Assembly, Official Documents, Fifty-Sixth Session, A/56/316.

————. 2002a. *Report of the UN Special Rapporteur on the Independence of Judges and Lawyers, Dato' Param Cumaraswamy, Submitted in Accordance with Commission on Human Rights Resolution 2001/39—Addendum: Report on the Mission to Mexico.* UN Commission on Human Rights, Fifty-Eighth Session, E/CN.4/2002/72/Add.1.

————. 2002b. *Report of the Special Rapporteur on Violence against Women, Ms. Radhika Coomaraswamy: Integration of the Human Rights of Women and the Gender Perspective, Violence against Women.* UN Commission on Human Rights, Fifty-Ninth Session, E/CN.4/2002/83.

————. 2002c. Rules of Procedure of the Committee on the Elimination of Discrimination against Women. General Assembly, Official Documents, Fifty-Sixth Session, A/56/38.

————. 2004. *A Report Submitted by the Special Rapporteur Katarina Tomaševski: Right to Education.* UN Commission on Human Rights, Sixtieth Session, E/CN.4/2004/45.

————. 2005a. *2005 World Summit Outcome.* UNGA A/60/L. 1.

————. 2005b. *Report Submitted by the Special Rapporteur on the Right to Education, Mr. Vernor Muñoz Villalobos: The Right to Education.* UN Commission on Human Rights, Sixty-First Session, E/CN.4/2005/50.

————. 2006a. *Report of the Secretary-General: In-Depth Study on All Forms of Violence against Women.* UN General Assembly, Sixty-First Session, A/61/122/Add.1.

————. 2006b. *Report of the Special Rapporteur on Violence against Women, Its Causes and Consequences, Yakin Ertürk. Addendum: Mission to Mexico.* UN Commission on Human Rights, Sixty-Second Session, E/CN.4/2006/61/Add.4.

————. 2006c. *Report Submitted by the Special Rapporteur on the Right to Education, Mr. Vernon Muñoz Villalobos: Girls' Right to Education.* UN Commission on Human Rights, Sixty-Second Session, E/CN.4/2006/45.

United Nations Commission on Human Rights. 2003. *Norms on the Responsibilities of Transnational Corporations and Other Business Enterprises with Regard to Human Rights.* E/CN.4/Sub.2/2003/12/Rev.2.

United Nations Security Council. 2000. *Resolution on Women, Peace and Security.* Res. 1325 (2000) of October 31. S/RES/1325.

Vogl, Frank. 2004. "The UN Convention against Corruption: A Milestone on the Road to Curbing Global Bribery." *UN Chronicle.* http://www.un.org/Pubs/chronicle/2004/issue3/0304p02.asp.

Wintersteen, Kristin. 1999. "Human Rights Issues and the WTO." Seattle, WA: University of Washington. http://www.washington.edu/wto/issues/humanrights.html.

World Trade Organization. 2005. *Ministerial Declaration.* December. http://www.wto.org/english/theWTO_e/minist_e/min05_e/final_text_e.htm.

Zdravomyslova, Olga M. 2003. *Family and Society: Gender Dimension of Russian Transformation.* Moscow: Editorial USSR.

CASE LAW
Case Law by Courts
Botswana

Attorney General of Botswana v. Unity Dow. 1992. Case No. 37, C.A. Botswana. July 3.

Fiji Islands

State v. Bechu. 2005. *Pacific Human Rights Law Digest,* I:53.

India

Apparel Exports Promotion Council v. A.K. Chopra. 1999. Supreme Court 625. http://orissagov.nic.in/wcd/pdf/judgement1.pdf.

Gita Hariharan v. Reserve Bank of India. 1999. 2 SCC 228.

Ranjit Hazarika v. State of Assam. 1998. 8 SCC 135.

Vishaka v. State of Rajasthan. 1997. 6 SCC 241.

Israel

Bavli v. Rabbinical Court of Appeals. 1994. HCJ 1000/92. 48(2) P.D 221.

Shakdiel v. Minister of Religions. 1998. 25(2) P.D. 221 (in Hebrew).

Kiribati

Balelah v. State, Republic of Kiribati v. Timiti and Robuti. 2005. *Pacific Human Rights Law Digest,* I:4, 47.

Nepal

FWLD v. Nepal Ministry of Law and Justice. 2002. Writ No. 55/2058 B.S. (2001–2002).

Mani Sharma v. Office of Prime Minister Nepal. 2005. Writ 31/661 (15.12.2005).

Meera Dhungana v. Minister of Law and Justice. 1995. Vol. 37. Nepal LJ: 462.

Meera Gurung v. Dept. of Immigration Nepal. 1991. *Nepal Law Journal* Vol. 2:479.

Rina Bajracharya v. H M's Government S.C. Nepal. 2000. June 8. 2812/054.

Sharmila Parajuli v. HMG Nepal. 2004. NKP 2061. Vol. 10: 1312.

South Africa

Government of RSA v. Grootboom & Others. 2000. (11) B CLR 1169 CC.

Minister of Health v. Treatment Action Campaign. 2002. 10 BCLR 1033 (CC).

Soobramany v. Minister of Health. 1998. Kwazulu Natal 1 SA 765 (CC).

Sri Lanka

Bandara v. State. 2001. 2 Sri L.R. 63.

Singarasa v. Attorney General of Sri Lanka CA. 2006. Appeal No. 208/95 SC Spl. LA No. 182/99 (15.09.2006).

Sriyani Silva v. Iddamalgoda. 2003. 2 Sri LR 63.

Yogalingam Vijitha v. Wijesekere SC. 2001. Sri Lanka 186/2001.

Tanzania

Ephrahim v. Pastory. 1990. Case No. 35 High Court of Tanzania (February 22).

United States

Geduldig v. Aiello. 1974. 417 U.S. 484.

Vanuatu

Noel v. Toto. 2005. *Pacific Human Rights Law Digest,* I:26.

International (Quasi-)Judicial Organs

European Court of Human Rights

Leyla Sahin v. Turkey. 2004. Application No. 44774/98, Judgement 29 June, European Human Rights Report, 18 (Grand Chamber).

Leyla Sahin v. Turkey. 2005. Application No. 44774/98, Judgement 10 November, European Human Rights Report, 18.

Refah Partisi (Welfare Party) and Others v. Turkey. 2003. Application No. 41340/98, 41342/98, 41343/98, and 41344/98. Judgement 13 February, European Human Rights Report, 37.

European Commission on Human Rights

D. v. France. 1983. Application No. 10180/82, D&R 35, 202.

Senay Karaduman v. Turkey. 1993. Application No. 16278/90. Decision, May 3. D&R 74, 93–110.

Inter-American Court of Human Rights

Velásquez Rodríguez v. Honduras. 1988. Judgement 4 July. Inter-Am.Ct.H.R.(Ser.C) No. 4.

UN Human Rights Committee

Aumeeruddy-Cziffra et al. v. Mauritius. 1981. Communication No. 35/1978, April 9, A/36/40, Annex XIII, 34–42.

Sandra Lovelace v. Canada. 1980. Communication No. 24/1977, July 30, A/36/40, Annex XVIII, 166–75.

CEDAW Committee

B.-J. v. Germany. 2004. Communication No. 1/2003. A/59/38, Annex VIII, 244–56.

A.T. v. Hungary. 2005. Communication No. 2/2004. A/60/38, Annex III, 80–92.

A.S. v. Hungary. 2006. Communication No. 4/2004. A/61/38, Annex VIII, 366–79.

Dung Thi Thuy Nguyen v. The Netherlands. 2006. Communication No. 3/2004. A/61/38, Annex VIII, 353–65.

Rahime Kayan v. Turkey. 2006. Communication No. 8/2005. A/61/38, Annex I. 69–78.

Salgado v. United Kingdom. 2007. Communication No. 11/2006. CEDAW/C/37/D/11/2006.

CONTRIBUTORS' BIOGRAPHIES

FORMER AND CURRENT CEDAW COMMITTEE MEMBERS

Essay Writers

CHARLOTTE ABAKA, *GHANA*
Dental surgeon in private practice in Kumasi, Ghana; Chairperson of the National Subcommittee on CEDAW from 1996–2001(an independent body to monitor implementation of the Convention and the Beijing Platform for Action); member of Board of Trustees of Ghana Education Trust Fund (2002–2005); UN Independent Expert on the Situation of Human Rights in Liberia from 2003–2008; member of the CEDAW Committee from 1991–2002; Chairperson of the Committee from 2000–2002.

SILVIA ROSE CARTWRIGHT, *NEW ZEALAND*
Currently, Judge Extraordinary Chambers of the Courts of Cambodia; Chair of the National Commission of UNESCO New Zealand; former Judge of the High Court of New Zealand (1993–2001) and Governor-General of New Zealand (2001–2006); Dame Commander of the Order of the British Empire (For Services to Women, 1989) and Principal Companion of the New Zealand Order of Merit (2001); member of the CEDAW Committee from 1993–2000.

IVANKA CORTI, *ITALY*
National and international political activist; former member of Executive Board of the Italian Social Democratic Party, in charge of international policy, and Deputy Chairperson of the party's women's organization; Deputy Chairperson of Socialist International Women (1985–1986); active participant in the Association of Italian Women for participation of Women in Developments process (AIDOS) and Italian Association of Business and Professional Women (FIDA-PA). In 2006 was granted with award "Women Who Make a Change" of the International Women's Forum (IMF); member of the Italian official delegation in Nairobi World Conference in 1985; member of the CEDAW Committee from 1987–2002; Chairperson of the Committee from 1993–1996; Chairperson of the Meeting of Chairpersons of the Human Rights Treaty Bodies from 1995–1996.

SHANTHI DAIRIAM, *MALAYSIA*
Former Director of the International Women's Rights Action Watch (IWRAW) Asia Pacific; activist; adviser to HAWA (Women's Affairs Department) Prime Minister's Office on the preparation of the Initial Report to CEDAW; Executive Committee member of the Women's Aid Organization (Vice President, 1999-

2001) and the National Council of Women's Organizations, Malaysia; member of the CEDAW Committee since 2005.

ELIZABETH EVATT, *AUSTRALIA*
Commissioner of the International Commission of Jurists; former Chief Judge of the Family Court of Australia (1976–1988) and President of the Australian Law Reform Commission (1988–1993); member of the UN Human Rights Committee (1993–2000); Judge of the World Bank Administrative Tribunal (1998–2006); member of the CEDAW Committee from 1984–1992; Chairperson of the Committee from 1989–1991.

YOLANDA FERRER GOMÉZ, *CUBA*
General Secretary of the Federation of Cuban Women since 1990; represented Cuba at the Commission on the Status of Women and UN Economic Commission for Latin America and the Caribbean (ECLAC); member of the CEDAW Committee from 1997–2004; one of the two members of the Committee designated to conduct the first inquiry under the Optional Protocol.

CEES FLINTERMAN, *THE NETHERLANDS*
Director and Professor of Human Rights, Netherlands Institute of Human Rights, Utrecht School of Law; member of the Editorial Board of the *Netherlands Quarterly of Human Rights* and the *Netherlands International Law Review*, and member of the Government Advisory Council on International Affairs; alternate member of the UN Sub-Commission on Prevention of Discrimination and Protection of Minorities (1987-1991), Vice-Chairperson of the 49th session of the UN Commission on Human Rights (1993) and Head of the Netherlands Delegation to the UN Commission on Human Rights (1993 and 1994) and to the World Conference on Human Rights (1993); member of the CEDAW Committee since 2003.

FRANÇOISE GASPARD, *FRANCE*
Currently, Senior Lecturer at the EHESS (Ecole des Hautes Etudes en Sciences Sociales); former mayor; former member of the French National Assembly; former Regional Councilor in France; former member of the European Parliament; French representative to the UN Commission on the Status of Women (1998–2000); member of the CEDAW Committee since 2001.

AÍDA GONZÁLEZ MARTÍNEZ, *MEXICO*
Retired Ambassador; responsible for the organization of the First UN World Conference on Women in 1975 in Mexico; Representative of Mexico to the Commission on the Status of Women and participant in the 1976 sessions in which the CEDAW Convention was prepared; member of the Delegation of Mexico to the First, Third and Fourth UN World Conferences on Women;

member of the CEDAW Committee from 1982–1992 and from 1996–2004; Chairperson of the Committee from 2001–2002.

SAVITRI GOONESEKERE, *SRI LANKA*

Emeritus Professor of Law, University of Colombo, Sri Lanka; formerly Professor of Law and also Vice Chancellor of this university from 1999–2002; member of several regional and international bodies concerned with human rights; has held fellowships in universities in the United States and the United Kingdom and acted as a consultant to several UN agencies working on law and human rights projects; former Chairperson and, currently, member of the Asian Development Bank External Forum on Gender; member of the Board of Trustees UN Voluntary Fund for Victims of Torture; member of the CEDAW Committee from 1999–2002.

ROSARIO G. MANALO, *PHILIPPINES*

Director of the European Studies Program of the Ateneo de Manila University; adviser to Fidel V. Ramos, former President and the Philippines' Eminent Person to draft the ASEAN Charter (2006–2007); former Career Officer of the Philippine Diplomatic Service including positions as Deputy Foreign Minister and Ambassador to various European countries and to UNESCO; Chairperson of the UN Commission on the Status of Women (1984–1985); member of the CEDAW Committee from 1999 to 2006; Chairperson of the Committee from 2005–2006.

ELVIRA NOVIKOVA, *RUSSIAN FEDERATION*

Ph.D., History; currently, Consultant and lecturer on women's, gender and human rights issues at NGOs; researcher specializing in women's and gender studies at the Institute of Socio-Political Studies, the USSR Academy of Sciences, Chief of Sector of Problems of Working Women, and the Trade Unions Research Center; member of the CEDAW Committee from 1986–1990.

PRAMILA PATTEN, *MAURITIUS*

Currently, a practicing Barrister in Mauritius and Consultant at the Ministry of Justice and Human Rights and the Vice-Chair of the African Centre for Democracy and Human Rights, Gambia; member of the CEDAW Committee since 2003; past Chair of the Working Group on Communications under the Optional Protocol to CEDAW (January 2005–December 2006).

SILVIA PIMENTEL, *BRAZIL*

Jurist and Ph.D., professor teaching Philosophy of Law at Catholic University of São Paulo (PUC/SP); one of the founders of International Women's Rights Action Watch (IWRAW) and one of the founders of the Latin American and Caribbean Committee for the Defense of Women's Rights (CLADEM); coordinated the national section of CLADEM-Brazil for fifteen years and is a member of CLADEM's Honorary Consulting Council; member of the CEDAW Committee since 2005.

FRANCES RADAY, *ISRAEL*

Professor of Law; Elias Lieberman Chair in Labor Law, Hebrew University of Jerusalem; Director of Concord, Research Institute for Integration of International Law in Israel, College of Management Academic Studies; Chair of the Israeli Association of Feminist and Gender Studies; Chief Editor, Israel Law Review; Chair, Lafer Center for Women's Studies, Hebrew University of Jerusalem; founding Chair, Israel Women's Network Legal Center; member of the CEDAW Committee (2001–2002).

HANNA BEATE SCHÖPP-SCHILLING, *GERMANY*

Ph.D. in American Studies; currently, Consultant, University Lecturer on human rights; researcher; activist; former Chief Representative to the Board of American Field Service (1999–2002), former Director (1992–2002); former Director General for Women's Affairs at the German Federal Ministry of Family, Women and Youth (1987–1992); member of the Board of Trustees of the German Institute for Human Rights (since 2004; Vice-Chairperson from 2001–2004); member of the National Institute for Human Rights, Ekaterinburg, Russian Federation (since 2006); member of the CEDAW Committee since 1989 (held positions of Rapporteur, Vice-Chair, Chair of the Standing Working Group on Communications).

CARMEL SHALEV, *ISRAEL*

Public interest lawyer and bioethicist; currently, an international consultant and member of the law faculty of Tel Aviv University; instructor in medical qi gong, and engaged in spiritual peacemaking inside Israel; former Director of the Unit of Health Rights and Ethics at the Gertner Institute for Health Policy Research, and chief legal adviser to the Israel Ministry of Health; member of the CEDAW Committee from 1994–2000.

HEISOO SHIN, *REPUBLIC OF KOREA*

Sociologist; activist on women's human rights for thirty years, particularly in the area of violence against women; co-represented the Korean Council for the Women Drafted for Military Sexual Slavery by Japan (2001); president of Korea Women's Hot Line as well as co-representative of Korea Women's Associations United; currently, working toward a "War and Women's Human Rights Museum," Commissioner of the Korean National Human Rights Commission; Visiting professor of Kyung Hee University in Seoul; member of the CEDAW Committee since 2001.

MARIA REGINA TAVARES DA SILVA, *PORTUGAL*
Academic; member of the Advisory Committee on the Framework Convention for the Protection of National Minorities of the Council of Europe; former president of the Commission on the Status of Women, later Commission for Equality and Women's Rights in Portugal (1986–1992); former president of the Committee on Equality between Women and Men of the Council of Europe (1987–1988 and 1991–1992); Portuguese expert in the Community Mission of Investigation on the rape of Muslim women in Bosnia and Herzegovina (1993); member of the CEDAW Committee since 2001.

Personal Reflections Writers
FERIDE ACAR, *TURKEY*
Professor, Department Chair at the Political Science and Public Administration Department in the Middle East Technical University (METU) in Ankara, Turkey; Founding Chair (1994–2002) of the Gender and Women's Studies Graduate Program in the same university; currently, member (2005–2008) of the Task Force to Combat Violence against Women of the Council of Europe; member of the CEDAW Committee from 1997 to 2005; Chairperson of the Committee from 2003 to 2004.

SJAMSIAH ACHMAD, *INDONESIA*
Head, Bureau of International Relations of the Indonesian Institute of Sciences (1967–1978); (Senior) Program Officer at the United Nations Headquarters in New York and Vienna (1978–1988); Deputy Minister for the Role of Women in Indonesia (1988–1995); founder (1999) and Chairperson of the Indonesian Center for the Empowerment of Women in Politics; member of the Indonesian National Commission on Violence against Women (2003–2009); member of the CEDAW Committee (2001–2004).

RYOKO AKAMATSU, *JAPAN*
President of Japanese Association of International Women's Rights (JAIWR); adviser to the President, Bunkyo-Gakuin University (Tokyo), and President of WINWIN (an NGO to promote women's political participation); former Minister of Education; Minister of the Permanent Mission of Japan to the United Nations, Ambassador to Uruguay, and Director General of the Women's Bureau (Ministry of Labor); member of the CEDAW Committee from 1987–1994.

EMNA AOUIJ, *TUNISIA*
Former Minister of Justice (first female magistrate) (1968); member of Parliament (1990–1998); President of Tunisian Court of Auditors (1998–2000); former Ambassador to The Netherlands and Denmark (2000–2005); current President of the National Committee of piloting of the Project for the Modernisation of

the Legal System in Tunisia (Tunisia-C.E.E.); member of the CEDAW Committee from 1991–2002.

MERIEM BELMIHOUB-ZERDANI, *ALGERIA*
Lawyer at the Supreme Court and Council of State; founding member of the National Association to combat illiteracy (1964); former Minister Counselor to the head of Government on legal and administrative affairs (1992–1993); former member of the Council of the Nation (1998–2001); former Chair of the Group of Independent Members of the Council of the Nation (Senate); former member of the Justice Reform Commission established by the President of the Republic in 1999; member of the CEDAW Committee since 2003.

DÉSIRÉE PATRICIA BERNARD, *GUYANA*
First female Judge of the High Court of the Supreme Court of Guyana (1980); Justice of the Court of Appeal (1992); Chief Justice of Guyana (1996), and Chancellor and Head of Judiciary of the Supreme Court of Guyana (2001); Judge of the Caribbean Court of Justice from 2005; member of the CEDAW Committee from 1982–1992 and 1995–1998; Chairperson of the Committee from 1985–1989.

MARIE CARON, *CANADA*
Member of the Quebec Bar; former positions include President of the Liberal Women of Canada; member of the National Parole Board of Canada; member of the University of Ottawa Board of Governors; member of the CEDAW Committee from 1982–1988.

AURORA JAVATE DE DIOS, *PHILIPPINES*
Associate Professor of International and Migration Studies at Miriam College in the Philippines and Executive Director of the Women and Gender Institute in the same institution; former Chairperson of the National Commission on the Role of Filipino Women; President of the Coalition against Trafficking in Women International Board of Trustees; member of the CEDAW Committee from 1994–1998.

HADJA ASSA DIALLO SOUMARÉ, *MALI*
Public health administrator; President and Founder of the Action Committee for Women's and Children's Rights (CADEF) and Adviser to the Embassy of Canada on women's rights and Canadian development projects in Mali; member of the CEDAW Committee (1987–1990).

MIRIAM ESTRADA-CASTILLO, *ECUADOR*
Former Technical Director of the Project to Support the Ecuadorian National Human Rights Plan, for the United Nations Office of the High Commission-

er for Human Rights (Geneva, Switzerland) (2002); member of the CEDAW Committee from 1995–1998.

FENG CUI, *CHINA*
Vice President of the China Association of Women Entrepreneurs (2003–present); Vice President of the China Children and Teenagers' Fund (2003–present); National Committee Member of the Chinese People's Political Consultative Conference (1998–present); member of the Secretariat of the All-China Women's Federation (1996–2002); Counselor of the Permanent Mission of China to the United Nations (1991–1996); member of the CEDAW Committee (1999–2002).

NORMA MONICA FORDE, *BARBADOS*
Former Chairperson of the Barbados National Commission on the Status of Women; former member of the Judicial Council, Constitutional Review Commission, and Privy Council, Barbados; former member of the International Council on Environmental Law; retired Senior Lecturer in Law at the University of the West Indies; member of the CEDAW Committee from 1987–1994.

NAELA GABR, *EGYPT*
Assistant Minister for Multilateral Relations of Egypt; former Permanent Representative of the Arab Republic of Egypt to the United Nations Office in Geneva (2002–2005); Ambassador Extraordinary and Plenipotentiary of the Arab Republic of Egypt to the Republic of South Africa and Ambassador Extraordinary and Plenipotentiary to the Republic of Botswana (nonresident) and to the Kingdom of Lesotho (nonresident) (1999–2002); member of the CEDAW Committee since 1999.

LUVSANDANZANGYN IDER, *MONGOLIA*
Chargé d'Affaires of Mongolia in France and Permanent Delegate of Mongolia to UNESCO (1986–1989); Director, Department of International Organizations and of Department of Treaty and Legal Affairs, Ministry of Foreign Affairs of Mongolia (1977–1979), (1981–1986), (1989–1992); adviser of the Supreme Court of Mongolia (1993–2005); Vice-Chairperson (1979) and Chairperson (1985) of the UN Commission for Social Development; member of the Committee on Economic, Social and Cultural Rights (1991–1994); Ambassador Extraordinary and Plenipotentiary; member of the CEDAW Committee (1982–1986); first Chairperson of the CEDAW Committee (1982–1984).

CHRISTINE KAPALATA, *UNITED REPUBLIC OF TANZANIA*
Political Affairs Officer of the United Nations Mission in Liberia (UNMIL); former Head of Chancery at the Tanzania High Commission to Nigeria in Lagos; former Minister Counselor of the Permanent Mission of the United Republic of

Tanzania to the United Nations in New York; member of the CEDAW Committee from 2002–2004.

SALMA KHAN, *BANGLADESH*
Currently, Ambassador of Bangladesh to Indonesia; member of the National Council on Women and Development, the National Education Commission, the Human Development Foundation, and the Grameen Trust; previously key decision maker in areas of development planning and WID, and first woman Division Chief in the Planning Commission; member of the CEDAW Committee from 1992–2000 and 2002–2006; Chairperson of the Committee from 1997–1998.

PIRKKO MÄKINEN, *FINLAND*
Ministry of Social Affairs and Health, Gender Equality Ombudsman; former Secretary General of the Parliamentary Ombudsman (Finland); member of the CEDAW Committee from 1993 to 1996.

GÖRAN MELANDER, *SWEDEN*
Former professor of Public International Law and Humanitarian, Lund University; founder and former Director of Raoul Wallenberg Institute of Human Rights, Lund University (1984–2000); President of the Board of Directors, Raoul Wallenberg Institute (2000–present); member of the CEDAW Committee from 2001–2004.

KRISTZINA MORVAI, *HUNGARY*
Professor of Law, Eötvös Lorand University (Budapest); founding member of the Movement for a Prostitution-Free Hungary; founder and Chairperson of the Women's Rights and Children's Rights Research and Training Center Foundation and of the Independent Lawyers' Committee for the Examination of Mass Police Brutality in Budapest on the 50th Anniversary of the 1956 Revolution; member of the CEDAW Committee from 2003–2006.

VICTORIA POPESCU, *ROMANIA*
Ambassador of Romania to Sweden since 2004; former Director General for the United Nations and Global Affairs, Ministry of Foreign Affairs (Romania); alternate member in the UN Sub-Commission on the Promotion and Protection of Human Rights (2000–2006); Rapporteur and Vice-Chair of the Third Committee of the General Assembly of the United Nations (1996–1997; 1998–1999); Chairperson of the Consultative Committee of UNIFEM (1998–2000); member of the CEDAW Committee (2003–2006).

DUBRAVKA ŠIMONOVIĆ, *CROATIA*

Head of the Human Rights Department, Ministry of Foreign Affairs (Croatia) since 2002; Chairperson of the Council of Europe Task Force to Combat Violence against Women, including Domestic Violence for 2006–2007 and its Vice-Chairperson for 2007–2008; representative of the Republic of Croatia on the Steering Committee on Human Rights (CDDH) and its Chair for 2003–2005, Council of Europe; Chairperson of the UN Commission on the Status of Women (CSW), New York (2000–2002); Vice-Chair of the UN GA Special Session on women, peace and security (2000); member of the CEDAW Committee since 2003, its Rapporteur for 2004–2005, Chairperson for 2007–2008.

KONGIT SINEGIORGIS, *ETHIOPIA*

Ambassador to Austria and Permanent Representative to the International Organizations in Vienna; previous ambassadorial posts were Geneva, Ottawa, Israel, the Organization of African Unity (OAU), Egypt, and the African Union; member of the CEDAW Committee from 1985–2000.

MERVAT TALLAWY, *EGYPT*

Under-Secretary-General of the United Nations and Executive Secretary of the Economic and Social Commission for Western Asia (ECSWA); former Minister of Insurance and Social Affairs in Egypt; Secretary-General of the Egyptian National Women's Council; Ambassador of Egypt to Austria and Japan; Egyptian Governor on the Board of Governors of the International Atomic Energy Agency and other United Nations agencies in Vienna; member of the CEDAW Committee from 1987–1998 and Chairperson from 1991–1992.

UN Staff

KOFI A. ANNAN, *GHANA*

Seventh Secretary-General of the United Nations (1997–2006); 2002 Nobel Peace Prize winner; various senior positions at the UN Headquarters in New York in a diverse range of areas, including human resources management (1987–1990), budget and finance (1990–1992), and peacekeeping (March 1992–December 1996); Under-Secretary-General for Peacekeeping at a time when nearly 70,000 military and civilian personnel were deployed in UN operations around the world.

JANE CONNORS, *AUSTRALIA*

Academic; Senior Human Rights Officer in the Treaties and Council Branch of the United Nations Office of the High Commissioner for Human Rights; former senior lecturer in law at the London School of Oriental and African Studies (SOAS 1982–1996); former Chief Women's Rights Section in the Division for the Advancement of Women (DAW) in the Department of Economic and Social Affairs of the United Nations (1996–2002).

INGEBORG CREYDT, *GERMANY*
Former Senior Social Affairs Officer; Former Chief of the International Standards, Instruments and Relations Section of the Division for the Advancement of Women (DAW) of the Department of International Social and Economic Affairs (DIESA) (1980–1993).

PHILOMENA KINTU, *UNITED REPUBLIC OF TANZANIA*
Former Social Affairs Officer at the UN Division for the Advancement of Women (DAW); currently, Secretary to the CEDAW Committee.

RACHEL N. MAYANJA, *UGANDA*
Assistant Secretary-General and Special Adviser to the Secretary-General on Gender Issues and Advancement of Women; former Director of the Human Resources Management Division at the UN Food and Agriculture Organization (FAO); held different senior positions in the UN Office of Human Resources Management, including Chief, Common System and Specialist Service; Secretary to the Secretary-General's Task Force on the reform of human resources management (1999); former Secretary to the Drafting Committee of CEDAW; served in peacekeeping missions in Namibia (UNTAG) from 1989–1990, and Iraq/Kuwait (UNIKOM) from 1992–1994.

TEXT OF THE CONVENTION

The States Parties to the present Convention,

Noting that the Charter of the United Nations reaffirms faith in fundamental human rights, in the dignity and worth of the human person and in the equal rights of men and women,

Noting that the Universal Declaration of Human Rights affirms the principle of the inadmissibility of discrimination and proclaims that all human beings are born free and equal in dignity and rights and that everyone is entitled to all the rights and freedoms set forth therein, without distinction of any kind, including distinction based on sex,

Noting that the States Parties to the International Covenants on Human Rights have the obligation to ensure the equal right of men and women to enjoy all economic, social, cultural, civil and political rights,

Considering the international conventions concluded under the auspices of the United Nations and the specialized agencies promoting equality of rights of men and women,

Noting also the resolutions, declarations and recommendations adopted by the United Nations and the specialized agencies promoting equality of rights of men and women,

Concerned, however, that despite these various instruments extensive discrimination against women continues to exist,

Recalling that discrimination against women violates the principles of equality of rights and respect for human dignity, is an obstacle to the participation of women, on equal terms with men, in the political, social, economic and cultural life of their countries, hampers the growth of the prosperity of society and the family and makes more difficult the full development of the potentialities of women in the service of their countries and of humanity,

Concerned that in situations of poverty women have the least access to food, health, education, training and opportunities for employment and other needs,

Convinced that the establishment of the new international economic order based on equity and justice will contribute significantly towards the promotion of equality between men and women,

Emphasizing that the eradication of apartheid, of all forms of racism, racial discrimination, colonialism, neo-colonialism, aggression, foreign occupation and domination and interference in the internal affairs of States is essential to the full enjoyment of the rights of men and women,

Affirming that the strengthening of international peace and security, relaxation of international tension, mutual co-operation among all States irrespective of their social and economic systems, general and complete disarmament, and in particular nuclear disarmament under strict and effective international control, the affirmation of the principles of justice, equality and mutual benefit in relations among countries and the realization of the right of peoples under alien and colonial domination and foreign occupation to self-determination and independence, as well as respect for national sovereignty and territorial integrity, will promote social progress and development and as a consequence will contribute to the attainment of full equality between men and women,

Convinced that the full and complete development of a country, the welfare of the world and the cause of peace require the maximum participation of women on equal terms with men in all fields,

Bearing in mind the great contribution of women to the welfare of the family and to the development of society, so far not fully recognized, the social significance of maternity and the role of both parents in the family and in the upbringing of children, and aware that the role of women in procreation should not be a basis for discrimination but that the upbringing of children requires a sharing of responsibility between men and women and society as a whole,

Aware that a change in the traditional role of men as well as the role of women in society and in the family is needed to achieve full equality between men and women,

Determined to implement the principles set forth in the Declaration on the Elimination of Discrimination against Women and, for that purpose, to adopt the measures required for the elimination of such discrimination in all its forms and manifestations,

Have agreed on the following:

PART I
Article 1

For the purposes of the present Convention, the term "discrimination against women" shall mean any distinction, exclusion or restriction made on the basis of sex which has the effect or purpose of impairing or nullifying the recognition, enjoyment or exercise by women irrespective of their marital status, on a basis of equality of men and women, of human rights and fundamental freedoms in the political, economic, social, cultural, civil or any other field.

Article 2

States Parties condemn discrimination against women in all its forms, agree to pursue by all appropriate means and without delay a policy of eliminating discrimination against women and, to this end, undertake:

(a) To embody the principle of the equality of men and women in their national constitutions or other appropriate legislation if not yet incorporated therein and to ensure, through law and other appropriate means, the practical realization of this principle;

(b) To adopt appropriate legislative and other measures, including sanctions where appropriate, prohibiting all discrimination against women;

(c) To establish legal protection of the rights of women on an equal basis with men and to ensure through competent national tribunals and other public institutions the effective protection of women against any act of discrimination;

(d) To refrain from engaging in any act or practice of discrimination against women and to ensure that public authorities and institutions shall act in conformity with this obligation;

(e) To take all appropriate measures to eliminate discrimination against women by any person, organization or enterprise;

(f) To take all appropriate measures, including legislation, to modify or abolish existing laws, regulations, customs and practices which constitute discrimination against women;

(g) To repeal all national penal provisions which constitute discrimination against women.

Article 3

States Parties shall take in all fields, in particular in the political, social, economic and cultural fields, all appropriate measures, including legislation, to ensure the full development and advancement of women, for the purpose of guaranteeing them the exercise and enjoyment of human rights and fundamental freedoms on a basis of equality with men.

Article 4

1. Adoption by States Parties of temporary special measures aimed at accelerating de facto equality between men and women shall not be considered discrimination as defined in the present Convention, but shall in no way entail as a consequence the maintenance of unequal or separate standards; these measures shall be discontinued when the objectives of equality of opportunity and treatment have been achieved.

2. Adoption by States Parties of special measures, including those measures contained in the present Convention, aimed at protecting maternity shall not be considered discriminatory.

Article 5

States Parties shall take all appropriate measures:

(a) To modify the social and cultural patterns of conduct of men and women, with a view to achieving the elimination of prejudices and customary and all other practices which are based on the idea of the inferiority or the superiority of either of the sexes or on stereotyped roles for men and women;

(b) To ensure that family education includes a proper understanding of maternity as a social function and the recognition of the common responsibility of men and women in the upbringing and development of their children, it being understood that the interest of the children is the primordial consideration in all cases.

Article 6

States Parties shall take all appropriate measures, including legislation, to suppress all forms of traffic in women and exploitation of prostitution of women.

PART II

Article 7

States Parties shall take all appropriate measures to eliminate discrimination against women in the political and public life of the country and, in particular, shall ensure to women, on equal terms with men, the right:

(a) To vote in all elections and public referenda and to be eligible for election to all publicly elected bodies;

(b) To participate in the formulation of government policy and the implementation thereof and to hold public office and perform all public functions at all levels of government;

(c) To participate in nongovernmental organizations and associations concerned with the public and political life of the country.

Article 8

States Parties shall take all appropriate measures to ensure to women, on equal terms with men and without any discrimination, the opportunity to represent their Governments at the international level and to participate in the work of international organizations.

Article 9

1. States Parties shall grant women equal rights with men to acquire, change or retain their nationality. They shall ensure in particular that neither marriage to an alien nor change of nationality by the husband during marriage shall automatically change the nationality of the wife, render her stateless or force upon her the nationality of the husband.

2. States Parties shall grant women equal rights with men with respect to the nationality of their children.

PART III

Article 10

States Parties shall take all appropriate measures to eliminate discrimination against women in order to ensure to them equal rights with men in the field of education and in particular to ensure, on a basis of equality of men and women:

(a) The same conditions for career and vocational guidance, for access to studies and for the achievement of diplomas in educational establishments of all categories in rural as well as in urban areas; this equality shall be ensured in pre-school, general, technical, professional and higher technical education, as well as in all types of vocational training;

(b) Access to the same curricula, the same examinations, teaching staff with qualifications of the same standard and school premises and equipment of the same quality;

(c) The elimination of any stereotyped concept of the roles of men and women at all levels and in all forms of education by encouraging coeducation and other types of education which will help to achieve this aim and, in particular, by the revision of textbooks and school programmes and the adaptation of teaching methods;

(d) The same opportunities to benefit from scholarships and other study grants;

(e) The same opportunities for access to programmes of continuing education including adult and functional literacy programmes, particularly those aimed at reducing, at the earliest possible time, any gap in education existing between men and women;

(f) The reduction of female student drop-out rates and the organization of programmes for girls and women who have left school prematurely;

(g) The same opportunities to participate actively in sports and physical education;

(h) Access to specific educational information to help to ensure the health and well being of families, including information and advice on family planning.

Article 11

1. States Parties shall take all appropriate measures to eliminate discrimination against women in the field of employment in order to ensure, on a basis of equality of men and women, the same rights, in particular:

(a) The right to work as an inalienable right of all human beings;

(b) The right to the same employment opportunities, including the application of the same criteria for selection in matters of employment;

(c) The right to free choice of profession and employment, the right to promotion, job security and all benefits and conditions of service and the right to receive vocational training and retraining, including apprenticeships, advanced vocational training and recurrent training;

(d) The right to equal remuneration, including benefits, and to equal treatment in respect of work of equal value, as well as equality of treatment in the evaluation of the quality of work;

(e) The right to social security, particularly in cases of retirement, unemployment, sickness, invalidity and old age and other incapacity to work, as well as the right to paid leave;

(f) The right to protection of health and to safety in working conditions, including the safeguarding of the function of reproduction.

2. In order to prevent discrimination against women on the grounds of marriage or maternity and to ensure their effective right to work, States Parties shall take appropriate measures:

(a) To prohibit, subject to the imposition of sanctions, dismissal on the grounds of pregnancy or of maternity leave and discrimination in dismissals on the basis of marital status;

(b) To introduce maternity leave with pay or with comparable social benefits without loss of former employment, seniority or social allowances;

(c) To encourage the provision of the necessary supporting social services to enable parents to combine family obligations with work responsibilities and participation in public life, in particular through promoting the establishment and development of a network of child-care facilities;

(d) To provide special protection to women during pregnancy in types of work proved to be harmful to them.

3. Protective legislation relating to matters covered in this article shall be reviewed periodically in the light of scientific and technological knowledge and shall be revised, repealed or extended as necessary.

Article 12

1. States Parties shall take all appropriate measures to eliminate discrimination against women in the field of health care in order to ensure, on a basis of equality of men and women, access to health care services, including those related to family planning.

2. Notwithstanding the provisions of paragraph 1 of this article, States Parties shall ensure to women appropriate services in connexion with pregnancy, confinement and the post-natal period, granting free services where necessary, as well as adequate nutrition during pregnancy and lactation.

Article 13

States Parties shall take all appropriate measures to eliminate discrimination against women in other areas of economic and social life in order to ensure, on a basis of equality of men and women, the same rights, in particular:

(a) The right to family benefits;

(b) The right to bank loans, mortgages and other forms of financial credit;

(c) The right to participate in recreational activities, sports and all aspects of cultural life.

Article 14

1. States Parties shall take into account the particular problems faced by rural women and the significant roles which rural women play in the economic survival of their families, including their work in the non-monetized sectors of the economy, and shall take all appropriate measures to ensure the application of the provisions of this Convention to women in rural areas.

2. States Parties shall take all appropriate measures to eliminate discrimination against women in rural areas in order to ensure, on a basis of equality of men and women, that they participate in and benefit from rural development and, in particular, shall ensure to such women the right:
   (a) To participate in the elaboration and implementation of development planning at all levels;
   (b) To have access to adequate health care facilities, including information, counselling and services in family planning;
   (c) To benefit directly from social security programmes;
   (d) To obtain all types of training and education, formal and non-formal, including that relating to functional literacy, as well as, inter alia, the benefit of all community and extension services, in order to increase their technical proficiency;
   (e) To organize self-help groups and co-operatives in order to obtain equal access to economic opportunities through employment or self-employment;
   (f) To participate in all community activities;
   (g) To have access to agricultural credit and loans, marketing facilities, appropriate technology and equal treatment in land and agrarian reform as well as in land resettlement schemes;
   (h) To enjoy adequate living conditions, particularly in relation to housing, sanitation, electricity and water supply, transport and communications.

PART IV
Article 15
1. States Parties shall accord to women equality with men before the law.
2. States Parties shall accord to women, in civil matters, a legal capacity identical to that of men and the same opportunities to exercise that capacity. In particular, they shall give women equal rights to conclude contracts and to administer property and shall treat them equally in all stages of procedure in courts and tribunals.
3. States Parties agree that all contracts and all other private instruments of any kind with a legal effect which is directed at restricting the legal capacity of women shall be deemed null and void.
4. States Parties shall accord to men and women the same rights with regard to the law relating to the movement of persons and the freedom to choose their residence and domicile.

Article 16
1. States Parties shall take all appropriate measures to eliminate discrimination against women in all matters relating to marriage and family relations and in particular shall ensure, on a basis of equality of men and women:

(a) The same right to enter into marriage;

(b) The same right freely to choose a spouse and to enter into marriage only with their free and full consent;

(c) The same rights and responsibilities during marriage and at its dissolution;

(d) The same rights and responsibilities as parents, irrespective of their marital status, in matters relating to their children; in all cases the interests of the children shall be paramount;

(e) The same rights to decide freely and responsibly on the number and spacing of their children and to have access to the information, education and means to enable them to exercise these rights;

(f) The same rights and responsibilities with regard to guardianship, wardship, trusteeship and adoption of children, or similar institutions where these concepts exist in national legislation; in all cases the interests of the children shall be paramount;

(g) The same personal rights as husband and wife, including the right to choose a family name, a profession and an occupation;

(h) The same rights for both spouses in respect of the ownership, acquisition, management, administration, enjoyment and disposition of property, whether free of charge or for a valuable consideration.

2. The betrothal and the marriage of a child shall have no legal effect, and all necessary action, including legislation, shall be taken to specify a minimum age for marriage and to make the registration of marriages in an official registry compulsory.

PART V
Article 17

1. For the purpose of considering the progress made in the implementation of the present Convention, there shall be established a Committee on the Elimination of Discrimination against Women (hereinafter referred to as the Committee) consisting, at the time of entry into force of the Convention, of eighteen and, after ratification of or accession to the Convention by the thirty-fifth State Party, of twenty-three experts of high moral standing and competence in the field covered by the Convention. The experts shall be elected by States Parties from among their nationals and shall serve in their personal capacity, consideration being given to equitable geographical distribution and to the representation of the different forms of civilization as well as the principal legal systems.

2. The members of the Committee shall be elected by secret ballot from a list of persons nominated by States Parties. Each State Party may nominate one person from among its own nationals.

3. The initial election shall be held six months after the date of the entry into

force of the present Convention. At least three months before the date of each election the Secretary-General of the United Nations shall address a letter to the States Parties inviting them to submit their nominations within two months. The Secretary-General shall prepare a list in alphabetical order of all persons thus nominated, indicating the States Parties which have nominated them, and shall submit it to the States Parties.

4. Elections of the members of the Committee shall be held at a meeting of States Parties convened by the Secretary-General at United Nations Headquarters. At that meeting, for which two thirds of the States Parties shall constitute a quorum, the persons elected to the Committee shall be those nominees who obtain the largest number of votes and an absolute majority of the votes of the representatives of States Parties present and voting.

5. The members of the Committee shall be elected for a term of four years. However, the terms of nine of the members elected at the first election shall expire at the end of two years; immediately after the first election the names of these nine members shall be chosen by lot by the Chairman of the Committee.

6. The election of the five additional members of the Committee shall be held in accordance with the provisions of paragraphs 2, 3 and 4 of this article, following the thirty-fifth ratification or accession. The terms of two of the additional members elected on this occasion shall expire at the end of two years, the names of these two members having been chosen by lot by the Chairman of the Committee.

7. For the filling of casual vacancies, the State Party whose expert has ceased to function as a member of the Committee shall appoint another expert from among its nationals, subject to the approval of the Committee.

8. The members of the Committee shall, with the approval of the General Assembly, receive emoluments from United Nations resources on such terms and conditions as the Assembly may decide, having regard to the importance of the Committee's responsibilities.

9. The Secretary-General of the United Nations shall provide the necessary staff and facilities for the effective performance of the functions of the Committee under the present Convention.

Article 18

1. States Parties undertake to submit to the Secretary-General of the United Nations, for consideration by the Committee, a report on the legislative, judicial, administrative or other measures which they have adopted to give effect to the provisions of the present Convention and on the progress made in this respect:

   (a) Within one year after the entry into force for the State concerned; and

   (b) Thereafter at least every four years and further whenever the Committee so requests.

2. Reports may indicate factors and difficulties affecting the degree of fulfilment of obligations under the present Convention.

Article 19
1. The Committee shall adopt its own rules of procedure.
2. The Committee shall elect its officers for a term of two years.

Article 20
1. The Committee shall normally meet for a period of not more than two weeks annually in order to consider the reports submitted in accordance with article 18 of the present Convention.
2. The meetings of the Committee shall normally be held at United Nations Headquarters or at any other convenient place as determined by the Committee.

Article 21
1. The Committee shall, through the Economic and Social Council, report annually to the General Assembly of the United Nations on its activities and may make suggestions and general recommendations based on the examination of reports and information received from the States Parties. Such suggestions and general recommendations shall be included in the report of the Committee together with comments, if any, from States Parties.
2. The Secretary-General shall transmit the reports of the Committee to the Commission on the Status of Women for its information.

Article 22
The specialized agencies shall be entitled to be represented at the consideration of the implementation of such provisions of the present Convention as fall within the scope of their activities. The Committee may invite the specialized agencies to submit reports on the implementation of the Convention in areas falling within the scope of their activities.

PART VI
Article 23
Nothing in this Convention shall affect any provisions that are
more conducive to the achievement of equality between men and women which may be contained:
(a) In the legislation of a State Party; or
(b) In any other international convention, treaty or agreement in force for that State.

Article 24

States Parties undertake to adopt all necessary measures at the national level aimed at achieving the full realization of the rights recognized in the present Convention.

Article 25

1. The present Convention shall be open for signature by all States.
2. The Secretary-General of the United Nations is designated as the depositary of the present Convention.
3. The present Convention is subject to ratification. Instruments of ratification shall be deposited with the Secretary-General of the United Nations.
4. The present Convention shall be open to accession by all States. Accession shall be effected by the deposit of an instrument of accession with the Secretary-General of the United Nations.

Article 26

1. A request for the revision of the present Convention may be made at any time by any State Party by means of a notification in writing addressed to the Secretary-General of the United Nations.
2. The General Assembly of the United Nations shall decide upon the steps, if any, to be taken in respect of such a request.

Article 27

1. The present Convention shall enter into force on the thirtieth day after the date of deposit with the Secretary-General of the United Nations of the twentieth instrument of ratification or accession.
2. For each State ratifying the present Convention or acceding to it after the deposit of the twentieth instrument of ratification or accession, the Convention shall enter into force on the thirtieth day after the date of the deposit of its own instrument of ratification or accession.

Article 28

1. The Secretary-General of the United Nations shall receive and circulate to all States the text of reservations made by States at the time of ratification or accession.
2. A reservation incompatible with the object and purpose of the present Convention shall not be permitted.
3. Reservations may be withdrawn at any time by notification to this effect addressed to the Secretary-General of the United Nations, who shall then inform all States thereof. Such notification shall take effect on the date on which it is received.

Article 29

1. Any dispute between two or more States Parties concerning the interpretation or application of the present Convention which is not settled by negotiation shall, at the request of one of them, be submitted to arbitration. If within six months from the date of the request for arbitration the parties are unable to agree on the organization of the arbitration, any one of those parties may refer the dispute to the International Court of Justice by request in conformity with the Statute of the Court.

2. Each State Party may at the time of signature or ratification of this Convention or accession thereto declare that it does not consider itself bound by paragraph 1 of this article. The other States Parties shall not be bound by that paragraph with respect to any State Party which has made such a reservation.

3. Any State Party which has made a reservation in accordance with paragraph 2 of this article may at any time withdraw that reservation by notification to the Secretary-General of the United Nations.

Article 30

The present Convention, the Arabic, Chinese, English, French, Russian and Spanish texts of which are equally authentic, shall be deposited with the Secretary-General of the United Nations.

TEXT OF THE OPTIONAL PROTOCOL TO THE CONVENTION

The States Parties to the present Protocol,

Noting that the Charter of the United Nations reaffirms faith in fundamental human rights, in the dignity and worth of the human person and in the equal rights of men and women,

Also noting that the Universal Declaration of Human Rights proclaims that all human beings are born free and equal in dignity and rights and that everyone is entitled to all the rights and freedoms set forth therein, without distinction of any kind, including distinction based on sex,

Recalling that the International Covenants on Human Rights and other international human rights instruments prohibit discrimination on the basis of sex,

Also recalling the Convention on the Elimination of All Forms of Discrimination against Women ("the Convention"), in which the States Parties thereto condemn discrimination against women in all its forms and agree to pursue by all appropriate means and without delay a policy of eliminating discrimination against women,

Reaffirming their determination to ensure the full and equal enjoyment by women of all human rights and fundamental freedoms and to take effective action to prevent violations of these rights and freedoms,

Have agreed as follows:

Article 1

A State Party to the present Protocol ("State Party") recognizes the competence of the Committee on the Elimination of Discrimination against Women ("the Committee") to receive and consider communications submitted in accordance with article 2.

Article 2

Communications may be submitted by or on behalf of individuals or groups of individuals, under the jurisdiction of a State Party, claiming to be victims of a violation of any of the rights set forth in the Convention by that State Party. Where a communication is submitted on behalf of individuals or groups of individuals, this shall be with their consent unless the author can justify acting on their behalf without such consent.

Article 3

Communications shall be in writing and shall not be anonymous. No communication shall be received by the Committee if it concerns a State Party to the Convention that is not a party to the present Protocol.

Article 4

1. The Committee shall not consider a communication unless it has ascertained that all available domestic remedies have been exhausted unless the application of such remedies is unreasonably prolonged or unlikely to bring effective relief.
2. The Committee shall declare a communication inadmissible where:
   (a) The same matter has already been examined by the Committee or has been or is being examined under another procedure of international investigation or settlement;
   (b) It is incompatible with the provisions of the Convention;
   (c) It is manifestly ill-founded or not sufficiently substantiated;
   (d) It is an abuse of the right to submit a communication;
   (e) The facts that are the subject of the communication occurred prior to the entry into force of the present Protocol for the State Party concerned unless those facts continued after that date.

Article 5

1. At any time after the receipt of a communication and before a determination on the merits has been reached, the Committee may transmit to the State Party concerned for its urgent consideration a request that the State Party take such interim measures as may be necessary to avoid possible irreparable damage to the victim or victims of the alleged violation.
2. Where the Committee exercises its discretion under paragraph 1 of the present article, this does not imply a determination on admissibility or on the merits of the communication.

Article 6

1. Unless the Committee considers a communication inadmissible without reference to the State Party concerned, and provided that the individual or individuals consent to the disclosure of their identity to that State Party, the Committee shall bring any communication submitted to it under the present Protocol confidentially to the attention of the State Party concerned.
2. Within six months, the receiving State Party shall submit to the Committee written explanations or statements clarifying the matter and the remedy, if any, that may have been provided by that State Party.

Article 7

1. The Committee shall consider communications received under the present Protocol in the light of all information made available to it by or on behalf

of individuals or groups of individuals and by the State Party concerned, provided that this information is transmitted to the parties concerned.

2. The Committee shall hold closed meetings when examining communications under the present Protocol.

3. After examining a communication, the Committee shall transmit its views on the communication, together with its recommendations, if any, to the parties concerned.

4. The State Party shall give due consideration to the views of the Committee, together with its recommendations, if any, and shall submit to the Committee, within six months, a written response, including information on any action taken in the light of the views and recommendations of the Committee.

5. The Committee may invite the State Party to submit further information about any measures the State Party has taken in response to its views or recommendations, if any, including as deemed appropriate by the Committee, in the State Party's subsequent reports under article 18 of the Convention.

Article 8

1. If the Committee receives reliable information indicating grave or systematic violations by a State Party of rights set forth in the Convention, the Committee shall invite that State Party to cooperate in the examination of the information and to this end to submit observations with regard to the information concerned.

2. Taking into account any observations that may have been submitted by the State Party concerned as well as any other reliable information available to it, the Committee may designate one or more of its members to conduct an inquiry and to report urgently to the Committee. Where warranted and with the consent of the State Party, the inquiry may include a visit to its territory.

3. After examining the findings of such an inquiry, the Committee shall transmit these findings to the State Party concerned together with any comments and recommendations.

4. The State Party concerned shall, within six months of receiving the findings, comments and recommendations transmitted by the Committee, submit its observations to the Committee.

5. Such an inquiry shall be conducted confidentially and the cooperation of the State Party shall be sought at all stages of the proceedings.

Article 9

1. The Committee may invite the State Party concerned to include in its report under article 18 of the Convention details of any measures taken in response to an inquiry conducted under article 8 of the present Protocol.

2. The Committee may, if necessary, after the end of the period of six months referred to in article 8.4, invite the State Party concerned to inform it of the measures taken in response to such an inquiry.

Article 10

1. Each State Party may, at the time of signature or ratification of the present Protocol or accession thereto, declare that it does not recognize the competence of the Committee provided for in articles 8 and 9.

2. Any State Party having made a declaration in accordance with paragraph 1 of the present article may, at any time, withdraw this declaration by notification to the Secretary-General.

Article 11

A State Party shall take all appropriate steps to ensure that individuals under its jurisdiction are not subjected to ill treatment or intimidation as a consequence of communicating with the Committee pursuant to the present Protocol.

Article 12

The Committee shall include in its annual report under article 21 of the Convention a summary of its activities under the present Protocol.

Article 13

Each State Party undertakes to make widely known and to give publicity to the Convention and the present Protocol and to facilitate access to information about the views and recommendations of the Committee, in particular, on matters involving that State Party.

Article 14

The Committee shall develop its own rules of procedure to be followed when exercising the functions conferred on it by the present Protocol.

Article 15

1. The present Protocol shall be open for signature by any State that has signed, ratified or acceded to the Convention.

2. The present Protocol shall be subject to ratification by any State that has ratified or acceded to the Convention. Instruments of ratification shall be deposited with the Secretary-General of the United Nations.

3. The present Protocol shall be open to accession by any State that has ratified or acceded to the Convention.

4. Accession shall be effected by the deposit of an instrument of accession with the Secretary-General of the United Nations.

Article 16

1. The present Protocol shall enter into force three months after the date of the deposit with the Secretary-General of the United Nations of the tenth instrument of ratification or accession.

2. For each State ratifying the present Protocol or acceding to it after its entry into force, the present Protocol shall enter into force three months after the date of the deposit of its own instrument of ratification or accession.

Article 17
No reservations to the present Protocol shall be permitted.

Article 18
1. Any State Party may propose an amendment to the present Protocol and file it with the Secretary-General of the United Nations. The Secretary-General shall thereupon communicate any proposed amendments to the States Parties with a request that they notify her or him whether they favour a conference of States Parties for the purpose of considering and voting on the proposal. In the event that at least one third of the States Parties favour such a conference, the Secretary-General shall convene the conference under the auspices of the United Nations. Any amendment adopted by a majority of the States Parties present and voting at the conference shall be submitted to the General Assembly of the United Nations for approval.
2. Amendments shall come into force when they have been approved by the General Assembly of the United Nations and accepted by a two-thirds majority of the States Parties to the present Protocol in accordance with their respective constitutional processes.
3. When amendments come into force, they shall be binding on those States Parties that have accepted them, other States Parties still being bound by the provisions of the present Protocol and any earlier amendments that they have accepted.

Article 19
1. Any State Party may denounce the present Protocol at any time by written notification addressed to the Secretary-General of the United Nations. Denunciation shall take effect six months after the date of receipt of the notification by the Secretary-General.
2. Denunciation shall be without prejudice to the continued application of the provisions of the present Protocol to any communication submitted under article 2 or any inquiry initiated under article 8 before the effective date of denunciation.

Article 20
The Secretary-General of the United Nations shall inform all States of:
(a) Signatures, ratifications and accessions under the present Protocol;
(b) The date of entry into force of the present Protocol and of any amendment under article 18;
(c) Any denunciation under article 19.

Article 21

1. The present Protocol, of which the Arabic, Chinese, English, French, Russian and Spanish texts are equally authentic, shall be deposited in the archives of the United Nations.

2. The Secretary-General of the United Nations shall transmit certified copies of the present Protocol to all States referred to in article 25 of the Convention.

SUMMARY LIST OF GENERAL RECOMMENDATIONS

As of January 2004, CEDAW had adopted 25 general recommendations, through which it interprets States Parties' obligations under the Convention.

To read these recommendations in their full text, most of which are discussed in this book, please visit: http://www.un.org/womenwatch/daw/cedaw/recommendations/index.html.

No. 1 (fifth session, 1986): Content of initial report
No. 2 (sixth session, 1987): Reporting guidelines
No. 3 (sixth session, 1987): Stereotyped conceptions of women
No. 4 (sixth session, 1987): Reservations
No. 5 (seventh session, 1988): Temporary special measures
No. 6 (seventh session, 1988): Effective national machinery and publicity
No. 7 (seventh session, 1988): Resources of the Committee
No. 8 (seventh session, 1988): Implementation of Article 8 of the Convention
No. 9 (eighth session, 1989): Statistical data concerning the situation of women
No. 10 (eighth session, 1989): Tenth anniversary of the adoption of the Convention
No. 11 (eighth session, 1989): Technical advisory services for reporting obligations
No. 12 (eighth session, 1989): Violence against women
No. 13 (eighth session, 1989): Equal remuneration for work of equal value
No. 14 (ninth session, 1990): Female circumcision
No. 15 (ninth session, 1990): Avoidance of discrimination against women in national strategies for the prevention and control of acquired immunodeficiency syndrome (AIDS)
No. 16 (tenth session, 1991): Unpaid women workers in rural and urban family enterprises
No. 17 (tenth session, 1991): Measurement and quantification of the unremunerated domestic activities of women and their recognition in the gross national product
No. 18 (tenth session, 1991): Disabled women
No. 19 (eleventh session, 1992): Violence against women
No. 20 (eleventh session, 1992): Reservations to the Convention
No. 21 (thirteenth session, 1994): Equality in marriage and family relations including with respect to nationality
No. 22 (fourteenth session, 1995): Amending Article 20 (1) of the Convention
No. 23 (sixteenth session, 1997): Political and public life
No. 24 (twentieth session, 1999): Women and health
No. 25 (thirtieth session, 2004): Temporary special measures

The Feminist Press at the City University of New York is a nonprofit literary and educational institution dedicated to publishing work by and about women. Our existence is grounded in the knowledge that women's writing has often been absent or underrepresented on bookstore and library shelves and in educational curricula—and that such absences contribute, in turn, to the exclusion of women from the literary canon, from the historical record, and from the public discourse.

The Feminist Press was founded in 1970. In its early decades, The Feminist Press launched the contemporary rediscovery of "lost" American women writers, and went on to diversify its list by publishing significant works by American women writers of color. More recently, the Press's publishing program has focused on international women writers, who remain far less likely to be translated than male writers, and on nonfiction works that explore issues affecting the lives of women around the world.

Founded in an activist spirit, The Feminist Press is currently undertaking initiatives that will bring its books and educational resources to underserved populations, including community colleges, public high schools and middle schools, literacy and ESL programs, and prison education programs. As we move forward into the twenty-first century, we continue to expand our work to respond to women's silences wherever they are found.

For information about events and for a complete catalog of the Press's 250 books, please refer to our website: www.feministpress.org.